750+
BLOCKBUSTER PROBLEMS in
PHYSICS
for NEET

Corporate Office

DISHA PUBLICATION

45, 2nd Floor, Maharishi Dayanand Marg,
Corner Market, Malviya Nagar, New Delhi - 110017
Tel : 49842349 / 49842350

Typeset by Disha DTP Team

www.dishapublication.com
Books & ebooks for School & Competitive Exams

www.mylearninggraph.com
Etests for Competitive Exams

Write to us at **feedback_disha@aiets.co.in**

Contents

PHYSICAL WORLD, UNITS AND MEASUREMENTS

1. If unit of length and force are increased 4 times. The unit of energy

   (a) is increased by 4 times

   (b) is increased by 16 times

   (c) is increased by 8 times

   (d) remains unchanged

2. The dimensions of the quantity $\vec{E} \times \vec{B}$ where $\vec{E}$ represents the electric field and $\vec{B}$ the magnetic field may be given as:

   (a) MT^{-3}

   (b) $M^2LT^{-5}A^{-2}$

   (c) $M^2LT^{-3}A^{-1}$

   (d) $MLT^{-2}A^{-2}$

3. If the length of rod A is 3.25 ± 0.01 cm and that of B is 4.19 ± 0.01 cm then how much rod B is longer than rod A?

   (a) 0.94 ± 0.00 cm

   (b) 0.94 ± 0.01 cm

   (c) 0.94 ± 0.02 cm

   (d) 0.94 ± 0.005 cm

4. Evaluate $\dfrac{25.2 \times 137.4}{33.3}$ and express the result with correct number of significant figures:

   (a) 10397

   (b) 104

   (c) 103.978

   (d) 103

5. Of the following quantities, which one has dimensions different from the remaining three?

   (a) Energy per unit volume

   (b) Force per unit area

   (c) Product of voltage and charge per unit volume

   (d) Angular momentum

6. The displacement of a body at a particular second n is given by the expression $S_{nth} = u + \dfrac{a}{2}(2n - 1)$. The dimensional formula of S_{nth} is

   (a) $[M^1L^0T^1]$

   (b) $[M^0L^1T^0]$

   (c) $[M^0L^1T^{-1}]$

   (d) $[M^0L^0T^0]$

7. The ratio of the dimensions of Planck's constant and that of the moment of inertia is the dimension(s) of

   (a) time

   (b) frequency

   (c) angular momentum

   (d) velocity

8. If force (X), acceleration (Y) and time (Z) are the fundamental units, then dimensions of work are

   (a) XYZ

   (b) XY^2Z

   (c) XYZ^2

   (d) XYZ^{-2}

9. The heat generated in a circuit is given by $Q = I^2Rt$, where I is current, R is resistance and t is time. If the percentage errors in measuring I, R and t are 2%, 1% and 1% respectively, then the maximum error in measuring heat will be

    (a) 2%
    (b) 3%
    (c) 4%
    (d) 6%

10. If force (F), length (L) and time (T) are assumed to be fundamental units, then the dimensional formula of the mass will be

    (a) $[FL^{-1}T^2]$
    (b) $[FL^{-1}T^{-2}]$
    (c) $[FL^{-1}T^{-1}]$
    (d) $[FL^2T^2]$

11. The velocity v of a particle at time t is given by

$$v = at + \frac{b}{t+c},$$ where a, b and c are constant.

    The dimensions of a, b and c are respectively

    (a) $[L^2], [T]$ and $[LT^2]$
    (b) $[LT^2], [LT]$ and $[L]$
    (c) $[L], [LT]$ and $[T^2]$
    (d) $[LT^{-2}], [L]$ and $[T]$

12. The time dependence of a physical quantity p is given by $p = p_0 \exp(-\alpha t^2)$, where α is a constant and t is the time. The constant α

    (a) is dimensionless
    (b) has dimensions $[T^{-2}]$
    (c) has dimensions $[T^2]$
    (d) has dimensions of p

13. The position x of a particle at time t is given by

$$x = \frac{V_0}{a}(1-e^{-at}),$$ where V_0 is constant and a > 0. The dimensions of V_0 and a are

    (a) $M^0 L T^{-1}$ and T^{-1}
    (b) $M^0 L T^0$ and T^{-1}
    (c) $M^0 L T^{-1}$ and $L T^{-2}$
    (d) $M^0 L T^{-1}$ and T

14. The dimensions of the quantities of the following pairs are the same. Identify the pair.

    (a) Torque and Work
    (b) Angular momentum and Work
    (c) Energy and Young's modulus
    (d) Light year and velocity

15. If E, m, J and G represent energy, mass, angular momentum and gravitational constant respectively, then the dimensional formula of EJ^2/m^5G^2 is same as that of

    (a) angle
    (b) length
    (c) mass
    (d) time

16. Which one of the following pairs of quantities and their units is a proper match?

    (a) Electric field – coulomb/m
    (b) Magnetic flux – weber
    (c) Power – farad
    (d) Capacitance – henry

17. Which of the following combinations has the dimension of electrical resistance (ϵ_0 is the permittivity of vacuum and μ_0 is the permeability of vacuum)?

    (a) $\sqrt{\dfrac{\mu_0}{\varepsilon_0}}$
    (b) $\dfrac{\mu_0}{\varepsilon_0}$
    (c) $\sqrt{\dfrac{\varepsilon_0}{\mu_0}}$
    (d) $\dfrac{\varepsilon_0}{\mu_0}$

18. A simple pendulum is being used to determine the value of gravitational acceleration g at a certain place. The length of the pendulum is 25.0 cm and a stop watch with 1 s resolution measures the time taken for 40 oscillations to be 50 s. The accuracy in g is:

    (a) 5.40%
    (b) 3.40%
    (c) 4.40%
    (d) 2.40%

19. The area of a square is 5.29 cm². The area of 7 such squares taking into account the significant figures is:

    (a) 37 cm²
    (b) 37.030 cm²
    (c) 37.03 cm²
    (d) 37.0 cm²

20. Using screw gauge of pitch 0.1 cm and 50 divisions on its circular scale, the thickness of an object is measured. It should correctly be recorded as :

(a) 2.121 cm

(b) 2.124 cm

(c) 2.125 cm

(d) 2.123 cm

21. A metal sample carrying a current along X-axis with density J_x is subjected to a magnetic field B_z (along z-axis). The electric field E_y developed along Y-axis is directly proportional to J_x as well as B_z. The constant of proportionality has SI unit

(a) $\dfrac{m^2}{A}$

(b) $\dfrac{m^3}{As}$

(c) $\dfrac{m^2}{As}$

(d) $\dfrac{As}{m^3}$

22. A body of mass m = 3.513 kg is moving along the x-axis with a speed of 5.00 ms^{-1}. The magnitude of its momentum is recorded as

(a) $17.6\,\text{kg ms}^{-1}$

(b) $17.565\,\text{kg ms}^{-1}$

(c) $17.56\,\text{kg ms}^{-1}$

(d) $17.57\,\text{kg ms}^{-1}$

23. A physical quantity z depends on four observables a, b, c and d, as $z = \dfrac{a^2 b^{\frac{2}{3}}}{\sqrt{c}\, d^3}$. The percentages of error in the measurement of a, b, c and d are 2%, 1.5%, 4% and 2.5% respectively. The percentage of error in z is :

(a) 12.25%

(b) 16.5%

(c) 13.5%

(d) 14.5%

24. The displacement of a particle moving along x-axis with respect to time t is $x = at + bt^2 - ct^3$. The dimensions of c are

(a) T^{-3}

(b) LT^{-2}

(c) LT^{-3}

(d) LT^3

25. In the relation displacement y = cos (ωt + kx), the dimension(s) of ω is [where t is time]

(a) $[M^0 LT]$

(b) $[M^0 L^{-1} T^0]$

(c) $[M^0 L^0 T^{-1}]$

(d) $[M^0 LT^{-1}]$

ANSWER KEY

1	(b)	4	(b)	7	(b)	10	(a)	13	(a)	16	(b)	19	(d)	22	(a)	25	(c)
2	(b)	5	(d)	8	(c)	11	(d)	14	(a)	17	(a)	20	(a)	23	(d)		
3	(c)	6	(b)	9	(d)	12	(b)	15	(a)	18	(c)	21	(b)	24	(c)		

MOTION IN A STRAIGHT LINE

1. A body moves in a straight line along Y-axis. Its distance y (in metre) from the origin is given by $y = 8t - 3t^2$. The average speed in the time interval from $t = 0$ second to $t = 1$ second is

   (a) $-4\ ms^{-1}$ (b) zero

   (c) $5\ ms^{-1}$ (d) $6\ ms^{-1}$

2. In 1.0 s, a particle goes from point A to point B, moving in a semicircle of radius 1.0 m (see Figure). The magnitude of the average velocity is

   (a) 3.14 m/s

   (b) 2.0 m/s

   (c) 1.0 m/s

   (d) Zero

3. If a body starts from rest and moves with uniform acceleration then distance covered by the body in t second is proportional to

   (a) t (b) t^2

   (c) t^3 (d) $\dfrac{1}{t^2}$

4. If the displacement of a particle varies with time as $\sqrt{x} = t + 7$, then

   (a) velocity of the particle is inversely proportional to t

   (b) velocity of the particle is proportional to t

   (c) velocity of the particle is proportional to $\sqrt{t}$

   (d) None of these

5. The displacement time graph of a moving particle is shown below

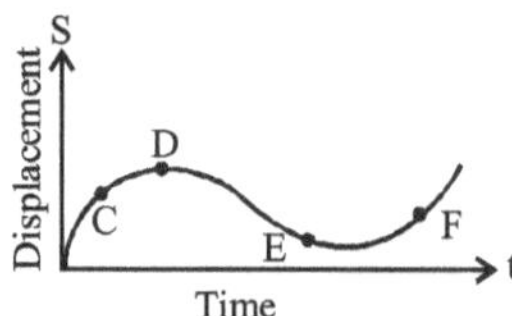

   The instantaneous velocity of the particle is negative at the point

   (a) D   (b) F

   (c) C   (d) E

6. A particle located at $x = 0$ at time $t = 0$, starts moving along with the positive x-direction with a velocity 'v' that varies as $v = \alpha\sqrt{x}$. The displacement of the particle varies with time as

   (a) t^2 (b) t

   (c) $t^{1/2}$ (d) t^3

7. A motor car moving with a uniform speed of 20 m/sec comes to stop on the application of brakes after travelling a distance of 10 m, its acceleration is

   (a) $20\ m/s^2$ (b) $-20\ m/s^2$

   (c) $-40\ m/s^2$ (d) $+2 m/s^2$

8. A body starts from rest from the origin with an acceleration of 6 m /s^2 along the x-axis and 8 m/s^2 along the y-axis. Its distance from the origin after 4 seconds will be

   (a) 56 m   (b) 64 m

   (c) 80 m   (d) 128 m

9. A particle accelerates from rest at a constant rate for some time and attains a velocity of 8 m/sec. Afterwards it decelerates with the constant rate and comes to rest. If the total time taken is 4 sec, the distance travelled is

   (a) 32 m   (b) 16 m

   (c) 4 m   (d) 8 m

10. Which of the following curve does not represent motion in one dimension?

    (a) 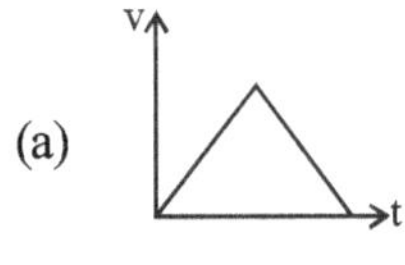   (b) 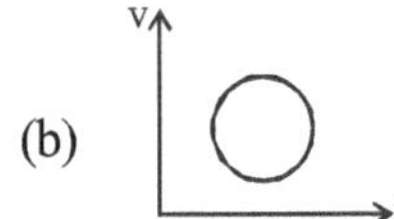

    (c) 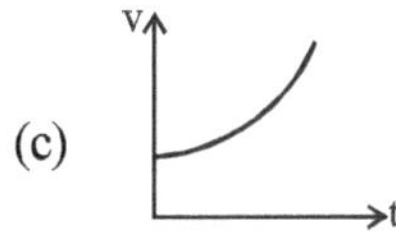   (d) 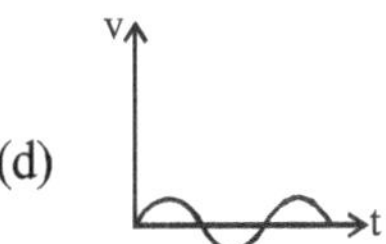

11. The displacement x of a particle at the instant when its velocity is v is given by $v = \sqrt{3x + 16}$. Its acceleration and initial velocity are

    (a) 1.5 units, 4 units   (b) 3 units, 4 units

    (b) 16 units, 1.6 units   (d) 16 units, 3 units

12. Three different objects of masses m_1, m_2 and m_3 are allowed to fall from rest from the same point along three different frictionless paths. The speeds of the three objects on reaching the ground will be in the ratio of

    (a) $m_1 : m_2 : m_3$ (b) $m_1 : 2m_2 : 3m_3$

    (c) $1 : 1 : 1$ (d) $\dfrac{1}{m_1} : \dfrac{1}{m_2} : \dfrac{1}{m_3}$

13. The $v - t$ plot of a moving object is shown in the figure. The average velocity of the object during the first 10 seconds is

    (a) 0

    (b) 2.5 ms^{-1}

    (c) 5 ms^{-1}

    (d) 2 ms^{-1}

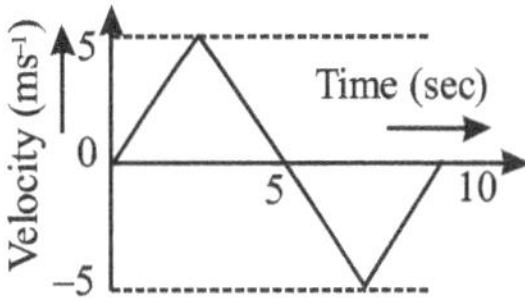

14. A boy walks up a stationary escalator in t_1 second. If he remains stationary on the escalator, then it can take him up in t_2 second. If the length of the escalator is L then time taken by him to walk up the moving escalator is

    (a) $t_2 - t_1$ (b) $\dfrac{t_1 t_2}{t_2 - t_1}$

    (c) $t_1 + t_2$ (d) $\dfrac{t_1 t_2}{t_1 + t_2}$

15. Two cars A and B are travelling in the same direction with velocities v_A and v_B ($v_A > v_B$). When the car A is at a distance d ahead the car B the driver of the car A applies brakes producing a uniform retardation a. There will be no collision when

    (a) $d < \dfrac{(v_A - v_B)^2}{2a}$ (b) $d < \dfrac{v_A^2 - v_B^2}{2a}$

    (c) $d > \dfrac{(v_A - v_B)^2}{2a}$ (d) $d > \dfrac{v_A^2 - v_B^2}{2a}$

16. A ball falls from height h. After 1 second, another ball falls freely from a point 20 m below the point where the first ball falls. Both of them reach the ground at the same time. What is the value of h?

    (a) 11.2 m   (b) 21.2 m

    (c) 31.2 m   (d) 41.2 m

17. A car, moving with a speed of 50 km/hr, can be stopped by brakes after at least 6 m. If the same car is moving at a speed of 100 km/hr, the minimum stopping distance is

    (a) 12 m   (b) 18 m

    (c) 24 m   (d) 6 m

18. The given figure represents the displacement (x) time (t) graph for a particle in one dimensional motion.

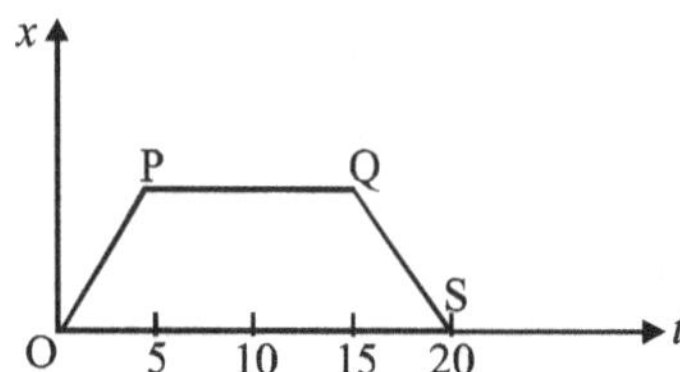

Which of the figure given below represents the variation in velocity of the particle with time

(a) 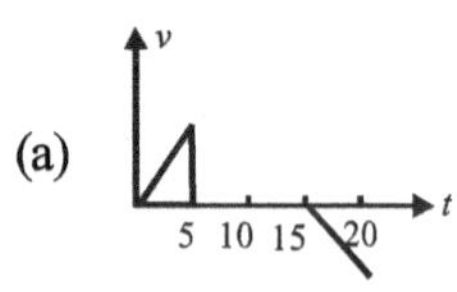

(b) 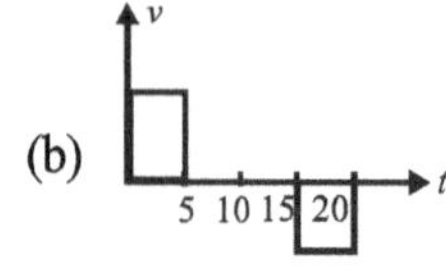

(c) 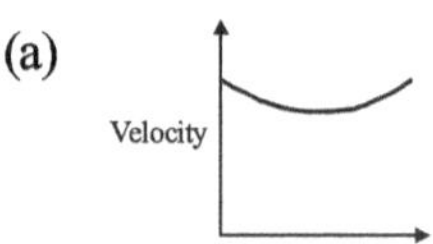

(d) 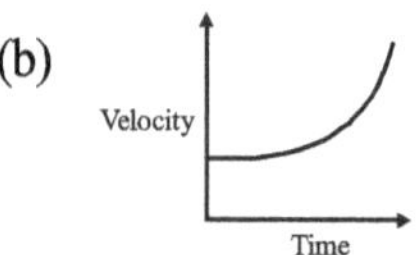

19. Which graph corresponds to an object moving with a constant negative acceleration and a positive velocity ?

(a) 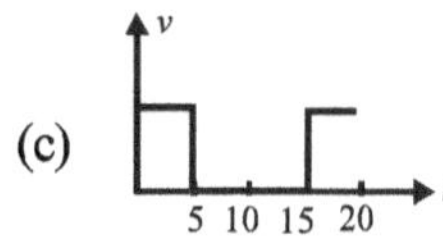

(b) 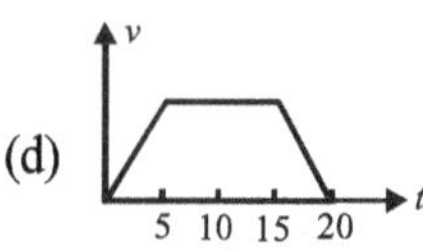

(c) 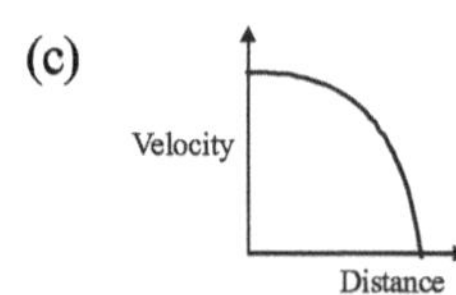

(d) 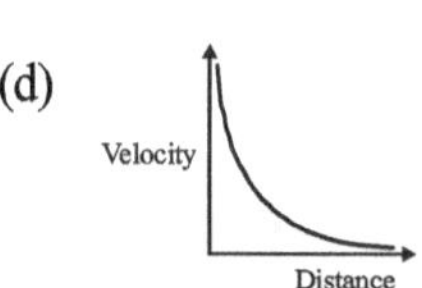

20. A car covers the first half of the distance between two places at 40 km/h and other half at 60 km/h. The average speed of the car is

  (a) 40 km/h   (b) 45 km/h

  (c) 48 km/h   (d) 60 km/h

21. In a car race on straight road, car A takes a time t less than car B at the finish and passes finishing point with a speed 'v' more than of car B. Both the cars start from rest and travel with constant acceleration a_1 and a_2 respectively. Then 'v' is equal to:

(a) $\dfrac{2a_1 a_2}{a_1 + a_2}\, t$ (b) $\sqrt{2a_1 a_2}\; t$

(c) $\sqrt{a_1 a_2}\; t$ (d) $\dfrac{a_1 + a_2}{2}\, t$

22. The acceleration of a moving body can be found from

  (a) area under velocity-time graph

  (b) area under distance-time graph

  (c) slope of the velocity-time graph

  (d) slope of distance-time graph

23. The graph (fig.) below describes the motion of a ball rebounding from a horizontal surface being released from a point above the surface. Assume the ball collides each time with the floor inelastically. The quantity represented on the y-axis is the ball's (take upward direction as positive)

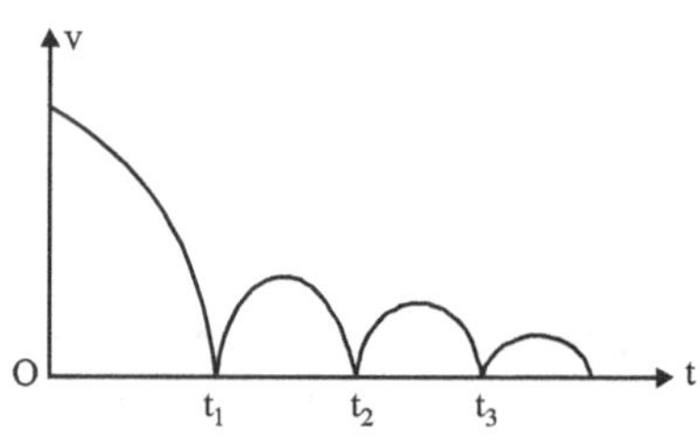

  (a) displacement   (b) velocity

  (c) acceleration   (d) momentum

24. A body moving with a uniform acceleration crosses a distance of 65 m in the 5 th second and 105 m in 9th second. How far will it go in 20 s?

  (a) 2040 m   (b) 240 m

  (c) 2400 m   (d) 2004 m

25. A particle moves along a straight line OX. At a time t (in second) the distance x (in metre) of the particle from O is given by $x = 40 + 12t - t^3$. How long would the particle travel before coming to rest?

(a) 40 m (b) 56 m

(c) 16 m (d) 24 m

26. A man in a balloon, throws a stone downwards with a speed of 5 m/s with respect to balloon. The balloon is moving upwards with constant acceleration of 5 m/s². Then velocity of the stone relative to the man after 2 second is

(a) 10 m/s (b) 30 m/s

(c) 15 m/s (d) 35 m/s

27. A balloon is rising vertically up with a velocity of 29 ms⁻¹. A stone is dropped from it and it reaches the ground in 10 seconds. The height of the balloon when the stone was dropped from it, was ($g = 9.8$ ms⁻²)

(a) 100 m (b) 200 m

(c) 400 m (d) 150 m

28. Two bodies, A (of mass 1 kg) and B (of mass 3 kg), are dropped from heights of 16 m and 25 m, respectively. The ratio of the time taken by them to reach the ground is

(a) $12 : 5$ (b) $5 : 12$

(c) $4 : 5$ (d) $5 : 4$

29. The graph of an object's motion (along the x-axis) is shown in the figure. The instantaneous velocity of the object at points A and B are v_A and v_B respectively. Then

(a) $v_A = v_B = 0.5$ m/s

(b) $v_A = 0.5$ m/s $< v_B$

(c) $v_A = 0.5$ m/s $> v_B$

(d) $v_A = v_B = 2$ m/s

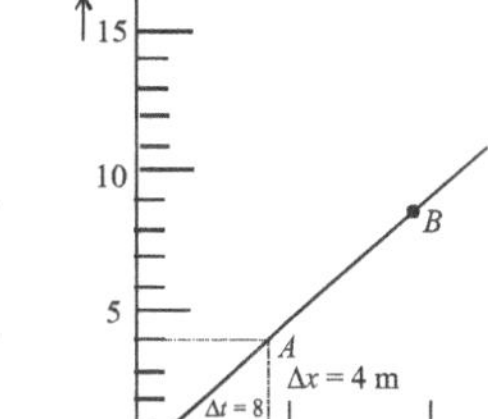

30. A body starts from rest with an acceleration a_1. After two seconds another body B starts from rest with an acceleration a_2. If they travel equal distances in fifth second, after the starts of A, the ratio $a_1 : a_2$ will be equal to

(a) $9 : 5$ (b) $5 : 7$

(c) $5 : 9$ (d) $7 : 9$

ANSWER KEY																												
1	(c)	4	(b)	7	(b)	10	(b)	13	(a)	16	(c)	19	(c)	22	(c)	25	(b)	28	(c)
2	(b)	5	(d)	8	(c)	11	(a)	14	(d)	17	(c)	20	(c)	23	(a)	26	(d)	29	(a)
3	(b)	6	(a)	9	(b)	12	(c)	15	(c)	18	(b)	21	(c)	24	(c)	27	(b)	30	(c)

MOTION IN A PLANE 

1. The vector that must be added to the vector $\hat{i} - 3\hat{j} + 2\hat{k}$ and $3\hat{i} + 6\hat{j} + 7\hat{k}$ so that the resultant vector is a unit vector along the positive y-axis, is

   (a) $4\hat{i} - 2\hat{j} + 5\hat{k}$
   (b) $-4\hat{i} - 2\hat{j} - 9\hat{k}$

   (c) $3\hat{i} - 4\hat{j} + 5\hat{k}$
   (d) null vector

2. Two stones are projected from the same point with same speed making angles $(45° + \theta)$ and $(45° - \theta)$ with the horizontal respectively. If $\theta \leq 45°$, then the horizontal ranges of the two stones are in the ratio of

   (a) $1:1$
   (b) $1:2$
   (c) $1:3$
   (d) $1:4$

3. The angle between the two vectors

   $$\vec{A} = 3\hat{i} + 4\hat{j} + 5\hat{k} \text{ and } \vec{B} = 3\hat{i} + 4\hat{j} - 5\hat{k} \text{ will be}$$

   (a) zero
   (b) $45°$
   (c) $90°$
   (d) $180°$

4. An aircraft moving with a speed of 250 m/s is at a height of 6000 m, just overhead of an anti aircraft gun. If the muzzle velocity is 500 m/s, the firing angle θ should be:

   (a) $30°$
   (b) $45°$
   (c) $60°$
   (d) $90°$.

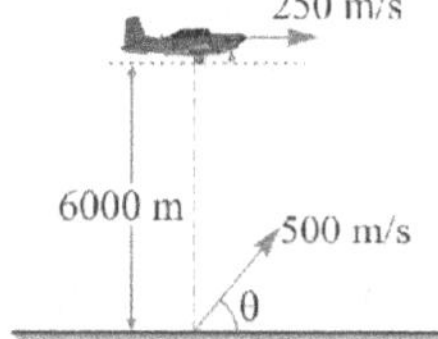

5. At the height 80 m, an aeroplane is moving with a speed of 150 m/s. A bomb is dropped from it so as to hit a target. At what distance from the target should the bomb be dropped (given g = 10 m/s²)

   (a) 605.3 m
   (b) 600 m
   (c) 80 m
   (d) 230 m

6. An object is projected with a velocity of 20 m/s making an angle of 45° with horizontal. The equation for the trajectory is $h = Ax - Bx^2$ where h is height, x is horizontal distance, A and B are constants. The ratio A : B is (g = 10 ms⁻²)

   (a) $1:5$
   (b) $5:1$
   (c) $1:40$
   (d) $40:1$

7. A large number of bullets are fired in all directions with the same speed v from ground. What is the maximum area on the ground on which these bullets will spread?

   (a) $\dfrac{\pi v^2}{g}$
   (b) $\dfrac{\pi v^4}{g^2}$
   (c) $\pi^2 \dfrac{v^2}{g^2}$
   (d) $\dfrac{\pi^2 v^4}{g^2}$

8. A man can swim in still water with a speed of 2 m/s. If he wants to cross a river of water current speed $\sqrt{3}$ m/s along the shortest possible path, then in which direction should he swim?
   (a) At an angle 120° to the water current.
   (b) At an angle 150° to the water current.
   (c) At an angle 90° to the water current.
   (d) None of these

9. Initial velocity with which a body is projected is 10 m/sec and angle of projection is 60° with horizontal, find the range R

   (a) $\dfrac{15\sqrt{3}\,\text{m}}{2}$
   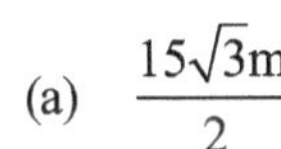

   (b) $\dfrac{40}{3}\,\text{m}$

   (c) $5\sqrt{3}\,\text{m}$

   (d) $\dfrac{20}{3}\,\text{m}$

10. If a_r and a_t represent radial and tangential accelerations, the motion of particle will be uniformly circular, if
    (a) $a_r = 0$ and $a_t = 0$
    (b) $a_r = 0$ but $a_t \neq 0$
    (c) $a_r \neq 0$ and $a_t = 0$
    (d) $a_r \neq 0$ and $a_t \neq 0$

11. If a body moving in circular path maintains constant speed of 10 ms⁻¹, then which of the following correctly describes relation between magnitude of acceleration and radius ?

   (a) 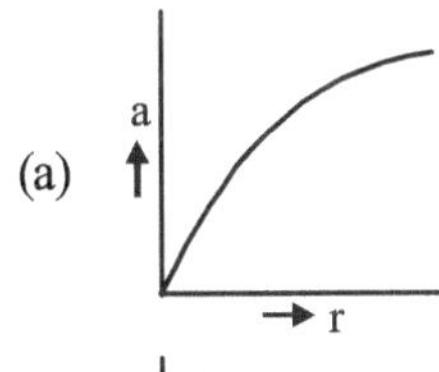
   (b) 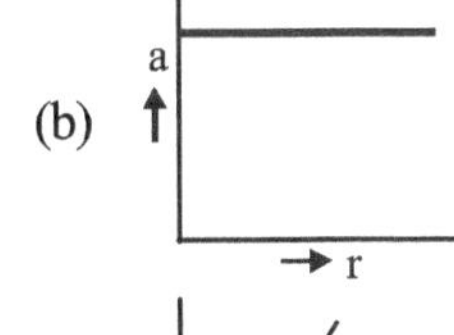
   (c) 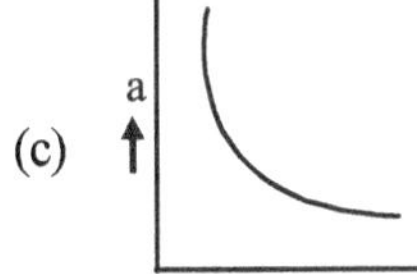
   (d) 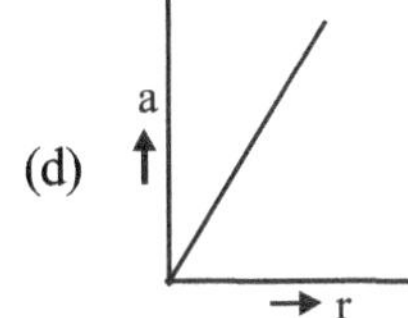

12. A projectile thrown with velocity v making angle θ with vertical gains maximum height 20m in the time for which the projectile remains in air, the time period is
    (a) 15 s
    (b) 25 s
    (c) 9 s
    (d) 4 s

13. A projectile is fired with a velocity v at right angle to the slope which is inclined at an angle θ with the horizontal. The range of the projectile along the inclined plane is:

   (a) $\dfrac{2v^2 \tan\theta}{g}$

   (b) $\dfrac{v^2 \sec\theta}{g} 0$

   (c) $\dfrac{2v^2 \tan\theta \sec\theta}{g}$

   (d) $\dfrac{v^2 \sin\theta}{g}$

   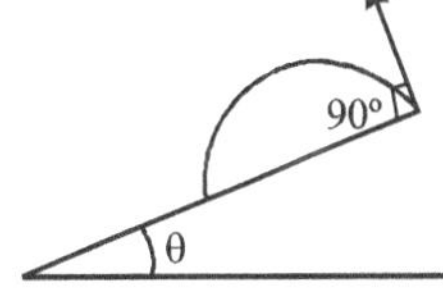

14. A car is moving along a circular path of radius 500 m with a speed of 30 m/s. If at some instant, its speed increases at the rate of 2 m/s², than at that instant the magnitude of resultant acceleration will be
    (a) 4.7 m/s²
    (b) 3.8 m/s²
    (c) 3 m/s²
    (d) 2.7 m/s²

15. A projectile reaches its highest point when it has covered exactly one half of its horizontal range. The corresponding point on the horizontal component of velocity-time (i.e. v_x–t) graph is characterized by
    (a) negative slope
    (b) negative slope and negative curvature
    (c) zero slope
    (d) positive slope

16. Two bodies are thrown up at angles of 45° and 60° respectively, with the horizontal. If both bodies attain same vertical height, then the ratio of velocities with which these are thrown is

(a) $\sqrt{\dfrac{2}{3}}$ (b) $\dfrac{2}{\sqrt{3}}$

(c) $\sqrt{\dfrac{3}{2}}$ (d) $\dfrac{\sqrt{3}}{2}$

17. Trajectories are shown in figure are for three kicked footballs, ignoring the effect of the air on the footballs. If T_1, T_2 and T_3 are their respective time of flights then:

(a) $T_1 > T_3$

(b) $T_1 < T_3$

(c) $T_2 = \dfrac{T_3}{2}$

(d) $T_1 = T_2 = T_3$

18. A projectile is given an initial velocity of $(\hat{i} + 2\hat{j})$ m/s, where $\hat{i}$ is along the ground and $\hat{j}$ is along the vertical. If g = 10 m/s², the equation of its trajectory is :

(a) $y = x - 5x^2$ (b) $y = 2x - 5x^2$

(c) $4y = 2x - 5x^2$ (d) $4y = 2x - 25x^2$

19. A clock has a continuously moving second's hand of 0.1 m length. The average acceleration of the tip of the hand (in units of ms⁻²) is of the order of:

(a) 10^{-3} (b) 10^{-4}

(c) 10^{-2} (d) 10^{-1}

20. A particle has an initial velocity of $3\hat{i} + 4\hat{j}$ and an acceleration of $0.4\hat{i} + 0.3\hat{j}$. Its speed after 10 s is :

(a) $7\sqrt{2}$ units (b) 7 units

(c) 8.5 units (d) 10 units

21. A particle is moving along a circular path with a constant speed of 10 ms⁻¹. What is the magnitude of the change in velocity of the particle, when it moves through an angle of 60° around the centre of the circle?

(a) $10\sqrt{3}$ m/s (b) zero

(c) $10\sqrt{2}$ m/s (d) 10 m/s

22. A projectile is thrown in the upward direction making an angle of 60° with the horizontal direction with a velocity of 147 ms⁻¹. Then the time after which its inclination with horizontal is 45°, is

(a) 15 s (b) 10.98 s

(c) 5.49 s (d) 2.745 s

23. A boy playing on the roof of a 20 m high tower throws a ball with a speed of 20m/s at an angle of 45° with the horizontal. How far from the throwing point will the ball be at the height of 20 m from the ground ? $[g = 10 \text{m}/\text{s}^2]$

(a) 20m (b) 4.33m

(c) 2.60m (d) 40m

24. A particle is projected from a tower as shown in figure, then the distance from the foot of the tower where it will strike the ground will be

(a) 4000/3 m

(b) 2000/m

(c) 1000/3 m

(d) 2500/3 m

25. An electric fan has blades of length 30 cm measured from the axis of rotation. If the fan is rotating at 120 rpm, the acceleration of a point on the tip of the blade is

(a) 1600 ms^{-2} (b) 47.4 ms^{-2}

(c) 23.7 ms^{-2} (d) 50.55 ms^{-2}

26. A ball projected from ground at an angle of $45°$ just clears a wall in front. If point of projection is 4 m from the foot of wall and ball strikes the ground at a distance of 6 m on the other side of the wall, the height of the wall is :

    (a) 4.4 m
    (b) 2.4 m
    (c) 3.6 m
    (d) 1.6 m

27. A particle is projected with a certain velocity at an angle α above the horizontal from the foot of an inclined plane of inclination $30°$. If the particle strikes the plane normally then α is

    (a) $30° + \tan^{-1}\left(\dfrac{\sqrt{3}}{2}\right)$
    (b) $30° + \tan^{-1}\dfrac{1}{2}$

    (c) $30° + \tan^{-1}1$
    (d) $60°$

28. A ball is thrown from a point with a speed $'v_0'$ at an elevation angle of θ. From the same point and at the same instant, a person starts running with a constant speed $\dfrac{'v_0'}{2}$ to catch the ball. Will the person be able to catch the ball? If yes, what should be the angle of projection θ?

    (a) No
    (b) Yes, $30°$
    (c) Yes, $60°$
    (d) Yes, $45°$

29. A shell is fired from a fixed artillery gun with an initial speed u such that it hits the target on the ground at a distance R from it. If t_1 and t_2 are the values of the time taken by it to hit the target in two possible ways, the product $t_1 t_2$ is :

    (a) R/4g
    (b) R/g
    (c) R/2g
    (d) 2R/g

30. Two particles are projected from the same point with the same speed u such that they have the same range R, but different maximum heights, h_1 and h_2. Which of the following is correct ?

    (a) $R^2 = 4 h_1 h_2$
    (b) $R^2 = 16 h_1 h_2$
    (c) $R^2 = 2 h_1 h_2$
    (d) $R^2 = h_1 h_2$

LAWS OF MOTION

1. A player caught a cricket ball of mass 150 g moving at a rate of 20 m/s. If the catching process is completed in 0.1s, the force of the blow exerted by the ball on the hand of the player is equal to

(a) 150 N

(b) 3 N

(c) 30 N

(d) 300 N

2. A ball is thrown vertically up (taken as $+z$-axis) from the ground. The correct momentum-height (p-h) diagram is:

(a) 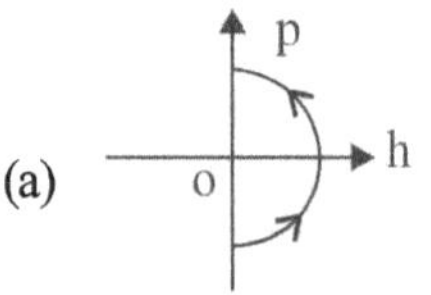

(b) 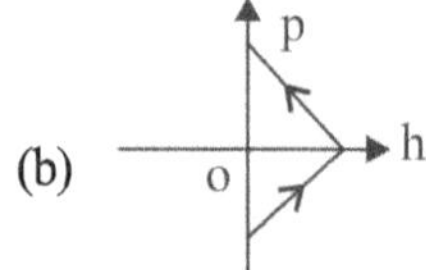

(c) 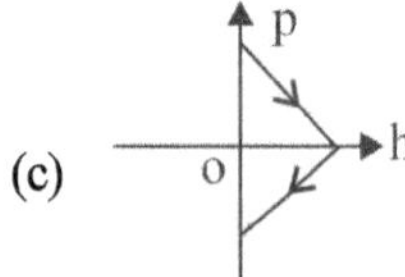

(d) 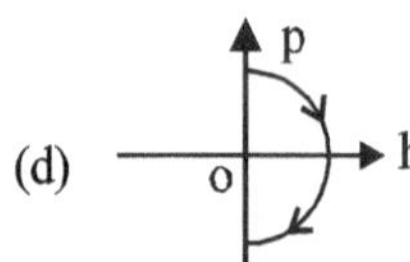

3. A rope of length 4 m having mass 1.5 kg/m lying on a horizontal frictionless surface is pulled at one end by a force of 12N. What is the tension in the rope at a point 1.6 m from the other end?

(a) 5N

(b) 4.8N

(c) 7.2N

(d) 6N

4. A 1 kg block and a 0.5 kg block move together on a horizontal frictionless surface. Each block exerts a force of 6 N on the other. The block move with a uniform acceleration of

(a) 3 ms^{-2}

(b) 6 ms^{-2}

(c) 9 ms^{-2}

(d) 12 ms^{-2}

5. An elevator weighing 6000 kg is pulled upward by a cable with an acceleration of 5 ms^{-2}. Taking g to be 10 ms^{-2}, then the tension in the cable is

(a) 6000 N

(b) 9000 N

(c) 60000 N

(d) 90000 N

6. A block A of mass 7 kg is placed on a frictionless table. A thread tied to it passes over a frictionless pulley and carries a body B of mass 3 kg at the other end. The acceleration of the system is (given $g = 10 \text{ ms}^{-2}$)

(a) 100 ms^{-2}

(b) 3 ms^{-2}

(c) 10 ms^{-2}

(d) 30 ms^{-2}

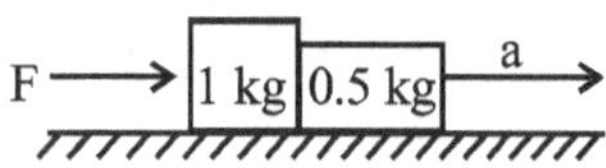

7. A block of mass M is pulled along a horizontal frictionless surface by a rope of mass m. If a force P is applied at the free end of the rope, the force exerted by the rope on the block is

(a) $\dfrac{Pm}{M+m}$

(b) $\dfrac{Pm}{M-m}$

(c) P

(d) $\dfrac{PM}{M+m}$

8. A block of mass 4 kg is suspended through two light spring balances A and B. Then A and B will read respectively :

(a) 4 kg and zero kg

(b) zero kg and 4 kg

(c) 4 kg and 4 kg

(d) 2 kg and 2 kg

9. The coefficient of friction between a body and the surface of an inclined plane at $45°$ is 0.5. If g = 9.8 m/s^2, the acceleration of the body in downwards in m/s^2 is

(a) $\dfrac{4.9}{\sqrt{2}}$

(b) $4.9\sqrt{2}$

(c) $19.6\sqrt{2}$

(d) 4.9

10. A block weighs W is held against a vertical wall having coefficient of friction μ by applying a horizontal force F. The value of F needed to hold the block is

(a) Less than W/μ

(b) Equal to $W/2\mu$

(c) Greater than or equal to W/μ

(d) Data is insufficient

11. A body of mass 0.4 kg is whirled in a vertical circle making 2 rev/sec. If the radius of the circle is 1.2 m, then tension in the string when the body is at the top of the circle, is

(a) 71.8 N

(b) 89.86 N

(c) 109.86 N

(d) 115.86 N

12. The rate of mass of the gas emitted from rear of a rocket is initially 0.1 kg/sec. If the speed of the gas relative to the rocket is 50 m/sec and mass of the rocket is 2 kg, then the acceleration of the rocket in m/sec^2 is

(a) 5

(b) 5.2

(c) 2.5

(d) 25

13. Two masses $m_1 = 5$g and $m_2 = 4.8$ kg tied to a string are hanging over a light frictionless pulley. What is the acceleration of m_1 when left free to move ? $(g = 9.8$ m/s$^2)$

(a) 5 m/s^2

(b) 9.8 m/s^2

(c) 0.2 m/s^2

(d) 4.8 m/s^2

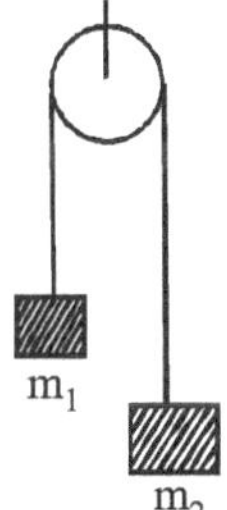

14. Consider a car moving along a straight horizontal road with a speed of 72 km/h. If the coefficient of static friction between the tyres and the road is 0.5, the shortest distance in which the car can be stopped is (taking g = 10 m/s^2)

(a) 30 m

(b) 40 m

(c) 72 m

(d) 20 m

15. A body of weight $2kg$ is suspended as shown in the figure. The tension T_1 in the horizontal string (in $kg\,wt$) is

(a) $2/\sqrt{3}$

(b) $\sqrt{3}/2$

(c) $2\sqrt{3}$

(d) 2

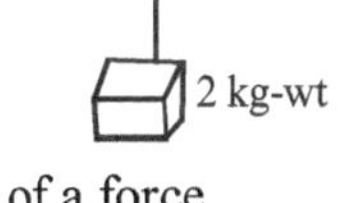

16. A body under the action of a force

$\bar{F} = 6\,\hat{i} - 8\,\hat{j} + 10\,\hat{k}$, acquires an acceleration of 1 m/s^2. The mass of this body must be

(a) 10 kg

(b) 20 kg

(c) $10\sqrt{2}$ kg

(d) $2\sqrt{10}$ kg

17. A particle of mass m is acted upon by a force F given by the empirical law $F = \dfrac{R}{t^2}\, v(t)$. If this law is to be tested experimentally by observing the motion starting from rest, the graph between which of the following gives a straight line?

(a) log v(t) against $\dfrac{1}{t}$ (b) v(t) against t^2

(c) log v(t) against $\dfrac{1}{t^2}$ (d) log v(t) against t

18. Three forces start acting simultaneously on a particle moving with velocity $\vec{v}$. These forces are represented in magnitude and direction by the three sides of a triangle ABC. The particle will now move with velocity

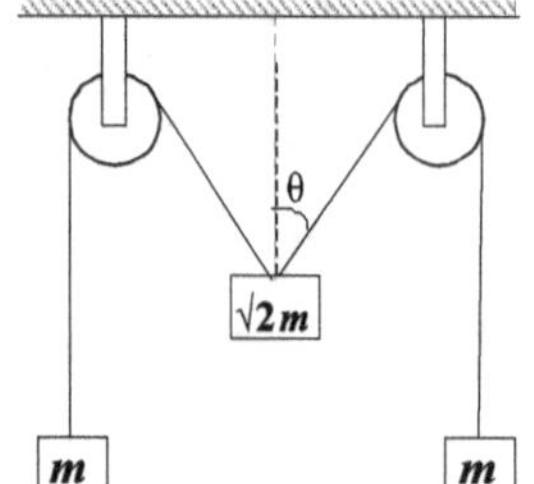

(a) less than $\vec{v}$

(b) greater than $\vec{v}$

(c) $|\vec{v}|$ in the direction of the largest force BC

(d) $\vec{v}$, remaining unchanged

19. A box of mass 8 kg is placed on a rough inclined plane of inclination 45°. Its downward motion can be prevented by applying an upward pull F and it can be made to slide upwards by applying a force 2F. The coefficient of friction between the box and the inclined plane is

(a) $\dfrac{1}{2}$ (b) $\dfrac{1}{\sqrt{2}}$

(c) $\dfrac{1}{2\sqrt{2}}$ (d) $\dfrac{1}{3}$

20. The pulleys and strings shown in the figure are smooth and of negligible mass. For the system to remain in equilibrium, the angle θ should be

(a) 0°

(b) 30°

(c) 45°

(d) 60°

21. A smooth block is released at rest on a 45° incline and then slides a distance 'd'. The time taken to slide is 'n' times as much to slide on rough incline than on a smooth incline. The coefficient of friction is

(a) $\mu_k = \sqrt{1 - \dfrac{1}{n^2}}$ (b) $\mu_k = 1 - \dfrac{1}{n^2}$

(c) $\mu_s = \sqrt{1 - \dfrac{1}{n^2}}$ (d) $\mu_s = 1 - \dfrac{1}{n^2}$

22. Consider a car moving on a straight road with a speed of 100 m/s. The distance at which car can be stopped is $[\mu_k = 0.5]$

(a) 1000 m   (b) 800 m

(c) 400 m   (d) 100 m

23. A block is kept on a frictionless inclined surface with angle of inclination 'α'. The incline is given an acceleration 'a' to keep the block stationary. Then a is equal to

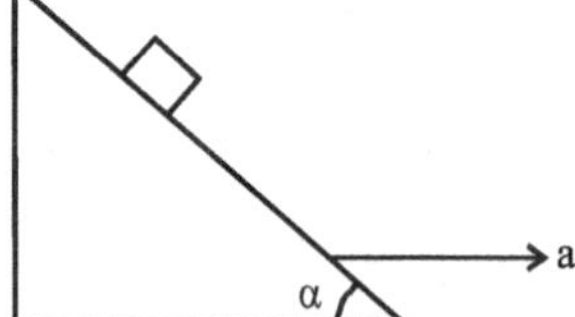

(a) g cosec α

(b) g / tan α

(c) g tan α

(d) g

24. A disc rotates about its axis of symmetry in a hoizontal plane at a steady rate of 3.5 revolutions per second. A coin placed at a distance of 1.25cm from the axis of rotation remains at rest on the disc. The coefficient of friction between the coin and the disc is (g = 10m/s²)

(a) 0.5   (b) 0.7

(c) 0.3   (d) 0.6

25. One end of a massless rope, which passes over a massless and frictionless pulley P is tied to a hook C while the other end is free. Maximum tension that the rope can bear is 360 N. With what value of maximum safe acceleration (in ms⁻²) can a man of 60 kg climb on the rope?

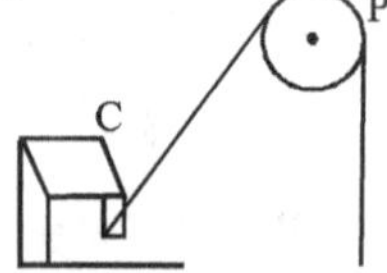

(a) 16

(b) 6

(c) 4

(d) 8

26. The upper half of an inclined plane with inclination ϕ is perfectly smooth while the lower half is rough. A body starting from rest at the top will again come to rest at the bottom if the coefficient of friction for the lower half is given by

    (a) $2\cos\phi$ (b) $2\sin\phi$

    (c) $\tan\phi$ (d) $2\tan\phi$

27. A 60 kg man stands on a spring scale in a lift. At some instant, he finds that the scale reading has changed from 60 kg to 50 kg for a while and then comes back to original mark. What should be concluded?

    (a) The lift was in constant motion upwards

    (b) The lift was in constant motion downwards

    (c) The lift while in downward motion suddenyl stopped

    (d) The lift while in upward motion suddenly stopped

28. In a rocket of mass 1000 kg fuel is consumed at a rate of 40 kg/s. The velocity of the gases ejected from the rocket is 5×10^4 m/s. The thrust on the rocket is

    (a) $2 \times 10^3\,\text{N}$ (b) $5 \times 10^4\,\text{N}$

    (c) $2 \times 10^6\,\text{N}$ (d) $2 \times 10^9\,\text{N}$

29. A particle describes a horizontal circle in a conical funnel whose inner surface is smooth with speed of 0.5 m/s. What is the height of the plane of circle from vertex of the funnel?

    (a) 0.25 cm   (b) 2 cm

    (c) 4 cm   (d) 2.5 cm

30. A car moves at a speed of 20 ms^{-1} on a banked track and describes an arc of a circle of radius $40\sqrt{3}$ m. The angle of banking is ($g = 10\,\text{ms}^{-2}$)

    (a) $25°$ (b) $60°$

    (c) $45°$ (d) $30°$

ANSWER KEY																			
1	(c)	4	(d)	7	(d)	10	(c)	13	(c)	16	(c)	19	(d)	22	(a)	25	(c)	28	(c)
2	(d)	5	(d)	8	(c)	11	(a)	14	(b)	17	(a)	20	(c)	23	(c)	26	(d)	29	(d)
3	(b)	6	(b)	9	(a)	12	(c)	15	(c)	18	(d)	21	(b)	24	(d)	27	(d)	30	(d)

WORK, ENERGY AND POWER

1. A body of mass 10 kg is dropped to the ground from a height of 10 metre. The work done by the gravitational force is ($g = 9.8$ m/sec^2)

   (a) -490 joule   (b) $+490$ joule

   (c) -980 joule   (d) $+980$ joule

2. A ball of mass 2 kg and another of mass 4 kg are dropped together from a 60 feet tall building. After a fall of 30 feet each towards earth, their respective kinetic energies will be in the ratio of

   (a) $1 : \sqrt2$ (b) $\sqrt2 : 1$

   (c) $1 : 4$ (d) $1 : 2$

3. A spring of spring constant 5×10^3 N/m is stretched initially by 5cm from the unstretched position. Then the work required to stretch it further by another 5 cm is

   (a) 12.50 Nm   (b) 18.75 Nm

   (c) 25.00 Nm   (d) 6.25 Nm

4. A force F acting on an object varies with distance x as shown in graph. The force is in N and x in m. The work done by the force in moving the object from $x = 0$ to $x = 6$ m is

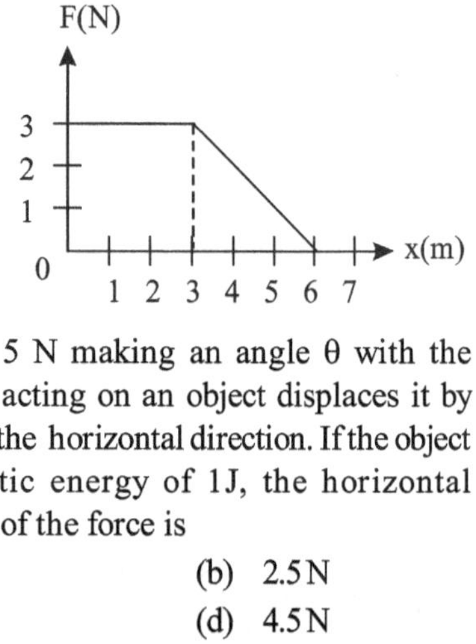

   (a) 18.0 J

   (b) 13.5 J

   (c) 9.0 J

   (d) 4.5 J

5. A force of 5 N making an angle θ with the horizontal, acting on an object displaces it by 0.4m along the horizontal direction. If the object gains kinetic energy of 1J, the horizontal component of the force is

   (a) 1.5 N   (b) 2.5 N

   (c) 3.5 N   (d) 4.5 N

6. A body of mass 10 kg moves with a velocity of 2 m/s along a circular path of radius 8 m. The power produced by the body will be (Assume motion of the body is uniform circular motion)

   (a) 10 J/s   (b) 98 J/s

   (c) 49 J/s   (d) zero

7. A body is initially at rest. It undergoes one dimensional motion with constant acceleration. The power delivered to it at time t is proportional to

   (a) $t^{1/2}$ (b) t^3

   (c) $t^{2/3}$ (d) t

8. Two identical balls A and B moving with velocities +0.5 m/s and –0.3 m/s respectively, collide head on elastically. The velocities of the balls A and B after collision, will be, respectively
(a) +0.5 m/s and +0.3 m/s
(b) – 0.3 m/s and +0.5 m/s
(c) +0.3 m/s and 0.5 m/s
(d) –0.5 m/s and +0.3 m/s

9. A shell of mass 20 kg at rest explodes into two fragments whose masses are in the ratio 2 : 3. The smaller fragment moves with a velocity of 6 m/s. The kinetic energy of the larger fragment is
(a) 360 J
(b) 96 J
(c) 144 J
(d) 216 J

10. In two separate collisions, the coefficients of restitutions 'e_1' and 'e_2' are in the ratio of 3 : 1. In the first collision the relative velocity of approach is twice the relative velocity of separation. Then the ratio between the relative velocity of approach and relative velocity of separation in the second collisions is
(a) 1 : 5
(b) 2 : 3
(c) 3 : 2
(d) 6 : 1

11. A ball drops from a celling of a room and after rebounding twice from the floor reaches a height equal to half that of the celling. Find the coefficient of restitution.
(a) $\dfrac{1}{\sqrt{3}}$
(b) $\left(\dfrac{1}{2}\right)^{1/4}$
(c) $\left(\dfrac{1}{3}\right)^{1/2}$
(d) $\left(\dfrac{1}{4}\right)^{1/2}$

12. The bob A of a simple pendulum is released when the string makes an angle of 45° with the vertical. It hits another bob B of the same material and same mass kept at rest on the table. If the collision is elastic

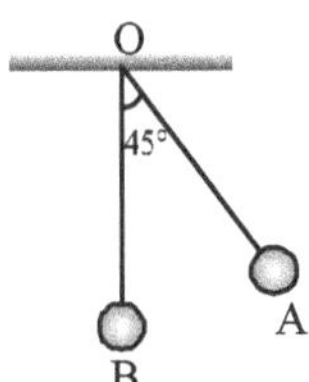

(a) both A and B rise to the same height
(b) both A and B come to rest at B
(c) both A and B move with the same velocity of A
(d) A comes to rest and B moves with the velocity of A

13. A car of mass m moving at a speed v is stopped at a distance x by the friction between the tyres and the road. If the kinetic energy of the car is doubled, its stopping distance will be
(a) 8x
(b) 4x
(c) 2x
(d) x

14. A ball of mass 2kg moving with velocity 3m/s, strikes with spring of natural length 2m and force constant 144 N/m. What will be length of compressed spring ?
(a) 2m
(b) 1.5m
(c) 1m
(d) 0.5m

15. A uniform rod of mass m and length l is held inclined at an angle of 60° with the vertical. What will be the potential energy of the rod in this position ?
(a) zero
(b) $\dfrac{mgl}{4}$
(c) $\dfrac{mgl}{2}$
(d) $mg\ell$

16. A particle is acted by a force $F = kx$, where k is a +ve constant. Its potential energy at $x = 0$ is zero. Which curve correctly represents the variation of potential energy of the block with respect to x?

(a) 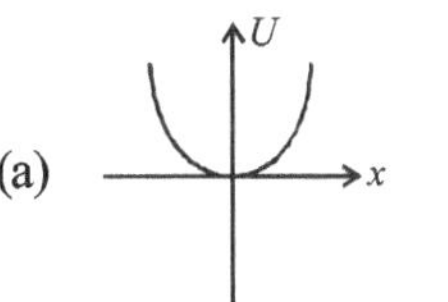
(b) 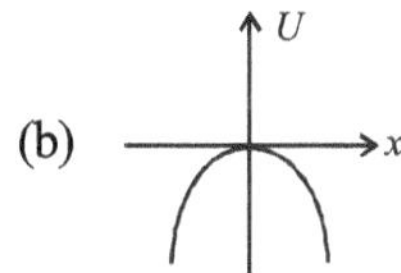
(c) 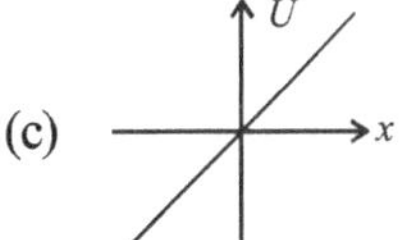
(d) 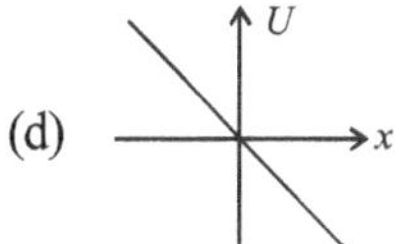

17. A metal ball of mass 2 kg moving with a velocity of 36 km/h has a head on collision with a stationary ball of mass 3 kg. If after the collision, the two balls move together, the loss in kinetic energy due to collision is

(a) 140 J   (b) 100 J

(c) 60 J   (d) 40 J

18. An object of mass 2.0 kg makes an elastic collision with another object of mass M at rest and continues to move in the original direction but with one-fourth of its original speed. What is the value of M ?

(a) 0.75 kg   (b) 1.0 kg

(c) 1.2 kg   (d) None of these

19. A bullet of mass 20g is moving with 600 m/s collides with a block of mass 4 kg hanging with the string. What is velocity of bullet when it comes out of block, if block rises to height 0.2 m after collision ?

(a) 200 m/s   (b) 150 m/s

(c) 400 m/s   (d) 300 m/s

20. Two particles A and B of equal mass m are moving with the same speed v as shown in the figure. They collide completely inelastically and move as a single particle C. The angle θ that the path of C makes with the X-axis is given by:

(a) $\tan\theta = \dfrac{\sqrt{3}+\sqrt{2}}{1-\sqrt{2}}$

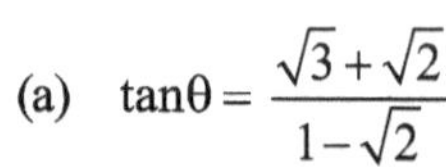

(b) $\tan\theta = \dfrac{\sqrt{3}-\sqrt{2}}{1-\sqrt{2}}$

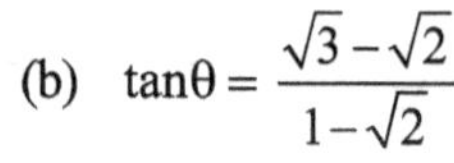

(c) $\tan\theta = \dfrac{1-\sqrt{2}}{\sqrt{2}(1+\sqrt{3})}$

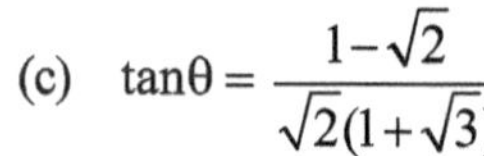

(d) $\tan\theta = \dfrac{1-\sqrt{3}}{1+\sqrt{2}}$

21. The potential energy of a 1 kg particle free to move along the x-axis is given by

$$V(x) = \left(\frac{x^4}{4} - \frac{x^2}{2}\right) J.$$

The total mechanical energy of the particle is 2 J. Then, the maximum speed (in m/s) is

(a) $\dfrac{3}{\sqrt{2}}$ (b) $\sqrt{2}$

(c) $\dfrac{1}{\sqrt{2}}$ (d) 2

22. A mass of M kg is suspended by a weightless string. The horizontal force that is required to displace it until the string makes an angle of 45° with the initial vertical direction is

(a) $Mg(\sqrt{2}+1)$ (b) $Mg\sqrt{2}$

(c) $\dfrac{Mg}{\sqrt{2}}$ (d) $Mg(\sqrt{2}-1)$

23. A particle is projected at 60° to the horizontal with a kinetic energy K. The kinetic energy at the highest point is

(a) $K/2$ (b) K

(c) Zero   (d) $K/4$

24. A particle is moving unidirectionally on a horizontal plane under the action of a constant power supplying energy source. The displacement (s) - time (t) graph that describes the motion of the particle is (graphs are drawn schematically and are not to scale) :

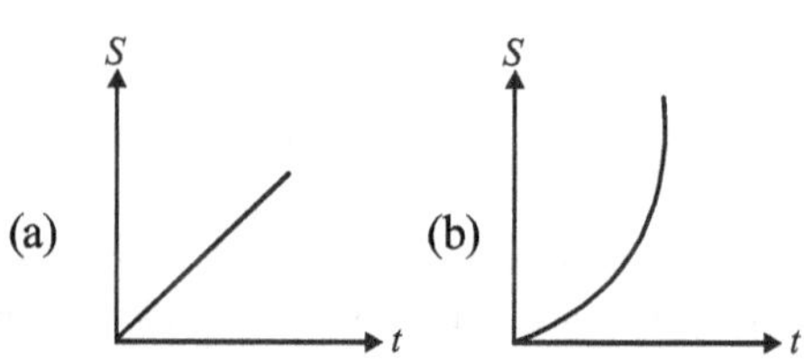

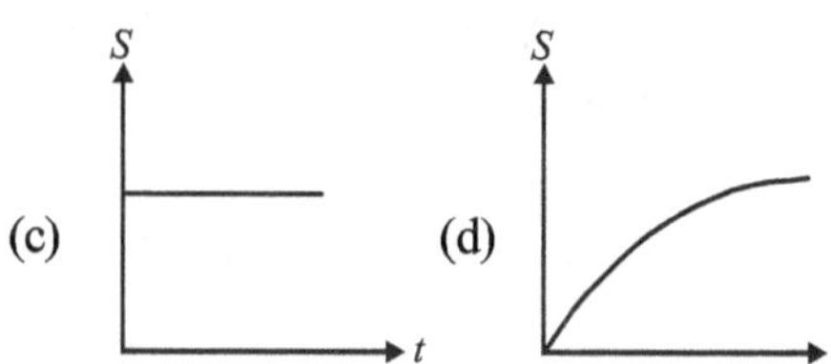

25. A bomb of mass 16kg at rest explodes into two pieces of masses 4 kg and 12 kg. The velolcity of the 12 kg mass is $4\,ms^{-1}$. The kinetic energy of the other mass is

(a) 144 J
(b) 288 J
(c) 192 J
(d) 96 J

26. A particle of mass M is moving in a circle of fixed radius R in such a way that its centripetal acceleration at time t is given by $n^2R\,t^2$ where n is a constant. The power delivered to the particle by the force acting on it, is :

(a) $\dfrac{1}{2}\,M\,n^2\,R^2t^2$
(b) $M\,n^2R^2t$
(c) $M\,n\,R^2t^2$
(d) $M\,n\,R^2t$

27. A bullet fired into a fixed target loses 20% of its kinetic energy in penetrating 1 cm. The total distance penetrated by the bullet before it comes to rest is

(a) 4 cm
(b) 5 cm
(c) 8 cm
(d) 6 cm

28. In a simple pendulum of length l the bob is pulled aside from its equilibrium position through an angle θ and then released. The bob passes through the equilibrium position with speed

(a) $\sqrt{2g\ell(1+\cos\theta)}$
(b) $\sqrt{2g\ell\sin\theta}$
(c) $\sqrt{2g\ell}$
(d) $\sqrt{2g\ell(1-\cos\theta)}$

29. A body of mass 2 kg initially at rest moves under the action of an applied horizontal force of 7N on a table with coefficient of kinetic friction = 0.1. Work done by friction in 10s and change in K.E. of the body in 10s are respectively

(a) 246.9 J, 635 J
(b) 200 J, 600 J
(c) 295 J, 625 J
(d) 500 J, 600 J

30. A force applied by an engine of a train of mass 2.05×10^6 kg and changes its velocity from 5m/s to 25 m/s in 5 minutes. The power of the engine is

(a) 1.025 MW
(b) 2.05 MW
(c) 5 MW
(d) 6 MW

<table>
<tr><td colspan="18" align="center">ANSWER KEY</td></tr>
<tr><td>1</td><td>(d)</td><td>4</td><td>(b)</td><td>7</td><td>(d)</td><td>10</td><td>(d)</td><td>13</td><td>(c)</td><td>16</td><td>(b)</td><td>19</td><td>(a)</td><td>22</td><td>(d)</td><td>25</td><td>(b)</td><td>28</td><td>(d)</td></tr>
<tr><td>2</td><td>(d)</td><td>5</td><td>(b)</td><td>8</td><td>(b)</td><td>11</td><td>(b)</td><td>14</td><td>(b)</td><td>17</td><td>(c)</td><td>20</td><td>(a)</td><td>23</td><td>(d)</td><td>26</td><td>(b)</td><td>29</td><td>(a)</td></tr>
<tr><td>3</td><td>(b)</td><td>6</td><td>(d)</td><td>9</td><td>(b)</td><td>12</td><td>(d)</td><td>15</td><td>(b)</td><td>18</td><td>(c)</td><td>21</td><td>(a)</td><td>24</td><td>(b)</td><td>27</td><td>(b)</td><td>30</td><td>(b)</td></tr>
</table>

SYSTEM OF PARTICLES AND ROTATIONAL MOTION

6

1. Two bodies of masses 2 kg and 4 kg are moving with velocities 2 m/s and 10 m/s respectively along the same direction. Then the velocity of their centre of mass will be

   (a) 8.1 m/s   (b) 7.3 m/s

   (c) 6.4 m/s   (d) 5.3 m/s

2. A ballet dancer, dancing on a smooth floor is spinning about a vertical axis with her arms folded with an angular velocity of 20 rad/s. When she stretches her arms fully, the spinning speed decreases by 10 rad/s. If I is the initial moment of inertia of the dancer, the new moment of inertia is

   (a) $2I$ (b) $3I$

   (c) $I/2$ (d) $I/3$

3. A circular disc of radius R and thickness $\dfrac{R}{6}$ has moment of inertia I about an axis passing through its centre perpendicular to its plane. It is melted and recasted into a solid sphere. The moment of inertia of the sphere about its diameter is

   (a) I (b) $\dfrac{2I}{8}$

   (c) $\dfrac{I}{5}$ (d) $\dfrac{I}{10}$

4. A uniform thin rod of length 2L and mass m lies on a horizontal table. An impulse J is given to the rod at one end. There is no friction. The total kinetic energy of the rod (just after the impulse) will be :

   (a) $\dfrac{J}{2m}$ (b) $\dfrac{J^2}{m}$

   (c) $\dfrac{2J^2}{m}$ (d) $\dfrac{6J^2}{m}$

5. Two discs of moment of inertia I_1 and I_2 and angular speeds ω_1 and ω_2 are rotating along collinear axes passing through their centre of mass and perpendicular to their plane. If the two are made to rotate combindly along the same axis the rotational KE of system will be

   (a) $\dfrac{I_1\omega_1 + I_2\omega_2}{2(I_1 + I_2)}$

   (b) $\dfrac{(I_1 + I_2)(\omega_1 + \omega_2)^2}{2}$

   (c) $\dfrac{(I_1\omega_1 + I_2\omega_2)^2}{2(I_1 + I_2)}$

   (d) None of these

6. A metre stick is held vertically with one end in contact of the floor and is then allowed to fall. If the end touching the floor is not allowed to slip, the other end will hit the ground with a velocity of ($g = 9.8$ m/s^2)

(a) 3.2 m/s

(b) 5.4 m/s

(c) 7.6 m/s

(d) 9.2 m/s

7. Particles of masses m, 2m, 3m, ..., nm grams are placed on the same line at distance ℓ, 2ℓ, 3ℓ, ..., $n\ell$ cm, from a fixed point. The distance of centre of mass of the particles from the fixed point in centimetre is

(a) $\dfrac{(2n+1)\,\ell}{3}$

(b) $\dfrac{\ell}{n+1}$

(c) $\dfrac{n\,(n^2+1)\,\ell}{2}$

(d) $\dfrac{2\ell}{n\,(n^2+1)}$

8. Four particles of masses m_1, m_2, m_3 and m_4 are placed at the vertices A, B, C and D respectively of a square as shown in figure. The COM of the system will lie at diagonal AC if

(a) $m_1 = m_4$

(b) $m_2 = m_4$

(c) $m_1 = m_2$

(d) $m_3 = m_4$

9. A small disc of radius 2 cm is cut from a disc of radius 6 cm. If the distance between their centres is 3.2 cm, what is the shift in the centre of mass of the disc?

(a) 0.4 cm

(b) 2.4 cm

(c) 1.8 cm

(d) 1.2 cm

10. Two racing cars of masses m and 4m are moving in circles of radii r and 2r respectively. If their speeds are such that each makes a complete circle in the same time, then the ratio of the angular speeds of the first to the second car is

(a) 8 : 1

(b) 4 : 1

(c) 2 : 1

(d) 1 : 1

11. A cubical block of side $a = 30$ cm is moving with velocity 2 ms^{-1} on a smooth horizontal surface. The surface has a bump at a point O as shown in figure. The angular velocity (in rad/s) of the block immediately after it hits the bump, is :

(a) 13.3

(b) 5.0

(c) 9.4

(d) 6.7

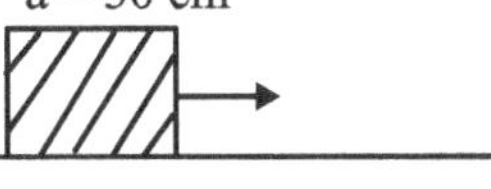

12. A ball of mass 160 g is thrown up at an angle of 60° to the horizontal at a speed of 10 ms^{-1}. The angular momentum of the ball at the highest point of the trajectory with respect to the point from which the ball is thrown is nearly ($g = 10$ ms^{-2})

(a) 1.73 kg m^2/s

(b) 3.0 kg m^2/s

(c) 3.46 kg m^2/s

(d) 6.0 kg m^2/s

13. When a ceiling fan is switched off, its angular velocity falls to half while it makes 36 rotations. How many more rotations will it make before coming to rest?

(a) 24

(b) 36

(c) 18

(d) 12

14. The figure shows a metallic plate of uniform density. The value of ℓ, in terms of L so that the centre of mass of the system lies at the common interface of the triangular and rectangular portion is

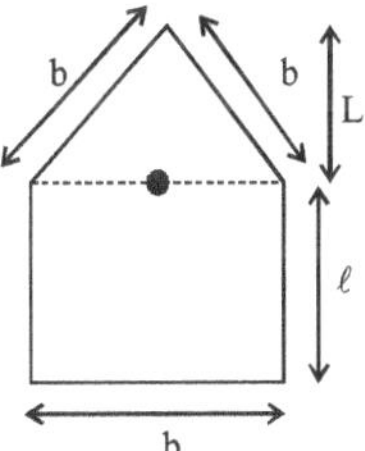

(a) $\sqrt{\dfrac{L}{3}}$

(b) $\dfrac{L}{3}$

(c) $\dfrac{L}{\sqrt{3}}$

(d) $L\sqrt{\dfrac{2}{3}}$

15. The angular velocity of a body changes from ω_1 to ω_2 without applying a torque but by changing the moment of inertia about its axis of rotation. The ratio of its corresponding radii of gyration is

(a) $\omega_1 : \omega_2$

(b) $\sqrt{\omega_1} : \sqrt{\omega_2}$

(c) $\omega_2 : \omega_1$

(d) $\sqrt{\omega_2} : \sqrt{\omega_1}$

16. Moment of inertia of an equilateral triangular lamina ABC, about the axis passing through its centre O and perpendicular to its plane is I_o as shown in the figure. A cavity DEF is cut out from the lamina, where D, E, F are the mid points of the sides. Moment of inertia of the remaining part of lamina about the same axis is :

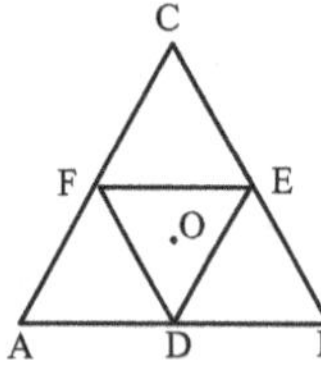

(a) $\dfrac{7}{8}I_o$

(b) $\dfrac{15}{16}I_o$

(c) $\dfrac{3I_o}{4}$

(d) $\dfrac{3II_o}{32}$

17. Two rods each of mass m and length ℓ are joined at the centre to form a cross. The moment of inertia of this cross about an axis passing through the common centre of the rods and perpendicular to the plane formed by them, is

(a) $\dfrac{m\ell^2}{12}$

(b) $\dfrac{m\ell^2}{6}$

(c) $\dfrac{m\ell^2}{3}$

(d) $\dfrac{m\ell^2}{2}$

18. A circular hole of diameter R is cut from a thin uniform disc of mass M and radius R. The circumference of the cut circular hole passes through the centre of the disc. The moment of inertia of the remaining portion of the disc about an axis perpendicular to the disc and passing through its centre is

(a) $\left(\dfrac{15}{32}\right)MR^2$

(b) $\left(\dfrac{1}{8}\right)MR^2$

(c) $\left(\dfrac{3}{8}\right)MR^2$

(d) $\left(\dfrac{13}{32}\right)MR^2$

19. A solid cylinder is released from the top of an inclined plane of inclination with the horizontal θ and length ℓ. If the cylinder rolls without slipping what will be its speed when it reaches the bottom?

(a) $\sqrt{3g\ell \sin\theta}$

(b) $\sqrt{\dfrac{4}{3}g\ell \sin\theta}$

(c) $\sqrt{\dfrac{5}{3}g\ell \sin\theta}$

(d) $\sqrt{6g\ell \sin\theta}$

20. A solid sphere is rolling on a surface as shown in figure, with a translational velocity v ms^{-1}. If it is to climb the inclined surface continuing to roll without slipping, then minimum velocity for this to happen is

(a) $\sqrt{2gh}$

(b) $\sqrt{\dfrac{7}{5}gh}$

(c) $\sqrt{\dfrac{7}{2}gh}$

(d) $\sqrt{\dfrac{10}{7}gh}$

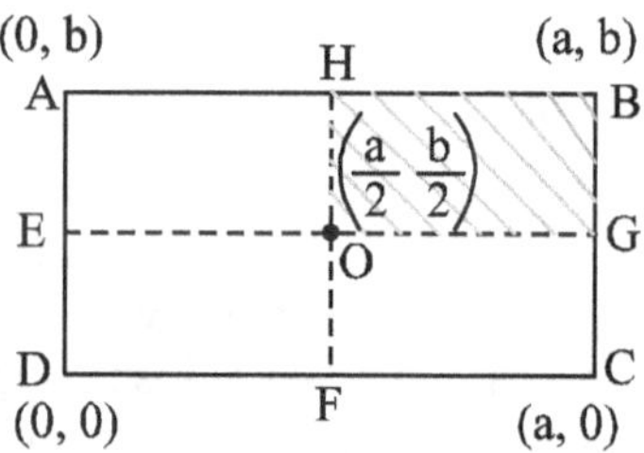

21. Consider a two particle system with particles having masses m_1 and m_2. If the first particle is pushed towards the centre of mass through a distance d, by what distance should the second particle is moved, so as to keep the centre of mass at the same position?

(a) $\dfrac{m_2}{m_1}d$

(b) $\dfrac{m_1}{m_1+m_2}d$

(c) $\dfrac{m_1}{m_2}d$

(d) d

22. A uniform rectangular thin sheet ABCD of mass M has length a and breadth b, as shown in the figure. If the shaded portion HBGO is cut-off, the coordinates of the centre of mass of the remaining portion will be :

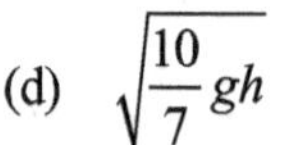

(a) $\left(\dfrac{3a}{4},\dfrac{3b}{4}\right)$

(b) $\left(\dfrac{5a}{3},\dfrac{5b}{3}\right)$

(c) $\left(\dfrac{2a}{3},\dfrac{2b}{3}\right)$

(d) $\left(\dfrac{5a}{12},\dfrac{5b}{12}\right)$

23. The magnitude of torque on a particle of mass 1 kg is 2.5 Nm about the origin. If the force acting on it is 1 N, and the distance of the particle from the origin is 5m, the angle between the force and the position vector is (in radians):

    (a) $\dfrac{\pi}{6}$
    (b) $\dfrac{\pi}{3}$
    (c) $\dfrac{\pi}{8}$
    (d) $\dfrac{\pi}{4}$

24. A uniform solid cylindrical roller of mass 'm' is being pulled on a horizontal surface with force F parallel to the surface and applied at its centre. If the acceleration of the cylinder is 'a' and it is rolling without slipping then the value of 'F' is:

    (a) ma
    (b) $\dfrac{5}{3}$ma
    (c) $\dfrac{3}{2}$ma
    (d) 2 ma

25. A round uniform body of radius R, mass M and moment of inertia I rolls down (without slipping) an inclined plane making an angle θ with the horizontal. Then its acceleration is

    (a) $\dfrac{g\sin\theta}{1-MR^2/I}$
    (b) $\dfrac{g\sin\theta}{1+I/MR^2}$
    (c) $\dfrac{g\sin\theta}{1+MR^2/I}$
    (d) $\dfrac{g\sin\theta}{1-I/MR^2}$

26. A thin spherical shell of radius R lying on a rouogh horizontal surface is hit sharply and horizontally by a cue. Where should it be hit so that the shell does not slip on the surface ? [above the ground level]

    (a) $\dfrac{5R}{3}$
    (b) $\dfrac{6R}{5}$
    (c) $\dfrac{7R}{5}$
    (d) $\dfrac{8R}{7}$

27. A solid cylinder of mass 20 kg rotates about its axis with angular speed 100 rad s^{-1}. The radius of the cylinder is 0.25m. What is the K.E. associated with the rotation of the cylinder?

    (a) 3125 J
    (b) 5135 J
    (c) 7215 J
    (d) 9615 J

28. The wheel of a car is rotating at the rate of 1200 revolutions per minute. On pressing the accelerator for 10 seconds, it starts rotating at 4500 revolutions per minute. The angular acceleration of the wheel is

    (a) 30 radian/second^2
    (b) 1880 degree/second^2
    (c) 40 radian/second^2
    (d) 1980 degree/second^2

29. Consider a thin uniform square lamina whose side is 'a' mass m and moment of inertia I about one of its diagonals, then :

    (a) $I > \dfrac{ma^2}{12}$
    (b) $\dfrac{ma^2}{24} < I < \dfrac{ma^2}{12}$
    (c) $I = \dfrac{ma^2}{24}$
    (d) $I = \dfrac{ma^2}{12}$

30. Three particles, each of mass m gram, are situated at the vertices of an equilateral triangle ABC of side ℓ cm (as shown in the figure). The moment of inertia of the system about a line AX perpendicular to AB and in the plane of ABC, in gram-cm^2 units will be

    (a) $\dfrac{3}{2}m\ell^2$
    (b) $\dfrac{3}{4}m\ell^2$
    (c) $2\,m\ell^2$
    (d) $\dfrac{5}{4}m\ell^2$

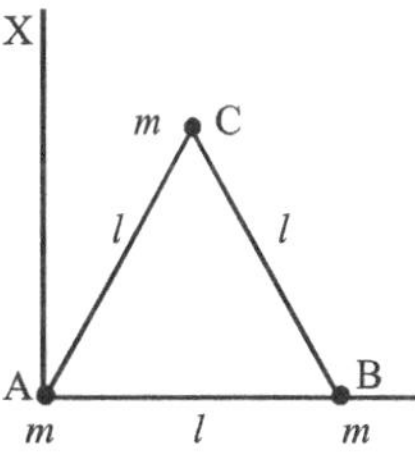

ANSWER KEY																													
1	(b)	4	(c)	7	(a)	10	(d)	13	(d)	16	(b)	19	(b)	22	(d)	25	(b)	28	(d)
2	(a)	5	(c)	8	(b)	11	(b)	14	(c)	17	(b)	20	(d)	23	(a)	26	(a)	29	(d)
3	(c)	6	(b)	9	(a)	12	(b)	15	(d)	18	(d)	21	(c)	24	(c)	27	(a)	30	(d)

1. Two particles of equal mass go round a circle of radius R under the action of their mutual gravitational attraction. The speed of each particle is

   (a) $v = \dfrac{1}{2R}\sqrt{\dfrac{1}{Gm}}$

   (b) $v = \sqrt{\dfrac{1}{Gm}}$

   (c) $v = \dfrac{1}{2}\sqrt{\dfrac{Gm}{R}}$

   (d) $v = \sqrt{\dfrac{4Gm}{R}}$

2. Two stars of mass m_1 and m_2 are parts of a binary system. The radii of their orbits are r_1 and r_2 respectively, measured from the C.M. of the system. The magnitude of gravitational force m_1 exerts on m_2 is

   (a) $\dfrac{m_1 m_2 G}{(r_1 + r_2)^2}$

   (b) $\dfrac{m_1 G}{(r_1 + r_2)^2}$

   (c) $\dfrac{m_2 G}{(r_1 + r_2)^2}$

   (d) $\dfrac{(m_1 + m_2)}{(r_1 + r_2)^2}$

3. A planet moves around the sun along an ellipse so that its minimum distance from the sun is equal to r and the maximum distance to R. Making use of Kepler's laws, find its period of revolution around the sun.

   (a) $\dfrac{\pi}{4}v\sqrt{\dfrac{(R+r)^3}{2GM}}$

   (b) $\dfrac{\pi R^2}{GM}$

   (c) $\dfrac{\pi}{3}\sqrt{\dfrac{R+r}{GM}}$

   (d) $\pi\sqrt{\dfrac{(R+r)^3}{2GM}}$

4. R is the radius of the earth and ω is its angular velocity and g_p is the value of g at the poles. The effective value of g at the latitude $\lambda = 60°$ will be equal to

   (a) $g_p - \dfrac{1}{4}R\omega^2$

   (b) $g_p - \dfrac{3}{4}R\omega^2$

   (c) $g_p - R\omega^2$

   (d) $g_p + \dfrac{1}{4}R\omega^2$

5. Two spherical bodies of mass M and $5M$ and radii R & $2R$ respectively are released in free space with initial separation between their centres equal to $12R$. If they attract each other due to gravitational force only, then the distance covered by the smaller body just before collision is

   (a) $2.5\,R$

   (b) $4.5\,R$

   (c) $7.5\,R$

   (d) $1.5\,R$

6. In order to make the effective acceleration due to gravity equal to zero at the equator, the angular velocity of rotation of the earth about its axis should be (g = 10 ms^{-2} and radius of earth is 6400 km)

   (a) Zero

   (b) $\dfrac{1}{800}$ rad sec^{-1}

   (c) $\dfrac{1}{80}$ rad sec^{-1}

   (d) $\dfrac{1}{8}$ rad sec^{-1}

7. A planet moving around sun sweeps area A_1 in 2 days, A_2 in 3 days and A_3 in 6 days. Then the relation between A_1, A_2 and A_3 is

(a) $3A_1 = 2A_2 = A_3$

(b) $2A_1 = 3A_2 = 6A_3$

(c) $3A_1 = 2A_2 = 6A_3$

(d) $6A_1 = 3A_2 = 2A_3$

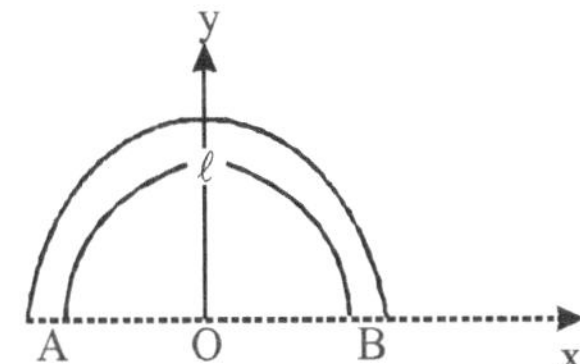

8. Gravitational field at the centre of a semicircle formed by a thin wire AB of mass m and length ℓ is

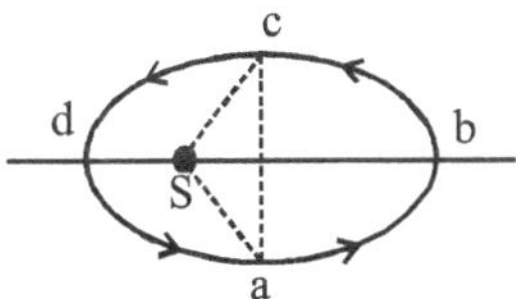

(a) $\dfrac{Gm}{\ell^2}$ along +x-axis

(b) $\dfrac{Gm}{\pi\ell^2}$ along +y-axis

(c) $\dfrac{2\pi Gm}{\ell^2}$ along + x-axis

(d) $\dfrac{2\pi Gm}{\ell^2}$ along +y-axis

9. Four particles each of mass M, are located at the vertices of a square with side L. The gravitational potential due to this at the centre of the square is

(a) $-\sqrt{32}\,\dfrac{GM}{L}$

(b) $-\sqrt{64}\,\dfrac{GM}{L^2}$

(c) zero

(d) $\sqrt{32}\,\dfrac{GM}{L}$

10. If the height of a satellite from the earth is negligible in comparison to the radius of the earth R, the orbital velocity of the satellite is

(a) gR

(b) gR/2

(c) $\sqrt{g/R}$

(d) $\sqrt{gR}$

11. If the radius of the earth were to shrink by 1%, with its mass remaining the same, the acceleration due to gravity on the earth's surface would

(a) decrease by 1%

(b) decrease by 2%

(c) increase by 1%

(d) increase by 2%

12. Figure shows elliptical path abcd of a planet around the sun S such that the area of triangle csa is $\dfrac{1}{4}$ the area of the ellipse. (See figure) With db as the semimajor axis, and ca as the semiminor axis. If t_1 is the time taken for planet to go over path abc and t_2 for path taken over cda then:

(a) $t_1 = 4t_2$

(b) $t_1 = 2t_2$

(c) $t_1 = 3t_2$

(d) $t_1 = t_2$

13. The escape velocity for a body projected vertically upwards from the surface of earth is 11 km/s. If the body is projected at an angle of 45° with the vertical, the escape velocity will be

(a) $11\sqrt{2}$ km / s

(b) 22 km/s

(c) 11 km/s

(d) $\dfrac{11}{\sqrt{2}}$ km / s

14. Assuming the radius of the earth as R, the change in gravitational potential energy of a body of mass m, when it is taken from the earth's surface to a height 3R above its surface, is

(a) 3 mg R

(b) $\dfrac{3}{4}$ mg R

(c) 1 mg R

(d) $\dfrac{3}{2}$ mg R

15. Inside a uniform sphere of density ρ there is a spherical cavity whose centre is at a distance ℓ from the centre of the sphere. Find the strength of the gravitational field inside the cavity at the point P.

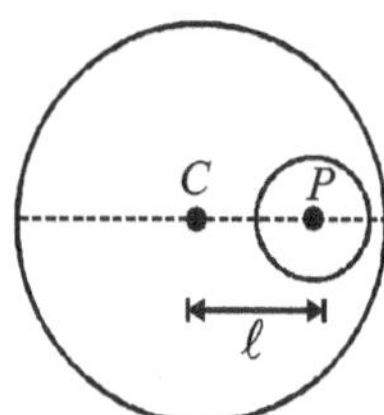

(a) $\dfrac{4}{3}G\pi\rho\ell$

(b) $\dfrac{1}{3}G\pi\rho\ell$

(c) $\dfrac{2}{3}G\pi\rho\ell$

(d) $\dfrac{1}{2}G\pi\rho\ell$

16. Two satellites of same mass are launched in the same orbit aroound the earth so as to rotate opposite to each other. If they collide inellastically and stick together as wreckage, the total energy of the system [where, M = mass of earth, m = mass of satellites, r = distance of satellite from centre of earth]

(a) $\dfrac{-2GMm}{r}$

(b) $\dfrac{-3}{2}\dfrac{GMm}{r}$

(c) $\dfrac{5}{2}\dfrac{GMm}{r}$

(d) $\dfrac{GMm}{r}$

17. A satellite of mass m is orbiting the earth at a height h from its surface. If M is the mass of the earth and R its radius, then how much energy must be spent to pull the satellite out of the earth's gravitational field ?

(a) $\dfrac{2GmM}{(R+h)^2}$

(b) $\dfrac{GmM}{2(R+h)^2}$

(c) $\dfrac{2GmM}{(R+h)}$

(d) $\dfrac{GmM}{2(R+h)}$

18. Escape velocity for earth surface is 11 km/s. If the radius of any planet is two times the radius of the earth but average density is same as that of earth. Then the escape velocity at the planet will be

(a) 15.5 km/s

(b) 5.5 km/sec

(c) 11 km/sec

(d) 22 km/sec

19. If the angular momentum of a planet of mass m, moving around the Sun in a circular orbit is L, about the center of the Sun, its areal velocity is:

(a) $\dfrac{L}{m}$

(b) $\dfrac{4L}{m}$

(c) $\dfrac{L}{2m}$

(d) $\dfrac{2L}{m}$

20. The maximum and minimum distance of a comet from the sun are 8×10^{12} m and 1.6×10^{12} m. If its velocity when nearest to the sun is 60 m/s, what will be its velocity (in m/s) when it is farthest?

(a) 12

(b) 60

(c) 112

(d) 6

21. The variation of acceleration due to gravity g with distance d from centre of the earth is best represented by (R = Earth's radius):

(a) 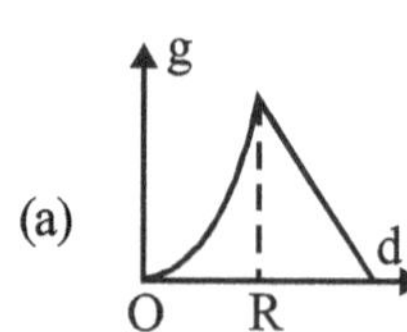

(b) 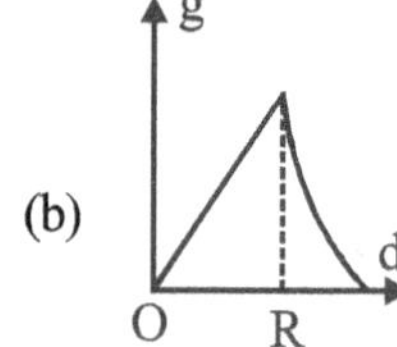

(c) 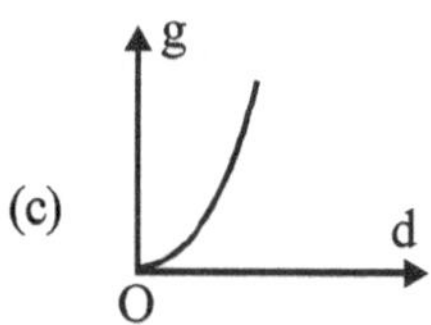

(d) 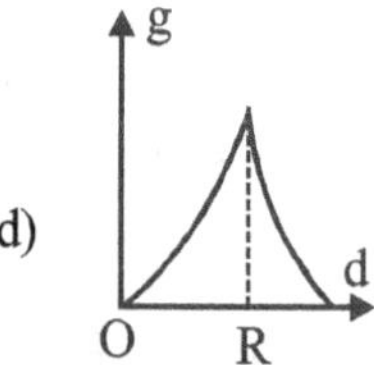

22. The ratio between the values of acceleration due to gravity at a height 1 km above and at a depth of 1 km below the earth's surface is (radius of earth is R km)

(a) $\dfrac{R-2}{R-1}$

(b) $\dfrac{R}{R-1}$

(c) $\dfrac{R-2}{R}$

(d) $\dfrac{2R}{R-1}$

23. The mass density of a planet of radius R varies with the distance r from its centre as

$$\rho(r) = \rho_0\left(1 - \frac{r^2}{R^2}\right).$$ Then the gravitational field is maximum at:

(a) $r - \sqrt{\frac{3}{4}}R$ (b) $r = R$

(c) $r = \frac{1}{\sqrt{3}}R$ (d) $r = \sqrt{\frac{5}{9}}R$

24. A body is moving in a low circular orbit about a planet of mass M and radius R. The radius of the orbit can be taken to be R itself. Then the ratio of the speed of this body in the orbit to the escape velocity from the planet is :

(a) $\frac{1}{\sqrt{2}}$ (b) 2

(c) 1 (d) $\sqrt{2}$

25. Two satellites, A and B, have masses m and 2m respectively. A is in a circular orbit of radius R, and B is in a circular orbit of radius 2R around the earth. The ratio of their kinetic energies, T_A/T_B, is :

(a) $\frac{1}{2}$ (b) 1

(c) 2 (d) $\sqrt{\frac{1}{2}}$

26. A solid sphere of mass 'M' and radius 'a' is surrounded by a uniform concentric spherical shell of thickness 2a and mass 2M. The gravitational field at distance '3a' from the centre will be:

(a) $\frac{2GM}{9a^2}$ (b) $\frac{GM}{9a^2}$

(c) $\frac{GM}{3a^2}$ (d) $\frac{2GM}{3a^2}$

27. If the earth is at one-fourth of its present distance from the sun, the duration of the year will be

(a) half the present year

(b) one-eighth the present year

(c) one-sixth the present year

(d) one-tenth the present year

28. Two bodies of masses M_1 and M_2 are placed at a distance d apart. What is the potential at the position where the gravitational field due to them is zero?

(a) $-\frac{G}{d}\left(M_1 + M_2 + 2\sqrt{M_1}\sqrt{M_2}\right)$

(b) $-\frac{G}{d}\left(M_1 + M_2 - 2\sqrt{M_1}\sqrt{M_2}\right)$

(c) $-\frac{G}{d}\left(2M_1 + M_2 + 2\sqrt{M_1}\sqrt{M_2}\right)$

(d) $-\frac{G}{2d}\left(M_1 + M_2 + 2\sqrt{M_1}\sqrt{M_2}\right)$

29. Acceleration due to gravity is 'g' on the suface of the earth. The value of acceleration due to gravity at a height of 32 km above earth's surface is (Radius of the earth = 6400 km)

(a) $0.9\,g$ (b) $0.99\,g$

(c) $0.8\,g$ (d) $1.01\,g$

30. The time period of a satellite of earth is 5 hours. If the separation between the earth and the satellite is increased to 4 times the previous value, the new time period will become

(a) 10 hours   (b) 80 hours

(c) 40 hours   (d) 20 hours

ANSWER KEY																			
1	(c)	4	(a)	7	(a)	10	(d)	13	(c)	16	(a)	19	(c)	22	(a)	25	(b)	28	(a)
2	(a)	5	(c)	8	(d)	11	(d)	14	(b)	17	(d)	20	(a)	23	(d)	26	(c)	29	(b)
3	(d)	6	(b)	9	(a)	12	(c)	15	(a)	18	(d)	21	(b)	24	(a)	27	(b)	30	(c)

MECHANICAL PROPERTIES OF SOLIDS

8

1. Two wires A and B are of the same material. Their lengths are in the ratio of 1 : 2 and the diameter are in the ratio 2 : 1. If they are pulled by the same force, then increase in length will be in the ratio of

   (a) $2:1$ (b) $1:4$

   (c) $1:8$ (d) $8:1$

2. A wire breaks when subjected to a stress S. If ρ is the density of the material of the wire, then the length of the wire so that it breaks by its own weight is

   (a) $\rho g S$ (b) $\dfrac{\rho g}{S}$

   (c) $\dfrac{g S}{\rho}$ (d) $\dfrac{S}{\rho g}$

3. A steel wire of length 4.7 m and cross-section 3×10^{-5} m^2 stretches by the same amount as a copper wire of length 3.5 m and cross-section 4×10^{-5} m^2 under a given load. The ratio of the Young's modulus of steel to that of copper is

   (a) $5/9$ (b) $9/5$

   (c) $6/7$ (d) $7/6$

4. A piece of copper having a rectangular cross-section 15.2 mm $\times$ 19.1 mm is pulled in tension with 44,500 N force, producing only elastic deformation. What is the resulting strain? [Young's modulus of elasticity of copper is 120×10^9 N/m^2.]

   (a) 0.127×10^{-2} (b) 1.27×10^{-2}

   (c) 12.7×10^{-2} (d) 127×10^{-2}

5. One end of a uniform rod of mass M and cross-sectional area A is suspended from a rigid support and an equal mass M is suspended from the other end. The stress at the mid-point of the rod is

   (a) $\dfrac{9Mg}{2A}$ (b) $\dfrac{3Mg}{2A}$

   (c) $\dfrac{8Mg}{3A}$ (d) $\dfrac{9Mg}{8A}$

6. The area of cross-section of a steel wire ($Y = 2.0 \times 10^{11}$ N/m^2) is 0.1 cm^2. The force required to double its length will be

   (a) 2×10^{12} N   (b) 2×10^{11} N

   (c) 2×10^{10} N   (d) 2×10^{6} N

7. Two wires of same diameter of the same material having the length l and $2l$. If the force F is applied on each, the ratio of the work done in the two wires will be

   (a) $1:2$ (b) $1:4$

   (c) $2:1$ (d) $1:1$

8. According to Hooke's law of elasticity, if stress is increased, the ratio of stress to strain

   (a) Increases

   (b) Decreases

   (c) Becomes zero

   (d) Remains constant

9. For a constant hydraulic stress on an object, the fractional change in the object volume $\left(\dfrac{\Delta V}{V}\right)$ and its bulk modulus (B) are related as

   (a) $\dfrac{\Delta V}{V} \propto B$ (b) $\dfrac{\Delta V}{V} \propto \dfrac{1}{B}$

   (c) $\dfrac{\Delta V}{V} \propto B^2$ (d) $\dfrac{\Delta V}{V} \propto B^{-2}$

10. The load versus elongation graphs for four wires of same length and made of the same material are shown in the figure. The thinnest wire is represented by the line

    (a) OA

    (b) OC

    (c) OD

    (d) OB

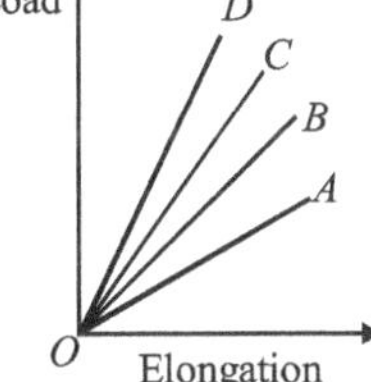

11. A wire elongates by ℓ mm when a load W is hanged from it. If the wire goes over a pulley and two weights W each are hung at two ends, the elongation of the wire will be (in mm)

    (a) 2ℓ (b) zero

    (c) $\ell/2$ (d) ℓ

12. What will be the volume contraction of a solid copper cube, 10 cm on an edge when subjected to a hydraulic pressure of 7×10^6 Pa? Bulk modulus of copper = 140 GPa

    (a) $5 \times 10^{-8}\,\text{m}^3$ (b) $9 \times 10^{-8}\,\text{m}^3$

    (c) $12 \times 10^{-8}\,\text{m}^3$ (d) $15 \times 10^{-8}\,\text{m}^3$

13. How much should the pressure on a litre of water be changed to compress it by 0.1%? (Bulk modulus of elasticity of water $= 2.2 \times 10^9$ N/m^2)

    (a) $2.2 \times 10^6\,\text{N/m}^2$ (b) $6.2 \times 10^6\,\text{N/m}^2$

    (c) $8.2 \times 10^6\,\text{N/m}^2$ (d) $12.1 \times 10^6\,\text{N/m}^2$

14. When a certain weight is suspended to a long uniform wire its length increases by one cm. If the same weight is suspended to another wire of the same material and length but having a diameter half of the first one, the increase in its length will be

    (a) 0.5 cm   (b) 2 cm

    (c) 4 cm   (d) 8 cm

15. A steel wire having a radius of 2.0 mm, carrying a load of 4kg, is hanging from a ceiling. Given that g $= 3.1\ \text{Å ms}^{-2}$, what will be the tensile stress that would be developed in the wire?

    (a) $6.2 \times 10^6\,\text{Nm}^{-2}$ (b) $5.2 \times 10^6\,\text{Nm}^{-2}$

    (c) $3.1 \times 10^6\,\text{Nm}^{-2}$ (d) $4.8 \times 10^6\,\text{Nm}^{-2}$

16. Two steel wires having same length are suspended from a ceiling under the same load. If the ratio of their energy stored per unit volume is $1:4$, the ratio of their diameters is:

    (a) $\sqrt{2}:1$ (b) $1:2$

    (c) $2:1$ (d) $1:\sqrt{2}$

17. In materials like aluminium and copper, the correct order of magnitude of various elastic modului is:

    (a) Young's modulus < shear modulus < bulk modulus.

    (b) Bulk modulus < shear modulus < Young's modulus

    (c) Shear modulus < Young's modulus < bulk modulus.

    (d) Bulk modulus < Young's modulus < shear modulus.

18. The breaking stress of a wire depends upon

(a) Length of the wire

(b) Radius of the wire

(c) Material of the wire

(d) Shape of the cross-section

19. If 'S' is stress and 'Y' is young's modulus of material of a wire, the energy stored in the wire per unit volume is

(a) $\dfrac{S^2}{2Y}$
(b) $2S^2Y$

(c) $\dfrac{S}{2Y}$
(d) $\dfrac{2Y}{S^2}$

20. A structural steel rod has a radius of 10 mm and length of 1.0 m. A 100 kN force stretches it along its length. Young's modulus of structural steel is 2×10^{11} Nm^{-2}. The percentage strain is about

(a) 0.16%
(b) 0.32%

(c) 0.08%
(d) 0.24%

21. When a force is applied on a wire of uniform cross-sectional area 3×10^{-6} m^2 and length 4 m, the increase in length is 1 mm. Energy stored in it will be ($Y = 2 \times 10^{11}$ N/m^2)

(a) 6250 J
(b) 0.177 J

(c) 0.075 J
(d) 0.150 J

22. The graph given is a stress-strain curve for

(a) elastic objects

(b) plastics

(c) elastomers

(d) None of these

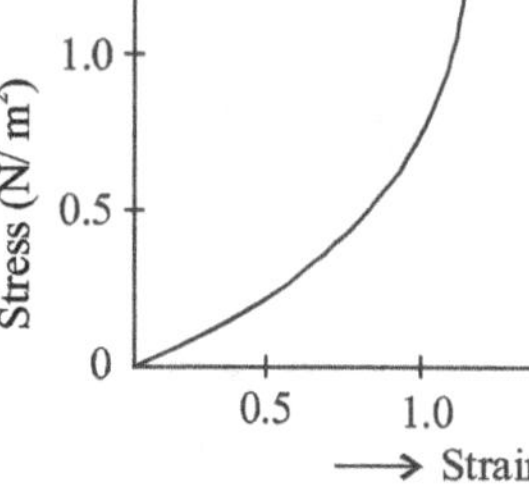

23. The fractional change in volume of a glass slab when subjected to a hydraulic pressure of 10 atmosphere is [Bulk modulus of elasticity of glass $= 37 \times 10^9$ N/m^2 and 1 atm $= 1.013 \times 10^5$ Pa.]

(a) 1.12×10^{-5}
(b) 2.74×10^{-5}

(c) 3.13×10^{-5}
(d) 8.81×10^{-5}

24. Steel ruptures when a shear of 3.5×10^8 N m^{-2} is applied. The force needed to punch a 1 cm diameter hole in a steel sheet 0.3 cm thick is nearly:

(a) 1.4×10^4 N
(b) 2.7×10^4 N

(c) 3.3×10^4 N
(d) 1.1×10^4 N

25. For a given material, the Young's modulus is 2.4 times that of rigidity modulus. Its Poisson's ratio is

(a) 2.4
(b) 1.2

(c) 0.4
(d) 0.2

ANSWER KEY																								
1	(c)	4	(a)	7	(a)	10	(a)	13	(a)	16	(a)	19	(a)	22	(c)	25	(d)
2	(d)	5	(b)	8	(d)	11	(d)	14	(c)	17	(c)	20	(a)	23	(b)		
3	(b)	6	(d)	9	(b)	12	(a)	15	(c)	18	(c)	21	(c)	24	(c)		

MECHANICAL PROPERTIES OF FLUIDS

1. A piece of steel floats in mercury, the specific gravity of mercury and steel are 13.6 and 7.8 respectively. For covering the whole piece, some water is filled above the mercury. What part of the piece is inside the mercury ?

   (a) 0.62   (b) 0.47

   (c) 0.50   (d) 0.54

2. Horizontal tube of non-uniform cross-section has radii of 0.1 m and 0.05 m respectively at M and N. For a streamline flow of liquid the rate of liquid flow is (Liquid is incompressible)

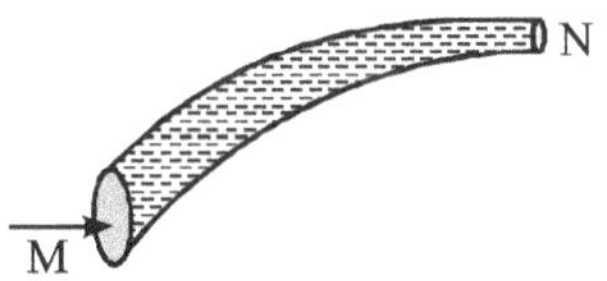

   (a) continuously changes with time

   (b) greater at M than at N

   (c) greater at N than at M

   (d) same at M and N

3. A hole is there in the bottom of tank having water. If total pressure at bottom is 3 atm (1 atm = $10^5 \, \text{Nm}^{-2}$), then the velocity of water flowing from hole is

   (a) $20 \, \text{ms}^{-1}$ (b) $30 \, \text{ms}^{-1}$

   (c) $40 \, \text{ms}^{-1}$ (d) None of these

4. When the temperature increases, the viscosity of

   (a) gases decreases and liquid increases

   (b) gases increases and liquid decreases

   (c) gases and liquids increases

   (d) gases and liquids decreases

5. A candle of diameter d is floating on a liquid in a cylindrical container of diameter D (D >> d) as shown in figure. If it is burning at the rate of 2 cm/hour then the top of the candle will

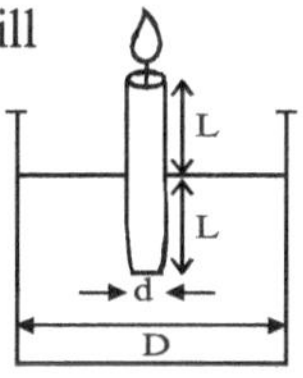

   (a) remain at the same height

   (b) fall at the rate of 1 cm/hour

   (c) fall at the rate of 2 cm/hour

   (d) go up at the rate of 1 cm/hour

6. The velocity of small ball of mass M and density d_1 when dropped in a container filled with glycerine becomes constant after sometime. If the density of glycerine is d_2, the viscous force acting on the ball will be :

   (a) $\dfrac{M d_1 g}{d_2}$ (b) $Mg\left(1 - \dfrac{d_2}{d_1}\right)$

   (c) $\dfrac{M(d_1 + d_2)}{g}$ (d) $m d_1 d_2$

7. Which of the following is the velocity time graph of a small spherical body falling through a long columns of a viscous liquid?

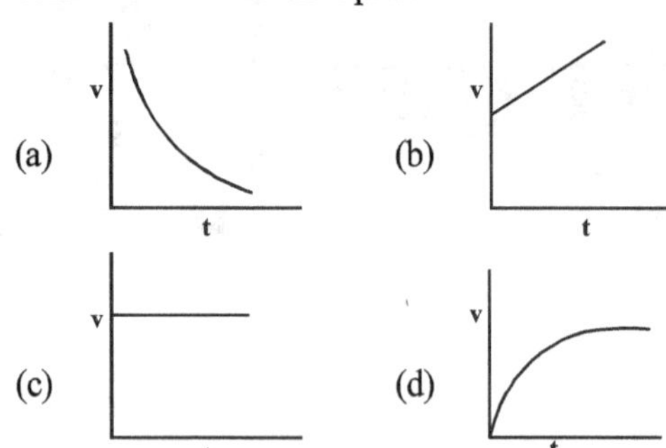

8. The radius R of the soap bubble is doubled under isothermal condition. If T be the surface tension of soap bubble, the work done in doing so is given by

(a) $32\pi R^2 T$ (b) $24\pi R^2 T$

(c) $8\pi R^2 T$ (d) $4\pi R^2 T$

9. A film of water is formed between two straight parallel wires of length 10 cm each separated by 0.5 cm. If their separation is increased by 1 mm while still maintaining their parallelism, how much work will have to be done? (Surface tension of water = 7.2×10^{-2} N/m)

(a) 7.22×10^{-6} joule   (b) 1.44×10^{-5} joule

(c) 2.88×10^{-5} joule   (d) 5.76×10^{-5} joule

10. A soap bubble of radius r_1 is placed on another soap bubble of radius r_2 ($r_1 < r_2$). The radius R of the soapy film separating the two bubbles is

(a) $r_2 + r_2$ (b) $\dfrac{r_2 - r_1}{r_1 r_2}$

(c) $\dfrac{r_1 r_2}{r_2 - r_1}$ (d) $\sqrt{r_1^2 + r_2^2}$

11. Two capillary tubes of length L and 2L and of radius R and 2R are connected in series. The net rate of flow of fluid through them will be (given rate of the flow through single capillary,

$$X = \frac{\pi P R^4}{8\eta L})$$

(a) $\dfrac{8}{9}X$ (b) $\dfrac{9}{8}X$

(c) $\dfrac{5}{7}X$ (d) $\dfrac{7}{5}X$

12. Two tubes of radii r_1 and r_2, and lengths l_1 and l_2, respectively, are connected in series and a liquid flows through them in streamline conditions. P_1 and P_2 are pressure differences across the two tubes. If P_2 is $4P_1$ and l_2 is $\dfrac{l_1}{4}$, then the radius r_2 will be equal to :

(a) r_1 (b) $2r_1$

(c) $4r_1$ (d) $\dfrac{r_1}{2}$

13. A cylindrical tank has a small hole at its botom of area of cross-section a. Liquid is being poured in the tank at the rate $V m^3/s$, the maximum level of liquid in the container will be (Area of tank A)

(a) $\dfrac{V}{gaA}$ (b) $\dfrac{V^2}{2ga^2}$

(c) $\dfrac{V^2}{gAa}$ (d) $\dfrac{V}{2gaA}$

14. A large tank filled with water to a height 'h' is to be emptied through a small hole at the bottom. The ratio of time taken for the level of water to fall from h to h/2 and from h/2 to zero is

(a) $\sqrt{2}$ (b) $\sqrt{2} - 1$

(c) $\dfrac{1}{\sqrt{2} - 1}$ (d) $\dfrac{1}{\sqrt{2}}$

15. What is the absolute pressure of the gas above the liquid surface in the tank shown in fig. Density of oil = 820 kg/m³, density of mercury = 13.6×10^3 kg/m³. Given 1 atmospheric pressure = 1.01×10^5 Pa.

(a) 3.81×10^5 Pa

(b) 6×10^6 Pa

(c) 5×10^7 Pa

(d) 4.6×10^2 Pa

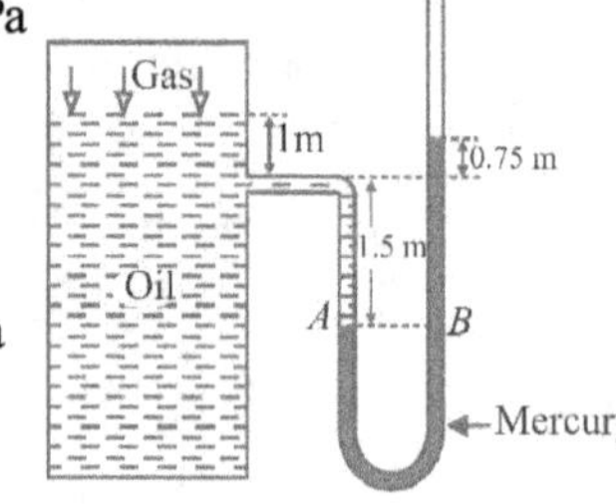

16. A capillary tube is immersed vertically in water and the height of the water column is x. When this arrangement is taken into a mine of depth d, the height of the water column is y. If R is the radius of earth, the ratio $\dfrac{x}{y}$ is:

(a) $\left(1-\dfrac{d}{R}\right)$

(b) $\left(1-\dfrac{2d}{R}\right)$

(c) $\left(\dfrac{R-d}{R+d}\right)$

(d) $\left(\dfrac{R+d}{R-d}\right)$

17. A ball of radius r and density ρ falls freely under gravity through a distance h before entering water. Velocity of ball does not change even on entering water. If viscosity of water is η the value of h is given by

(a) $\dfrac{2}{9}r^2\left(\dfrac{1-\rho}{\eta}\right)g$

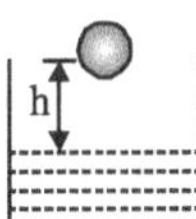

(b) $\dfrac{2}{81}r^2\left(\dfrac{\rho-1}{\eta}\right)g$

(c) $\dfrac{2}{81}r^4\left(\dfrac{\rho-1}{\eta}\right)^2 g$

(d) $\dfrac{2}{9}r^4\left(\dfrac{\rho-1}{\eta}\right)^2 g$

18. Two parallel glass plates are dipped partly in the liquid of density 'd' keeping them vertical . If the distance between the plates is 'x', surface tension for this liquid is T and angle of contact is θ, then the height of capillary rise between two parallel plates will be

(a) $\dfrac{T\cos\theta}{xd}$

(b) $\dfrac{2T\cos\theta}{xdg}$

(c) $\dfrac{2T}{xdg\cos\theta}$

(d) $\dfrac{T\cos\theta}{xdg}$

19. A plate of area 100 cm^2 is placed on the upper surface of castor oil, 2 mm thick. Taking the coefficient of viscosity to be 15.5 poise, calculate the hoizontal force necessary to move the plate with a velocity 3 cms^{-1}.

(a) zero

(b) 0.4525 N

(c) 0.2325 N

(d) 0.1550 N

20. Two liquids of densities d_1 and d_2 are flowing in identical capillary tubes under the same pressure difference. If t_1 and t_2 are time taken for the flow of equal quantities (mass) of liquids, then the ratio of coefficient of viscosity of liquids must be

(a) $\dfrac{d_1 t_1}{d_2 t_2}$

(b) $\dfrac{t_1}{t_2}$

(c) $\dfrac{d_2}{d_1}\dfrac{t_2}{t_1}$

(d) $\sqrt{\dfrac{d_1 t_1}{d_2 t_2}}$

21. In the diagram shown, the difference in the two tubes of the manometer is 5 cm, the cross section of the tube at A and B is 6 mm^2 and 10 mm^2 respectively. The rate at which water flows through the tube is (g = 10 ms^{-2})

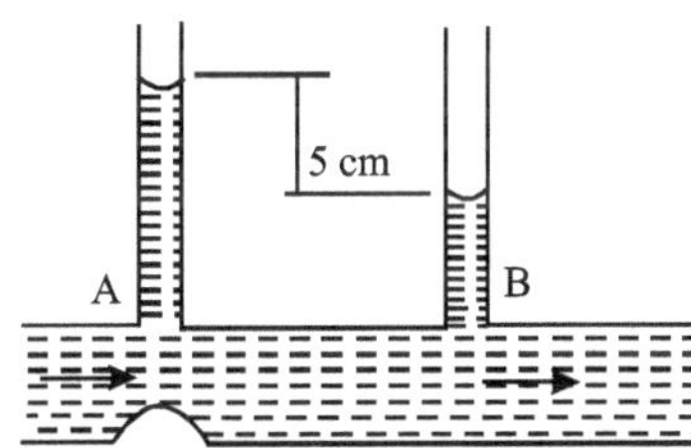

(a) 7.5 cc/s

(b) 8.0 cc/s

(c) 10.0 cc/s

(d) 12.5 cc/s

22. Wax is coated on the inner wall of a capillary tube and the tube is then dipped in water. Then, compared to the unwaxed capillary, the angle of contact θ and the height h upto which water rises change. These changes are :

(a) θ increases and h also increases

(b) θ decreases and h also decreases

(c) θ increases and h decreases

(d) θ decreases and h increases

23. Radius of a capillary tube is 2×10^{-3} m. A liquid of weight 6.28×10^{-4} N may remain in the capillary then the surface tension of the liquid will be

    (a) 5 N/m
    (b) 50 N/m
    (c) 5×10^{-2} N/m
    (d) 5×10^{-3} N/m

24. A body floats with two-fifth of its volume outside water. And same body flows with one-fourth of its volume inside another liquid. The specific gravity of this liquid (x) is

    (a) 8/5
    (b) 12/5
    (c) 4/5
    (d) 8/3

25. Glycerine flows steadily through a horizontal tube of length 1.5 m and radius 1.0 cm. If the amount of glycerine collected per second at one end is 4.0×10^{-3} kg s^{-1}, what is the pressure difference between the two ends of the tube? (density of glycerine $= 1.3 \times 10^3$ kg m^{-3} and viscosity of glycerine $= 0.83$ Pas).

    (a) 975.37 Pa
    (b) 625.53 Pa
    (c) 312.29 Pa
    (d) 125.58 Pa

26. The cylindrical tube of a spray pump has a cross - section of 8.0 cm^2, one end of which has 40 fine holes each of diameter 1.0 mm. If the liquid flow inside the tube is 1.5 m per minute, what is the speed of ejection of the liquid through the holes?

    (a) 0.637 ms^{-1}
    (b) 1.882 ms^{-1}
    (c) 5.123 ms^{-1}
    (d) 9.921 ms^{-1}

27. Excess pressure inside a drop of mercury of radius 3 mm at room temperature is (Surface tension of mercury at that temperature (20° C) is 4.65×10^{-1} Nm^{-1}, atmospheric pressure is 1.01×10^5 Pa).

    (a) 110 Pa
    (b) 310 Pa
    (c) 610 Pa
    (d) 910 Pa

28. In a hydraulic lift, compressed air exerts a force F_1 on a small piston having a radius of 5 cm. This pressure is transmitted to a second piston of radius 15 cm. If the mass of the load to be lifted is 1350 kg, then find the value of F_1.

    (a) 1.4×10^5 N
    (b) 2×10^5 N
    (c) 1.5×10^3 N
    (d) 1.9×10^3 N

29. In the figure, the velocity V_3 will be

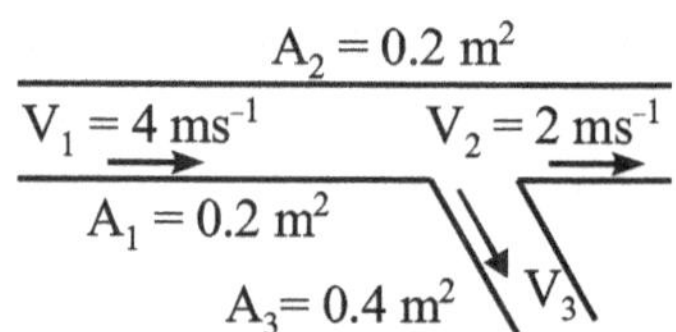

    (a) Zero
    (b) 4 ms^{-1}
    (c) 1 ms^{-1}
    (d) 3 ms^{-1}

30. A bird of mass 1.23 kg is able to hover by imparting a downward velocity 10 m/s uniformly to air of density ρ kg/m^3 over an effective area 0.1 m^2. If the acceleration due to gravity is 10 m/s^2, then the magnitude of ρ in kg/m^3 is

    (a) 0.0123
    (b) 0.123
    (c) 1.23
    (d) 1.32

ANSWER KEY																			
1	(d)	4	(b)	7	(d)	10	(c)	13	(b)	16	(a)	19	(c)	22	(c)	25	(a)	28	(c)
2	(d)	5	(b)	8	(b)	11	(a)	14	(b)	17	(c)	20	(a)	23	(c)	26	(a)	29	(c)
3	(a)	6	(b)	9	(b)	12	(d)	15	(a)	18	(b)	21	(a)	24	(b)	27	(b)	30	(c)

THERMAL PROPERTIES OF MATTER

1. A bar of iron is 10 cm at 20°C. At 19°C it will be (α of iron = $11 \times 10^{-6}/°C$)
   (a) 11×10^{-6} cm longer
   (b) 11×10^{-6} cm shorter
   (c) 11×10^{-5} cm shorter
   (d) 11×10^{-5} cm longer

2. The two ends of a rod of length L and a uniform cross-sectional area A are kept at two temperatures T_1 and T_2 ($T_1 > T_2$). The rate of heat transfer, $\dfrac{dQ}{dt}$ through the rod in a steady state is given by:
   (a) $\dfrac{k(T_1 - T_2)}{LA}$
   (b) $kLA\,(T_1 - T_2)$
   (c) $\dfrac{kA\,(T_1 - T_2)}{L}$
   (d) $\dfrac{kL\,(T_1 - T_2)}{A}$

3. In order that the heat flows from one part of a solid to another part, what is required?
   (a) Uniform density
   (b) Temperature gradient
   (c) Density gradient
   (d) Uniform temperature

4. The graph AB shown in figure is a plot of temperature of a body in degree celsius and degree Fahrenheit. Then slope of line AB is
   (a) 9/5
   (b) 5/9
   (c) 1/9
   (d) 3/9

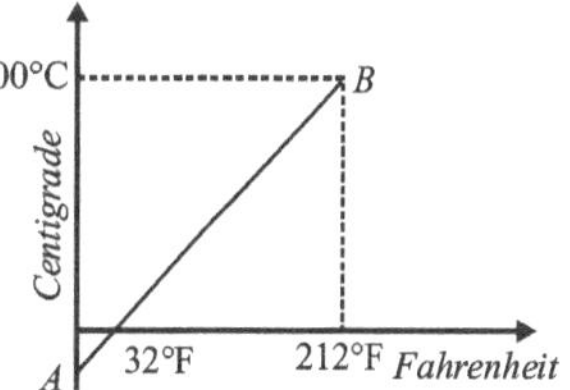

5. If two rods A and B of equal length L, and different areas of cross-section A_1 and A_2 have one end of each at temperature T_1 and other end at T_2, have equal rates of flow of heat, then
   (a) $A_1 = A_2$
   (b) $\dfrac{A_1}{A_2} = \dfrac{K_1}{K_2}$
   (c) $\dfrac{A_1}{A_2} = \dfrac{K_2}{K_1}$
   (d) $K_1 = K_2$

6. The radiation energy density per unit wavelength at a temperature T has a maximum at a wavelength λ_0. At temperature 2T, it will have a maximum wavelength
   (a) $4\lambda_0$
   (b) $2\lambda_0$
   (c) $\dfrac{\lambda_0}{2}$
   (d) $\dfrac{\lambda_0}{4}$

7. A lead ball moving with velocity v strikes a wall and stops. If 50% of its energy is converted into heat, then what will be the increase in temperature? (Specific heat of lead is s cal/kg°c and J is the mechanical equivalent of heat.)

(a) $\dfrac{2v^2}{Js}$

(b) $\dfrac{v^2}{4Js}$

(c) $\dfrac{v^2 s}{J}$

(d) $\dfrac{v^2 s}{2J}$

8. Two rods of the same length and diameter having thermal conductivities K_1 and K_2 are joined in parallel. The equivalent thermal conductivity of the combination is

(a) $\dfrac{K_1 K_2}{K_1 + K_2}$

(b) $K_1 + K_2$

(c) $\dfrac{K_1 + K_2}{2}$

(d) $\sqrt{K_1 K_2}$

9. A water fall is 84 m high. If half of the potential energy of the falling water gets converted to heat, the rise in temperature of water will be

(a) 9.8°C

(b) 0.98°C

(c) 0.098°C

(d) 0.0098°C

10. A copper block of mass 2.5 kg is heated in a furnace to a temperature of 500°C and then placed on a large ice block. What is the maximum amount of ice that can melt?

Specific heat of copper is $= 0.39\ \mathrm{Jg^{-1}\ K^{-1}}$, heat of fusion of water $= 335\mathrm{Jg^{-1}}$

(a) 1255 g

(b) 1355 g

(c) 1155 g

(d) 1455 g

11. If a piece of metal is heated to temperature θ and then allowed to cool in a room which is at temperature θ_0, the graph between the temperature T of the metal and time t will be closest to

(a)

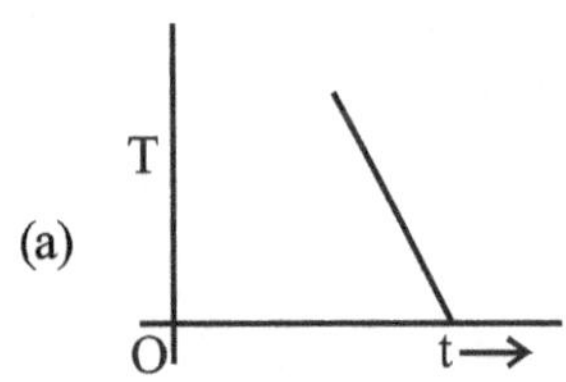

12. In a room where the temperature is 30°C, a body cools from 61°C to 59°C in 4 minutes. The time (in minutes) taken by the body to cool from 51°C to 49°C will be :

(a) 8

(b) 5

(c) 6

(d) 4

13. A black body emits radiation at the rate P when its temperature is T. At this temperature the wavelength at which the radiation has maximumm intensity is λ_0. If at another temperature T' the power radiated is P' and wavelength at maximum intensity is $\dfrac{\lambda_0}{2}$ then P' T' equals to

(a) 32 PT

(b) 16 PT

(c) 8 PT

(d) 4 PT

14. In a surrounding medium of temperature 10°C, a body takes 7 min for a fall of temperature from 60°C to 40°C. In what time the temperature of the body will fall from 40°C to 28°C?

(a) 7 min

(b) 11 min

(c) 14 min

(d) 21 min

(b)

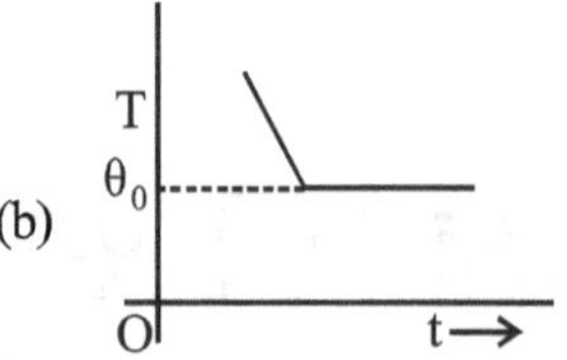

(c)

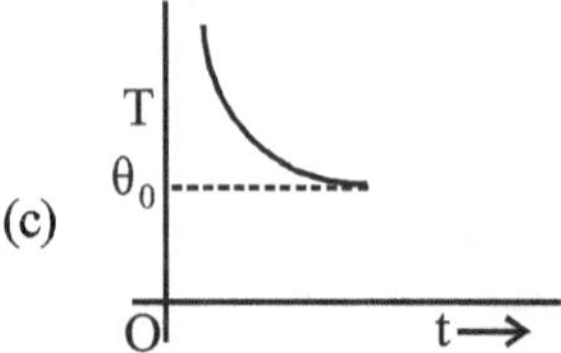

(d)

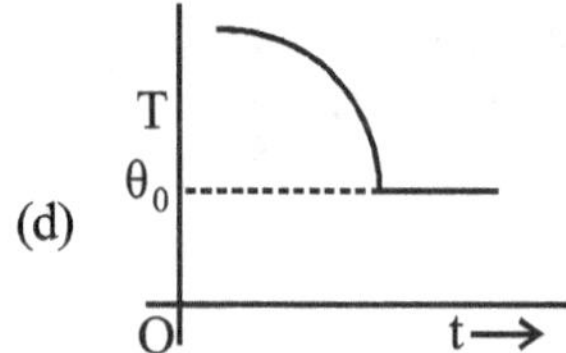

15. 50g of water and an equal volume of alcohol (relative density 0.8) are placed one after the other in the same calorimeter. They are found to cool from 60°C to 50°C in 2 minutes and 1 minute respectively. If the water equivalent of the calorimeter is 2g then the specific heat of the alcohol is

(a) 0.3 Cal/g°C   (b) 0.6 Cal/g°C

(c) 1.3 Cal/g°C   (d) 0.7 Cal/g°C

16. The reading of Centigrade thermometer coincides with that of Fahrenheit thermometer in a liquid. The temperature of the liquid is

(a) -40°C   (b) 313°C

(c) 0°C   (d) 100°C

17. Three bodies A, B and C have equal area which are painted red, yellow and black respectively. If they are at same temperature, then emissive power of

(a) A is maximum.

(b) B is maximum.

(c) C is maximum.

(d) A, B and C are equal.

18. A hole is drilled in a copper sheet. The diameter of the hole is 4.24 cm at 27.0°C. What is the change in the diameter of the hole when the sheet is heated to 227°C? Coefficient of linear expansion of copper $= 1.70 \times 10^{-5}$ K^{-1}

(a) 14.4 cm   (b) 0.0144 cm

(c) 0.144 cm   (d) 1.44 cm

19. If a bar is made of copper whose coefficient of linear expansion is one and a half times that of iron, the ratio of force developed in the copper bar to the iron bar of identical lengths and cross-sections, when heated through the same temperature range (Young's modulus of copper may be taken to be equal to that of iron) is

(a) 3/2   (b) 2/3

(c) 9/4   (d) 4/9

20. A vertical column 50 cm long at 50°C balances another column of same liquid 60 cm long at 100°C. The coefficient of absolute expansion of the liquid is

(a) 0.005/°C   (b) 0.0005/°C

(c) 0.002/°C   (d) 0.0002/°C

21. The plots of intensity versus wavelength for three black bodies at temperatures T_1, T_2 and T_3 respectively are as shown. Their temperature are such that

(a) $T_1 > T_2 > T_3$

(b) $T_1 > T_3 > T_2$

(c) $T_2 > T_3 > T_1$

(d) $T_3 > T_2 > T_1$

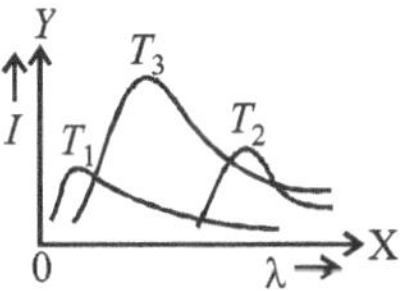

22. A calorimter of water equivalent 20 g contains 180 g of water at 25°C. 'm' grams of steam at 100°C is mixed in it till the temperature of the mixture is 31°C. The value of 'm' is close to (Latent heat of water $= 540$ cal g^{-1}, specific heat of water $= 1$ cal g^{-1} °C^{-1})

(a) 2   (b) 4

(c) 3.2   (d) 2.6

23. When 100 g of a liquid A at 100°C is added to 50 g of a liquid B at temperature 75°C, the temperature of the mixture becomes 90°C. The temperature of the mixture, if 100 g of liquid A at 100°C is added to 50 g of liquid B at 50°C, will be :

(a) 85°C   (b) 60°C

(c) 80°C   (d) 70°C

24. 100g of water is heated from 30°C to 50°C. Ignoring the slight expansion of the water, the change in its internal energy is (specific heat of water is 4184 J/kg/K):

(a) 8.4 kJ   (b) 84 kJ

(c) 2.1 kJ   (d) 4.2 kJ

25. One end of a thermally insulated rod is kept at a temperature T_1 and the other at T_2. The rod is composed of two sections of length l_1 and l_2 and thermal conductivities K_1 and K_2 respectively. The temperature at the interface of the two section is

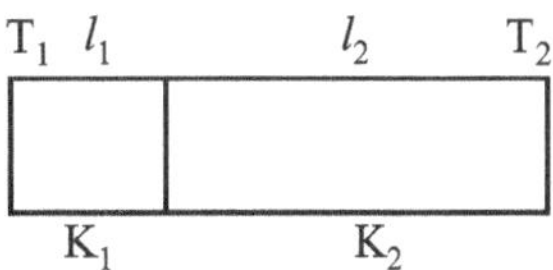

(a) $\dfrac{(K_1 l_1 T_1 + K_2 l_2 T_2)}{(K_1 l_1 + K_2 l_2)}$

(b) $\dfrac{(K_2 l_2 T_1 + K_1 l_1 T_2)}{(K_1 l_1 + K_2 l_2)}$

(c) $\dfrac{(K_2 l_1 T_1 + K_1 l_2 T_2)}{(K_2 l_1 + K_1 l_2)}$

(d) $\dfrac{(K_1 l_2 T_1 + K_2 l_1 T_2)}{(K_1 l_2 + K_2 l_1)}$

26. A bucket full of hot water is kept in a room and it cools from 75°C to 70°C in T_1 minutes, from 70°C to 65°C in T_2 minutes and from 65°C to 60°C in T_3 minutes. Then

(a) $T_1 = T_2 = T_3$ 　　(b) $T_1 < T_2 < T_3$

(c) $T_1 > T_2 > T_3$ 　　(d) $T_1 < T_2 > T_3$

27. When the temperature of a metal wire is increased from 0°C to 10°C, its length increased by 0.02%. The percentage change in its mass density will be closest to :

(a) 0.06 　　(b) 2.3

(c) 0.008 　　(d) 0.8

28. In the given pressure-temperature diagram, for water, which point indicates triple point?

(a) A

(b) C

(c) P

(d) E

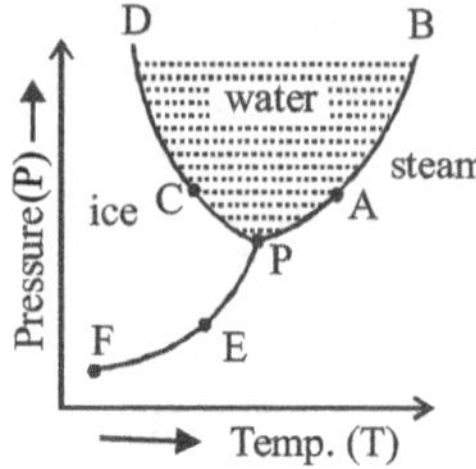

29. From what height should a piece of ice fall so that it melts completely? Only one-quarter of the heat produced is absorbed by the ice. The latent heat of ice is 3.4×10^5 J/kg and g = 10 N/kg.

(a) 136 km 　　(b) 140 km

(c) 68 km 　　(d) 48 km

30. The filament of an evacuated light bulb has a length 10 cm, diameter 0.2 mm and emissivity 0.2. Calculate the power it radiates at 2000 K. ($\sigma = 5.67 \times 10^{-8}$ W/m^2 K^4)

(a) 21.5 W 　　(b) 15.5 W

(c) 8.9 W 　　(d) 11.4 W

ANSWER KEY																			
1	(c)	4	(b)	7	(b)	10	(d)	13	(a)	16	(a)	19	(a)	22	(a)	25	(d)	28	(c)
2	(c)	5	(c)	8	(c)	11	(c)	14	(a)	17	(c)	20	(a)	23	(c)	26	(b)	29	(a)
3	(b)	6	(c)	9	(c)	12	(c)	15	(b)	18	(b)	21	(b)	24	(a)	27	(a)	30	(d)

THERMODYNAMICS 

1. 4 kg of oxygen gas is heated so as to raise its temperature from 20 to 120°C. If the heating is done at constant pressure, the external work done by the gas is (C_p = 0.219 cal/g°C and C_v = 0.157 cal/g°C)

   (a) 628 kJ
   (b) 104 kJ
   (c) 366 kJ
   (d) 206 kJ

2. In a given process on an ideal gas, $dW = 0$ and $dQ < 0$. Then for the gas

   (a) the temperature will decrease
   (b) the volume will increase
   (c) the pressure will remain constant
   (d) the temperature will increase

3. A system X is neither in thermal equilibrium with Y nor with Z. The systems Y and Z

   (a) must be in thermal equilibrium
   (b) cannot be in thermal equilibrium
   (c) may be in thermal equilibrium
   (d) None of these

4. A system performs work ΔW when an amount of heat is ΔQ added to the system, the corresponding change in the internal energy is ΔU. A unique function of the initial and final states (irrespective of mode of change) is

   (a) ΔQ
   (b) ΔW
   (c) ΔU and ΔQ
   (d) ΔU

5. In the equation PV^γ = constant, the value of γ is unity. Then the process is

   (a) isothermal
   (b) adiabatic
   (c) isobaric
   (d) irreversible

6. The slopes of isothermal and adiabatic curves are related as

   (a) isothermal curve slope = adiabatic curve slope
   (b) isothermal curve slope = $\gamma \times$ adiabatic curve slope
   (c) adiabatic curve slope = $\gamma \times$ isothermal curve slope
   (d) adiabatic curve slope = $\dfrac{1}{2} \times$ isothermal curve slope

7. If C_P and C_V are specific heat capacities at constant pressure and constant volume respectively, then for an adiabatic process of an ideal gas $\left[\text{where } \dfrac{C_P}{C_V} = \gamma \right]$

(a) PV = constant

(b) $PV^{-\gamma}$ = constant

(c) PV^{γ} = constant

(d) $\dfrac{P}{V^{\gamma}}$ = constant

8. Two samples A and B of a gas initially at the same pressure and temperature are compressed from volume V to V/2 (A isothermally and B adiabatically). The final pressure of A is

(a) greater than the final pressure of B

(b) equal to the final pressure of B

(c) less than the final pressure of B

(d) twice the final pressure of B

9. Volume of one mole gas changes according to the V = a/T. If temperature change is ΔT, then work done by the gas will be

(a) $R\Delta T$

(b) $-R\Delta T$

(c) $\dfrac{R}{\gamma - 1}\Delta T$

(d) $R(\gamma - 1)\Delta T$

10. A gas is compressed from a volume of $2m^3$ to a volume of $1m^3$ at a constant pressure of 100 N/m^2. Then it is heated at constant volume by supplying 150 J of energy. As a result, the internal energy of the gas:

(a) increases by 250 J

(b) decreases by 250 J

(c) increases by 50 J

(d) decreases by 50 J

11. A perfect gas goes from a state A to another state B by absorbing 8×10^5 J of heat and doing 6.5×10^5 J of external work. It is now transferred between the same two states in another process in which it absorbs 10^5 J of heat. In the second process

(a) work done by gas is 10^5 J

(b) work done on gas is 10^5 J

(c) work done by gas is 0.5×10^5 J

(d) work done on the gas is 0.5×10^5 J

12. A diatomic gas is compressed adiabatically to 1/32 of its initial volume. If the initial temperature of the gas is T_i (in Kelvin) and the final temperature is aT_i, the value of a is

(a) 8

(b) 4

(c) 3

(d) 5

13. An ideal gas at atmospheric pressure is adiabatically compressed so that its density becomes 32 times of its initial value. If the final pressure of gas is 128 atmospheres, the value of 'γ' of the gas is :

(a) 1.5

(b) 1.4

(c) 1.3

(d) 1.6

14. For an ideal gas graph is shown for three process. Process 1, 2 and 3 are respectively.

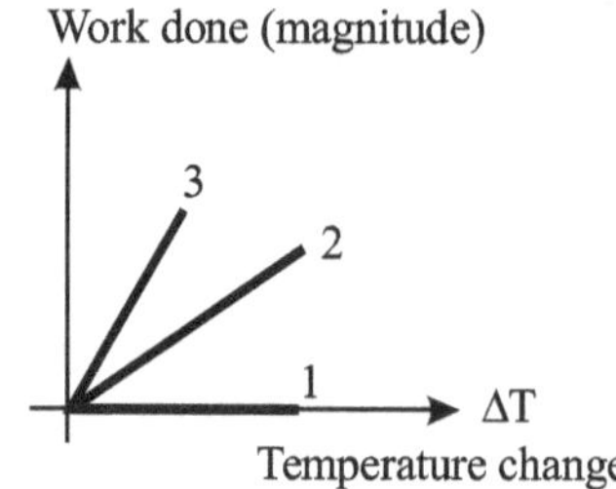

(a) Isobaric, adiabatic, isochoric

(b) Adiabatic, isobaric, isochoric

(c) Isochoric, adiabatic, isobaric

(d) Isochoric, isobaric, adiabatic

15. A system is taken from state a to state c by two paths adc and abc as shown in the figure. The internal energy at a is $U_a = 10$ J. Along the path adc the amount of heat absorbed $\delta Q_1 = 50$ J and the work done $\delta W_1 = 20$ J whereas along the path abc the heat absorbed $\delta Q_2 = 36$ J. The amount of work done along the path abc is

(a) 6 J

(b) 10 J

(c) 12 J

(d) 36 J

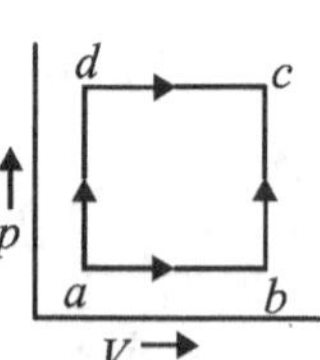

16. A Carnot's engine works as a refrigerator between 250 K and 300 K. It receives 500 cal heat from the reservoir at the lower temperature. The amount of work done in each cycle to operate the refrigerator is:

(a) 420 J (b) 2100 J

(c) 772 J (d) 2520 J

17. In which process the PV indicator diagram is a straight line parallel to volume axis

(a) Isothermal (b) Isobaric

(c) Ineversible (d) Adiabatic

18. In a Carnot engine, the temperature of reservoir is 927°C and that of sink is 27°C. If the work done by the engine when it transfers heat from reservoir to sink is 12.6×10^6 J, the quantity of heat absorbed by the engine from the reservoir is

(a) 16.8×10^6 J (b) 4×10^6 J

(c) 7.6×10^6 J (d) 4.2×10^6 J

19. A reversible engine converts one-fourth of the heat input into work. When the temperature of the sink is reduced by 70K, the efficiency of the engine is doubled. The temperatures of the source and sink are

(a) 280 K and 210 K (b) 290 K and 230 K

(c) 250 K and 220 K (d) 240 K and 210 K

20. A Carnot engine absorbs an amount Q of heat from a reservoir at an abosolute temperature T and rejects heat to a sink at a temperature of $T/3$. The amount of heat rejected is

(a) $Q/4$ (b) $Q/3$

(c) $Q/2$ (d) $2Q/3$

21. An ideal gas has volume V_0 at 27°C. It is heated at constant pressure so that its volume becomes $2V_0$. The final temperature is.

(a) 54°C (b) 32.6°C

(c) 327°C (d) 150 K

22. A Carnot engine takes 3×10^6 cal. of heat from a reservoir at 627°C, and gives it to a sink at 27°C. The work done by the engine is

(a) 4.2×10^6 J (b) 8.4×10^6 J

(c) 16.8×10^6 J (d) zero

23. For the given cyclic process CAB as shown for gas, the work done is:

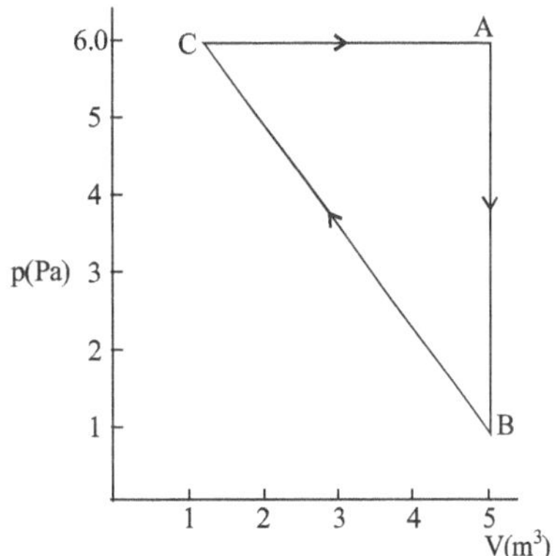

(a) 30 J (b) 10 J

(c) 1 J (d) 5 J

24. A litre of dry air at STP expands adiabatically to a volume of 3 litres. If $\gamma = 1.40$, the work done by air is: $(3^{1.4} = 4.6555)$ [Take air to be an ideal gas]

(a) 60.7 J (b) 90.5 J

(c) 100.8 J (d) 48 J

25. A refrigerator works between 3°C and 40°C. To keep the temperature of the refrigerator constant, 600 calories of heat are to be removed every second. The power required is

(a) 337.8 watt (b) 6.77 watt

(c) 7.77 watt (d) 10.77 watt

26. 200g water is heated from 40°C to 60°C. Ignoring the slight expansion of water, the change in its internal energy is close to (Given specific heat of water = 4184 J/kgK):

(a) 167.4 kJ (b) 8.4 kJ

(c) 4.2 kJ (d) 16.7 kJ

27. n moles of an ideal gas undergo a process $A \to B$ as shown in the figure. Maximum temperature of the gas during the process is

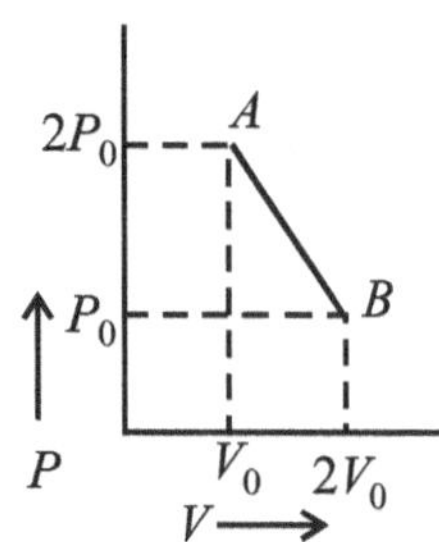

(a) $\dfrac{9P_0V_0}{nR}$ (b) $\dfrac{3P_0V_0}{2nR}$

(c) $\dfrac{9P_0V_0}{2nR}$ (d) $\dfrac{9P_0V_0}{4nR}$

28. A sample of an ideal gas is taken through the cyclic process abca as shown in the figure. The change in the internal energy of the gas along the path ca is -180 J, The gas absorbs 250 J of heat along the path ab and 60 J along the path bc. The work down by the gas along the path abc is:

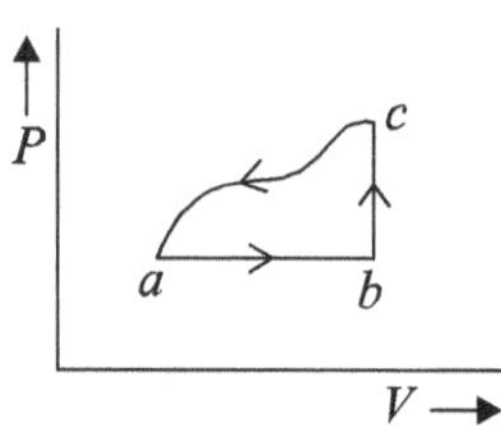

(a) 120 J   (b) 130 J
(c) 100 J   (d) 140 J

29. A certain amount of ideal monoatomic gas undergoes, process given by $UV^{1/2} = C$ where U is the internal energy of the gas. The molar specific heat of the gas for the process will be

(a) $R/2$ (b) $3R$
(c) $5R/2$ (d) $-R/2$

30. When a gas ($\gamma = 5/3$) is heated under constant pressure, then what percentage of given heat energy will be utilised in doing external work?

(a) 40%   (b) 30%
(c) 60%   (d) 20%

ANSWER KEY

1	(b)	4	(d)	7	(c)	10	(a)	13	(b)	16	(a)	19	(a)	22	(b)	25	(a)	28	(b)
2	(a)	5	(a)	8	(c)	11	(d)	14	(d)	17	(b)	20	(b)	23	(b)	26	(d)	29	(d)
3	(c)	6	(c)	9	(b)	12	(b)	15	(a)	18	(a)	21	(c)	24	(b)	27	(b)	30	(a)

KINETIC THEORY

1. At constant pressure, the ratio of increase in volume of an ideal gas per degree rise in kelvin temperature to its original volume is (T = absolute temperature of the gas) is
   (a) T^2 (b) T
   (c) $1/T$ (d) $1/T^2$

2. A graph is plotted with PV/T on y-axis and mass of the gas along x-axis for different gases. The graph is
   (a) a straight line parallel to x-axis for all the gases
   (b) a straight line passing through origin with a slope having a constant value for all the gases
   (c) a straight line passing through origin with a slope having different values for different gases
   (d) a straight line parallel to y-axis for all the gases

3. The relation PV = nRT can describe the behaviour of a real gas at
   (a) high temperature and high pressure
   (b) high temperature and low pressure
   (c) low temperature and low pressure
   (d) low temperature and high pressure

4. A gas is found to obey the law P^2V = constant. The initial temperature and volume are T_0 and V_0. If the gas expands to a volume $2V_0$, its final temperature becomes
   (a) $\sqrt{2}T_0$ (b) $2T_0$
   (c) $T_0/2$ (d) $T_0/\sqrt{2}$

5. At 0°C the density of a fixed mass of a gas divided by pressure is x. At 100°C, the ratio will be
   (a) x (b) $\dfrac{273}{373}x$
   (c) $\dfrac{373}{273}x$ (d) $\dfrac{100}{273}x$

6. Three containers of the same volume contain three different gases. The masses of the molecules are m_1, m_2 and m_3 and the number of molecules in their respective containers are N_1, N_2 and N_3. The gas pressure in the containers are P_1, P_2 and P_3 respectively. All the gases are now mixed and put in one of these containers. The pressure P of the mixture is
   (a) $P < (P_1 + P_2 + P_3)$ (b) $P = \dfrac{P_1 + P_2 + P_3}{3}$
   (c) $P = P_1 + P_2 + P_3$ (d) $P > (P_1 + P_2 + P_3)$

7. For a gas at a temperature T the root-mean-square velocity v_{rms}, the most probable speed v_{mp}, and the average speed v_{av} obey the relationship
   (a) $v_{av} > v_{rms} > v_{mp}$ (b) $v_{rms} > v_{av} > v_{mp}$
   (c) $v_{mp} > v_{av} > v_{rms}$ (d) $v_{mp} > v_{rms} > v_{av}$

8. The rms velocity of the molecules of a gas at temperature 120 K is v. At what temperature will the rms velocity be 2 v?
   (a) 120 K   (b) 240 K
   (c) 480 K   (d) 1120 K

9. The density of a gas is 6×10^{-2} kg/m^3 and the root mean square velocity of the gas molecules is 500 m/s. The pressure exerted by the gas on the walls of the vessel is
(a) 5×10^3 N/m^2
(b) 1.2×10^{-4} N/m^2
(c) 0.83×10^{-4} N/m^2
(d) 30 N/m^2

10. In the degree of freedom of a gas are f, then the ratio of two specific heats C_p/C_V is given by
(a) $\dfrac{2}{f}+1$
(b) $1-\dfrac{2}{f}$
(c) $1+\dfrac{1}{f}$
(d) $1-\dfrac{1}{f}$

11. For the P-V diagram given for an ideal gas,

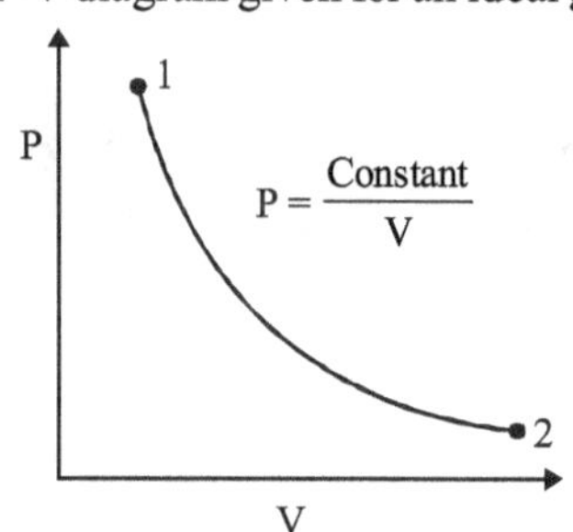

out of the following which one correctly represents the T-P diagram ?

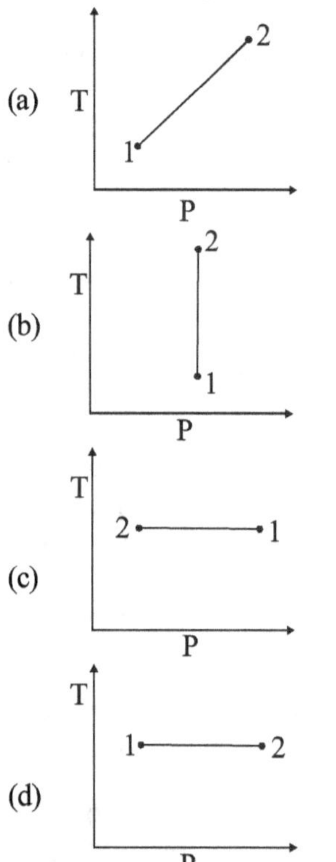

12. Two moles of an ideal gas with $\dfrac{C_p}{C_V}=\dfrac{5}{3}$ are mixed with 3 moles of another ideal gas with $\dfrac{C_p}{C_V}=\dfrac{4}{3}$. The value of $\dfrac{C_p}{C_V}$ for the mixture is:
(a) 1.45
(b) 1.50
(c) 1.47
(d) 1.42

13. A 25×10^{-3} m^3 volume cylinder is filled with 1 mol of O_2 gas at room temperature (300 K). The molecular diameter of O_2, and its root mean square speed, are found to be 0.3 nm and 200 m/s, respectively. What is the average collision rate (per second) for an O_2 molecule?
(a) $\sim 10^{12}$
(b) $\sim 10^{11}$
(c) $\sim 10^{10}$
(d) $\sim 10^{13}$

14. The plot that depicts the behavior of the mean free time τ (time between two successive collisions) for the molecules of an ideal gas, as a function of temperature (T), qualitatively, is: (Graphs are schematic and not drawn to scale)

(a) 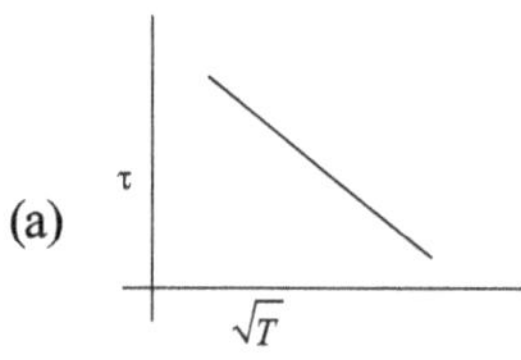

(b) 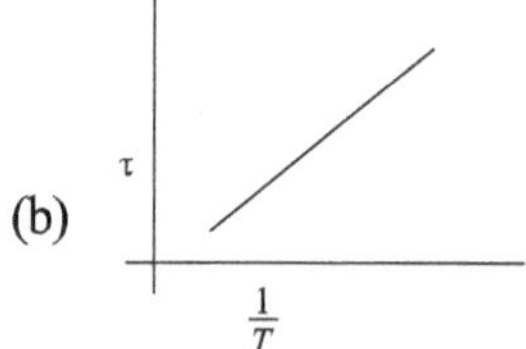

(c) 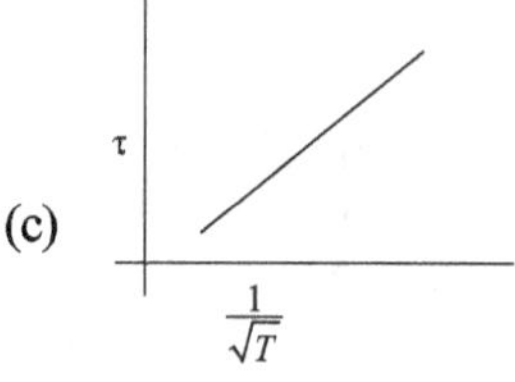

(d) 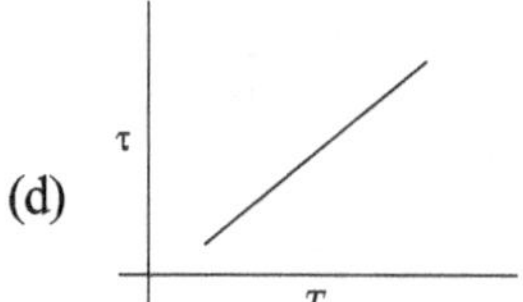

15. To raise the temperature of a certain mass of gas by 50°C at a constant pressure, 160 calories of heat is required. When the same mass of gas is cooled by 100°C at constant volume, 240 calories of heat is released. How many degrees of freedom does each molecule of this gas have (assume gas to be ideal)?

(a) 5   (b) 6
(c) 3   (d) 7

16. Molecules of an ideal gas are known to have three translational degrees of freedom and two rotational degrees of freedom. The gas is maintained at a temperature of T.

The total internal energy, U of a mole of this gas, and the value of $\gamma\left(=\dfrac{C_p}{C_v}\right)$ are given, respectively, by:

(a) $U = \dfrac{5}{2}RT$ and $\gamma = \dfrac{6}{5}$

(b) $U = 5RT$ and $\gamma = \dfrac{7}{5}$

(c) $U = \dfrac{5}{2}RT$ and $\gamma = \dfrac{7}{5}$

(d) $U = 5RT$ and $\gamma = \dfrac{6}{5}$

17.

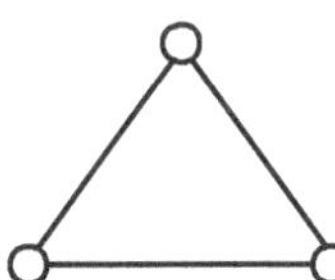

Consider a gas of triatomic molecules. The molecules are assumed to be triangular and made of massless rigid rods whose vertices are occupied by atoms. The internal energy of a mole of the gas at temperature T is :

(a) $\dfrac{5}{2}RT$ (b) $\dfrac{3}{2}RT$

(c) $\dfrac{9}{2}RT$ (d) $3RT$

18. An ideal gas has molecules with 5 degrees of freedom. The ratio of specific heats at constant pressure (C_p) and at constant volume (C_v) is :

(a) 6   (b) $\dfrac{7}{2}$

(c) $\dfrac{5}{2}$ (d) $\dfrac{7}{5}$

19. An ideal gas is enclosed in a cylinder at pressure of 2 atm and temperature, 300 K. The mean time between two successive collisions is 6×10^{-8} s. If the pressure is doubled and temperature is increased to 500 K, the mean time between two successive collisions wiil be close to:

(a) 2×10^{-7} s   (b) 4×10^{-8} s
(c) 0.5×10^{-8} s   (d) 3×10^{-6} s

20. A 15 g mass of nitrogen gas is enclosed in a vessel at a temperature 27°C. Amount of heat transferred to the gas, so that rms velocity of molecules is doubled, is about: [Take R = 8.3 J/K mole]

(a) 0.9 kJ   (b) 6 kJ
(c) 10 kJ   (d) 14 kJ

21. At room temperature a diatomic gas is found to have an r.m.s. speed of 1930 ms^{-1}. The gas is:

(a) H_2 (b) Cl_2
(c) O_2 (d) F_2

22. One mole of monoatomic gas and three moles of diatomic gas are put together in a container. The molar specific heat (in $JK^{-1} mol^{-1}$) at constant volume is ($R = 8.3 \, JK^{-1} mol^{-1}$)

(a) 18.7   (b) 20.32
(c) 19.2   (d) None of these

23. P, V, T respectively denote pressure, volume and temperature of two gases. On mixing, new temperature and volume are respectively T and V. Final pressure of the mixture is

(a) P (b) $2P$
(c) zero   (d) $3P$

24. For a gas, difference between two specific heats is 5000 J/mole°C. If the ratio of specific heat is 1.6, the two specific heats in J/mole-°C are

(a) $C_P = 1.33 \times 10^5, C_V = 2.66 \times 10^4$
(b) $C_P = 13.3 \times 10^5, C_V = 8.33 \times 10^4$
(c) $C_P = 1.33 \times 10^4, C_V = 8.33 \times 10^3$
(d) $C_P = 2.6 \times 10^4, C_V = 8.33 \times 10^4$

25. The molar heat capacities of a mixture of two gases at constant volume is 13R/6. The ratio of number of moles of the first gas to the second is $1:2$. The respective gases may be

  (a) O_2 and N_2 (b)   He and Ne

  (c)   He and N_2 (d) N_2 and He

26. Two vessels separately contain two ideal gases A and B at the same temperature. The pressure of A being twice that of B. Under such conditions, the density of A is found to be 1.5 times the density of B. The ratio of molecular weight of A and B is:

  (a)   3/4   (b)   2

  (c)   1/2   (d)   2/3

27. The speed of sound in oxygen (O_2) at a certain temperature is $460\ ms^{-1}$. The speed of sound in helium (He) at the same temperature will be (assume both gases to be ideal)

  (a) $1421\ ms^{-1}$ (b) $500\ ms^{-1}$

  (c) $650\ ms^{-1}$ (d) $330\ ms^{-1}$

28. A fixed mass of gas at constant pressure occupies a volume V. The gas undergoes a rise in temperature at constant pressure so that the root mean square velocity of its molecules is doubled. The new volume will be

  (a)   V/2   (b) $V/\sqrt{2}$

  (c)   2V   (d)   4V

29. If at the same temperature and pressure, the densities of two diatomic gases are d_1 and d_2 respectively, the ratio of mean kinetic energy per molecule of gases will be

  (a) $1:1$ (b) $d_1:d_2$

  (c) $\sqrt{d_1}:\sqrt{d_2}$ (d) $\sqrt{d_2}:\sqrt{d_1}$

30. Two monatomic ideal gases 1 and 2 of molecular masses m_1 and m_2 respectively are enclosed in separate containers of same volume kept at the same temperature. The ratio of the root mean square speed of molecules of gas 1 to that of gas 2 is given by

  (a) $\sqrt{\dfrac{m_1}{m_2}}$ (b) $\sqrt{\dfrac{m_2}{m_1}}$

  (c) $\dfrac{m_1}{m_2}$ (d) $\dfrac{m_2}{m_1}$

ANSWER KEY

1	(c)	4	(a)	7	(b)	10	(a)	13	(c)	16	(c)	19	(b)	22	(a)	25	(c)	28	(d)
2	(c)	5	(b)	8	(c)	11	(c)	14	(c)	17	(d)	20	(c)	23	(b)	26	(a)	29	(a)
3	(b)	6	(c)	9	(a)	12	(d)	15	(b)	18	(d)	21	(a)	24	(c)	27	(a)	30	(b)

OSCILLATIONS

1. Which of the following expressions does not represent simple harmonic motion?

   (a) $x = A \cos(\omega t + \delta)$

   (b) $x = B \cos(\omega t + \phi)$

   (c) $x = A \tan(\omega t + \phi)$

   (d) $x = A \sin \omega t \cos \omega t$

2. Two simple harmonic motions with the same frequency act on a particle at right angles i.e., along x and y axis. If the two amplitudes are equal and the phase difference is $\pi/2$, the resultant motion will be

   (a) a circle

   (b) an ellipse with the major axis along y-axis

   (c) an ellipse with the major axis along x-axis

   (d) a straight line inclined at 45° to the x-axis

3. A simple harmonic wave having an amplitude a and time period T is represented by the equation $y = 5 \sin \pi(t + 4)m$. Then the value of amplitude (a) in (m) and time period (T) in second are [y is in (m) and t is in (sec)]

   (a) $a = 10, T = 2$ (b) $a = 5, T = 1$

   (c) $a = 10, T = 1$ (d) $a = 5, T = 2$

4. The amplitude of a particle executing SHM is 4 cm. At the mean position the speed of the particle is 16 cm/sec. The distance of the particle from the mean position at which the speed of the particle becomes $8\sqrt{3}$ cm/s, will be

   (a) $2\sqrt{3}$ cm   (b) $\sqrt{3}$ cm

   (c) 1 cm   (d) 2 cm

5. A body executes simple harmonic motion have amplitude A. The potential energy (P.E.), the kinetic energy (K.E.) and total energy (T.E.) are measured as a function of displacement x. Which of the following statement is true?

   (a) P.E. is maximum when $x = 0$.

   (b) K.E. = P.E. at $x = \pm \dfrac{A}{\sqrt{2}}$

   (c) T.E. is zero when $x = \pm A$.

   (d) K.E. is maximum when $x = A$

6. The total energy of a particle executing S.H. M. is 80 J. What is the potential energy when the particle is at a distance of 3/4 of amplitude from the mean position?

   (a) 60 J   (b) 10 J

   (c) 40 J   (d) 45 J

7. A graph of the square of the velocity against the square of the acceleration of a given simple harmonic motion is

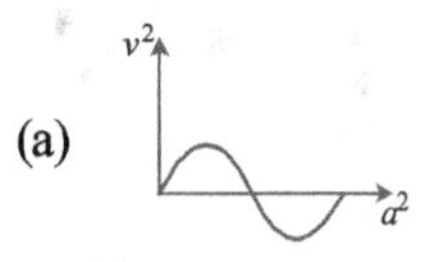

(a)

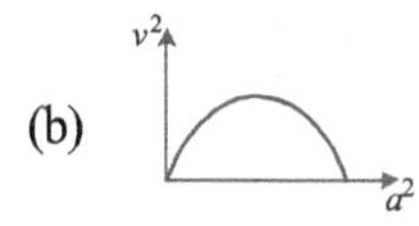

(b)

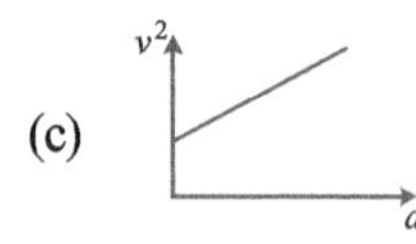

(c)

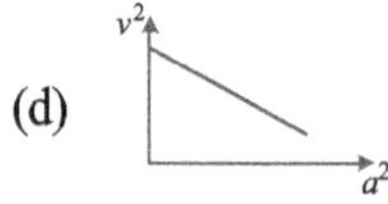

(d)

8. A mass M is suspended from a spring of negligible mass. The spring is pulled a little and then released so that the mass executes SHM of time period T. If the mass is increased by m, the time period becomes $\dfrac{5T}{3}$. Then the ratio of $\dfrac{m}{M}$ is

(a) 3/5

(b) 25/9

(c) 16/9

(d) 5/3

9. A simple pendulum performs SHM about $x = 0$ with an amplitude a and time period T. What is the speed of the pendulum at $x = a/2$?

(a) $\dfrac{a\pi\sqrt{3}}{T}$

(b) $\dfrac{a^2\pi^2\sqrt{3}}{T^2}$

(c) $\dfrac{a}{T}$

(d) $\dfrac{a\pi}{T}$

10. For a particle executing S.H.M. the displacement x is given by $x = A\cos\omega t$. Identify the graph which represents the variation of potential energy (P.E.) as a function of time t and displacement x.

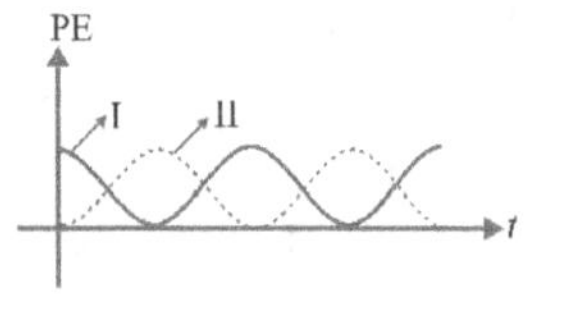
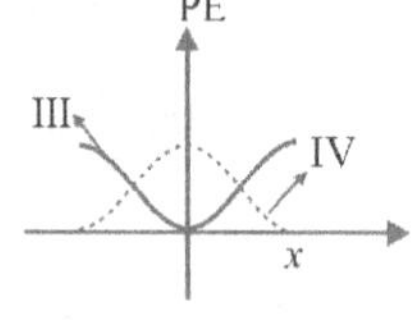

(a) I, III

(b) II, IV

(c) II, III

(d) I, IV

11. A spring balance has a scale that reads from 0 to 50 kg. The length of the scale is 20 cm. A body suspended from this balance, when displaced and released, oscillates with a period of 0.6s. What is the weight of the body?

(a) 219.1 N

(b) 518.2 N

(c) 132.2 N

(d) 612.1 N

12. A mass M is suspended from a massless spring. An additional mass m stretches it further by a distance x. The combined mass will oscillate on the spring with time period

(a) $2\pi\sqrt{\dfrac{(M+m)x}{mg}}$

(b) $2\pi\sqrt{\dfrac{mg}{(M+m)x}}$

(c) $\dfrac{1}{2\pi}\sqrt{\dfrac{mg}{(M+m)x}}$

(d) $\dfrac{\pi}{2}\sqrt{\dfrac{mg}{(M+m)x}}$

13. The displacement-time graph of a harmonic oscillator is shown below. The frequency of the oscillator is

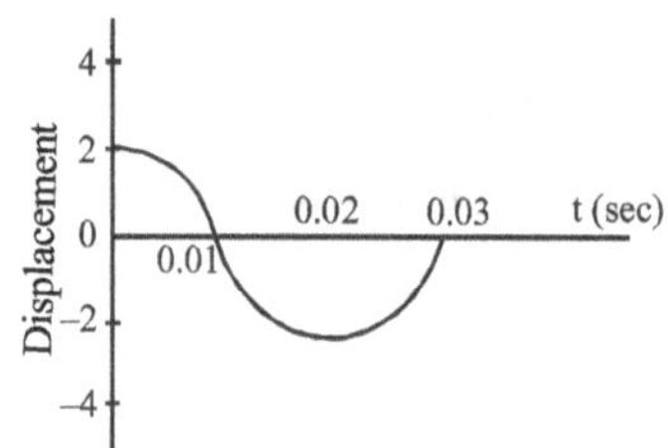

(a) 25 Hz

(b) 100 Hz

(c) 12.5 Hz

(d) 33.3 Hz

14. A cylindrical piece of cork of density of base area A and height h floats in a liquid of density ρ_1. The cork is depressed slightly and then released. What is the time period of the cork oscillating up and down simple harmonically.

(a) $2\pi\sqrt{\dfrac{h\rho}{\rho_l g}}$

(b) $4\pi\sqrt{\dfrac{h\rho}{\rho_l g}}$

(c) $6\pi\sqrt{\dfrac{h\rho}{\rho_l g}}$

(d) $8\pi\sqrt{\dfrac{h\rho}{\rho_l g}}$

where ρ is the density of cork. (Ignore damping due to viscosity of the liquid).

15. Two simple pendulums of length 1 m and 4 m respectively are both given small displacement in the same direction at the same instant. They will be again in phase after the shorter pendulum has completed number of oscillations equal to :

(a) 2
(b) 7
(c) 5
(d) 3

16. A mass m is suspended by means of two coiled spring which have the same lenght in unstretched condition as in figure. Their force constant are k_1 and k_2 respectively. When set into vertical vibrations, the period will be

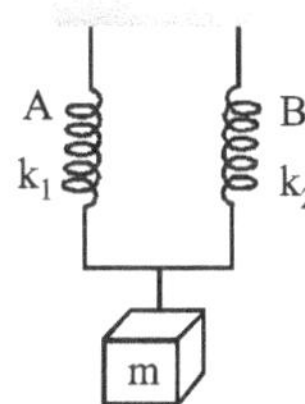

(a) $2\pi\sqrt{\left(\dfrac{m}{k_1 k_2}\right)}$
(b) $2\pi\sqrt{m\left(\dfrac{k_1}{k_2}\right)}$

(c) $2\pi\sqrt{\left(\dfrac{m}{k_1 - k_2}\right)}$
(d) $2\pi\left(\sqrt{\dfrac{m}{k_1 + k_2}}\right)$

17. Two identical springs of spring constant k are attached to a block of mass m and to fixed supports as shown in figure. When the mass is displaced from equilibrium position by a distance x towards right, then the restoring force will be.

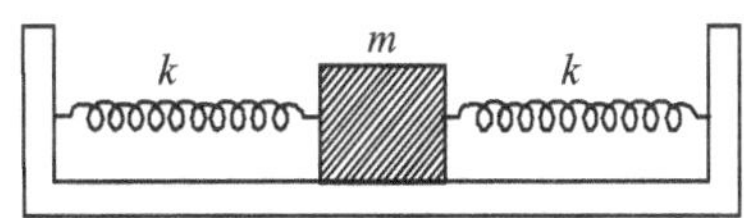

(a) $2\,kx$
(b) $5\,kx$
(c) $6\,kx^2$
(d) $8\,kx^2$

18. A simple harmonic oscillator of angular frequency 2 rad s^{-1} is acted upon by an external force $F = \sin t$ N. If the oscillator is at rest in its equilibrium position at $t = 0$, its position at later times is proportional to :

(a) $\sin t + \dfrac{1}{2}\cos 2t$
(b) $\cos t - \dfrac{1}{2}\sin 2t$

(c) $\sin t - \dfrac{1}{2}\sin 2t$
(d) $\sin t + \dfrac{1}{2}\sin 2t$

19. The time period of a simple pendulum of length L as measured in an elevator descending with acceleration $\dfrac{g}{3}$ is

(a) $2\pi\sqrt{\dfrac{3L}{g}}$
(b) $\pi\left(\sqrt{\dfrac{3L}{g}}\right)$

(c) $2\pi\left(\sqrt{\dfrac{3L}{2g}}\right)$
(d) $2\pi\sqrt{\dfrac{2L}{3g}}$

20. The function $\sin^2(\omega t)$ represents
(a) a periodic, but not simple harmonic motion with a period $\dfrac{\pi}{\omega}$
(b) a periodic, but not simple harmonic motion with a period $\dfrac{2\pi}{\omega}$
(c) a simple harmonic motion with a period $\dfrac{\pi}{\omega}$
(d) a simple harmonic motion with a period $\dfrac{2\pi}{\omega}$

21. A pendulum is executing simple harmonic motion and its maximum kinetic energy is K_1. If the length of the pendulum is doubled and it performs simple harmonic motion with the same amplitude as in the first case, its maximum kinetic energy is K_2.

(a) $K_2 = 2K_1$
(b) $K_2 = \dfrac{K_1}{2}$

(c) $K_2 = \dfrac{K_1}{4}$
(d) $K_2 = K_1$

22. A particle is executing simple harmonic motion (SHM) of amplitude A, along the x-axis, about $x = 0$. When its potential Energy (PE) equals kinetic energy (KE), the position of the particle will be:

(a) $\dfrac{A}{2}$
(b) $\dfrac{A}{2\sqrt{2}}$

(c) $\dfrac{A}{\sqrt{2}}$
(d) A

23. A pendulum with time period of 1s is losing energy. At certain time its energy is 45 J. If after completing 15 oscillations, its energy has become 15 J, its damping constant (in s^{-1}) is

(a) $\dfrac{1}{2}$

(b) $\dfrac{1}{30}\ln 3$

(c) 2

(d) $\dfrac{1}{15}\ln 3$

24. A particle of mass m executes simple harmonic motion with amplitude a and frequency v. The average kinetic energy during its motion from the position of equilibrium to the end is

(a) $2\pi^2 ma^2 v^2$

(b) $\pi^2 ma^2 v^2$

(c) $\dfrac{1}{4}ma^2 v^2$

(d) $4\pi^2 ma^2 v^2$

25. Starting from the origin a body oscillates simple harmonically with a period of 2 s. After what time will its kinetic energy be 75% of the total energy?

(a) $\dfrac{1}{6}$s

(b) $\dfrac{1}{4}$s

(c) $\dfrac{1}{3}$s

(d) $\dfrac{1}{12}$s

26. A simple harmonic motion is represented by :

$y = 5(\sin 3\pi t + \sqrt{3}\,\cos 3\pi t)\,cm$

The amplitude and time period of the motion are:

(a) $10\,cm, \dfrac{2}{3}$ s

(b) $10\,cm, \dfrac{3}{2}$ s

(c) $5\,cm, \dfrac{3}{2}$ s

(d) $5\,cm, \dfrac{2}{3}$ s

27. The mass and the diameter of a planet are three times the respective values for the Earth. The period of oscillation of a simple pendulum on the Earth is 2s. The period of oscillation of the same pendulum on the planet would be:

(a) $\dfrac{\sqrt{3}}{2}$s

(b) $\dfrac{2}{\sqrt{3}}$s

(c) $\dfrac{3}{2}$s

(d) $2\sqrt{3}$s

28. A damped harmonic oscillator has a frequency of 5 oscillations per second. The amplitude drops to half its value for every 10 oscillations. The time it will take to drop to $\dfrac{1}{1000}$ of the original amplitude is close to :

(a) 50s

(b) 100s

(c) 20s

(d) 10s

29. In forced oscillation of a particle the amplitude is maximum for a frequency ω_1 of the force while the energy is maximum for a frequency ω_2 of the force; then

(a) $\omega_1 < \omega_2$ when damping is small and $\omega_1 > \omega_2$ when damping is large

(b) $\omega_1 > \omega_2$

(c) $\omega_1 = \omega_2$

(d) $\omega_1 < \omega_2$

30. A block of mass m attached to a massless spring is performing oscillatory motion of amplitude 'A' on a frictionless horizontal plane. If half of the mass of the block breaks off when it is passing through its equilibrium point, the amplitude of oscillation for the remaining system become fA. The value of f is :

(a) $\dfrac{1}{\sqrt{2}}$

(b) 1

(c) $\dfrac{1}{2}$

(d) $\sqrt{2}$

ANSWER KEY																			
1	(c)	**4**	(d)	**7**	(d)	**10**	(a)	**13**	(a)	**16**	(d)	**19**	(c)	**22**	(c)	**25**	(a)	**28**	(c)
2	(a)	**5**	(b)	**8**	(c)	**11**	(a)	**14**	(a)	**17**	(a)	**20**	(a)	**23**	(d)	**26**	(a)	**29**	(c)
3	(d)	**6**	(d)	**9**	(a)	**12**	(a)	**15**	(a)	**18**	(c)	**21**	(a)	**24**	(b)	**27**	(d)	**30**	(a)

WAVES

1. The equation of a travelling wave is $y = 60 \cos (180\,t - 6x)$ where y is in microns, t in second and x in metres. The ratio of maximum particle velocity to velocity of wave propagation is
   (a) 3.6
   (b) 3.6×10^{-4}
   (c) 3.6×10^{-6}
   (d) 3.6×10^{-11}

2. Sound waves are travelling in a medium whose adiabatic elasticity is E and isothermal elasticity E'. The velocity of sound waves is proportional to
   (a) E
   (b) $\sqrt{E}$
   (c) $\sqrt{E'}$
   (d) $\dfrac{E}{E'}$

3. A stretched wire 60 cm long is vibrating with its fundamental frequency of 256 Hz. If the length of the wire is decreased to 15 cm and the tension remains the same, then the fundamental freuqency of the vibration of the wire will be
   (a) 1024
   (b) 572
   (c) 256
   (d) 64

4. Two coherent sources of different intensities send waves which interfere. The ratio of maximum intensity to the minimum intensity is 25. The intensities of the sources are in the ratio of
   (a) $25 : 1$
   (b) $5 : 1$
   (c) $9 : 4$
   (d) $25 : 16$

5. 41 forks are so arranged that each produces 5 beats per sec when sounded with its near fork. If the frequency of last fork is double the frequency of first fork, then the frequencies (in Hz) of the first and the last fork are respectively.
   (a) 200, 400
   (b) 205, 410
   (c) 195, 390
   (d) 100, 200

6. 26 tuning forks are placed in a series such that each tuning fork produces 4 beats with its previous tuning fork. If the frequency of last tuning fork be three times the frequency of first tuning fork then the frequency of first tuning fork will be
   (a) 76 Hz
   (b) 75 Hz
   (c) 50 Hz
   (d) 25 Hz

7. The speed of longitudinal wave in a wire is 100 times the speed of transverse wave. If Young's modulus of the wire material is 1×10^{11} N/m^2, then the stress in the wire is
   (a) 1×10^{7} N/m^2
   (b) 1.5×10^{7} N/m^2
   (c) 1×10^{11} N/m^2
   (d) 1.5×10^{11} N/m^2

8. The vibrations of a string of length 60 cm fixed at both the ends are represented by the equation
   $$y = 2 \sin\left(\dfrac{4\pi x}{15}\right) \cos (96\pi t)$$
   where x and y are in cm. The maximum number of loops that can be formed in it is
   (a) 4
   (b) 16
   (c) 5
   (d) 15

9. An air column in a pipe, which is closed at one end, will be in resonance wtih a vibrating tuning fork of frequency 264 Hz if the length of the column in cm is (velocity of sound = 330 m/s)

(a) 125.00   (b) 93.75

(c) 62.50   (d) 187.50

10. Two vibrating tuning forks producing waves given by $y_1 = 27 \sin 600\pi t$ and $y_2 = 27 \sin 604\,\pi t$ are held near the ear of a person, how many beats will be heard in three seconds by him ?

(a) 4   (b) 2

(c) 6   (d) 12

11. The frequencies of two tuning forks A and B are respectively 1.5% more and 2.5% less than that of the tuning fork C. When A and B are sounded together, 12 beats are produced in 1 sec. The frequency of the tuning fork C is

(a) 200 Hz   (b) 240 Hz

(c) 360 Hz   (d) 300 Hz

12. A man is watching two trains, one leaving and the other coming in with equal speeds of 4m/ sec. If they sound their whistles, each of frequency 240 Hz, the number of beats heard by the man will be equal to (velocity of sound in air = 320 m/sec)

(a) 6   (b) 3

(c) 0   (d) 12

13. A sound source S is moving along a straight track with speed v, and is emitting sound of frequency v_o (see figure). An observer is standing at a finite distance, at the point O, from the track. The time variation of frequency heard by the observer is best represented by:

(t_0 represents the instant when the distance between the source and observer is minimum)

(a) 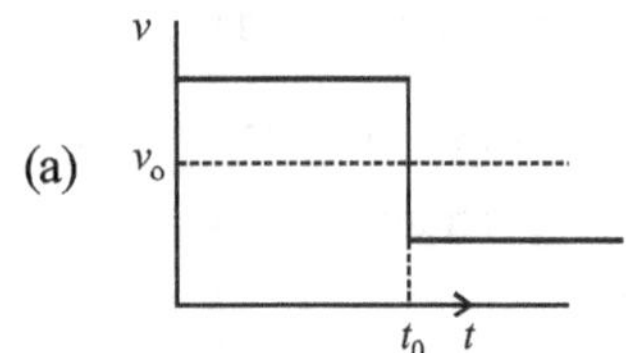

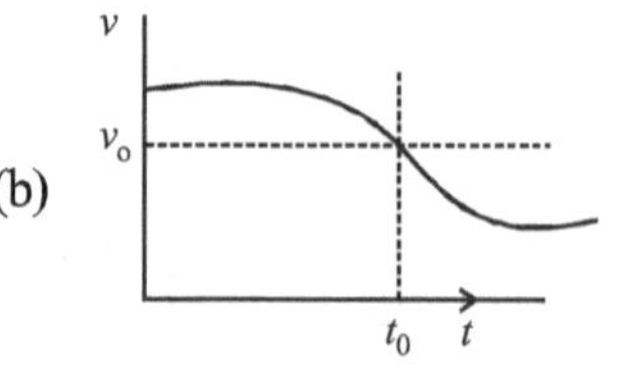

(b)

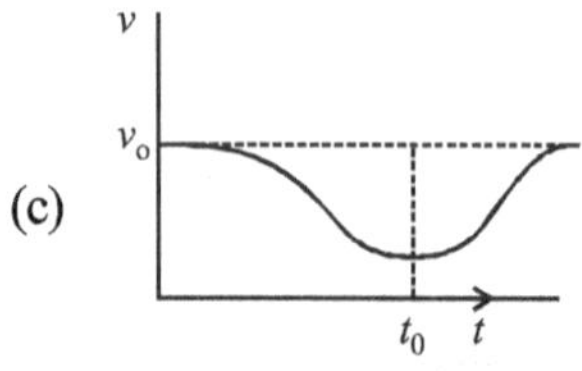

(c)

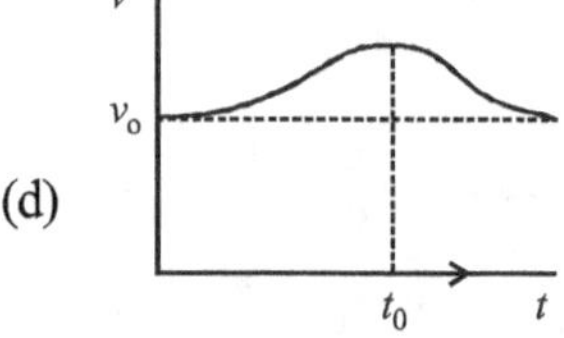

(d)

14. Two cars are moving on two perpendicular roads towards a crossing with uniform speeds of 72 km/hr and 36 km/hr. If first car blows horn of frequency 280 Hz, then the frequency of horn heard by the driver of second car when line joining the cars make 45° angle with the roads; will be

(a) 321 Hz   (b) 298 Hz

(c) 289 Hz   (d) 280 Hz

15. A progressive sound wave of frequency 500 Hz is travelling through air with a speed of 350 ms^{-1}. A compression maximum appears at a place at a given instant. The minimum time interval after which the rarefraction maximum occurs at the same point, is

(a) 200 s   (b) $\dfrac{1}{250}$ s

(c) $\dfrac{1}{500}$ s   (d) $\dfrac{1}{1000}$ s

16. Two points are located at a distance of 10 m and 15 m from the source of oscillation. The period of oscillation is 0.05 sec and the velocity of the wave is 300 m/sec. What is the phase difference between the oscillations of two points?

(a) $\dfrac{\pi}{3}$ (b) $\dfrac{2\pi}{3}$

(c) π (d) $\dfrac{\pi}{6}$

17. The total length of a sonometer wire between fixed ends is 110 cm. Two bridges are placed to divide the length of wire in ratio 6 : 3 : 2. The tension in the wire is 400 N and the mass per unit length is 0.01 kg/m. What is the minimum common frequency with which three parts can vibrate?

(a)   1100 Hz   (b)   1000 Hz

(c)   166 Hz   (d)   100 Hz

18. There are three sources of sound of equal intensity with frequencies 400, 401 and 402 vib/sec. The number of beats heard per second is

(a)   0   (b)   1

(c)   2   (d)   3

19. Velocity of sound measured in hydrogen and oxygen gas at a given temperature and pressure will be in the ratio of

(a)   1 : 1   (b)   2 : 1

(c)   1 : 4   (d)   4 : 1

20. With the propagation of a longitudinal wave through a material medium, the quantities transmitted in the propagation direction are

(a)   energy, momentum and mass

(b)   energy

(c)   energy and mass

(d)   energy and linear momentum

21. The correct figure that shows, schematically, the wave pattern produced by superposition of two waves of frequencies 9 Hz and 11 Hz is :

(a)   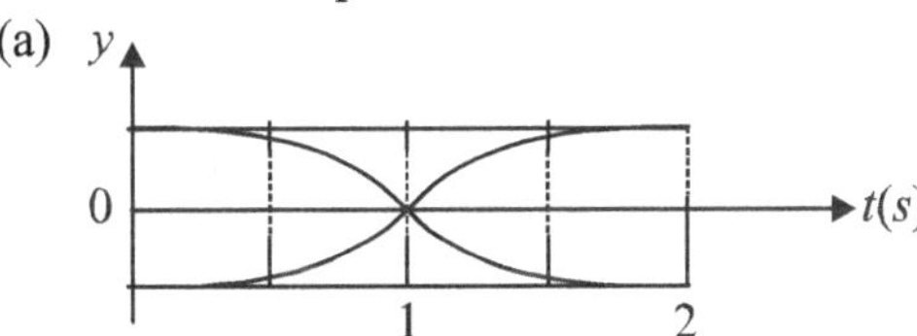

(b)   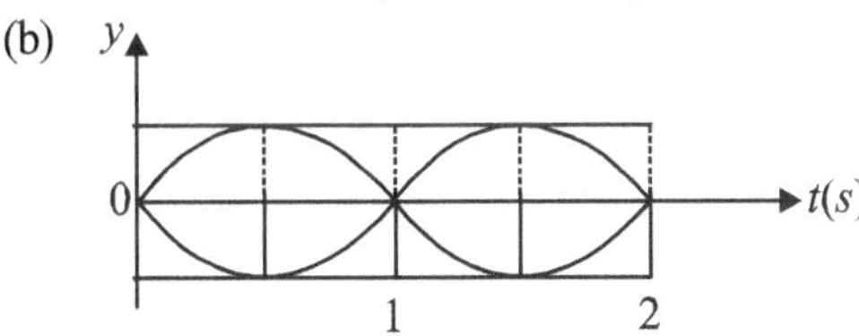

(c)   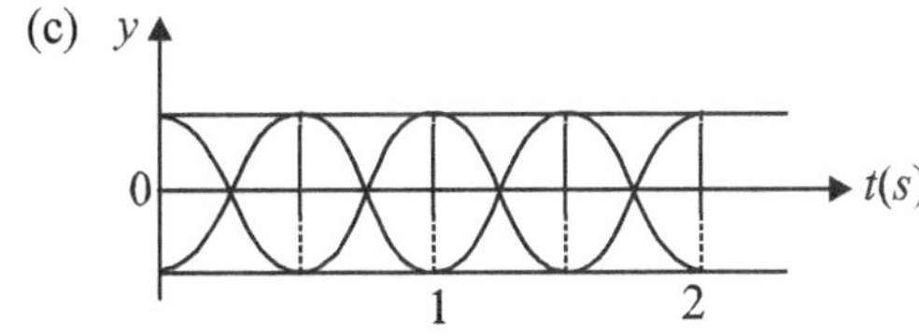

(d)   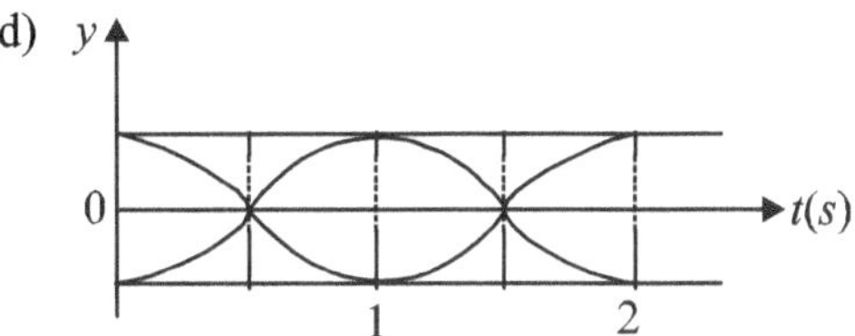

22. A sound absorber attenuates the sound level by 20 dB. The intensity decreases by a factor of

(a)   100   (b)   1000

(c)   10000   (d)   10

23. A granite rod of 60 cm length is clamped at its middle point and is set into longitudinal vibrations. The density of granite is 2.7×10^3 kg/m^3 and its Young's modulus is 9.27×10^{10} Pa. What will be the fundamental frequency of the longitudinal vibrations?

(a)   5 kHz   (b)   2.5 kHz

(c)   10 kHz   (d)   7.5 kHz

24. The end correction of a resonance column is 1 cm. If the shortest length resonating with the tuning fork is 10 cm, the next resonating length should be

(a)   32 cm   (b)   40 cm

(c)   28 cm   (d)   36 cm

25. A uniform string of length 20 m is suspended from a rigid support. A short wave pulse is introduced at its lowest end. It starts moving up the string. The time taken to reach the supports is : (take g = 10 ms^{-2})

(a) $2\sqrt{2}$ s   (b) $\sqrt{2}$ s

(c) $2\pi\sqrt{2}$ s   (d)   2 s

26. A pipe open at both ends has a fundamental frequency f in air. The pipe is dipped vertically in water so that half of it is in water. The fundamental frequency of the air column is now:

(a)   2f   (b)   f

(c) $\dfrac{f}{2}$ (d) $\dfrac{3f}{4}$

27. A pipe of length 85 cm is closed from one end. Find the number of possible natural oscillations of air column in the pipe whose frequencies lie below 1250 Hz. The velocity of sound in air is 340 m/s.

   (a) 12   (b) 8

   (c) 6   (d) 4

28. Three sound waves of equal amplitudes have frequencies $(v-1)$, v, $(v+1)$. They superpose to give beats. The number of beats produced per second will be :

   (a) 3   (b) 2

   (c) 1   (d) 4

29. A tuning fork of known frequency 256 Hz makes 5 beats per second with the vibrating string of a piano. The beat frequency decreases to 2 beats per second when the tension in the piano string is slightly increased. The frequency of the piano string before increasing the tension was

   (a) $(256+2)\,\text{Hz}$ (b) $(256-2)\,\text{Hz}$

   (c) $(256-5)\,\text{Hz}$ (d) $(256+5)\,\text{Hz}$

30. A bat moving at $10\ \text{ms}^{-1}$ towards a wall sends a sound signal of 8000 Hz towards it. On reflection it hears a sound of frequency f. The value of f in Hz is close to (speed of sound $= 320\ \text{ms}^{-1}$)

   (a) 8516   (b) 8258

   (c) 8424   (d) 8000

ANSWER KEY																			
1	(b)	**4**	(c)	**7**	(a)	**10**	(c)	**13**	(b)	**16**	(b)	**19**	(d)	**22**	(a)	**25**	(a)	**28**	(b)
2	(b)	**5**	(a)	**8**	(b)	**11**	(d)	**14**	(b)	**17**	(b)	**20**	(d)	**23**	(a)	**26**	(b)	**29**	(c)
3	(a)	**6**	(c)	**9**	(b)	**12**	(a)	**15**	(d)	**18**	(b)	**21**	(c)	**24**	(a)	**27**	(c)	**30**	(a)

ELECTRIC CHARGES AND FIELDS

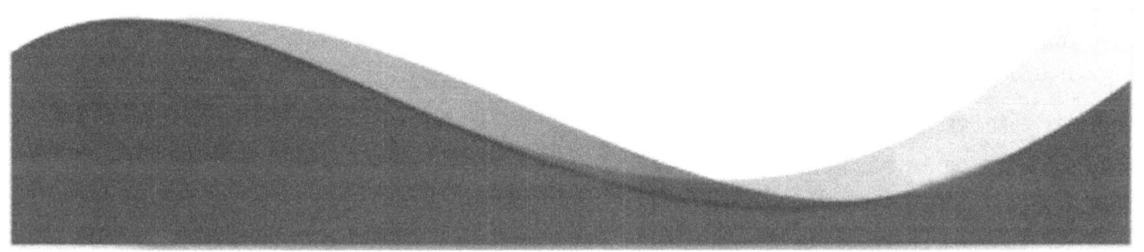

1. The charges on two spheres are $+7\mu C$ and $-5\mu C$ respectively. They experience a force F. If each of them is given and additional charge of $-2\mu C$, the new force of attraction will be

   (a) F
   (b) F / 2
   (c) $F/\sqrt{3}$
   (d) 2F

2. If E_a be the electric field strength of a short dipole at a point on its axial line and E_e that on the equatorial line at the same distance, then

   (a) $E_e = 2E_a$
   (b) $E_a = 2E_e$
   (c) $E_a = E_e$
   (d) $E_a = 3E_e$

3. There is an electric field E in x-direction. If the work done on moving a charge of 0.2 C through a distance of 2 m along a line making an angle 60° with x-axis is 4 J, then what is the value of E?

   (a) 3 N/C
   (b) 4 N/C
   (c) 5 N/C
   (d) 20 N/C

4. If the electric flux entering and leaving an enclosed surface respectively is ϕ_1 and ϕ_2, the electric charge inside the surface will be

   (a) $2(\phi_2 + \phi_1) \times \varepsilon_o$
   (b) $2(\phi_1 - \phi_2) \times \varepsilon_o$
   (c) $(\phi_1 + \phi_2) \times \varepsilon_o$
   (d) $(\phi_2 - \phi_1) \times \varepsilon_o$

5. Two point charges $-Q$ and $+2Q$ are placed at a distance R apart. Where should a third point charge q placed so that it is in equilibrium?

   (a) At a point on the right of $+2Q$
   (b) At a point on the left of charge $-Q$
   (c) Between $-Q$ and $+2Q$
   (d) At a point on a line perpendicular to the line joining $-Q$ and $+2Q$

6. Two point charges $+8q$ and $-2q$ are located at $x = 0$ and $x = L$ respectively. The location of a point on the x axis at which the net electric field due to these two point charges is zero is

   (a) $\dfrac{L}{4}$
   (b) $2L$
   (c) $4L$
   (d) $8L$

7. A conducting spherical shell having inner radius a and outer radius b carries a net charge Q. If a point charge q is placed at the centre of this shell, then the surface charge density on the outer surface of the shell is

   (a) $\dfrac{Q - q}{4\pi b^2}$
   (b) $\dfrac{Q}{4\pi b^2}$
   (c) $\dfrac{Q + q}{4\pi b^2}$
   (d) zero

8. An electric dipole consists of two opposite charges each of magnitude 1.0×10^{-6} coulomb separated by a distance of 2.0 cm. The dipole is placed in an external field of 1.0×10^5 N/C. The maximum torque on the dipole is

(a) 0.2×10^{-3}Nm   (b) 1.0×10^{-3}Nm

(c) 2.0×10^{-3}Nm   (d) 4×10^{-3}Nm

9. A spherical portion has been removed from a solid sphere having a charge distributed uniformly in its volume in the figure. The electric field inside the emptied space is

(a) Zero everywhere

(b) Non-zero and uniform

(c) Non-uniform

(d) Zero only at its centre

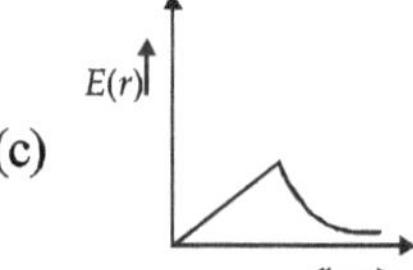

10. A negatively charged oil drop is prevented from falling under gravity by applying a vertical electric field 100 Vm^{-1}. If the mass of the drop is 1.6×10^{-3} g, the number of electrons carried by the drop is (g = 10 ms^{-2})

(a) 10^{18} (b) 10^{15}

(c) 10^6 (d) 10^{12}

11. Two identical charged spheres suspended from a common point by two massless strings of length l are initially a distance $d(d << l)$ apart because of their mutual repulsion. The charge begins to leak from both the spheres at a constant rate. As a result charges approach each other with a velocity v. Then as a function of distance x between them,

(a) $v \propto x^{-1}$ (b) $v \propto x^{½}$

(c) $v \propto x$ (d) $v \propto x^{-½}$

12. If a charge q is placed at the centre of the line joining two equal charges Q such that the system is in equilibrium then the value of q is

(a) $Q/2$ (b) $-Q/2$

(c) $Q/4$ (d) $-Q/4$

13. A charge Q is placed at a distance a/2 above the centre of the square surface of edge a as shown in the figure. The electric flux through the square surface is:

(a) $\dfrac{Q}{3\varepsilon_0}$

(b) $\dfrac{Q}{6\varepsilon_0}$

(c) $\dfrac{Q}{2\varepsilon_0}$

(d) $\dfrac{Q}{\varepsilon_0}$

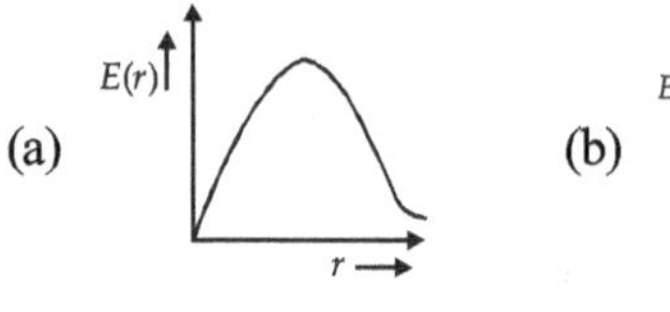

14. An electric field of 1000 V/m is applied to an electric dipole at angle of $45°$. The value of electric dipole moment is 10^{-29} C.m. What is the potential energy of the electric dipole?

(a) -20×10^{-18} J   (b) -7×10^{-27} J

(c) -10×10^{-29} J   (d) -9×10^{-20} J

15. In a uniformly charged sphere of total charge Q and radius R, the electric field E is plotted as function of distance from the centre, The graph which would correspond to the above will be:

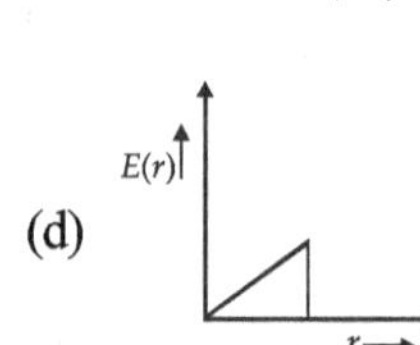

(a)   (b)   (c)   (d)

16. An electric dipole is formed by two equal and opposite charges q with separation d. The charges have same mass m. It is kept in a uniform electric field E. If it is slightly rotated from its equilibrium orientation, then its angular frequency ω is :

(a) $\sqrt{\dfrac{qE}{md}}$ (b) $\sqrt{\dfrac{2qE}{md}}$

(c) $2\sqrt{\dfrac{qE}{md}}$ (d) $\sqrt{\dfrac{qE}{2md}}$

17. Let $r(r) = \dfrac{Q}{p\,R^4} r$ be the charge density distribution for a solid sphere of radius R and total charge Q. For a point 'P' inside the sphere at distance r_1 from the centre of the sphere, the magnitude of electric field is :

(a) $\dfrac{Q}{4\pi \in_0 r_1^2}$

(b) $\dfrac{Q r_1^2}{4\pi \in_0 R^4}$

(c) $\dfrac{Q r_1^2}{3\pi \in_0 R^4}$

(d) 0

18. Two point charges q_1 ($\sqrt{10}$ μC) and q_2 (-25 μC) are placed on the x-axis at $x = 1$ m and $x = 4$ m respectively. The electric field (in V/m) at a point $y = 3$ m on y-axis is,

$$\left[\text{take } \frac{1}{4\pi \in_0} = 9 \times 10^9 \text{ Nm}^2\text{C}^{-2} \right]$$

(a) $(63\,\hat{i} - 27\,\hat{j}) \times 10^2$

(b) $(-63\,\hat{i} + 27\,\hat{j}) \times 10^2$

(c) $(81\,\hat{i} - 81\,\hat{j}) \times 10^2$

(d) $(-81\,\hat{i} + 81\,\hat{j}) \times 10^2$

19. A point charge causes an electric flux of -1.0×10^3 Nm^2/C to pass through a spherical Gaussian surface of 10.0 cm radius centred on the charge of the radius of the Gaussian surface were three times, how much flux would pass through the surface.

(a) 3.0×10^3 Nm^2/C

(b) -1.0×10^3 Nm^2/C

(c) -3.0×10^3 Nm^2/C

(d) -2.0×10^3 Nm^2/C

20. The inward and outward electric flux for a closed surface in units of N-m^2/C are respectively 8×10^3 and 4×10^3. Then the total charge inside the surface is [where ε_0 = permittivity constant]

(a) $4 \times 10^3\,C$

(b) $-4 \times 10^3\,C$

(c) $\dfrac{(-4 \times 10^3)}{\varepsilon}\,C$

(d) $-4 \times 10^3\,\varepsilon_0 C$

21. Two parallel large thin metal sheets have equal surface charge densities ($\sigma = 26.4 \times 10^{-12}$ C/m^2) of same signs. The electric field between these sheets is

(a) 1.5 N/C

(b) 1.5×10^{-10} N/C

(c) zero

(d) 3×10^{-10} N/C

22. Two parallel metal plates having charges $+Q$ and $-Q$ face each other at a certain distance between them. If the plates are now dipped in kerosine oil tank the electric field between the plates will.

(a) become zero

(b) increases

(c) decreases

(d) remain same

23. Two spheres A and B of radius 4 cm and 6 cm are given charges of 80 μC and 40 μC respectively. If they are connected by a fine wire, the amount of charge flowing from one to the other is

(a) 20 μC from A to B

(b) 16 μC from A to B

(c) 32 μC from B to A

(d) 32 μC from A to B

24. Three charges each of magnitude q are placed at the corners of an equitorial triangle, the electrostatic force on the charge placed at the centre is (each side of triangle is L):

(a) zero

(b) $\dfrac{1 q^2}{4\pi\varepsilon_0 L^2}$

(c) $\dfrac{1}{4\pi\varepsilon_0}\dfrac{3q^2}{L^2}$

(d) $\dfrac{1}{12\pi\varepsilon_0}\dfrac{q^2}{L^2}$

25. The electric field intensity just sufficient to balance the earth's gravitational attraction on an electron will be: (given mass and charge of an electron respectively are 9.1×10^{-31} kg and 1.6×10^{-19} C.)

(a) -5.6×10^{-11} N/C

(b) -4.8×10^{-15} N/C

(c) -1.6×10^{-19} N/C

(d) -3.2×10^{-19} N/C

26. Figure shows some of the electric field lines corresponding to an electric field. The figure suggests that

(a) $E_A > E_B > E_C$

(b) $E_A = E_B = E_C$

(c) $E_A = E_C > E_B$

(d) $E_A = E_C < E_B$

27. Two particle of equal mass m and charge q are placed at a distance of 16 cm. They do not experience any force. The value of $\dfrac{q}{m}$ is

(a) 1

(b) $\sqrt{\dfrac{\pi\varepsilon_0}{G}}$

(c) $\sqrt{\dfrac{G}{4\pi\varepsilon_0}}$

(d) $\sqrt{4\pi\varepsilon_0 G}$

28. If an electron has an initial velocity in a direction perpendicular to the electric field, the path of the electron is

(a) a straight line

(b) a circle

(c) an ellipse

(d) a parabola

29. An electric dipole of moment $\vec{p}$ is lying along a uniform electric field $\vec{E}$. The work done in rotating the dipole by 90° is

(a) $\dfrac{pE}{2}$

(b) $2pE$

(c) pE

(d) $\sqrt{2}\,pE$

30. Figure shows three electric field lines. If F_A, F_B and F_C are the forces on a test charge q at the positions A, B and C respectively, then

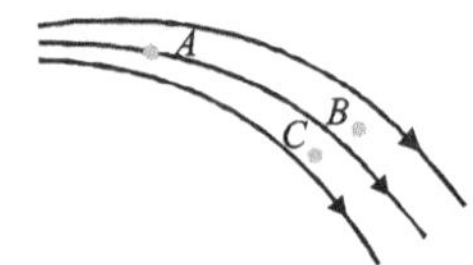

(a) $F_A > F_B > F_C$

(b) $F_A < F_B < F_C$

(c) $F_A > (F_B = F_C)$

(d) $F_A < (F_B = F_C)$

<table>
<tr><td colspan="16">ANSWER KEY</td></tr>
<tr><td>1</td><td>(a)</td><td>4</td><td>(d)</td><td>7</td><td>(c)</td><td>10</td><td>(d)</td><td>13</td><td>(b)</td><td>16</td><td>(b)</td><td>19</td><td>(b)</td><td>22</td><td>(c)</td><td>25</td><td>(a)</td><td>28</td><td>(d)</td></tr>
<tr><td>2</td><td>(b)</td><td>5</td><td>(b)</td><td>8</td><td>(c)</td><td>11</td><td>(d)</td><td>14</td><td>(b)</td><td>17</td><td>(b)</td><td>20</td><td>(d)</td><td>23</td><td>(d)</td><td>26</td><td>(c)</td><td>29</td><td>(c)</td></tr>
<tr><td>3</td><td>(d)</td><td>6</td><td>(b)</td><td>9</td><td>(b)</td><td>12</td><td>(d)</td><td>15</td><td>(a)</td><td>18</td><td>(a)</td><td>21</td><td>(c)</td><td>24</td><td>(a)</td><td>27</td><td>(d)</td><td>30</td><td>(c)</td></tr>
</table>

ELECTROSTATIC POTENTIAL AND CAPACITANCE **16**

1. A charge of total amount Q is distributed over two concentric hollow spheres of radii r and R $(R > r)$ such that the surface charge densities on the two spheres are equal. The electric potential at the common centre is

   (a) $\dfrac{1}{4\pi\varepsilon_0}\dfrac{(R-r)Q}{\left(R^2+r^2\right)}$

   (b) $\dfrac{1}{4\pi\varepsilon_0}\dfrac{(R+r)Q}{2\left(R^2+r^2\right)}$

   (c) $\dfrac{1}{4\pi\varepsilon_0}\dfrac{(R+r)Q}{\left(R^2+r^2\right)}$

   (d) $\dfrac{1}{4\pi\varepsilon_0}\dfrac{(R-r)Q}{2\left(R^2+r^2\right)}$

2. Two thin wire rings each having a radius R are placed at a distance d apart with their axes coinciding. The charges on the two rings are $+q$ and $-q$. The potential difference between the centres of the two rings is

   (a) $\dfrac{q}{2\pi\,\varepsilon_0}\left[\dfrac{1}{R}-\dfrac{1}{\sqrt{R^2+d^2}}\right]$

   (b) $\dfrac{qR}{4\pi\,\varepsilon_0\,d^2}$

   (c) $\dfrac{q}{8\pi\,\varepsilon_0}\left[\dfrac{1}{R}-\dfrac{1}{\sqrt{R^2+d^2}}\right]$

   (d) zero

3. Four charges $q_1 = 2 \times 10^{-8}$ C, $q_2 = -2 \times 10^{-8}$ C, $q_3 = -3 \times 10^{-8}$ C, and $q_4 = 6 \times 10^{-8}$ C are placed at four corners of a square of side $\sqrt{2}$ m. What is the potential at the centre of the square?

   (a) 270 V   (b) 300 V

   (c) Zero   (d) 100 V

4. Two concentric conducting spherical shells of radii a_1 and a_2 $(a_2 > a_1)$ are charged to potentials ϕ_1 and ϕ_2, respectively. Find the charge on the inner shell.

   (a) $q_1 = 4\pi\varepsilon_0\left(\dfrac{\phi_1-\phi_2}{a_2-a_1}\right)a_1a_2$

   (b) $q_1 = 4\pi\varepsilon_0\left(\dfrac{\phi_1+\phi_2}{a_2+a_1}\right)a_1a_2$

   (c) $q_1 = \pi\varepsilon_0\left(\dfrac{\phi_1-\phi_2}{a_2+a_1}\right)a_1a_2$

   (d) $q_1 = 2\pi\varepsilon_0\left(\dfrac{\phi_1+\phi_2}{a_2-a_1}\right)a_1a_2$

5. The electric potential V is given as a function of distance x (metre) by $V = (5x^2 + 10x - 9)$ volt. Value of electric field at $x = 1$ is

(a) $-20 V/m$

(b) $6 V/m$

(c) $11 V/m$

(d) $-23 V/m$

6. Four point charges q, q, q and $-3q$ are placed at the vertices of a regular tetrahedron of side L. The work done by electric force in taking all the charges to the centre of the tetrahedron is (where $k = \dfrac{1}{4\pi\varepsilon_0}$)

(a) $\dfrac{6kq^2}{5L}$

(b) $\dfrac{-6kq^2}{L}$

(c) $\dfrac{12kq^2}{L}$

(d) zero

7. Three point charges $+q$, $+2q$ and $-4q$ where q $= 0.1$ µC, are placed at the vertices of an equilateral triangle of side 10 cm as shown in figure. The potential energy of the system is

(a) 3×10^{-3} J

(b) -3×10^{-3} J

(c) 10×10^{-3} J

(d) -9×10^{-3} J

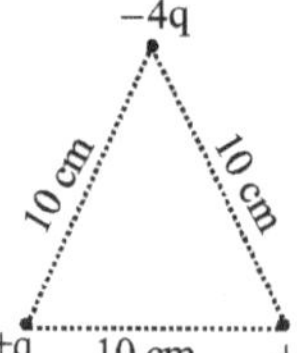

8. Two charges q_1 and q_2 are placed 30 cm apart, as shown in the figure. A third charge q_3 is moved along the arc of a circle of radius 40 cm from C to D. The change in the potential energy of the system is $\dfrac{q_3}{4\pi\,\epsilon_0}k$, where k is

(a) $9q_1$

(b) $6q_1$

(c) $8q_2$

(d) $6q_2$

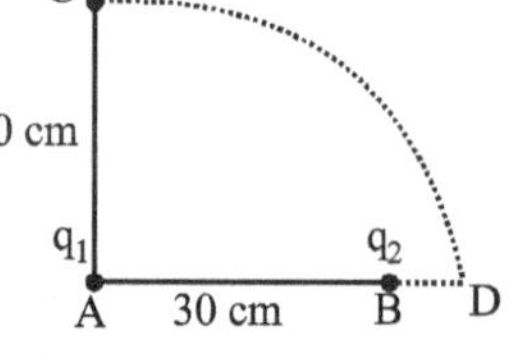

9. Identical charges $-q$ each are placed at 8 corners of a cube of each side b. Electrostatic potential energy of a charge $+q$ which is placed at the centre of cube will be

(a) $\dfrac{-4\sqrt{2}\,q^2}{\pi\,\varepsilon_0 b}$

(b) $\dfrac{-8\sqrt{2}\,q^2}{\pi\,\varepsilon_0 b}$

(c) $\dfrac{-4q^2}{\sqrt{3}\,\pi\varepsilon_0 b}$

(d) $\dfrac{8\sqrt{2}\,q^2}{\pi\varepsilon_0 b}$

10. A parallel plate condenser is filled with two dielectrics as shown. Area of each plate is A m^2 and the separation is t m. The dielectric constants are k_1 and k_2 respectively. Its capacitance in farad will be

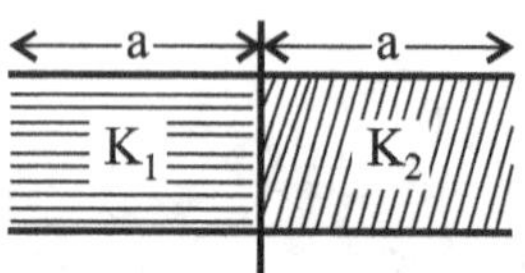

(a) $\dfrac{\varepsilon_0 A}{t}(k_1 + k_2)$

(b) $\dfrac{\varepsilon_0 A}{t}\cdot\dfrac{k_1 + k_2}{2}$

(c) $\dfrac{2\varepsilon_0 A}{t}(k_1 + k_2)$

(d) $\dfrac{\varepsilon_0 A}{t}\cdot\dfrac{k_1 - k_2}{2}$

11. A capacitor C_1 is charged to a potential difference V. The charging battery is then removed and the capacitor is connected in parallel to an uncharged capacitor C_2. The potential difference across the combination is

(a) $\dfrac{VC_1}{(C_1 + C_2)}$

(b) $V\left(1 + \dfrac{C_2}{C_1}\right)$

(c) $V\left(1 + \dfrac{C_1}{C_2}\right)$

(d) $\dfrac{VC_2}{(C_1 + C_2)}$

12. Figure shows charge (q) versus voltage (V) graph for series and parallel combination of two given capacitors. The capacitances are :

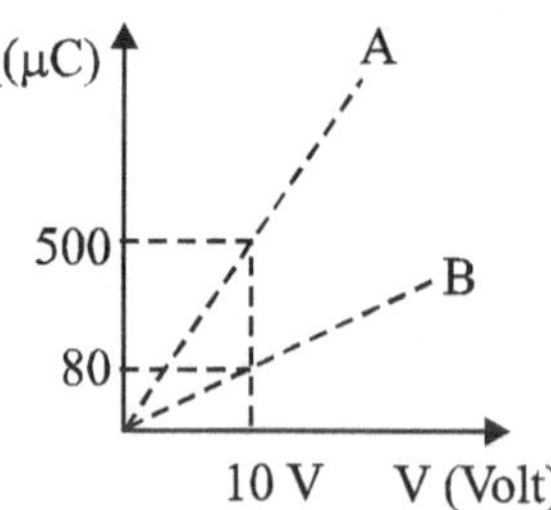

(a) 40 µF and 10 µF

(b) 60 µF and 40 µF

(c) 50 µF and 30 µF

(d) 20 µF and 30 µF

13. Effective capacitance of parallel combination of two capacitors C_1 and C_2 is 10 µF. When these capacitors are individually connected to a voltage source of 1 V, the energy stored in the capacitor C_2 is 4 times that of C_1. If these capacitors are connected in series, their effective capacitance will be:

(a) 4.2 µF　　　　　(b) 3.2 µF

(c) 1.6 µF　　　　　(d) 8.4 µF

14. In the figure shown, after the switch 'S' is turned from position 'A' to position 'B', the energy dissipated in the circuit in terms of capacitance 'C' and total charge 'Q' is:

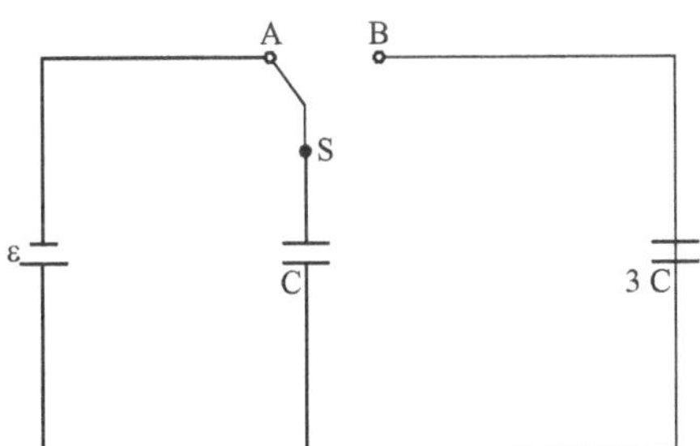

(a) $\dfrac{1}{8}\dfrac{Q^2}{C}$　　　　　(b) $\dfrac{3}{8}\dfrac{Q^2}{C}$

(c) $\dfrac{5}{8}\dfrac{Q^2}{C}$　　　　　(d) $\dfrac{3}{4}\dfrac{Q^2}{C}$

15. A parallel plate capacitor with plates of area 1 m² each, are at a separation of 0.1 m. If the electric field between the plates is 100 N/C, the magnitude of charge on each plate is :

(Take $\epsilon_0 = 8.85 \times 10^{-12}\ \dfrac{C^2}{N-m^2}$)

(a) $7.85 \times 10^{-10}\,C$　　　　　(b) $6.85 \times 10^{-10}\,C$

(c) $8.85 \times 10^{-10}\,C$　　　　　(d) $9.85 \times 10^{-10}\,C$

16. Two metal pieces having a potential difference of 800 V are 0.02 m apart horizontally. A particle of mass 1.96×10^{-15} kg is suspended in equilibrium between the plates. If e is the elementary charge, then charge on the particle is ne. Find n.

(a) 8　　　　　(b) 6

(c) 0.1　　　　　(d) 3

17. If a slab of insulating material 4×10^{-5} m thick is introduced between the plates of a parallel plate capacitor, the distance between the plates has to be increased by 3.5×10^{-5} m to restore the capacity to original value. Then the dielectric constant of the material of slab is

(a) 8　　　　　(b) 6

(c) 12　　　　　(d) 10

18. A capacitor of capacitance $C_1 = 1\mu F$ can withstand maximum voltage $V_1 = 6kV$ (*kilo-volt*) and another capacitor of capacitance $C_2 = 3\mu F$ can withstand maximum voltage $V_2 = 4k\bar{V}$. When the two capcitors are connected in series, the combined system can withstand a maximum voltage of

(a) 4kV　　　　　(b) 6kV

(c) 8kV　　　　　(d) 10kV

19. A capacitor of capacitance $C_1 = 1$ µF charged up to a voltage V = 110 V is then connected in parallel to the terminals connected in series and possessing capacitances $C_2 = 2$ µF and $C_3 = 3$ µF. Then, the amount of charge that will flow through the connecting wires is

(a) 40 µC　　　　　(b) 50 µC

(c) 60 µC　　　　　(d) 110 µC

20. Figure given below shows two identical parallel plate capacitors connected to a battery with switch S closed. The switch is now opened and the free space between the plate of capacitors is filled with a dielectric of dielectric constant 3. What will be the ratio of total electrostatic energy stored in both capacitors before and after the introduction of the dielectic

(a) 3 : 1

(b) 5 : 1

(c) 3 : 5

(d) 5 : 4

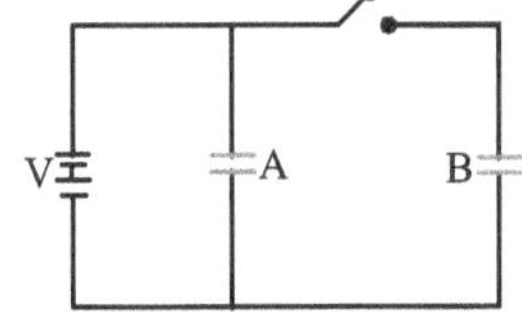

21. Figure shows a network of capacitors where the numbers indicates capacitances in micro Farad. The value of capacitance C if the equivalent capacitance between point A and B is to be 1 μF is :

(a) $\dfrac{32}{23}\,\mu F$

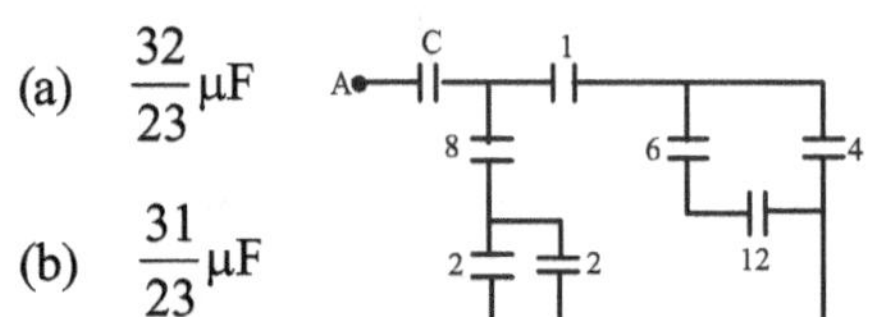

(b) $\dfrac{31}{23}\,\mu F$

(c) $\dfrac{33}{23}\,\mu F$

(d) $\dfrac{34}{23}\,\mu F$

22. A 5 μF capacitor is charged fully by a 220 V supply. It is then disconnected from the supply and is connected in series to another uncharged 2.5 μF capacitor. The energy change during the charge redistribution is

(a) $6 \times 10^{-2}\,J$ (b) $5 \times 10^{-2}\,J$

(c) $8 \times 10^{-2}\,J$ (d) $4 \times 10^{-2}\,J$

23. A capacitance of 2μF is required in an electrical circuit across a potential difference of 1.0 kV. A large number of 1μF capacitors are available which can withstand a potential difference of not more than 300 V. The minimum number of capacitors required to achieve this is

(a) 24   (b) 32

(c) 2   (d) 16

24. A parallel plate capacitor with area $200\,cm^2$ and separation between the plates 1.5cm, is connected across a battery of emf V. If the force of attraction between the plates is $25 \times 10^{-6}N$, the value of V is approximately:

$$\left(\varepsilon_0 = 8.85 \times 10^{-12}\,\dfrac{C^2}{N.m^2} \right)$$

(a) 150V   (b) 100V

(c) 250V   (d) 300V

25. A 60 pF capacitor is fully charged by a 20 V supply. It is then disconnected from the supply and is connected to another uncharged 60 pF capacitor in parallel. The electrostatic energy that is lost in this process by the time the charge is redistributed between them is

(a) 6 nJ   (b) 4 nJ

(c) 8 nJ   (d) 2 nJ

ANSWER KEY																								
1	(c)	4	(a)	7	(d)	10	(b)	13	(c)	16	(d)	19	(c)	22	(d)	25	(a)
2	(a)	5	(a)	8	(c)	11	(a)	14	(b)	17	(a)	20	(c)	23	(c)		
3	(a)	6	(b)	9	(c)	12	(a)	15	(c)	18	(c)	21	(a)	24	(c)		

CURRENT ELECTRICITY

1. The resistance of a wire at room temperature 30°C is found to be 10 Ω. Now to increase the resistance by 10%, the temperature of the wire must be [The temperature coefficient of resistance of the material of the wire is 0.002 per °C]

  (a) 36°C   (b) 83°C

  (c) 63°C   (d) 33°C

2. The plot represent the flow of current through a wire at three different time intervals. The ratio of charges flowing through the wire corresponding to these time intervals is (Fig.)

  (a) 2 : 1 : 2

  (b) 1 : 3 : 3

  (c) 1 : 1 : 1

  (d) 2 : 3 : 4

3. A current of 2A flows through a 2Ω resistor when connected across a battery. The same battery supplies a current of 0.5 A when connected across a 9Ω resistor. The internal resistance of the battery is

  (a) 0.5 Ω   (b) 1/3 Ω

  (c) 1/4 Ω   (d) 1 Ω

4. The n rows each containing m cells in series are joined in parallel. Maximum current is taken from this combination across an exernal resistance of 3Ω resistance. If the total number of cells are 24 and internal resistance of each cells is 0.5Ω, then

  (a) m = 8, n = 3   (b) m = 6, n = 4

  (c) m = 12, n = 2   (d) m = 2, n = 12

5. Five cells each of emf E and internal resistance r send the same amount of current through an external resistance R whether the cells are connected in parallel or in series. Then the ratio $\left(\dfrac{R}{r}\right)$ is

  (a) 2   (b) 1/2

  (c) 1/5   (d) 1

6. A wire when connected to 220 V mains supply has power dissipation P_1. Now the wire is cut into two equal pieces which are connected in parallel to the same supply. Power dissipation in this case is P_2. Then $P_2 : P_1$ is

  (a) 1   (b) 4

  (c) 2   (d) 3

7. In the electric network shown, when no current flows through the 4Ω resistor in the arm EB, the potential difference between the points A and D will be :

  (a) 6 V

  (b) 3 V

  (c) 5 V

  (d) 4 V

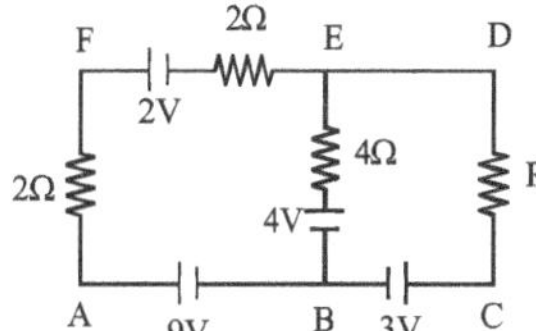

8. In a meter bridge experiment null point is obtained at 20 cm. from one end of the wire when resistance X is balanced against another resistance Y. If $X < Y$, then where will be the new position of the null point from the same end, if one decides to balance a resistance of $4X$ against Y

(a) 40 cm   (b) 80 cm

(c) 50 cm   (d) 70 cm

9. The figure shows a meter-bridge circuit, $X = 12\,\Omega$ and $R = 18\,\Omega$. The jockey J is at the null point. If R is made $8\,\Omega$, through the jockey J have to be moved by $4 \times A$ cm to obtain null point again then find the value of A.

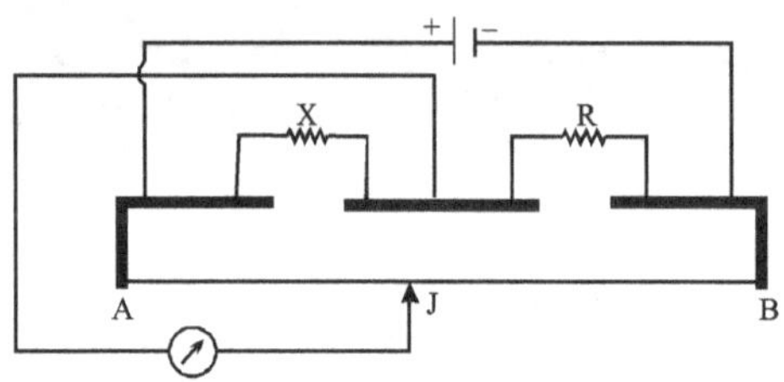

(a) 2   (b) 5

(c) 8   (d) 6

10. When a wire of uniform cross–section a, length l and resistance R is bent into a complete circle, equivalent resistance between any two of diametrically opposite points will be

(a) $\dfrac{R}{4}$ (b) 4R

(c) $\dfrac{R}{8}$ (d) $\dfrac{R}{2}$

11. A student measures the terminal potential difference (V) of a cell (of emf E and internal resistance r) as a function of the current (I) flowing through it. The slope and intercept, of the graph between V and I, respectively, are

(a) $-r$ and E   (b) r and $-E$

(c) $-E$ and r   (d) E and $-r$

12. A heater boils a certain quantity of water in time t_1 Another heater boils the same quantity of water in time t_2. If both heaters are connected in parallel, the combination will boil the same quantity of water in time

(a) $\dfrac{1}{2}(t_1 + t_2)$ (b) $(t_1 + t_2)$

(c) $\dfrac{t_1 t_2}{t_1 + t_2}$ (d) $\sqrt{t_1 t_2}$

13. A battery of emf E produces currents I_1 and I_2 when connected to external resistances R_1 and R_2 respectively. The internal resistance of the battery is

(a) $\dfrac{I_1 R_2 - I_2 R_1}{I_2 - I_1}$ (b) $\dfrac{I_1 R_2 + I_2 R_1}{I_1 - I_2}$

(c) $\dfrac{I_1 R_1 + I_2 R_2}{I_1 - I_2}$ (d) $\dfrac{I_1 R_1 - I_2 R_2}{I_2 - I_1}$

14. Suppose the drift velocity v_d in a material varied with the applied electric field E as $v_d \propto \sqrt{E}$. Then V – I graph for a wire made of such a material is best given by :

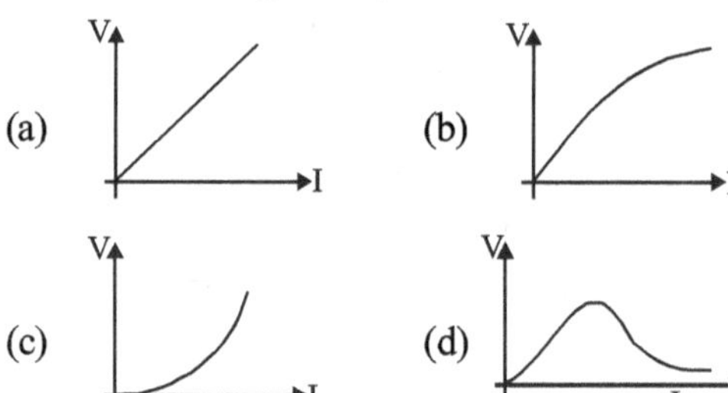

15. The potential difference across the terminals of a battery is 50 V when 11A current is drawn and 60 V when 1A current is drawn. The e.m.f. and the internal resistance of the battery are

(a) $62V, 2\Omega$ (b) $63V, 1\Omega$

(c) $61V, 1\Omega$ (d) $64V, 2\Omega$

16. In a large building, there are 15 bulbs of 40 W, 5 bulbs of 100 W, 5 fans of 80 W and 1 heater of 1 kW. The voltage of electric mains is 220 V. The minimum capacity of the main fuse of the building will be:

(a) 8 A   (b) 10 A

(c) 12 A   (d) 14 A

17. Two sources of equal emf are connected to an external resistance R. The internal resistance of the two sources are R_1 and R_2 $(R_1 > R_1)$. If the potential difference across the source having internal resistance R_2 is zero, then

(a) $R = R_2 - R_1$

(b) $R = R_2 \times (R_1 + R_2)/(R_2 - R_1)$

(c) $R = R_1 R_2 /(R_2 - R_1)$

(d) $R = R_1 R_2 /(R_1 - R_2)$

18. A current of 5 A passes through a copper conductor (resistivity) $= 1.7 \times 10^{-8} \Omega m$) of radius of cross-section 5 mm. Find the mobility of the charges if their drift velocity is 1.1×10^{-3} m/s.

(a) $1.8 \, m^2/Vs$ (b) $1.5 \, m^2/Vs$

(c) $1.3 \, m^2/Vs$ (d) $1.0 \, m^2/Vs$

19. An electric current passes through a circuit containing two wires of the same material connected in parallel. If the lengths of the wires are in the ratio of 4/3 and radius of the wires are in the ratio of 2/3, then the ratio of the currents passing through the wires will be

(a) 3   (b) 1/3

(c) 3/9   (d) 4/9

20. Two identical cells connected in series send 1.0A current through a 5 Ω resistor. When they are connected in parallel, they send 0.8 A current through the same resistor. What is the internal resistance of the cell?

(a) $0.5 \, \Omega$ (b) $1.0 \, \Omega$

(c) $1.5 \, \Omega$ (d) $2.5 \, \Omega$

21. A battery is charged at a potential of 15V for 8 hours when the current flowing is 10A. The battery on discharge supplies a current of 5A for 15 hours. The mean terminal voltage during discharge is 14V. The "watt-hour" efficiency of the battery is

(a) 87.5%   (b) 82.5%

(c) 80%   (d) 90%

22. In an experiment to measure the internal reistance of a cell by a potential, it is found that the balance point is at a length of 2 m when the cell is shunted by a 5 Ω resistance and is at a length of 3 m when the cell is shunted by a 10 Ω resistance, the internal resistance of the cell is then

(a) $1.5 \, \Omega$ (b) $10 \, \Omega$

(c) $15 \, \Omega$ (d) $1 \, \Omega$

23. When 5V potential difference is applied across a wire of length 0.1 m, the drift speed of electrons is $2.5 \times 10^{-4} \, ms^{-1}$. If the electron density in the wire is $8 \times 10^{28} \, m^{-3}$, the resistivity of the material is close to :

(a) $1.6 \times 10^{-6} \, \Omega m$ (b) $1.6 \times 10^{-5} \, \Omega m$

(c) $1.6 \times 10^{-8} \, \Omega m$ (d) $1.6 \times 10^{-7} \, \Omega m$

24. Four resistances of 15 Ω, 12 Ω, 4 Ω and 10 Ω respectively in cyclic order to form Wheatstone's network. The resistance that is to be connected in parallel with the resistance of 10 Ω to balance the network is

(a) $10 \, \Omega$ (b) $15 \, \Omega$

(c) $20 \, \Omega$ (d) $25 \, \Omega$

25. A potentiometer wire PQ of 1 m length is connected to a standard cell E_1. Another cell E_2 of emf 1.02 V is connected with a resistance 'r' and switch S (as shown in figure). With switch S open, the null position is obtained at a distance of 49 cm from Q. The potential gradient in the potentiometer wire is :

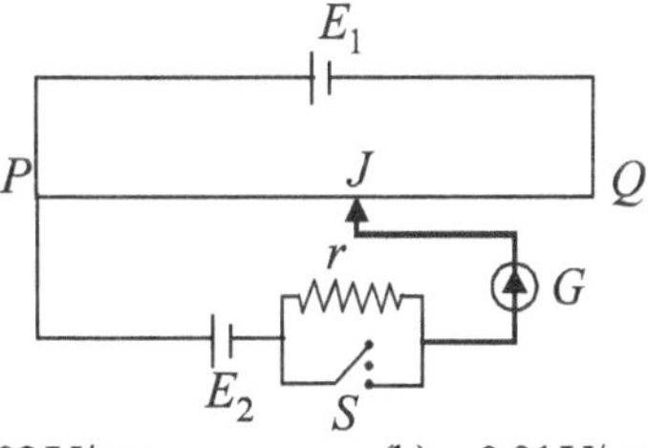

(a) 0.02 V/cm   (b) 0.01 V/cm

(c) 0.03 V/cm   (d) 0.04 V/cm

ANSWER KEY																								
1	(b)	**4**	(c)	**7**	(c)	**10**	(a)	**13**	(d)	**16**	(c)	**19**	(b)	**22**	(b)	**25**	(a)
2	(c)	**5**	(d)	**8**	(c)	**11**	(a)	**14**	(c)	**17**	(a)	**20**	(d)	**23**	(b)		
3	(b)	**6**	(b)	**9**	(b)	**12**	(c)	**15**	(c)	**18**	(d)	**21**	(a)	**24**	(a)		

MOVING CHARGES AND MAGNETISM

18

1. A proton (mass = 1.67×10^{-27} kg and charge $= 1.6 \times 10^{-19}$ C) enters perpendicular to a magnetic field of intensity 2 weber/m^2 with a velocity 3.4×10^7 m/sec. The acceleration of the proton should be
   (a) 6.5×10^{15} m/sec^2
   (b) 6.5×10^{13} m/sec^2
   (c) 6.5×10^{11} m/sec^2
   (d) 6.5×10^9 m/sec^2

2. A uniform magnetic field acts at right angles to the direction of motion of electron. As a result, the electron moves in a circular path of radius 2cm. If the speed of electron is doubled, then the radius of the circular path will be
   (a) 2.0 cm
   (b) 0.5 cm
   (c) 4.0 cm
   (d) 1.0 cm

3. A charged particle of mass m and charge q travels on a circular path of radius r that is perpendicular to a magnetic field B. The time taken by the particle to complete one revolution is
   (a) $\dfrac{2\pi q^2 B}{m}$
   (b) $\dfrac{2\pi mq}{B}$
   (c) $\dfrac{2\pi m}{qB}$
   (d) $\dfrac{2\pi qB}{m}$

4. The magnetic induction at a point P which is at a distance of 4 cm from a long current carrying wire is 10^{-3} T. The field of induction at a distance 12 cm from the current will be

   (a) 3.33×10^{-4} T
   (b) 1.11×10^{-4} T
   (c) 3×10^{-3} T
   (d) 9×10^{-3} T

5. A current i ampere flows in a circular arc of wire whose radius is R, which subtends an angle $3\pi/2$ radian at its centre. The magnetic induction B at the centre is

   (a) $\dfrac{\mu_0 i}{R}$

   (b) $\dfrac{\mu_0 i}{2R}$

   (c) $\dfrac{2\mu_0 i}{R}$

   (d) $\dfrac{3\mu_0 i}{8R}$

6. A straight section PQ of a circuit lies along the X-axis from $x = -\dfrac{a}{2}$ to $x = \dfrac{a}{2}$ and carries a steady current i. The magnetic field due to the section PQ at a point $X = + a$ will be
   (a) proportional to a
   (b) proportional to a^2
   (c) proportional to $1/a$
   (d) zero

7. A long solenoid carrying a current produces a magnetic field B along its axis. If the current is double and the number of turns per cm is halved, the new value of the magnetic field is
   (a) $4B$
   (b) $B/2$
   (c) B
   (d) $2B$

8. A straight wire of length 0.5 metre and carrying a current of 1.2 ampere is placed in uniform magnetic field of induction 2 tesla. The magnetic field is perpendicular to the length of the wire. The force on the wire is
   (a) 2.4 N
   (b) 1.2 N
   (c) 3.0 N
   (d) 2.0 N

9. Two long parallel wires are at a distance of 1 metre. Both of them carry 5 ampere of current. The force of attraction per unit length between the two wires is
   (a) 50×10^{-7} N/m
   (b) 2×10^{-8} N/m
   (c) 5×10^{-8} N/m
   (d) 10^{-7} N/m

10. A moving coil galvanometer has resistance of $10\,\Omega$ and full scale deflection of 0.01 A. It can be converted into voltmeter of 10 V full scale by connecting into resistance of
    (a) $9.90\,\Omega$ in series
    (b) $10\,\Omega$ in series
    (c) $990\,\Omega$ in series
    (d) $0.10\,\Omega$

11. The distance between the wires of electric mains is 12 cm. These wires experience 4 mg wt. per unit length. The value of current flowing in each wire will be
    [assume equal current flows in both wires]
    (a) 4.85 A
    (b) 0
    (c) 4.85×10^{-2} A
    (d) 4.85×10^{-4} A

12. An electron moves in a circular arc of radius 10 m at a constant speed of 2×10^7 ms^{-1} with its plane of motion normal to a magnetic flux density of 10^{-5} T. What will be the value of specific charge of the electron?
    (a) 2×10^4 C kg^{-1}
    (b) 2×10^5 C kg^{-1}
    (c) 5×10^6 C kg^{-1}
    (d) 2×10^{11} C kg^{-1}

13. A beam of proton with velocity 4×10^5 ms^{-1} enters a uniform magnetic field of 0.3T. The velocity makes an angle $60°$ with magnetic field. The pitch of the helix path will be
    (a) 4.4 cm
    (b) 5.8 cm
    (c) 6.1 cm
    (d) 7.2 cm

14. A deuteron of kinetic energy 50 keV is describing a circular orbit of radius 0.5 metre in a plane perpendicular to the magnetic field B. The kinetic energy of the proton that describes a circular orbit of radius 0.5 metre in the same plane with the same B is
    (a) 25 keV
    (b) 50 keV
    (c) 200 keV
    (d) 100 kcV

15. A particle of charge 16×10^{-16} C moving with velocity 10 ms^{-1} along x-axis enters a region where magnetic field of induction $\vec{B}$ is along the y-axis and an electric field of magnitude 10^4 Vm^{-1} is along the negative z-axis. If the charged particle continues moving along x-axis, the magnitude of $\vec{B}$ is :
    (a) 16×10^3 Wb m^{-2}
    (b) 2×10^3 Wb m^{-2}
    (c) 1×10^3 Wb m^{-2}
    (d) 4×10^3 Wb m^{-2}

16. A cyclotron's oscillator frequency is 10 MHz. If the radius of its **'dees'** is 60 cm, what is the kinetic energy of the proton beam produced by the accelerator ?
    Given $e = 1.60 \times 10^{-19}$ C, $m = 1.67 \times 10^{-27}$ kg.
    $1\,MeV = 1.6 \times 10^{-13}$ J)
    (a) 3.421 MeV
    (b) 4.421 MeV
    (c) 5.421 MeV
    (d) 7.421 MeV

17. Two wires with currents 2 A and 1 A are enclosed in a circular loop. Another wire with current 3 A is situated outside the loop as shown. The $\oint \vec{B}.\vec{dl}$ around the loop is
    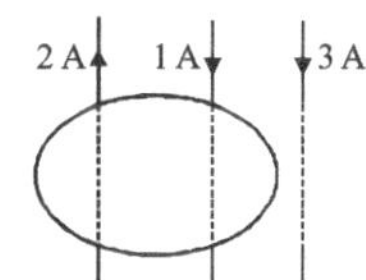

    (a) μ_0
    (b) $3\mu_0$
    (c) $6\mu_0$
    (d) $2\mu_0$

18. The magnetic field due to a current carrying circular loop of radius 3 cm at a point on the axis at a distance of 4 cm from the centre is 54 μT. What will be its value at the centre of loop?
    (a) 125 μT
    (b) 150 μT
    (c) 250 μT
    (d) 75 μT

19. A current I flows in an infinitely long wire with cross section in the form of a semi-circular ring of radius R. The magnitude of the magnetic induction along its axis is:

(a) $\dfrac{\mu_0 I}{2\pi^2 R}$

(b) $\dfrac{\mu_0 I}{2\pi R}$

(c) $\dfrac{\mu_0 I}{4\pi R}$

(d) $\dfrac{\mu_0 I}{\pi^2 R}$

20. A wire in the form of a square of side 'a' carries a current i. Then the magnetic induction at the centre of the square wire is (Magnetic permeability of free space $= \mu_0$)

(a) $\dfrac{\mu_0 i}{2\pi a}$

(b) $\dfrac{\mu_0 i \sqrt{2}}{\pi a}$

(c) $\dfrac{2\sqrt{2}\mu_0 i}{\pi a}$

(d) $\dfrac{\mu_0 i}{\sqrt{2}\pi a}$

21. A galvanometer having a coil resistance of 100 Ω gives a full scale deflection, when a currect of 1 mA is passed through it. The value of the resistance, which can convert this galvanometer into ammeter giving a full scale deflection for a current of 10 A, is :

(a) 0.1Ω

(b) 3Ω

(c) 0.01Ω

(d) 2Ω

22. A square loop of side 2m carries a current of 5 A is suspended freely in a uniform magnetic field of strength 0.8T. Net force acting on the loop is

(a) 2×10^{-5} N

(b) 4.8×10^{-5} N

(c) Zero

(d) 2.6×10^{-7} N

23. Proton, deuteron and alpha particle of same kinetic energy are moving in circular trajectories in a constant magnetic field. The radii of proton, deuteron and alpha particle are respectively r_p, r_d and r_α. Which one of the following relation is correct?

(a) $r_\alpha = r_p = r_d$

(b) $r_\alpha = r_p < r_d$

(c) $r_\alpha > r_d > r_p$

(d) $r_\alpha = r_d > r_p$

24. If an electron and a proton having same momenta enter perpendicular to a magnetic field, then

(a) curved path of electron and proton will be same (ignoring the sense of revolution)

(b) they will move undeflected

(c) curved path of electron is more curved than that of the proton

(d) path of proton is more curved.

25. Two concentric coils each of radius equal to 2π cm are placed at right angles to each other. 3 ampere and 4 ampere are the currents flowing in each coil respectively. The magnetic induction in Weber/m^2 at the centre of the coils will be

$(\mu_0 = 4\pi \times 10^{-7} \text{ Wb / A.m})$

(a) 10^{-5}

(b) 12×10^{-5}

(c) 7×10^{-5}

(d) 5×10^{-5}

26. A rigid square of loop of side 'a' and carrying current I_2 is lying on a horizontal surface near a long current I_1 carrying wire in the same plane as shown in figure. The net force on the loop due to the wire will be:

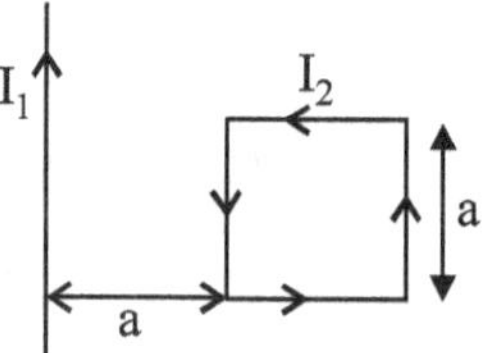

(a) Repulsive and equal to $\dfrac{\mu_0 I_1 I_2}{2\pi}$

(b) Attractive and equal to $\dfrac{\mu_0 I_1 I_2}{3\pi}$

(c) Repulsive and equal to $\dfrac{\mu_0 I_1 I_2}{4\pi}$

(d) Zero

27. Two long conductors, separated by a distance d carry current I_1 and I_2 in the same direction. They exert a force F on each other. Now the current in one of them is increased to two times and its direction is reversed. The distance is also increased to $3d$. The new value of the force between them is

(a) $-\dfrac{2F}{3}$

(b) $\dfrac{F}{3}$

(c) $-2F$

(d) $-\dfrac{F}{3}$

28. A current of 1A is flowing on the sides of an equilateral triangle of side 4.5×10^{-2} m . The magnetic field at the centre of the triangle will be:

(a) 4×10^{-5} Wb/m^2 (b) Zero

(c) 2×10^{-5} Wb/m^2 (d) 8×10^{-5} Wb/m^2

29. If in a circular coil A of radius R, current I is flowing and in another coil B of radius $2R$ a current $2I$ is flowing, then the ratio of the magnetic fields B_A and B_B, produced by them will be

(a) 1 (b) 2

(c) 1/2 (d) 4

30. A moving coil galvanometer has a coil with 175 turns and area 1 cm^2. It uses a torsion band of torsion constant 10^{-6} N-m/rad. The coil is placed in a magnetic field B parallel to its plane. The coil deflects by 1° for a current of 1mA. The value of B (in Tesla) is approximately:

(a) 10^{-4} (b) 10^{-2}

(c) 10^{-1} (c) 10^{-3}

<table>
<tr><td colspan="18" align="center">ANSWER KEY</td></tr>
<tr><td>1</td><td>(a)</td><td>4</td><td>(a)</td><td>7</td><td>(c)</td><td>10</td><td>(c)</td><td>13</td><td>(a)</td><td>16</td><td>(d)</td><td>19</td><td>(d)</td><td>22</td><td>(c)</td><td>25</td><td>(d)</td><td>28</td><td>(a)</td></tr>
<tr><td>2</td><td>(c)</td><td>5</td><td>(d)</td><td>8</td><td>(b)</td><td>11</td><td>(a)</td><td>14</td><td>(d)</td><td>17</td><td>(a)</td><td>20</td><td>(c)</td><td>23</td><td>(b)</td><td>26</td><td>(c)</td><td>29</td><td>(a)</td></tr>
<tr><td>3</td><td>(c)</td><td>6</td><td>(d)</td><td>9</td><td>(a)</td><td>12</td><td>(d)</td><td>15</td><td>(c)</td><td>18</td><td>(c)</td><td>21</td><td>(c)</td><td>24</td><td>(a)</td><td>27</td><td>(a)</td><td>30</td><td>(d)</td></tr>
</table>

MAGNETISM AND MATTER 19

1. If a magnet is suspended at angle 30° to the magnetic meridian, the dip needle makes an angle of 45° with the horizontal. The real dip is

   (a) $\tan^{-1}(\sqrt{3/2})$
   (b) $\tan^{-1}(\sqrt{3})$
   (c) $\tan^{-1}(\sqrt{3}/2)$
   (d) $\tan^{-1}(2/\sqrt{3})$

2. The net magnetic moment of two identical magnets each of magnetic moment M_0, inclined at 60° with each other is

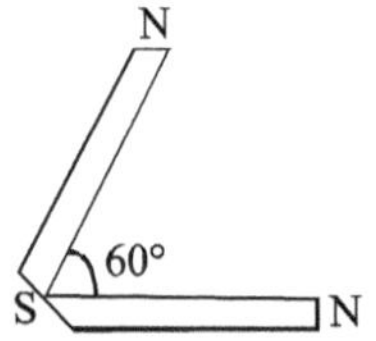

   (a) M_0
   (b) $\sqrt{2}\ M_0$
   (c) $\sqrt{3}\ M_0$
   (d) $2M_0$

3. A torque of 10^{-5} Nm is required to hold a magnet at 90° with the horizontal component H of the earth's magnetic field. The torque to hold it at 30° will be

   (a) 5×10^{-6} Nm
   (b) data is insufficient
   (c) $\dfrac{1}{3} \times 10^{-5}$ Nm
   (d) $5\sqrt{3} \times 10^{-6}$ Nm

4. For substances hysteresis (B - H) curves are given as shown in figure. For making temporary magnet which of the following is the best

   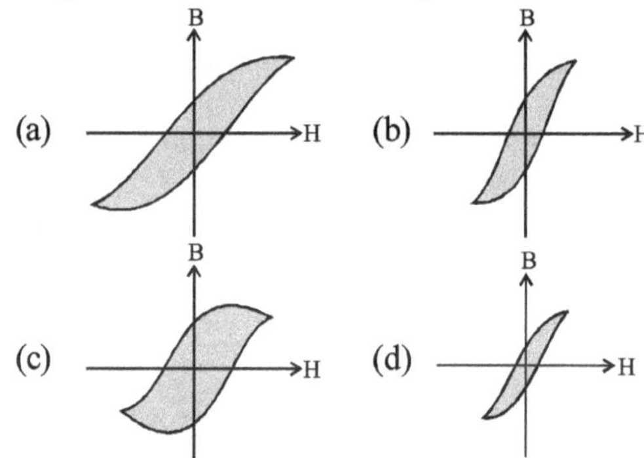

5. The magnetic needle has magnetic moment 8.7×10^{-2} Am^2 and moment of inertia 11.5×10^{-6} kgm^2. It performs 10 complete oscillations in 6.70 s, what is the magnitude of the magnetic field?

   (a) 0.012 T
   (b) 0.120 T
   (c) 1.200 T
   (d) 2.10 T

6. The force between two short bar magnets with magnetic moments M_1 and M_2 whose centres are r metres apart is 8 N when their axes are in same line. If the separation is increased to 2 r, the force between them is reduced to [length of magnet $<<$r]

   (a) 4 N
   (b) 2 N
   (c) 1 N
   (d) 0.5 N

7. The magnetic moment of a magnet is $0.1 \, \text{amp} \times \text{m}^2$. It is suspended in a magnetic field of intensity 3×10^{-4} weber/m^2. The torque acting upon it when deflected by $30°$ from the magnetic field is

   (a) $1 \times 10^{-5} \, \text{N m}$
   (b) $1.5 \times 10^{-5} \, \text{N m}$
   (c) $2 \times 10^{-5} \, \text{N m}$
   (d) $2.5 \times 10^{-5} \, \text{N m}$

8. A bar magnet of length 10 cm and having the pole strength equal to 10^{-3} weber is kept in a magnetic field having magnetic induction (B) equal to $4\pi \times 10^{-3}$ tesla. It makes an angle of $30°$ with the direction of magnetic induction. The value of the torque acting on the magnet is

   (a) $2\pi \times 10^{-7} \, \text{N} \times \text{m}$
   (b) $2\pi \times 10^{-5} \, \text{N} \times \text{m}$
   (c) $0.5 \, \text{N} \times \text{m}$
   (d) $0.5 \times 10^{2} \, \text{N} \times \text{m}$

   $(\mu = 4\pi \times 10^{-7} \, \text{weber}/\text{amp} \times \text{m})$

9. A magnetic dipole is under the influence of two magnetic fields. The angle between the field directions is $60°$ and one of the fields has a magnitude of 1.2×10^{-2} T. If the dipole comes to stable equilibrium at an angle of $15°$ with this field, what is the magnitude of other field ?

   (a) 4.4×10^{-3} tesla
   (b) 5.2×10^{-4} tesla
   (c) 3.4×10^{-5} tesla
   (d) 7.8×10^{-6} tesla

10. Two short bar magnets of magnetic moments $1000 \, \text{Am}^2$ are placed as shown at the corners of a square of side 10 cm. The net magnetic induction at P is

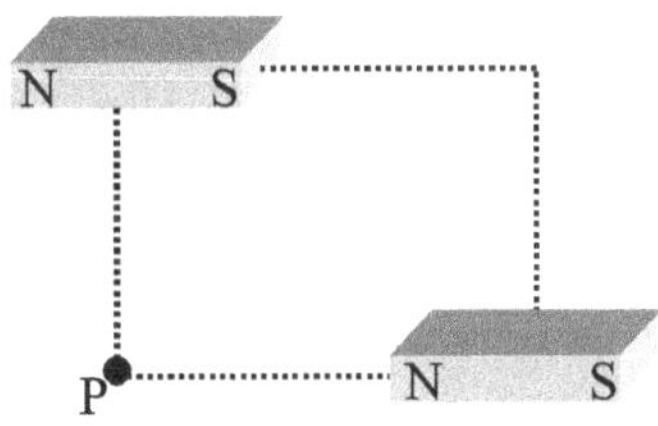

   (a) $0.1 \, T$
   (b) $0.2 \, T$
   (c) $0.3 \, T$
   (d) $0.4 \, T$

11. A coil in the shape of an equilateral triangle of side l is suspended between the pole pieces of a permanent magnet such that $\vec{B}$ is in the plane of the coil. If due to a current i in the triangle a torque τ acts on it, the side l of the triangle is

   (a) $\dfrac{2}{\sqrt{3}}\left(\dfrac{\tau}{\text{B.i}}\right)^{\frac{1}{2}}$
   (b) $2\left(\dfrac{\tau}{\sqrt{3}\text{B.i}}\right)^{\frac{1}{2}}$
   (c) $\dfrac{2}{\sqrt{3}}\left(\dfrac{\tau}{\text{B.i}}\right)$
   (d) $\dfrac{1}{\sqrt{3}}\dfrac{\tau}{\text{B.i}}$

12. Two identical short bar magnets, each having magnetic moment of $10 \, \text{Am}^2$, are arranged such that their axial lines are perpendicular to each other and their centres be along the same straight line in a horizontal plane. If the distance between their centres is 0.2 m, the resultant magnetic induction at a point midway between them is $(\mu_0 = 4\pi \times 10^{-7} \, \text{Hm}^{-1})$

   (a) $\sqrt{2} \times 10^{-7}$ tesla
   (b) $\sqrt{5} \times 10^{-7}$ tesla
   (c) $\sqrt{2} \times 10^{-3}$ tesla
   (d) $\sqrt{5} \times 10^{-3}$ tesla

13. A dip needle lies initially in the magnetic meridian when it shows an angle of dip θ at a place. The dip circle is rotated through an angle x in the horizontal plane and then it shows an angle of dip θ'. Then $\dfrac{\tan \theta'}{\tan \theta}$ is

   (a) $\dfrac{1}{\cos x}$
   (b) $\dfrac{1}{\sin x}$
   (c) $\dfrac{1}{\tan x}$
   (d) $\cos x$

14. Needles N_1, N_2 and N_3 are made of a ferromagnetic, a paramagnetic and a diamagnetic substance respectively. A magnet when brought close to them will

   (a) attract N_1, N_2 and N_3
   (b) attract N_1 strongly, N_2 weakly and repel N_3 weakly
   (c) attract N_1 strongly, but repel N_2 and N_3 weakly
   (d) none of these

15. A domain in a ferromagnetic substance is in the form of a cube of side length 1 μm. If it contains 8×10^{10} atoms and each atomic dipole has a dipole moment of 9×10^{-24} A m^2, then the magnetization of the domain is

(a) 7.2×10^5 A m^{-1}
(b) 7.2×10^3 A m^{-1}
(c) 7.2×10^9 A m^{-1}
(d) 7.2×10^{12} Am^{-1}

16. Three identical bars A, B and C are made of different magnetic materials. When kept in a uniform magnetic field, the field lines around them look as follows:

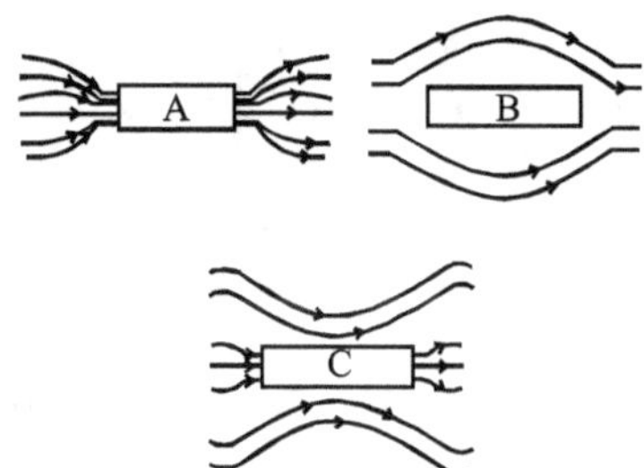

Make the correspondence of these bars with their material being diamagnetic (D), ferromagnetic (F) and paramagnetic (P):

(a) $A \leftrightarrow D, B \leftrightarrow P, C \leftrightarrow F$
(b) $A \leftrightarrow F, B \leftrightarrow D, C \leftrightarrow P$
(c) $A \leftrightarrow P, B \leftrightarrow F, C \leftrightarrow D$
(d) $A \leftrightarrow F, B \leftrightarrow P, C \leftrightarrow D$

17. When a piece of a ferromagnetic substance is put in a uniform magnetic field, the flux density inside it is four times the flux density away from the piece. The magnetic permeability of the material is

(a) 1
(b) 2
(c) 3
(d) 4

18. A vibration magnetometer placed in magnetic meridian has a small bar magnet. The magnet executes oscillations with a time period of 2 sec in earth's horizontal magnetic field of 24 microtesla. When a horizontal field of 18 microtesla is produced opposite to the earth's field by placing a current carrying wire, the new time period of magnet will be

(a) 1 s
(b) 2 s
(c) 3 s
(d) 4 s

19. The mid points of two small magnetic dipoles of length d in end-on positions, are separated by a distance x, (x >> d). The force between them is proportional to x^{-n} where n is:

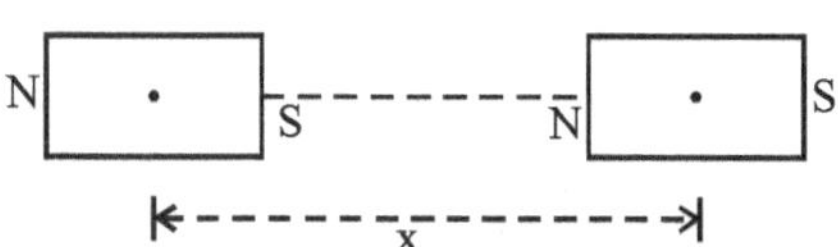

(a) 1
(b) 2
(c) 3
(d) 4

20. The magnetic field of earth at the equator is approximately 4×10^{-5} T. The radius of earth is 6.4×10^6 m. Then the dipole moment of the earth will be nearly of the order of

(a) 10^{23} A m^2
(b) 10^{12} A m^2
(c) 10^{16} A m^2
(d) 10^{10} A m^2

21. The earth's magnetic field lines resemble that of a dipole at the centre of the earth. If the magnetic moment of this dipole is close to 8×10^{22} Am^2, the value of earth's magnetic field near the pole is close to (radius of the earth = 6.4×10^6 m)

(a) 0.6 Gauss
(b) 1.2 Gauss
(c) 1.8 Gauss
(d) 0.32 Gauss

22. A compass needle whose magnetic moment is 60 Am^2, is directed towards geographical north at any place experiencing moment of force of 1.2×10^{-3} Nm. At that place the horizontal component of earth field is 40 micro W/m^2. What is the value of dip angle at that place?

(a) 30°
(b) 60°
(c) 45°
(d) 15°

23. A 10 cm long bar magnet of magnetic moment 1.34 Am^2 is placed in the magnetic meridian with its south pole pointing geographical south. The neutral point is obtained at a distance of 15 cm from the centre of the magnet. Calculate the horizontal component of earth's magnetic field.

(a) 0.12×10^{-4} T
(b) 0.21×10^{-4} T
(c) 0.34×10^{-4} T
(d) 0.87×10^{-7} T

24. A short bar magnet is placed in the magnetic meridian of the earth with north pole pointing north. Neutral points are found at a distance of 30 cm from the magnet on the East – West line, drawn through the middle point of the magnet. The magnetic moment of the magnet in Am^2 is close to (Given $\dfrac{\mu_0}{4\pi} = 10^{-7}$ in SI units and B_H =Horizontal component of earth's magnetic field $= 3.6 \times 10^{-5}$ tesla)

(a)   14.6

(b)   19.4

(c)   9.7

(d)   4.9

25. Two tangent galvanometers A and B have coils of radii 8 cm and 16 cm respectively and resistance 8 Ω each. They are connected in parallel with a cell of emf 4 V and negligible internal resistance. The deflections produced in the tangent galvanometers A and B are 30° and 60° respectively. If A has 2 truns, then B must have

(a)   18 turns

(b)   12 turns

(c)   6 turns

(d)   2 turns

ANSWER KEY

1	(c)	4	(d)	7	(b)	10	(a)	13	(a)	16	(b)	19	(d)	22	(a)	25	(b)
2	(c)	5	(a)	8	(a)	11	(b)	14	(b)	17	(d)	20	(a)	23	(c)		
3	(a)	6	(d)	9	(a)	12	(d)	15	(a)	18	(d)	21	(a)	24	(c)		

ELECTROMAGNETIC INDUCTION

1. A solenoid has 2000 turns wound over a length of 0.3 m. Its cross-sectional area is 1.2×10^{-3} m^2. Around its central section a coil of 300 turns is wound. If an initial current of 2 A flowing in the solenoid is reversed in 0.25 s, the emf induced in the coil will be

   (a) 2.4×10^{-4} V
   (b) 2.4×10^{-2} V
   (c) 4.8×10^{-4} V
   (d) 4.8×10^{-2} V

2. A boat is moving due east in a region where the earth's magnetic field is 5.0×10^{-5} NA^{-1} m^{-1} due north and horizontal. The boat carries a vertical aerial 2 m long. If the speed of the boat is 1.50 ms^{-1}, the magnitude of the induced emf in the wire of aerial is:

   (a) 0.75 mV
   (b) 0.50 mV
   (c) 0.15 mV
   (d) 1 mV

3. A coil having n turns and resistance R Ω is connected with a galvanometer of resistance 4R Ω. This combination is moved in time t seconds from a magnetic field W_1 weber to W_2 weber. The induced current in the circuit is

   (a) $-\dfrac{(W_1 - W_2)}{Rnt}$
   (b) $-\dfrac{n(W_2 - W_1)}{5\,Rt}$
   (c) $-\dfrac{(W_2 - W_1)}{3\,Rnt}$
   (d) $-\dfrac{n(W_2 - W_1)}{Rt}$

4. A conducting rod AB moves parallel to X-axis in a uniform magnetic field, pointing in the positive X-direction. The end A of the rod gets

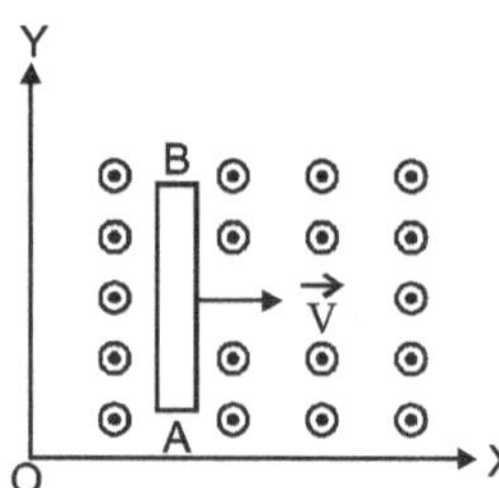

   (a) positively charged
   (b) negatively charged
   (c) neutral
   (d) first positively charged and then negatively charged

5. One conducting U tube can slide inside another as shown in figure, maintaining electrical contacts between the tubes. The magnetic field B is perpendicular to the plane of the figure. If each tube moves towards the other at a constant speed v, then the emf induced in the circuit in terms of B, l and v where l is the width of each tube, will be

   (a) $- Blv$
   (b) Blv
   (c) $2\,Blv$
   (d) zero

6. A coil 10 turns and a resistance of 20Ω is connected in series with B.G. of resistance 30Ω. The coil is placed with its plane perpendicular to the direction of a uniform magnetic field of induction 10^{-2} T. If it is now turned through an angle of $60°$ about an axis in its plane. Find the charge induced in the coil.

(Area of a coil $= 10^{-2}$ m^2)

(a) 10^{-5}C (b) 10^{-7}C

(c) 10^{-9}C (d) 10^{-10}C

7. A flexible wire loop in the shape of a circle has radius that grown linearly with time. There is a magnetic field perpendicular to the plane of the loop that has a magnitude inversely proportional to the distance from the center of the loop, $B(r) \propto \dfrac{1}{r}$. How does the emf E vary with time?

(a) $E \propto t^2$ (b) $E \propto t$

(c) $E \propto \sqrt{t}$ (d) E is constant

8. Magnetic flux linked with a stationary loop of resistance R varies with respect to time during the time period T as follows: $\phi = at(T - t)$. The amount of heat generated in the loop during that time (inductance of the coil is negligible) is

(a) $\dfrac{aT}{3R}$ (b) $\dfrac{a^2T^2}{3R}$

(c) $\dfrac{a^2T^2}{R}$ (d) $\dfrac{a^2T^3}{3R}$

9. A copper wire of length 40cm, diameter 2mm and resistivity 1.7×10^{-8} Ωm forms a square frame. If a uniform magnetic field B exists in a direction perpendicular to the plane of square frame and it changes at a steady rate $\dfrac{dB}{dt} = 0.02$ T/s, then find the current induced in the frame.

(a) 9.3×10^{-2} amp (b) 9.3×10^{-5} amp

(c) 3.3×10^{-2} amp (d) 19.3×10^{-6} amp

10. The figure shows certain wire segments joined together to form a coplanar loop. The loop is placed in a perpendicular magnetic field in the direction going into the plane of the figure. The magnitude of the field increases with time. I_1 and I_2 are the currents in the segments ab and cd. Then,

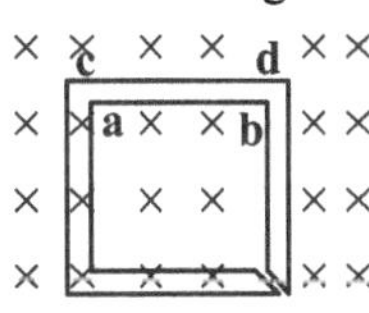

(a) $I_1 > I_2$

(b) $I_1 + I_2 = 0$

(c) I_1 is in the direction ba and I_2 is in the direction cd

(d) I_1 is in the direction ab and I_2 is in the direction dc

11. A thin non-conductinging of mass m carrying a charge q can rotate freely about its axis. At $t = 0$, the ring was at rest and no magnetic field was present. Then suddenly a magnetic field B was set perpendicular to the plane. Find the angular velocity acquired by the ring.

(a) $\dfrac{3qB}{2m}$ (b) $\dfrac{2qB}{3m}$

(c) $\dfrac{qB}{2m}$ (d) $\dfrac{q}{Bm}$

12. A circular and an elliptical loop, all in the $(x - y)$ plane, are moving out of a uniform magnetic field with a constant velocity, $\vec{V} = v\hat{i}$. The magnetic field is directed along the negative z axis direction. The induced emf, during the passage of these loops, out of the field region, will not remain constant for

(a) both circular and elliptical loops

(b) only elliptical loop

(c) only circular loop

(d) none of these

13. The current i in an induction coil varies with time t according to the graph shown in figure.

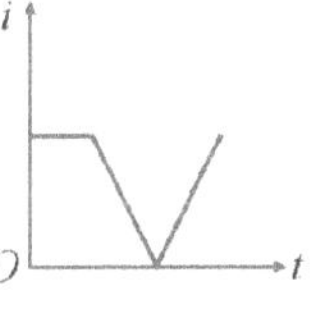

Which of the following graphs shows the induced emf (E) in the coil with time?

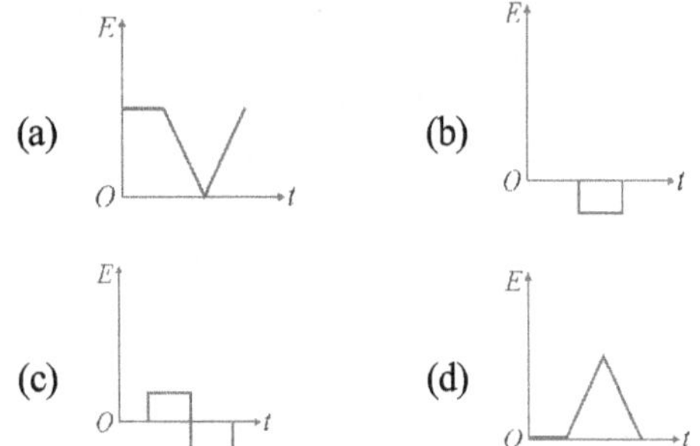

14. The total number of turns and cross-section area in a solenoid is fixed. However, its length L is varied by adjusting the separation between windings. The inductance of solenoid will be proportional to:

(a) L
(b) L^2
(c) $1/L^2$
(d) $1/L$

15. Two coils 'P' and 'Q' are separated by some distance. When a current of 3A flows through coil 'P', a magnetic flux of 10^{-3} Wb passes through 'Q'. No current is passed through 'Q'. When no current passes through 'P' and a current of 2A passes through 'Q', the flux through 'P' is:

(a) 6.67×10^{-4} Wb
(b) 3.67×10^{-3} Wb
(c) 6.67×10^{-3} Wb
(d) 3.67×10^{-4} Wb

16. A planar loop of wire rotates in a uniform magnetic field. Initially, at $t = 0$, the plane of the loop is perpendicular to the magnetic field. If it rotates with a period of 10 s about an axis in its plane then the magnitude of induced emf will be maximum and minimum, respectively at:

(a) 2.5 s and 7.5 s
(b) 2.5 s and 5.0 s
(c) 5.0 s and 7.5 s
(d) 5.0 s and 10.0 s

17. If the rod is moving with a constant velocity of 12 cm/s then the power that must be supplied by an external force in maintaining the speed and the reading of ammeter are respectively.

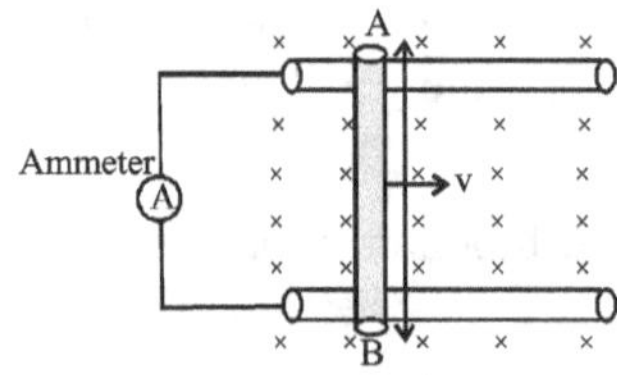

(Given B = 0.5 Tesla, l = 15 cm, v = 12 cm/s, Resistance of rod R_{AB} = 9.0 mΩ)

(a) 9×10^{-5} W, 0.5 A
(b) 0.5×10^{-5} W, 1A
(c) 9×10^{-3} W, 1 A
(d) 1×10^{-3} W, 3A

18. The number of turns in the coil of an AC generator is 5000 and the area of the coil is 0.25 m^2, the coil is rotated at the rate of 100 cycle per second in a magnetic field of 0.2 Weber/m^2. The peak value of the emf generated is nearly

(a) 786 kV
(b) 440 kV
(c) 220 kV
(d) 157 kV

19. A 100 turns coil of area of cross section 200 cm^2 having 2 Ω resistance is held perpendicular to a magnetic field of 0.1 T. If it is removed from the magnetic field in one second, find the charge flows in it during this process.

(a) 0.2 C
(b) 2 C
(c) 0.1 C
(d) 1 C

20. The coefficient of self inductance of a solenoid is 0.18 mH. If a core of soft iron of relative permeability 900 is inserted, then the coefficient of self inductance will become nearly.

(a) 5.4 mH
(b) 162 mH
(c) 0.006 mH
(d) 0.0002 mH

21. Two coaxial solenoids are made by winding thin insulated wire over a pipe of cross-sectional area A = 10 cm^2 and length = 20 cm. If one of the solenoids has 300 turns and the other 400 turns, their mutual inductance is ($\mu_0 = 4\pi \times 10^{-7}$ TmA^{-1})

(a) $4.8\pi \times 10^{-4}$ H
(b) $4.8\pi \times 10^{-5}$ H
(c) $2.4\pi \times 10^{-4}$ H
(d) $4.8\pi \times 10^4$ H

22. A copper wire is wound on a wooden frame, whose shape is that of an equilateral triangle. If the linear dimension of each side of the frame is increased by a factor of 3, keeping the number of turns of the coil per unit length of the frame the same, then the self inductance of the coil:

(a) decreases by a factor of 9

(b) increases by a factor of 27

(c) increases by a factor of 3

(d) decreases by a factor of $9\sqrt{3}$

23. Two coaxial solenoids are made by winding thin insulated wire over a pipe of cross-sectional area $A = 10$ cm^2 and length $= 20$ cm. If one of the solenoid has 300 turns and the other 400 turns, their mutual inductance is

$(\mu_0 = 4\pi \times 10^{-7}$ Tm A$^{-1})$

(a) $2.4\pi \times 10^{-5}$ H

(b) $4.8\pi \times 10^{-4}$ H

(c) $4.8\pi \times 10^{-5}$ H

(d) $2.4\pi \times 10^{-4}$ H

24. When the current changes from $+2$ A to -2A in 0.05 second, an e.m.f. of 8 V is induced in a coil. The coefficient of self-induction of the coil is

(a) 0.2 H

(b) 0.4 H

(c) 0.8 H

(d) 0.1 H

25. A conducting circular loop made of a thin wire, has area 3.5×10^{-3} m^2 and resistance 10Ω. It is placed perpendicular to a time dependent magnetic field $B(t) = (0.4T)\sin(50\pi t)$. The net charge flowing through the loop during $t = 0$ s and $t = 10$ ms is close to:

(a) 1.4×10^{-4} mC

(b) 7.0×10^{-4} mC

(c) 21×10^{-4} mC

(d) 6×10^{-4} mC

ANSWER KEY																
1	(d)	4	(a)	7	(d)	10	(d)	13	(c)	16	(b)	19	(c)	22	(c)	25	(a)
2	(c)	5	(c)	8	(d)	11	(c)	14	(d)	17	(c)	20	(b)	23	(d)		
3	(b)	6	(a)	9	(a)	12	(a)	15	(a)	18	(d)	21	(c)	24	(d)		

1. The voltage of an ac source varies with time according to the equation $V = 100 \sin 100\,\pi t \cos 100\,\pi t$ where t is in seconds and V is in volt. Then the peak voltage of the source is

   (a) 100 volt
   (b) 50 volt
   (c) $100/\sqrt{2}$ volt
   (d) 150 volt

2. An inductor ($L = 100$ mH), a resistor ($R = 100\,\Omega$) and a battery ($E = 100$ V) are initially connected in series as shown in the figure. After a long time the battery is disconnected after short circuiting the points A and B. The current in the circuit 1 ms after the short circuit is

   (a) $1/e$ A
   (b) e A
   (c) 0.1 A
   (d) 1 A

3. If a current I given by $I_0 \sin\left(\omega t - \dfrac{\pi}{2}\right)$ flows in an ac circuit across which an ac potential of $E = E_0 \sin \omega t$ has been applied, then the power consumption P in the circuit will be

   (a) $P = \dfrac{E_0 I_0}{\sqrt{2}}$
   (b) $P = \sqrt{2} E_0 I_0$
   (c) $P = \dfrac{E_0 I_0}{2}$
   (d) $P = 0$

4. In an alternating current circuit in which an inductance and capacitance are joined in series, current is found to be maximum when the value of inductance is 0.5 henry and the value of capacitance is 8 μF. The angular frequency of applied alternating voltage will be

   (a) 5000 rad/sec
   (b) 4000 rad/sec
   (c) 2×10^5 rad/sec
   (d) 500 rad/sec

5. In a circuit, L, C and R are connected in series with an alternating voltage source of frequency f. The current leads the voltage by 45°. The value of C is

   (a) $\dfrac{1}{\pi f(2\pi f L - R)}$
   (b) $\dfrac{1}{2\pi f(2\pi f L - R)}$
   (c) $\dfrac{1}{\pi f(2\pi f L + R)}$
   (d) $\dfrac{1}{2\pi f(2\pi f L + R)}$

6. For an RLC circuit driven with voltage of amplitude V_m and frequency $\omega_0 = \dfrac{1}{\sqrt{LC}}$ the current exhibits resonance the quality factor, Q is given by

   (a) $\dfrac{\omega_0}{L}$
   (b) $\dfrac{\omega_0 L}{R}$
   (c) $\dfrac{R}{\omega_0 C}$
   (d) $\dfrac{CR}{\omega_0}$

7. An e.m.f. of 15 volt is applied in a circuit containing 5 henry inductance and 10 ohm resistance. The ratio of the currents at time $t = \infty$ and at $t = 1$ second is

(a) $\dfrac{e^{1/2}}{e^{1/2-1}}$

(b) $\dfrac{e^2}{e^2-1}$

(c) $1-e^{-1}$

(d) e^{-1}

8. In a region of uniform magnetic induction $B = 10^{-2}$ tesla, a circular coil of radius 30 cm and resistance π^2 ohm is rotated about an axis which is perpendicular to the direction of B and which forms a diameter of the coil. If the coil rotates at 200 rpm the amplitude of the alternating current induced in the coil is

(a) 40 mA

(b) 30 mA

(c) 6 mA

(d) 200 mA

9. A capacitor of 10 μF and an inductor of 1 H are joined in series. An ac of 50 Hz is applied to this combination. What is the impedance of the combination?

(a) $\dfrac{5(\pi^2-5)}{\pi}\Omega$

(b) $\dfrac{100(10-\pi^2)}{\pi}\Omega$

(c) $\dfrac{10(\pi^2-5)}{\pi}\Omega$

(d) $\dfrac{5(10-\pi^2)}{\pi}\Omega$

10. A bulb is rated at 100 V, 100 W, it can be treated as a resistor. Find out the inductance of an inductor (called choke coil) that should be connected in series with the bulb to operate the bulb at its rated power with the help of an ac source of 200 V and 50 Hz.

(a) $\dfrac{\pi}{\sqrt{3}}$ H

(b) 100 H

(c) $\dfrac{\sqrt{2}}{\pi}$ H

(d) $\dfrac{\sqrt{3}}{\pi}$ H

11. In a series LCR circuit with an ideal ac source of peak voltage $E_0 = 50$ V, frequency $v = \dfrac{50}{\pi}$ Hz and $R = 300\,\Omega$. The average electric field energy stored in the capacitor and average magnetic energy stored in the coil are 25 mJ and 5 mJ

respectively. The value of RMS current in the circuit is 0.1 A. Then find : Capacitance (C) of the capacitor is

(a) 10 μF

(b) 15 μF

(c) 20 μF

(d) 25 μF

12. A series LR circuit is connected to an ac source of frequency ω and the inductive reactance is equal to 2R. A capacitance of capacitive reactance equal to R is added in series with L and R. The ratio of the new power factor to the old one is :

(a) $\sqrt{\dfrac{2}{3}}$

(b) $\sqrt{\dfrac{2}{5}}$

(c) $\sqrt{\dfrac{3}{2}}$

(d) $\sqrt{\dfrac{5}{2}}$

13. A sinusoidal voltage of peak value 283 V and angular frequency 320/s is applied to a series LCR circuit. Given that $R = 5\,\Omega$, $L = 25$ mH and $C = 1000$ μF. The total impedance, and phase difference between the voltage across the source and the current will respectively be :

(a) $10\ \Omega$ and $\tan^{-1}\left(\dfrac{5}{3}\right)$

(b) $7\ \Omega$ and $45°$

(c) $10\ \Omega$ and $\tan^{-1}\left(\dfrac{8}{3}\right)$

(d) $7\ \Omega$ and $\tan^{-1}\left(\dfrac{5}{3}\right)$

14. An ac source of angular frequency ω is fed across a resistor r and a capacitor C in series. The current registered is I. If now the frequency of source is changed to ω/3 (but maintaining the same voltage), the current in the circuit is found to be halved. Calculate the ratio of reactance to resistance at the original frequency ω

(a) $\sqrt{\dfrac{3}{5}}$

(b) $\sqrt{\dfrac{2}{5}}$

(c) $\sqrt{\dfrac{1}{5}}$

(d) $\sqrt{\dfrac{4}{5}}$

15. In a series resonant LCR circuit, the voltage across R is 100 volts and $R = 1\,k\Omega$ with $C = 2\mu F$. The resonant frequency ω is 200 rad/s. At resonance the voltage across L is

(a) $2.5 \times 10^{-2}\,V$ (b) $40\,V$

(c) $250\,V$ (d) $4 \times 10^{-3}\,V$

16. The voltage time (V-t) graph for triangular wave having peak value V_0 is as shown in figure. The rms value of V in time interval from $t = 0$ to T/4 is

$\dfrac{V_0}{\sqrt{x}}$ then find the value of x.

(a) 5

(b) 4

(c) 7

(d) 3

17. A resistor 'R' and $2\mu F$ capacitor in series is connected through a switch to 200 V direct supply. Across the capacitor is a neon bulb that lights up at 120 V. Calculate the value of R to make the bulb light up 5 s after the switch has been closed. $(\log_{10} 2.5 = 0.4)$

(a) $1.7 \times 10^5\,\Omega$ (b) $2.7 \times 10^6\,\Omega$

(c) $3.3 \times 10^7\,\Omega$ (d) $1.3 \times 10^4\,\Omega$

18. The peak value of an alternating emf E given by

$$E = E_0 \cos \omega t$$

is 10 V and frequency is 50 Hz. At time $t = (1/600)$ s, the instantaneous value of emf is

(a) $10\,V$ (b) $5\sqrt{3}\,V$

(c) $5\,V$ (d) $1\,V$

19. If $i_1 = 3 \sin \omega t$, $i_2 = 4 \cos \omega t$, and $i_3 = i_0 \sin (\omega t + 53°)$, find the value of i_0.

(a) 5

(b) 7

(c) 6

(d) 4

20. Combination of two identical capacitors, a resistor R and $a\,dc$ voltage source of voltage 6V is used in an experiment on a $(C\text{-}R)$ circuit. It is found that for a parallel combination of the capacitor the time in which the voltage of the fully charged combination reduces to half its original voltage is 10 second. For series combination the time for needed for reducing the voltage of the fully charged series combination by half is

(a) 10 second   (b) 5 second

(c) 2.5 second   (d) 20 second

21. In an electrical circuit R, L, C and an a.c. voltage source are all connected in series. When L is removed from the circuit, the phase difference between the voltage the current in the circuit is $\pi/3$. If instead, C is removed from the circuit, the phase difference is again $\pi/3$. The power factor of the circuit is:

(a) 1/2   (b) $1/\sqrt{2}$

(c) 1   (d) $\sqrt{3}/2$

22. Combination of two identical capacitors, a resistor R and $a\,dc$ voltage source of voltage 6V is used in an experiment on a $(C\text{-}R)$ circuit. It is found that for a parallel combination of the capacitor the time in which the voltage of the fully charged combination reduces to half its original voltage is 10 second. For series combination the time needed for reducing the voltage of the fully charged series combination by half is

(a) 10 second   (b) 5 second

(c) 2.5 second   (d) 20 second

23. An inductance coil has a reactance of 100 Ω. When an AC signal of frequency 1000 Hz is applied to the coil, the applied voltage leads the current by 45°. The self-inductance of the coil is:

(a) $1.1 \times 10^{-2}\,H$ (b) $1.1 \times 10^{-1}\,H$

(c) $5.5 \times 10^{-5}\,H$ (d) $6.7 \times 10^{-7}\,H$

24. When the rms voltages V_L, V_C and V_R are measured respectively across the inductor L, the capacitor C and the resistor R in a series LCR circuit connected to an AC source, it is found that the ratio $V_L : V_C : V_R = 1 : 2 : 3$. If the rms voltage of the AC sources is 100 V, the V_R is close to:

(a) 50 V   (b) 70 V

(c) 90 V   (d) 100 V

25. The plot given below is of the average power delivered to an LRC circuit versus frequency. The quality factor of the circuit is :

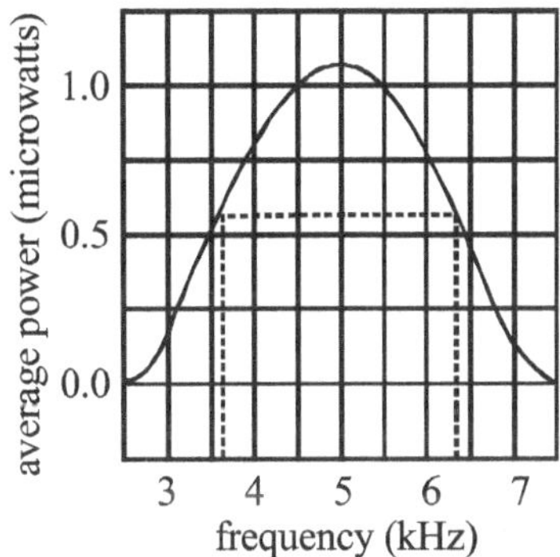

(a) 5.0   (b) 2.0

(c) 2.5   (d) 0.4

<table>
<tr><td colspan="16" align="center">ANSWER KEY</td></tr>
<tr><td>1</td><td>(b)</td><td>4</td><td>(d)</td><td>7</td><td>(b)</td><td>10</td><td>(d)</td><td>13</td><td>(b)</td><td>16</td><td>(d)</td><td>19</td><td>(a)</td><td>22</td><td>(c)</td><td>25</td><td>(b)</td></tr>
<tr><td>2</td><td>(a)</td><td>5</td><td>(d)</td><td>8</td><td>(c)</td><td>11</td><td>(c)</td><td>14</td><td>(a)</td><td>17</td><td>(b)</td><td>20</td><td>(c)</td><td>23</td><td>(a)</td><td></td><td></td></tr>
<tr><td>3</td><td>(d)</td><td>6</td><td>(b)</td><td>9</td><td>(b)</td><td>12</td><td>(d)</td><td>15</td><td>(c)</td><td>18</td><td>(b)</td><td>21</td><td>(c)</td><td>24</td><td>(c)</td><td></td><td></td></tr>
</table>

ELECTROMAGNETIC WAVES | 22

1. When an electromagnetic wave with poynting vector $\bar{S}$ is incident an a perfectly absorbing surface, then radiation pressure on surface is

   (a) $P = \dfrac{S}{c}$

   (b) $P = \dfrac{S}{2c}$

   (c) $\dfrac{2S}{3c}$

   (d) Sc

2. An electromagnetic wave passes through space and its equation is given by $E = E_0 \sin(\omega t - kx)$ where E is electric field. Energy density of electromagnetic wave in space is

   (a) $\dfrac{1}{2}\varepsilon_0 E_0^2$

   (b) $\dfrac{1}{4}\varepsilon_0 E_0^2$

   (c) $\varepsilon_0 E_0^2$

   (d) $2\varepsilon_0 E_0^2$

3. A plane electromagnetic wave is incident on a plane surface of area A, normally and is perfectly reflected. If energy E strikes the surface in time t then force exerted on the surface is (c = speed of light)

   (a) $\dfrac{2E}{Atc}$

   (b) $\dfrac{E}{2c}$

   (c) $\dfrac{2E}{ct}$

   (d) zero

4. A plane electromagnetic wave is incident on a material surface. If the wave delivers momentum p and energy E, then
   (a) $p = 0, E = 0$
   (b) $p \neq 0, E \neq 0$
   (c) $p \neq 0, E = 0$
   (d) $p = 0, E \neq 0$

5. The pressure exerted by an electromagnetic wave of intensity I (watts/m^2) on a nonreflecting surface is [c is the velocity of light]
   (a) Ic
   (b) Ic^2
   (c) I/c
   (d) None

6. The electric field of an electromagnetic wave travelling through vaccum is given by the equation $E = E_0 \sin(kx - \omega t)$. The quantity that is independent of wavelength is
   (a) $k\omega$
   (b) $\dfrac{k}{\omega}$
   (c) $k^2\omega$
   (d) ω

7. The magnetic field in a travelling electromagnetic wave has a peak value of 20 nT. The peak value of electric field strength is
   (a) $3\,V/m$
   (b) $4\,V/m$
   (c) $6\,V/m$
   (d) $9\,V/m$

8. In an electromagnetic wave, the amplitudes of magnetic field B_0 and electric field E_0 in free space are related as:
   (a) $B_0 = E_0$
   (b) $B = \dfrac{E_0}{c}$
   (c) $B_0 = E_0\sqrt{\mu_0\varepsilon_0}$
   (d) $B_0 = E_0\sqrt{\dfrac{\varepsilon_0}{\mu_0}}$

9. The magnetic field in a plane electromagnetic wave is given by

$$B_y = 2 \times 10^{-7} \sin (0.5 \times 10^3 x + 1.5 \times 10^{11} t)$$

The electromagnetic wave is

(a) A visible light

(b) An infrared wave

(c) A micro wave

(d) A radio wave

10. If microwaves, X rays, infrared, gamma rays, ultra-violet, radio waves and visible parts of the electromagnetic spectrum are denoted by M, X, I, G, U, R and V then which of the following is the arrangement in ascending order of wavelength ?

(a) R, M, I, V, U, X and G

(b) M, R, V, X, U, G and I

(c) G, X, U, V, I, M and R

(d) I, M, R, U, V, X and G

11. An electromagnetic wave going through vacuum is described by $E = E_0 \sin(kx - \omega t); B = B_0 \sin (kx - \omega t)$. Which of the following equations is true

(a) $E_0 k = B_0 \omega$ (b) $E_0 \omega = B_0 k$

(c) $E_0 B_0 = \omega k$ (d) None of these

12. A plane electromagnetic wave travels in free space along X-direction. If the value of $\vec{B}$ (in tesla) at a particular point in space and time is $1.2 \times 10^{-8} \, \hat{k} T$. The value of $\vec{E}$ (in Vm^{-1}) at that point is

(a) $2.2 \, \hat{j}$ (b) $2.6 \, \hat{k}$

(c) $3.2 \, \hat{k}$ (d) $3.6 \, \hat{j}$

13. The magnetic field in the plane electromagnetic field is given by: $B_y = 2 \times 10^{-7} \sin (0.5 \times 10^3 z + 1.5 \times 10^{11} t) T$

The expression for the electric field may be given by

(a) $E_y = 2 \times 10^{-7} \sin(2.5 \times 10^3 z + 1.5 \times 10^{11} t) V/m$

(b) $E_x = 2 \times 10^{-7} \sin(2.5 \times 10^3 z + 1.5 \times 10^{11} t) V/m$

(c) $E_y = 60 \sin(0.5 \times 10^3 z + 1.5 \times 10^{11} t) V/m$

(d) $E_x = 60 \sin(0.5 \times 10^3 z + 1.5 \times 10^{11} t) V/m$

14. A plane electromagnetic wave propagating in the X-direction has wavelength of 6.0 mm. The electric field is in the Y-direction and its maximum magnitude is 33 Vm^{-1}. The equation for the electric field as a function of x and t is

(a) $11 \sin \pi \left(t - \dfrac{x}{c} \right)$

(b) $33 \sin \left[\pi \times 10^{11} \left(t - \dfrac{x}{c} \right) \right]$

(c) $33 \sin \pi \left(t - \dfrac{x}{c} \right)$

(d) $11 \sin \left[\pi \times 10^{11} \left(t - \dfrac{x}{c} \right) \right]$

15. Given below is a list of electromagnetic spectrum and its mode of production. Which one does not match?

(a) Gamma rays – Radioactive decay of the nucleus

(b) Ultraviolet rays – Magnetron valve

(c) Radio wave – Rapid acceleration and deceleration of electrons in conducting wires

(d) X-rays – X-ray tubes or inner shell electrons

16. A lamp emits monochromatic green light uniformly in all directions. The lamp is 3% efficient in converting electrical power to electromagnetic waves and consumes 100 W of power. The amplitude of the electric field associated with the electromagnetic radiation at a distance of 5 m from the lamp will be nearly:

(a) 1.34 V/m   (b) 2.68 V/m

(c) 4.02 V/m   (d) 5.36 V/m

17. An electromagnetic wave of frequency 1×10^{14} hertz is propagating along z-axis. The amplitude of electric field is 4 V/m. If $\varepsilon_0 = 8.8 \times 10^{-12} C^2/N\text{-}m^2$, then average energy density of electric field will be:

(a) $35.2 \times 10^{-8} J/m^3$ (b) $35.2 \times 10^{-7} J/m^3$

(c) $35.2 \times 10^{-12} J/m^3$ (d) $35.2 \times 10^{-9} J/m^3$

18. A plane electromagnetic wave travels in free space along x-axis. At a particular point in space, the electric field along y-axis is 9.3 V m^{-1}. The magnetic induction (B) along z-axis is

  (a) 3.1×10^{-8} T   (b) 3×10^{-5} T

  (c) 3×10^{-6} T   (d) 9.3×10^{-6} T

19. The electric field associated with an e.m. wave in vacuum is given by $\vec{E} = \hat{i}\, 40 \cos (kz - 6 \times 10^8 t)$, where E, z and t are in volt/m, meter and seconds respectively. The value of wave vector k is

  (a) $2\, \text{m}^{-1}$ (b) $0.5\, \text{m}^{-1}$

  (c) $6\, \text{m}^{-1}$ (d) $3\, \text{m}^{-1}$

20. A 27 mW laser beam has a cross-sectional area of 10 mm^2. The magnitude of the maximum electric field in this electromagnetic wave is given by :

[Given permittivity of space $\epsilon_0 = 9 \times 10^{-12}$ SI units, Speed of light c $= 3 \times 10^8$ m/s]

  (a)   2kV/m   (c)   0.7kV/m

  (b)   1kV/m   (d)   1.4kV/m

21. If the magnetic field of a plane electromagnetic wave is given by (The speed of light $= 3 \times 10^8$ m/s)

$$B = 100 \times 10^{-6} \sin\left[2\pi \times 2 \times 10^{15} \left(t - \frac{x}{c} \right) \right]$$

then the maximum electric field associated with it is:

  (a) 6×10^4 N/C   (b) 3×10^4 N/C

  (c) 4×10^4 N/C   (d) $4.5\, 10^4$ N/C

22. A plane electromagnetic wave of frequency 50 MHz travels in free space along the positive x-direction. At a particular point in space and time, $\vec{E} = 6.3\, \hat{j}$ V / m. The corresponding magnetic field $\vec{B}$, at that point will be:

  (a) $18.9 \times 10^{-8}\, \hat{k}$T   (b) $2.1 \times 10^{-8}\, \hat{k}$T

  (c) $6.3 \times 10^{-8}\, \hat{k}$T   (d) $18.9 \times 10^{8}\, \hat{k}$T

23. The mean intensity of radiation on the surface of the Sun is about 10^8 W/m^2. The rms value of the corresponding magnetic field is closest to :

  (a)   1 T   (b) 10^2 T

  (c) 10^{-2} T   (d) 10^{-4} T

24. An electron is constrained to move along the y-axis with a speed of 0.1 c (c is the speed of light) in the presence of electromagnetic wave, whose electric field is $\vec{E} = 30\hat{j} \sin(1.5 \times 10^7 t - 5 \times 10^{-2} x)$ V/m. The maximum magnetic force experienced by the electron will be :

(given $c = 3 \times 10^8$ ms^{-1} & electron charge $= 1.6 \times 10^{-19}$C)

  (a) 3.2×10^{-18} N   (b) 2.4×10^{-18} N

  (c) 4.8×10^{-19} N   (d) 1.6×10^{-19} N

25. A plane electromagnetic wave, has frequency of 2.0×10^{10} Hz and its energy density is 1.02×10^{-8} J/m^3 in vacuum. The amplitude of the magnetic field of the wave is close to

$\left(\dfrac{1}{4\pi\varepsilon_0} = 9 \times 10^9\, \dfrac{Nm^2}{C^2} \right.$ and speed of light $= 3 \times 10^8$ ms^{-1}) :

  (a)   150 nT   (b)   160 nT

  (c)   180 nT   (d)   190 nT

ANSWER KEY

1	(a)	4	(b)	7	(c)	10	(c)	13	(d)	16	(b)	19	(a)	22	(b)	25	(b)
2	(a)	5	(c)	8	(c)	11	(a)	14	(b)	17	(c)	20	(d)	23	(d)		
3	(c)	6	(b)	9	(c)	12	(d)	15	(b)	18	(a)	21	(b)	24	(c)		

RAY OPTICS AND OPTICAL INSTRUMENTS

23

1. A car is fitted with a convex side-view mirror of focal length 20 cm. A second car 2.8 m behind the first car is overtaking the first car at a relative speed of 15 m/s. The speed of the image of the second car as seen in the mirror of the first one is:

   (a) $\dfrac{1}{15}$ m/s
   (b) 10 m/s
   (c) 15 m/s
   (d) $\dfrac{1}{10}$ m/s

2. A fish looking up through the water sees the outside world contained in a circular horizon. If the refractive index of water is $\dfrac{4}{3}$ and the fish is 12 cm below the surface of water, the radius of this circle in cm is

   (a) $\dfrac{36}{\sqrt{7}}$
   (b) $36\sqrt{7}$
   (c) $4\sqrt{5}$
   (d) $36\sqrt{5}$

3. A planoconcave lens is placed on a paper on which a flower is drawn. How far above its actual position does the flower appear to be?

   (a) 10 cm
   (b) 15 cm
   (c) 50 cm
   (d) None of these

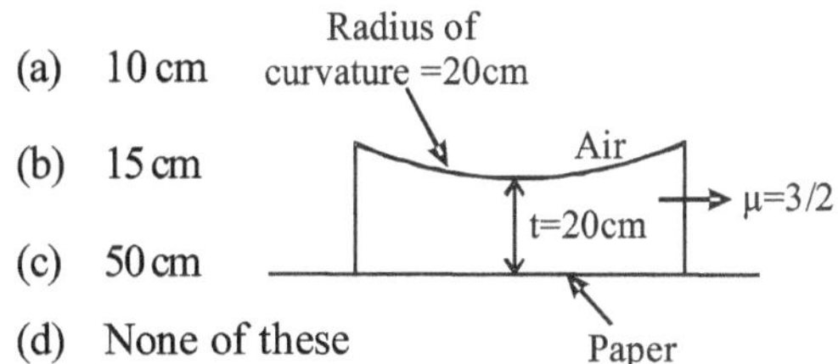

4. A bi-convex lens is formed with two thin plano-convex lenses as shown in the figure. Refractive index n of the first lens is 1.5 and that of the second lens is 1.2. Both the curved surfaces are of the same radius of curvature $R = 14$ cm. For this bi-convex lens, for an object distance of 40 cm, the image distance will be

   (a) -280.0 cm
   (b) 40.0 cm
   (c) 21.5 cm
   (d) 13.3 cm

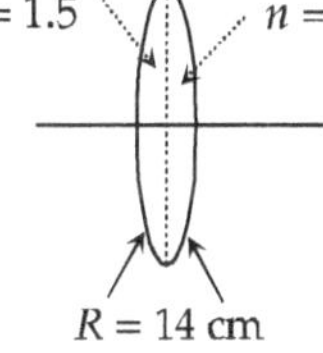

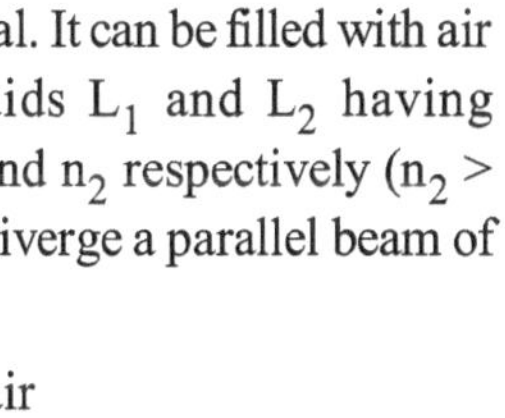

5. A hollow double concave lens is made of very thin transparent material. It can be filled with air or either of two liquids L_1 and L_2 having refractive indices n_1 and n_2 respectively ($n_2 > n_1 > 1$). The lens will diverge a parallel beam of light if it is filled with

   (a) air and placed in air
   (b) air and immersed in L_1
   (c) L_1 and immersed in L_2
   (d) L_2 and immersed in L_1

6. There is a prism with refractive index equal to $\sqrt{2}$ and the refracting angle equal to 60°. One of the refracting surfaces of the prism is polished. A beam of monochromatic light will retrace its

path if its angle of incidence over the refracting surface of the prism is

(a) $\sin^{-1}\left(\sqrt{2}\right)$

(b) $\sin^{-1}\left(2\sqrt{3}\right)$

(c) $\sin^{-1}\left(\dfrac{\sqrt{3}}{\sqrt{2}}\right)$

(d) $\sin^{-1}\left(\dfrac{1}{\sqrt{2}}\right)$

7. If the refractive index of the material of a prism is $\cot\dfrac{A}{2}$ and the angle of prism is A, then angle of minimum deviation is

(a) $\pi - 2A$

(b) $\pi - A$

(c) $\dfrac{\pi}{2} - 2A$

(d) $\dfrac{\pi}{2} - A$

8. The focal length of the objective and the eye-piece of an astronomical telescope are 60 cm and 5 cm respectively. What is the length of the telescope when the final image is formed at least distance of distinct vision (25 cm) approx.

(a) 61 cm

(b) 62 cm

(c) 64 cm

(d) 65 cm

9. An astronomical telescope has an angular magnification of magnitude 5 for distant objects. The separation between the objective and the eye-piece is 36 cm and the final image is formed at infinity. The focal length f_0 of the objective and f_e of the eye piece are

(a) $f_0 = 45$ cm and $f_2 = -8$ cm

(b) $f_0 = 50$ cm and $f_e = 10$ cm

(c) $f_0 = 7.2$ cm and $f_e = 5$ cm

(d) $f_0 = 30$ cm and $f_e = 6$ cm

10. A transparent solid cylindrical rod has a refractive index of $\dfrac{2}{\sqrt{3}}$. It is surrounded by air. A light ray is incident at the mid-point of one end of the rod as shown in the figure.

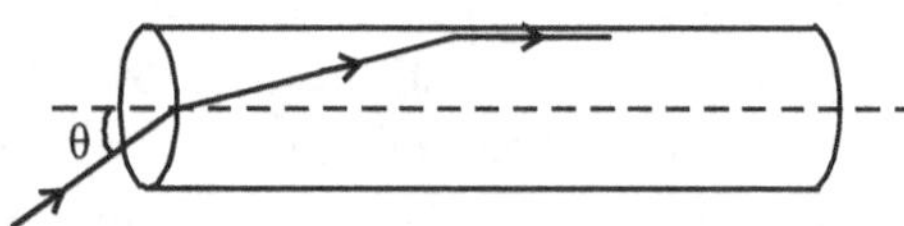

The incident angle θ for which the light ray grazes along the wall of the rod is :

(a) $\sin^{-1}\left(\sqrt{3}/2\right)$

(b) $\sin^{-1}\left(\dfrac{2}{\sqrt{3}}\right)$

(c) $\sin^{-1}\left(\dfrac{1}{\sqrt{3}}\right)$

(d) $\sin^{-1}\left(1/2\right)$

11. A thin glass (refractive index 1.5) lens has optical power of $-5\,D$ in air. Its optical power in a liquid medium with refractive index 1.6 will be

(a) $-1D$

(b) $1D$

(c) $-25\,D$

(d) $25\,D$

12. The graph shows how the magnification m produced by a thin lens varies with image distance v. What is the focal length of the lens used ?

(a) $\dfrac{b^2}{ac}$

(b) $\dfrac{b^2 c}{a}$

(c) $\dfrac{a}{c}$

(d) $\dfrac{b}{c}$

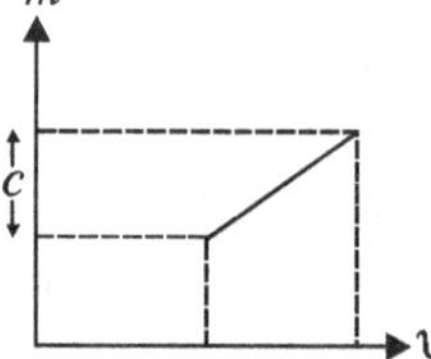

13. Two plane mirrors are inclined to each other such that a ray of light incident on the first mirror (M_1) and parallel to the second mirror (M_2) is finally reflected from the second mirror (M_2) parallel to the first mirror (M_1). The angle between the two mirrors will be:

(a) $45°$

(b) $60°$

(c) $75°$

(d) $90°$

14. A printed page is pressed by a glass of water. The refractive index of the glass and water is 1.5 and 1.33, respectively. If the thickness of the bottom of glass is 1 cm and depth of water is 5 cm, how much the page will appear to be shifted if viewed from the top ?

(a) 1.033 cm

(b) 3.581 cm

(c) 1.3533 cm

(d) 1.90 cm

15. A beam of light consisting of red, green and blue colours is incident on a right-angled prism on face *AB*. The refractive indices of the material for the above red, green and blue colours are 1.39, 1.44 and 1.47 respectively. A person looking on surface *AC* of the prism will see

(a) no light

(b) green and blue colours

(c) red and green colours

(d) red colour only

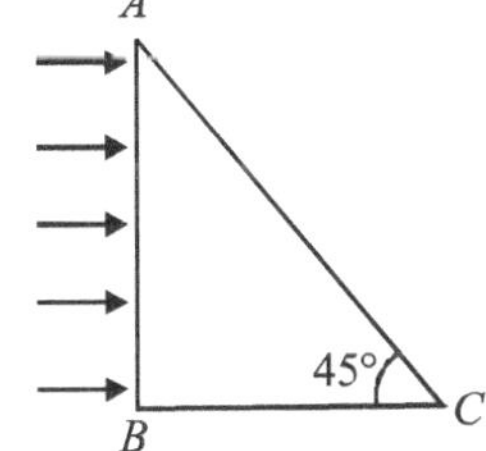

16. Water (with refractive index $= \dfrac{4}{3}$) in a tank is 18 cm deep. Oil of refractive index $\dfrac{7}{4}$ lies on water making a convex surface of radius of curvature 'R = 6 cm' as shown. Consider oil to act as a thin lens. An object 'S' is placed 24 cm above water surface. The location of its image is at 'x' cm above the bottom of the tank. Then 'x' is

(a) 5

(b) 2

(c) 8

(d) 9

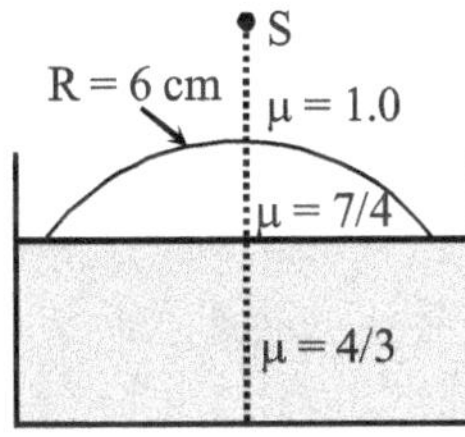

17. A ray PQ incident on the refracting face BA is refracted in the prism BAC as shown in the figure and emerges from the other refracting face AC as RS such that AQ = AR. If the angle of prism A = 60° and the refractive index of the material of prism is $\sqrt{3}$, then the angle of deviation of the ray is

(a) 60°

(b) 45°

(c) 30°

(d) 90°

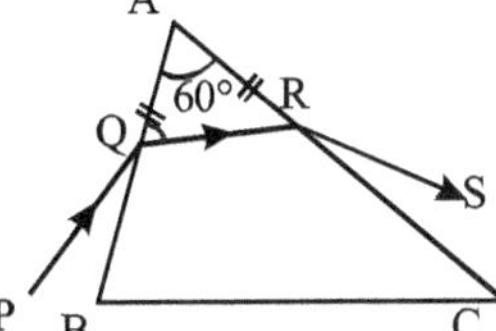

18. When plane face of planoconvex lens is silvered, it behaves as a concave mirror of focal length 30cm. But when its curved surface is silvered, it behaves as a concave mirror of focal length 10cm. The refractive index of lens material is

(a) 1.25

(b) 1.33

(c) 1.732

(d) 1.5

19. For a prism kept in air it is found that for an angle of incidence 60°, the angle of prism A, angle of deviation δ and angle of emergence 'e' become equal. Then the refractive index of the material of prism is

(a) 1.73

(b) 1.15

(c) 1.5

(d) 1.33

20. The distance between an object and a screen is 100 cm. A lens can produce real image of the object on the screen for two different positions between the screen and the object. The distance between these two positions is 40 cm. If the power of the lens is close to $\left(\dfrac{N}{100}\right) D$ where N is an integer, the value of N is

(a) 476

(b) 532

(c) 339

(d) 454

21. A point object in air is in front of the curved surface of a *plano-convex* lens. The radius of curvature of the curved surface is 30 cm and the refractive index of the lens material is 1.5, then the focal length of the lens is

(a) 40 cm

(b) 50 cm

(c) 60 cm

(d) 80 cm

22. A convex lens of focal length 20 cm produces images of the same magnification 2 when an object is kept at two distances x_1 and x_2 ($x_1 > x_2$) from the lens. The ratio of x_1 and x_2 is:

(a) 2 : 1

(b) 3 : 1

(c) 5 : 3

(d) 4 : 3

23. A compound microscope consists of an objective lens of focal length 1 cm and an eye piece of focal length 5 cm with a separation of 10 cm.

The distance between an object and the objective lens, at which the strain on the eye is minimum is

(a) -1.25 cm (b) -3.50 cm

(c) -4.50 cm (d) -6 cm

24. In a compound microscope, the magnified virtual image is formed at a distance of 25 cm from the eye-piece. The focal length of its objective lens is 1 cm. If the magnification is 100 and the tube length of the microscope is 20 cm, then the focal length of the eye-piece lens (in cm) is

(a) 4.48 cm (b) 5.60 cm

(c) 3 cm (d) 9 cm

25. When light falls on a given plate at angle of incidence of 60°, the reflected and refracted rays are found to be normal to each other. The refractive index of the matertial of the plate is then

(a) 0.866 (b) 1.5

(c) 1.732 (d) 2

ANSWER KEY																	
1	(a)	4	(b)	7	(a)	10	(c)	13	(b)	16	(b)	19	(a)	22	(b)	25	(c)
2	(a)	5	(d)	8	(c)	11	(b)	14	(c)	17	(a)	20	(a)	23	(a)		
3	(a)	6	(c)	9	(d)	12	(d)	15	(d)	18	(d)	21	(c)	24	(a)		

WAVE OPTICS

24

1. Two beams of light having intensities I and 4I interfere to produce a fringe pattern on a screen. The phase difference between the beams is $\dfrac{\pi}{2}$ at point A and π at point B. Then the difference between the resulting intensities at A and B is
   (a) 2 I
   (b) 4 I
   (c) 5 I
   (d) 7 I

2. Figure shows wavefront P passing through two systems A and B, and emerging as Q and then as R. The system A and B could, respectively, be
   (a) a prism and a convergent lens
   (b) a convergent lens and a prism
   (c) a divergent lens and a prism
   (d) a convergent lens and a divergent lens

   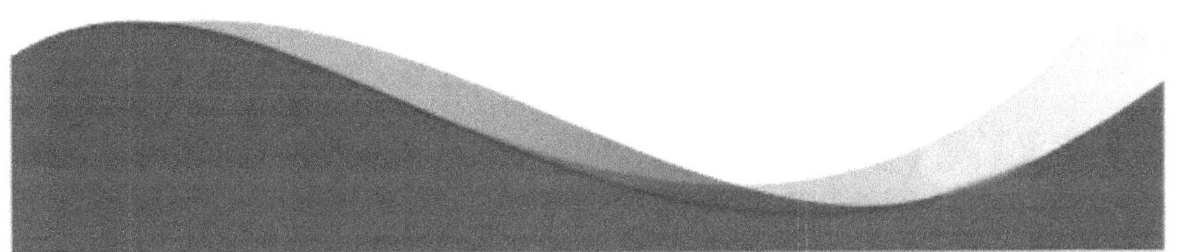

3. The interference pattern in obtained with two coherent light sources of intensity ratio n. In the interference pattern, the ratio $\dfrac{I_{max} - I_{min}}{I_{max} + I_{min}}$ will be
   (a) $\dfrac{2\sqrt{n}}{(n+1)^2}$
   (b) $\dfrac{\sqrt{n}}{n+1}$
   (c) $\dfrac{2\sqrt{n}}{n+1}$
   (d) $\dfrac{\sqrt{n}}{(n+1)^2}$

4. Two light waves having the same wavelength λ in vacuum are in phase initially. Then the first ray travels a path of length L_1 through a medium of refractive index μ_1. The of refractive index μ_2. The two waves are then combined to observe interference effects. The phase difference between the two, when they interfere, is
   (a) $\dfrac{2\pi}{\lambda}\left(L_1 - L_2\right)$
   (b) $\dfrac{2\pi}{\lambda}\left(\mu_1 L_1 - \mu_2 L_2\right)$
   (c) $\dfrac{2\pi}{\lambda}\left(\mu_2 L_1 - \mu_1 L_2\right)$
   (d) $\dfrac{2\pi}{\lambda}\left[\dfrac{L_1}{\mu_1} - \dfrac{L_2}{\mu_2}\right]$

5. A ray of light of intensity I is incident on a parallel glass slab at point A as shown in diagram. It undergoes partial reflection and refraction. At each reflection, 25% of incident energy is reflected. The rays AB and A'B' undergo interference. The ratio of I_{max} and I_{min} is :
   (a) 49 : 1
   (b) 7 : 1
   (c) 4 : 1
   (d) 8 : 1

   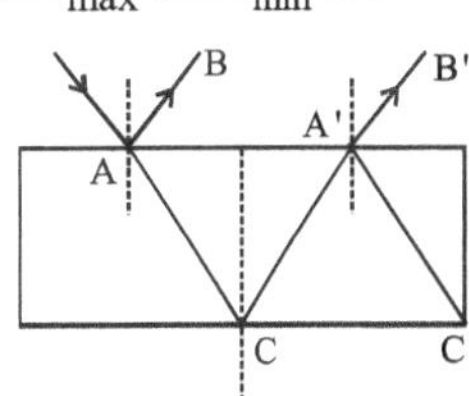

6. In a Young's double slit experiment with light of wavelength λ the separation of slits is d and distance of screen is D such that D >> d >> λ. If the fringe width is β, the distance from point of maximum intensity to the point where intensity falls to half of maximum intensity on either side is:

(a) $\dfrac{\beta}{6}$

(b) $\dfrac{\beta}{3}$

(c) $\dfrac{\beta}{4}$

(d) $\dfrac{\beta}{2}$

7. A parallel beam of monochromatic light of wavelength 5000Å is incident normally on a single narrow slit of width 0.001 mm. The light is focussed by a convex lens on a screen placed in focal plane. The first minimum will be formed for the angle of diffraction equal to

(a) $0°$

(b) $15°$

(c) $30°$

(d) $50°$

8. In Young's double slit experiment shown in figure S_1 and S_2 are coherent sources and S is the screen having a hole at a point 1.0mm away from the central line. White light (400 to 700nm) is sent through the slits. Which wavelength passing through the hole has strong intensity?

(a) 400 nm

(b) 700 nm

(c) 500 nm

(d) 667 nm

9. The diameter of the objective lens of microscope makes an angle β at the focus of the microscope. Further, the medium between the object and the lens is an oil of refractive index n. Then the resolving power of the microscope

(a) increases with decreasing value of n

(b) increases with decreasing value of β

(c) increases with increasing value of n

(d) increases with increasing value of $\dfrac{1}{n \sin 2\beta}$

10. A beam of light is incident on a glass slab ($\mu = 1.54$) in a direction as shown in the figure. The reflected light is analysed by a polaroid prism. On rotating the polaroid, ($\tan 57° = 1.54$)

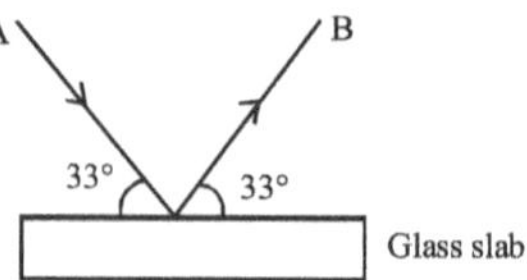

(a) the intensity remains unchanged

(b) the intensity is reduced to zero and remains at zero

(c) the intensity gradually reduces to zero and then again increase

(d) the intensity increases continuously

11. A single slit of width b is illuminated by a coherent monochromatic light of wavelength λ. If the second and fourth minima in the diffraction pattern at a distance 1 m from the slit are at 3 cm and 6 cm respectively from the central maximum, what is the width of the central maximum? (i.e. distance between first minimum on either side of the central maximum)

(a) 1.5 cm

(b) 3.0 cm

(c) 4.5 cm

(d) 6.0 cm

12. Two stars are 10 light years away from the earth. They are seen through a telescope of objective diameter 30 cm. The wavelength of light is 600 nm. To see the stars just resolved by the telescope, the minimum distance between them should be (1 light year = 9.46×10^{15} m) of the order of:

(a) 10^8 km

(b) 10^{10} km

(c) 10^{11} km

(d) 10^6 km

13. Unpolarised light of intensity 32 W m^{-2} passes through three polarizers such that transmission axis of the first and second polarizer makes an angle 30° with each other and the transmission axis of the last polarizer is crossed with that of the first The intensity of final emerging light is will be

(a) 32 W m^{-2}

(b) 3 W m^{-2}

(c) 8 W m^{-2}

(d) 4 W m^{-2}

14. The value of numerical aperature of the objective lens of a microscope is 1.25. If light of wavelength 5000 Å is used, the minimum separation between two points, to be seen as distinct, will be :

(a) 0.24 μm   (b) 0.38 μm

(c) 0.12 μm   (d) 0.48 μm

15. Consider a Young's double slit experiment as shown in figure. What should be the slit separation d in terms of wavelength λ such that the first minima occurs directly in front of the slit (S_1)?

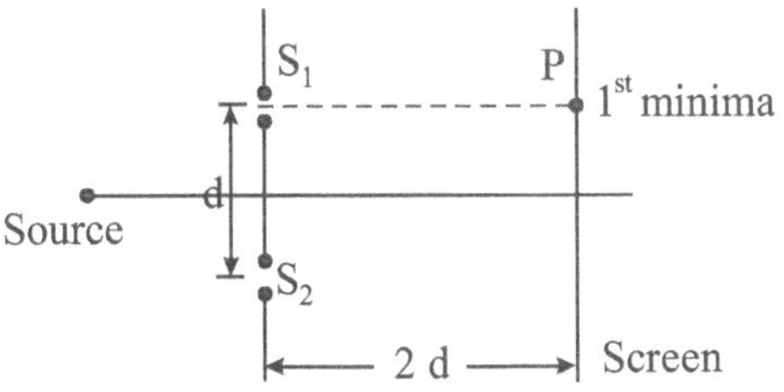

(a) $\dfrac{\lambda}{2\left(\sqrt{5}-2\right)}$ (b) $\dfrac{\lambda}{\left(\sqrt{5}-2\right)}$

(c) $\dfrac{\lambda}{2\left(5-\sqrt{2}\right)}$ (d) $\dfrac{\lambda}{\left(5-\sqrt{2}\right)}$

16. Light of wavelength 550 nm falls normally on a slit of width 22.0×10^{-5} cm. The angular position of the second minima from the central maximum will be (in radians)

(a) $\dfrac{\pi}{8}$ (b) $\dfrac{\pi}{12}$

(c) $\dfrac{\pi}{4}$ (d) $\dfrac{\pi}{6}$

17. Unpolarized light of intensity I is incident on a system of two polarizers, A followed by B. The intensity of emergent light is I/2. If a third polarizer C is placed between A and B, the intensity of emergent light is reduced to I/3. The angle between the polarizers A and C is θ. Then

(a) $\cos\theta = \left(\dfrac{2}{3}\right)^{1/4}$ (b) $\cos\theta = \left(\dfrac{1}{3}\right)^{1/4}$

(c) $\cos\theta = \left(\dfrac{1}{3}\right)^{1/2}$ (d) $\cos\theta = \left(\dfrac{2}{3}\right)^{1/2}$

18. Calculate the limit of resolution of a telescope objective having a diameter of 200 cm, if it has to detect light of wavelength 500 nm coming from a star.

(a) 305×10^{-9} radian

(b) 610×10^{-9} radian

(c) 152.5×10^{-9} radian

(d) 457.5×10^{-9} radian

19. A light of wavelength 6000 Å shines on two narrow slits separated by a distance 1.0 mm and illuminates a screen at a distance 1.5 m away. When one slit is covered by a thin glass plate of refractive index 1.8 and othe rslit by a thin glass plate of refractive index μ, the central maxima shifts by 0.1 rad. Both plates have the same thickness of 0.5 mm. The value of refractive index μ of the glass is

(a) 1.4   (b) 1.5

(c) 1.6   (d) 1.3

20. In young's double slit experiment, if the width of 4th bright fringe is 2×10^{-2} cm, then the width of 6th bright fringe will be

(a) 10^{-2} cm   (b) 3×10^{-2} cm

(c) 2×10^{-2} cm   (d) 1.5×10^{-2} cm

(Where the symbols have their usual meanings)

21. In Young's double slit experiment the two slits are illuminated by light of wavelenght 5890Å and the distance between the fringes obtained on the screen is 0.2°. If the whole apparatus is immersed in water then the angular fringe width will be, if the refractive index of water is 4/3.

(a) 0.30°   (b) 0.15°

(c) 19°   (d) 30°

22. In Young's experiment the wavelength of red light is 7.5×10^{-5} cm. and that of blue light 5.0×10^{-5} cm. What will be the value of n for which (n +1)th blue bright band coincides with nth red bright band ?

(a) 2   (b) 3

(c) 4   (d) 5

23. A young's double-slit experiment is performed using monocromatic light of wavelength λ. The inntensity of light at a point on the screen, where the path difference is λ, is K units. The intensity of light at a point where the path difference is $\dfrac{\lambda}{6}$ is given by $\dfrac{nK}{12}$, where n is an integer. The value of n is

(a) 9
(b) 7
(c) 5
(d) 4

24. In a double-slit experiment, green light (5303Å) falls on a double slit having a separation of 19.44 μm and a width of 4.05 μm. The number of bright fringes between the first and the second diffraction minima is :

(a) 10
(b) 05
(c) 04
(d) 09

25. A ray of light is incident from a denser to a rarer medium. The critical angle for total internal reflection is θ_{iC} and Brewster's angle of incidence is θ_{iB}, such that $\sin\theta_{iC}/\sin\theta_{iB} = \eta = 1.28$. The relative refractive index of the two media is:

(a) 0.2
(b) 0.4
(c) 0.8
(d) 0.9

ANSWER KEY																								
1	(b)	4	(b)	7	(c)	10	(c)	13	(b)	16	(a)	19	(c)	22	(a)	25	(c)
2	(b)	5	(a)	8	(c)	11	(b)	14	(a)	17	(a)	20	(c)	23	(a)		
3	(c)	6	(c)	9	(c)	12	(a)	15	(a)	18	(a)	21	(b)	24	(b)		

DUAL NATURE OF RADIATION AND MATTER

1. Two particles move at right angle to each other. Their de Broglie wavelengths are λ_1 and λ_2 respectively. The particles suffer perfectly inelastic collision. The de Broglie wavelength λ, of the final particle, is given by :

(a) $\dfrac{1}{\lambda^2} = \dfrac{1}{\lambda_1^2} + \dfrac{1}{\lambda_2^2}$
(b) $\lambda = \sqrt{\lambda_1 + \lambda_2}$

(c) $\lambda = \dfrac{\lambda_2 + \lambda_2}{2}$
(d) $\dfrac{2}{\lambda} = \dfrac{1}{\lambda_1} + \dfrac{1}{\lambda_2}$

2. An electron of mass m and charge e initially at rest gets accelerated by a constant electric field E. The rate of change of de-Broglie wavelength of this electron at time t ignoring relativistic effects is

(a) $\dfrac{-h}{e\,E t^2}$
(b) $\dfrac{-eht}{E}$

(c) $\dfrac{-mh}{e\,E t^2}$
(d) $\dfrac{-h}{e E}$

3. Two identical metal plates show photoelectric effect. Light of wavelength λ_A falls on plate A and λ_B fall on plate B, $\lambda_A = 2\lambda_B$. The maximum KE of the photoelectrons are K_A and K_B, respectively. Which one of the following is true?

(a) $2K_A = K_B$
(b) $K_A = 2K_B$
(c) $K_A < K_B/2$
(d) $K_A > 2K_B$

4. Monochromatic light of wavelength 667 nm is produced by a helium neon laser. The power emitted is 9 mW. The number of photons arriving per sec on the average at a target irradiated by this beam is:

(a) 3×10^{16}
(b) 9×10^{15}
(c) 3×10^{19}
(d) 9×10^{17}

5. There are n_1 photons of frequency y_1 in a beam of light. In an equally energetic beam, there are n_2 photons of frequency y_2. Then the correct relation is

(a) $\dfrac{n_2}{n_1} = 1$
(b) $\dfrac{n_1}{n_2} = \dfrac{y_1}{y_2}$

(c) $\dfrac{n_1}{n_2} = \dfrac{y_2}{y_1}$
(d) $\dfrac{n_1}{n_2} = \dfrac{y_1^2}{y_2^2}$

6. Electrons are accelerated through a potential difference V and protons are accelerated through a potential difference 4 V. The de-Broglie wavelengths are λ_e and λ_p for electrons and protons respectively. The ratio of $\dfrac{\lambda_e}{\lambda_p}$ is given by : (given m_e is mass of electron and m_p is mass of proton).

(a) $\sqrt{\dfrac{m_p}{m_e}}$
(b) $\sqrt{\dfrac{m_e}{m_p}}$

(c) $\dfrac{1}{2}\sqrt{\dfrac{m_e}{m_p}}$
(d) $2\sqrt{\dfrac{m_p}{m_e}}$

7. In photoelectric effect, stopping potential for a light of frequency n_1 is V_1. If light is replaced by another having a frequency n_2 then its stopping potential will be

(a) $V_1 - \dfrac{h}{e}(n_2 - n_1)$

(b) $V_1 + \dfrac{h}{e}(n_2 + n_1)$

(c) $V_1 + \dfrac{h}{e}(n_2 - 2n_1)$

(d) $V_1 + \dfrac{h}{e}(n_2 - n_1)$

8. In a photoelectric effect measurement, the stopping potential for a given metal is found to be V_0 when radiation of wavelength λ_0 is used. If radiation of wavelength $2\lambda_0$ is used with the same metal, the stopping potential (in volt) is

(a) $\dfrac{V_0}{2}$

(b) $2V_0$

(c) $V_0 + \dfrac{hc}{2e\lambda_0}$

(d) $V_0 - \dfrac{hc}{2e\lambda_0}$

9. A particle A of mass m and initial velocity v collides with a particle B of mass $\dfrac{m}{2}$ which is at rest. The collision is head on, and elastic. The ratio of the de-Broglie wavelengths λ_A to λ_B after the collision is

(a) $\dfrac{\lambda_A}{\lambda_B} = \dfrac{2}{3}$

(b) $\dfrac{\lambda_A}{\lambda_B} = \dfrac{1}{2}$

(c) $\dfrac{\lambda_A}{\lambda_B} = \dfrac{1}{3}$

(d) $\dfrac{\lambda_A}{\lambda_B} = 2$

10. The figure shows a plot of photo current versus anode potential for a photo sensitive surface for three different radiations. Which one of the following is a correct statement?

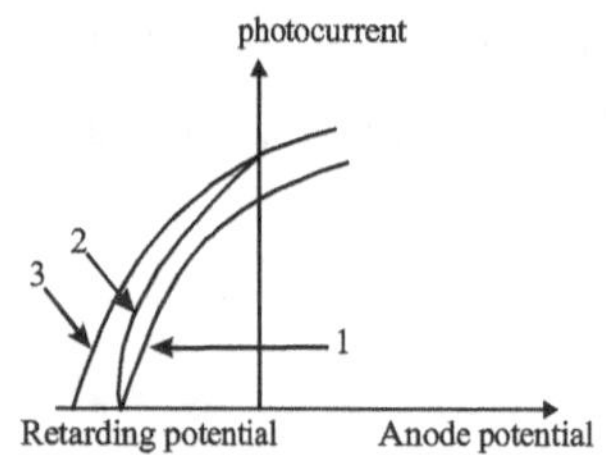

(a) Curves (1) and (2) represent incident radiations of same frequency but of different intensities.

(b) Curves (2) and (3) represent incident radiations of different frequencies and different intensities.

(c) Curves (2) and (3) represent incident radiations of same frequency having same intensity.

(d) Curves (1) and (2) represent incident radiations of different frequencies and different intensities.

11. Two identical photocathodes receive light of frequencies f_1 and f_2. If the velocites of the photoelectrons (of mass m) coming out are v_1 and v_2 respectively, then

(a) $v_1^2 - v_2^2 = \dfrac{2h}{m}(f_1 - f_2)$

(b) $v_1 + v_2 = \left[\dfrac{2h}{m}(f_1 + f_2)\right]^{1/2}$

(c) $v_1^2 + v_2^2 = \dfrac{2h}{m}(f_1 + f_2)$

(d) $v_1 - v_2 = \left[\dfrac{2h}{m}(f_1 - f_2)\right]^{1/2}$

12. A sensor is exposed for time t to a lamp of power P placed at a distance l. The sensor has an opening that is 4d in diameter. Assuming all energy of the lamp is given off as light, as number of photons entering the sensor if the wavelength of light is λ is

(a) $N = P\lambda d^2 t/hcl^2$

(b) $N = 4P\lambda d^2 t/hcl^2$

(c) $N = P\lambda d^2 t / 4hcl^2$

(d) $N = P\lambda d^2 t/16\,hcl^2$

13. Which one of the following graphs represents the variation of maximum kinetic energy (E_K) of the emitted electrons with frequency υ in photoelectric effect correctly ?

(a) 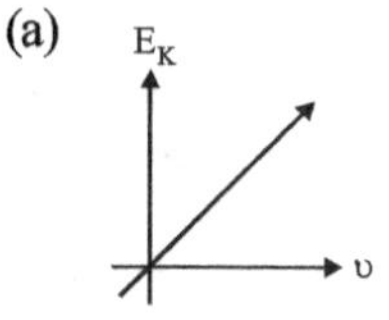

(b) 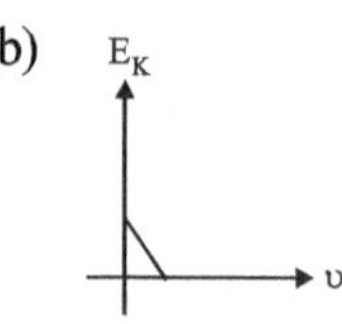

(c) 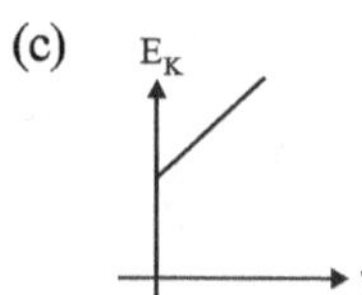

(d) 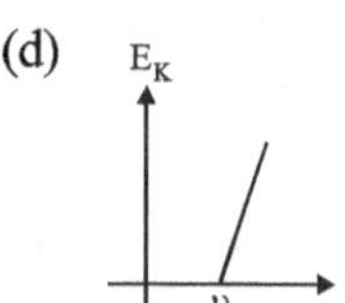

14. The maximum velocity of the photoelectrons emitted from the surface is v when light of frequency n falls on a metal surface. If the incident frequency is increased to 3n, the maximum velocity of the ejected photoelectrons will be :

(a) less than $\sqrt{3}$v   (b) v

(c) more than $\sqrt{3}$v   (d) equal to $\sqrt{3}$v

15. A 2 mW laser operates at a wavelength of 500 nm. The number of photons that will be emitted per second is : [Given Planck's constant h= 6.6×10^{-34} Js, speed of light $c=3.0\times10^8$ m/s]

(a) 5×10^{15} (b) 1.5×10^{16}

(c) 2×10^{16} (d) 1×10^{16}

16. A Laser light of wavelength 660 nm is used to weld Retina detachment. If a Laser pulse of width 60 ms and power 0.5 kW is used the approximate number of photons in the pulse are :

[Take Planck's constant h = 6.62×10^{-34} Js]

(a) 10^{20} (b) 10^{18}

(c) 10^{22} (d) 10^{19}

17. When photons of wavelength λ_1 are incident on an isolated sphere, the corresponding stopping potential is found to be V. When photons of wavelength λ_2 are used, the corresponding stopping potential was thrice that of the above value. If light of wavelength λ_3 is used then find the stopping potential for this case :

(a) $\dfrac{hc}{e}\left[\dfrac{1}{\lambda_3}+\dfrac{1}{\lambda_2}-\dfrac{1}{\lambda_1}\right]$

(b) $\dfrac{hc}{e}\left[\dfrac{1}{\lambda_3}+\dfrac{1}{2\lambda_2}-\dfrac{1}{\lambda_1}\right]$

(c) $\dfrac{hc}{e}\left[\dfrac{1}{\lambda_3}-\dfrac{1}{\lambda_2}-\dfrac{1}{\lambda_1}\right]$

(d) $\dfrac{hc}{e}\left[\dfrac{1}{\lambda_3}+\dfrac{1}{2\lambda_2}-\dfrac{3}{2\lambda_1}\right]$

18. A photosensitive metallic surface has work function, hv_0. If photons of energy $2 hv_0$ fall on this surface, the electrons come out with a maximum velocity of 4×10^6 m/s. When the photon energy is increased to 5 hv_0, then maximum velocity of photoelectrons will be

(a) 2×10^7 m/s   (b) 2×10^6 m/s

(c) 8×10^6 m/s   (d) 8×10^5 m/s

19. Light of wavelength 0.6 μm from a sodium lamp falls on a photocell and causes the emission of photoelectrons for which the stopping potential is 0.5 V. With light of wavelength 0.4 μm from a mercury vapor lamp, the stopping potential is 1.5 V. Then, the work function [in electron volts] of the photocell surface is

(a) 0.75 eV   (b) 1.5 eV

(c) 3 eV   (d) 2.5 eV

20. Light from a hydrogen discharge tube is incident on the cathode of a photoelectric cell, the work function of the cathode surface is 4.2 eV. In order to reduce the photocurrent to zero the voltage of the anode relative to the cathode must be made

(a) -4.2 V   (b) -9.4 V

(c) -17.8 V   (d) $+9.4$ V

21. All electrons ejected from a surface by incident light of wavelength 200nm can be stopped before travelling 1m in the direction of uniform electric field of 4N/C. The work function of the surface is

(a) 4 eV   (b) 6.2 eV

(c) 8 eV   (d) 2.2 eV

22. The surface of a metal is illuminated alternately with photons of energies $E_1 = 4$ eV and $E_2 = 2.5$ eV respectively. The ratio of maximum speeds of the photoelectrons emitted in the two cases is 2. The work function of the metal in (eV) is

(a) 2   (b) 5

(c) 7   (d) 9

23. When photon of energy 4.0 eV strikes the surface of a metal A, the ejected photoelectrons have maximum kinetic energy T_A eV and de-Broglie wavelength λ_A. The maximum kinetic energy of photoelectrons liberated from another metal B by photon of energy 4.50 eV is $T_B=(T_A-1.5)$eV. If the de-Broglie wavelength of these photoelectrons $\lambda_B = 2\lambda_A$, then the work function of metal B is:

(a) 4 eV   (b) 2 eV

(c) 1.5 eV   (d) 3 eV

24. The electric field of light wave is given as

$$\vec{E} = 10^3 \cos\left(\frac{2\pi x}{5\times10^{-7}} - 2\pi\times6\times10^{14}\,t\right)\hat{x}\,\frac{N}{C}$$

This light falls on a metal plate of work function 2eV. The stopping potential of the photo-electrons is:

Given, E (in eV) $= \dfrac{12375}{\lambda\,(\text{in Å})}$

(a) 2.0 V
(b) 0.72 V
(c) 0.48 V
(d) 2.48 V

25. Surface of certain metal is first illuminated with light of wavelength $\lambda_1 = 350$ nm and then, by light of wavelength $\lambda_2 = 540$ nm. It is found that the maximum speed of the photo electrons in the two cases differ by a factor of (2) The work function of the metal (in eV) is close to:

(Energy of photon $= \dfrac{1240}{\lambda\,(\text{in nm})}$eV)

(a) 1.8
(b) 2.5
(c) 5.6
(d) 1.4

ANSWER KEY

1	(a)	4	(a)	7	(d)	10	(a)	13	(d)	16	(a)	19	(b)	22	(a)	25	(a)
2	(a)	5	(c)	8	(d)	11	(a)	14	(c)	17	(d)	20	(b)	23	(a)		
3	(c)	6	(d)	9	(d)	12	(a)	15	(a)	18	(c)	21	(d)	24	(c)		

ATOMS

1. Energy E of a hydrogen atom with principal quantum number n is given by $E = \dfrac{-13.6}{n^2}\,\text{eV}$. The energy of a photon ejected when the electron jumps from n = 3 state to n = 2 state of hydrogen is approximately

   (a) 1.5 eV (b) 0.85 eV

   (c) 3.4 eV (d) 1.9 eV

2. An alpha nucleus of energy $\dfrac{1}{2}mv^2$ bombards a heavy nuclear target of charge Ze. Then the distance of closest approach for the alpha nucleus will be proportional to

   (a) $1/m$ (b) $1/v^4$

   (c) $1/Ze$ (d) v^2

3. The largest wavelength in the ultraviolet region of the hydrogen spectrum is 122 nm. The smallest wavelength in the infrared region of the hydrogen spectrum (to the nearest integer) is

   (a) 1802 nm (b) 823 nm

   (c) 1882 nm (d) 1648 nm

4. A beam of fast moving alpha particles were directed towards a thin film of gold. The parts A', B' and C' of the transmitted and reflected beams corresponding to the incident parts A, B and C of the beam, are shown in the adjoining diagram. The number of alpha particles in

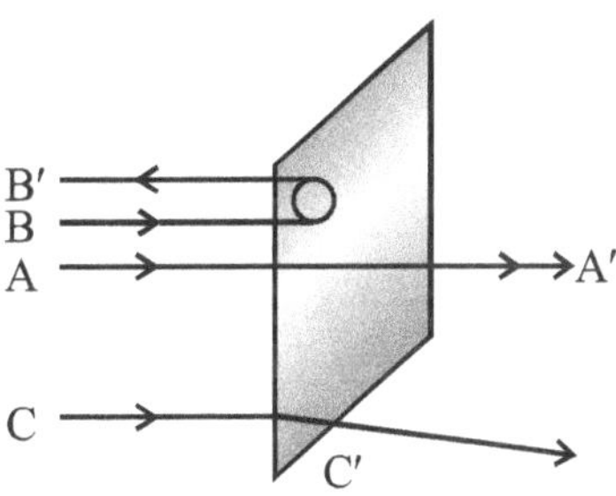

   (a) B' will be minimum and in C' maximum

   (b) A' will be maximum and in B' minimum

   (c) A' will be minimum and in B' maximum

   (d) C' will be minimum and in B' maximum

5. The wavelength of radiation is λ_0 when an electron jumps from third to second orbit of hydrogen atom. For the electron to jump from the fourth to the second orbit of the hydrogen atom, the wavelength of radiation emitted will be

   (a) $\dfrac{16}{25}\lambda_0$ (b) $\dfrac{20}{27}\lambda_0$

   (c) $\dfrac{27}{20}\lambda_0$ (d) $\dfrac{25}{16}\lambda_0$

6. The distance of the closest approach of an alpha particle fired at a nucleus with kinetic energy K is r_0. The distance of the closest approach when the α particle is fired at the same nucleus with kinetic energy 2K will be

(a) $\dfrac{r_0}{2}$ (b) $4r_0$

(c) $\dfrac{r_0}{4}$ (d) $2r_0$

7. The energy of electron in the nth orbit of hydrogen atom is expressed as $E_n = \dfrac{-13.6}{n^2}$ eV. The longest wavelength of Lyman series will be

(a) $1213\,\text{Å}$ (b) $7858\,\text{Å}$
(c) $1530\,\text{Å}$ (d) None of these

8. The ionization energy of the electron in the hydrogen atom in its ground state is 13.6 eV. The atoms are excited to higher energy levels to emit radiations of 6 wavelengths. Maximum wavelength of emitted radiation corresponds to the transition between

(a) $n = 3$ to $n = 1$ states
(b) $n = 2$ to $n = 1$ states
(c) $n = 4$ to $n = 3$ states
(d) $n = 3$ to $n = 2$ states

9. A hypothetical atom has only three energy levels. The ground level has energy, $E_1 = -8$ eV. The two excited states have energies, $E_2 = -6$ eV and $E_3 = -2$ eV. Then which of the following wavelengths will not be present in the emission spectrum of this atom?

(a) $207\,\text{nm}$ (b) $465\,\text{nm}$
(c) $310\,\text{nm}$ (d) $620\,\text{nm}$

10. In hydrogen atom, an electron changes its position from orbit $n = 4$ to the orbit In hydrogen atom, $n = 2$ of an atom. The wavelength of the emitted radiation is (R = Rydberg's constant)

(a) $\dfrac{16}{R}$ (b) $\dfrac{16}{3R}$

(c) $\dfrac{16}{5R}$ (d) $\dfrac{16}{7R}$

11. The diagram shows the energy levels for an electron in a certain atom. Which transition shown represents the emission of a photon with the most energy?

(a) IV
(b) III
(c) II
(d) I

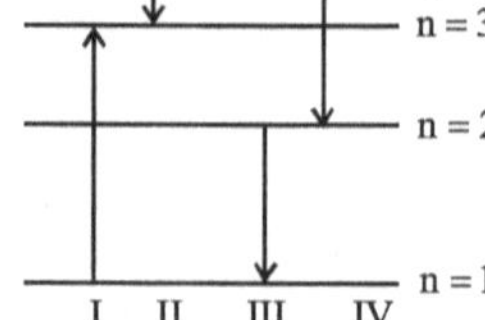

12. The wavelength of the first spectral line in the Balmer series of hydrogen atom is 6561 Å. If the wavelength of the spectral line in the Balmer series of singly-ionized helium atom is 1215Å when electron jumps from n_2 to n_1, then n_2 and n_1 are

(a) $4, 2$ (b) $5, 3$
(c) $6, 3$ (d) $6, 2$

13. In the Bohr model of a hydrogen atom, the centripetal force is furnished by the coulomb attraction between the proton and the electron. If a_0 is the radius of the ground state orbit, m is the mass, e is the charge on the electron and ε_0 is the vacuum permittivity, the speed of the electron is

(a) 0 (b) $\dfrac{e}{\sqrt{\varepsilon_0 a_0 m}}$

(c) $\dfrac{e}{\sqrt{4\pi\varepsilon_0 a_0 m}}$ (d) $\dfrac{\sqrt{4\pi\varepsilon_0\, a_0 m}}{e}$

14. A hydrogen atom, initially in the ground state is excited by absorbing a photon of wavelength 980Å. The radius of the atom in the excited state, in terms of Bohr radius a_0, will be:

(a) $25a_0$ (b) $9a_0$
(c) $16a_0$ (d) $4a_0$

15. A He^+ ion is in its first excited state. Its ionization energy is:

(a) $48.36\,\text{eV}$ (b) $54.40\,\text{eV}$
(c) $13.60\,\text{eV}$ (d) $6.04\,\text{eV}$

16. In Li^{++}, electron in first Bohr orbit is excited to a level by a radiation of wavelength λ. When the ion gets deexcited to the ground state in all possible ways (including intermediate emissions), a total of six spectral lines are observed. What is the value of λ? (Given : $h = 6.63\times10^{-34}$ Js; $c = 3 \times 10^8\,\text{ms}^{-1}$)

(a) $11.4\,\text{nm}$ (b) $9.4\,\text{nm}$
(c) $12.3\,\text{nm}$ (d) $10.8\,\text{nm}$

17. The electron in a hydrogen atom first jumps from the third excited state to the second excited state and subsequently to the first excited state. The ratio of the respective wavelengths, λ_1/λ_2, of the photons emitted in this process is :

(a) 20/7 (b) 27/5

(c) 7/5 (d) 9/7

18. The time period of revolution of electron in its ground state orbit in a hydrogen atom is 1.6×10^{-16} s. The frequency of revolution of the electron in its first excited state (in s^{-1}) is:

(a) 1.6×10^{14} (b) 7.8×10^{14}

(c) 6.2×10^{15} (d) 5.6×10^{12}

19. The electron in the hydrogen atom jumps from excited state (n = 3) to its ground state (n = 1) and the photons thus emitted irradiate a photosensitive material. If the work function of the material is 5.1 eV, the stopping potential is estimated to be (the energy of the electron in n^{th} state $E_n = -\dfrac{13.6}{n^2} eV$)

(a) 5.1 V (b) 12.1 V

(c) 17.2 V (d) 7 V

20. Which of the plots shown in the figure represents speed (v) of the electron in a hydrogen atom as a function of the principal quantum number (n)

(a) B

(b) D

(c) C

(d) A

21. One of the lines in the emission spectrum of Li^{2+} has the same wavelength as that of the 2nd line

of Balmer series in hydrogen spectrum. The electronic transition corresponding to this line is $n = 12 \rightarrow n = x$. Find the value of x.

(a) 8 (b) 6

(c) 7 (c) 5

22. The ionisation energy of hydrogen atom is 13.6 eV. An electron in the ground state of a hydrogen atom absorbs a photon of energy 12.75 eV. How many different spectral lines can one expect when the electron make a downward trnasition

(a) 1 (b) 4

(c) 2 (d) 6

23. In a hypothetical system, a particle of mass m and charge $-3q$ is moving around a very heavy particle of charge q. Assume that Bohr's model is applicable to this system, then velocity of mass m in the first orbit is

(a) $\dfrac{3q^2}{2\varepsilon_0 h}$ (b) $\dfrac{3q^2}{4\varepsilon_0 h}$

(c) $\dfrac{3q}{2\pi\varepsilon_0 h}$ (d) $\dfrac{3q}{4\pi\varepsilon_0 h}$

24. A hydrogen atom makes a transition from n = 2 to n = 1 and emits a photon. This photon strikes a doubly ionized lithium atom (z = 3) in excited state and completely removes the orbiting electron. The least quantum number for the excited state of the ion for the process is :

(a) 2 (b) 4

(c) 5 (d) 3

25. If 13.6 eV energy is required to ionize the hydrogen atom, then the energy required to remove an electron from $n = 2$ is

(a) 10.2 eV (b) 0 eV

(c) 3.4 eV (d) 6.8 eV

ANSWER KEY																								
1	(d)	4	(b)	7	(a)	10	(b)	13	(c)	16	(d)	19	(d)	22	(d)	25	(c)
2	(a)	5	(b)	8	(c)	11	(b)	14	(c)	17	(a)	20	(a)	23	(a)		
3	(b)	6	(a)	9	(b)	12	(a)	15	(c)	18	(b)	21	(b)	24	(b)		

1. The nuclear radius of $_8O^{16}$ is 3×10^{-15} m. If an atomic mass unit is 1.67×10^{-27} kg, then the nuclear density is approximately

   (a) 2.35×10^{17} g cm^{-3}

   (b) 2.35×10^{17} kg m^{-3}

   (c) 2.35×10^{17} gm^{-3}

   (d) 2.35×10^{17} kg mm^{-3}

2. Binding energy per nucleon plot against the mass number for stable nuclei is shown in the figure. Which curve is correct?

   (a) A

   (b) B

   (c) C

   (d) D

3. The ratio of the mass densities of nuclei of ^{40}Ca and ^{16}O is close to :

   (a) 1

   (b) 0.1

   (c) 5

   (d) 2

4. In the reaction, $_1^2H + _1^3H \longrightarrow _2^4He + _0^1n$, if the binding energies of $_1^2H$, $_1^3H$ and $_2^4He$ are respectively, a, b and c (in MeV), then the energy (in MeV) released in this reaction is

   (a) $a + b + c$

   (b) $a + b - c$

   (c) $c - a - b$

   (d) $c + a - b$

5. Two radioactive substances A and B have decay constants 5λ and λ respectively. At t = 0 they have the same number of nuclei. The ratio of number of nuclei of A to those of B will be $(1/e)$ after a time interval

   (a) 4λ

   (b) 2λ

   (c) $1/2\lambda$

   (d) $1/4\lambda$

6. In the uranium radioactive series, the initial nucleus is $_{92}U^{238}$ and that the final nucleus is $_{82}Pb^{206}$. When uranium nucleus decays to lead, the number of α particles and β particles emitted are

   (a) $8\alpha, 6\beta$

   (b) $6\alpha, 7\beta$

   (c) $6\alpha, 8\beta$

   (d) $4\alpha, 3\beta$

7. A radioactive nucleus A with a half life T, decays into a nucleus B. At t = 0, there is no nucleus B. At sometime t, the ratio of the number of B to that of A is 0.3. Then, t is given by

   (a) $t = T \log (1.3)$

   (b) $t = \dfrac{T}{\log(1.3)}$

   (c) $t = T \dfrac{\log 2}{\log 1.3}$

   (d) $t = \dfrac{\log 1.3}{\log 2} T$

8. A piece of wood from a recently cut tree shows 20 decays per minute. A wooden piece of same size placed in a museum (obtained from a tree cut many years back) shows 2 decays per minute. If half life of C^{14} is 5730 years, then age of the wooden piece placed in the museum is approximately:

(a) 10439 years   (b) 13094 years

(c) 19039 years   (d) 39049 years

9. In a radioactive material, fraction of active material remaining after time t is 9/16. The fraction that was remaining after $t/2$ is :

(a) $\dfrac{4}{5}$ (b) $\dfrac{3}{5}$

(c) $\dfrac{3}{4}$ (d) $\dfrac{7}{8}$

10. A radioactive nucleus (initial mass number A and atomic number Z) emits 3α particles and 2 positrons. The ratio of number of neutrons to that of protons in the final nucleus will be

(a) $\dfrac{A-Z-4}{Z-2}$ (b) $\dfrac{A-Z-8}{Z-4}$

(c) $\dfrac{A-Z-4}{Z-8}$ (d) $\dfrac{A-Z-12}{Z-4}$

11. If the binding energies of $^{2}_{1}H$, $^{4}_{2}He$, $^{56}_{26}Fe$ & $^{235}_{92}U$ nuclei are 2.22, 28.3, 492 and 1786 MeV respectively, identify the most stable nucleus of the following.

(a) $^{56}_{26}Fe$ (b) $^{2}_{1}H$ (c) $^{235}_{92}U$ (d) $^{4}_{2}He$

12. The radius of germanium (Ge) nuclide is measured to be twice the radius of $^{9}_{4}Be$. The number of nucleons in Ge are

(a) 74   (b) 75   (c) 72   (d) 73

13. The masses of neutron and proton are 1.0087 a.m.u. and 1.0073 a.m.u. respectively. If the neutrons and protons combine to form a helium nucleus (alpha particles) of mass 4.0015 a.m.u the binding energy of the helium nucleus will be (1 a.m.u. = 931 MeV)

(a) 28.4 MeV   (b) 20.8 MeV

(c) 27.3 MeV   (d) 14.2 MeV

14. A radioactive nucleus decays by two different processes. The half life for the first process is 10 s and that for the second is 100 s. The effective half life of the nucleus is close to :

(a) 9 sec.   (b) 6 sec.

(c) 55 sec.   (d) 12 sec.

15. Let N_{β} be the number of β particles emitted by 1 gram of Na^{24} radioactive nuclei (half life = 15 hrs) in 7.5 hours, N_{β} is close to (Avogadro number = 6.023×10^{23}/g. mole):

(a) 6.2×10^{21} (b) 7.5×10^{21}

(c) 1.25×10^{22} (d) 1.75×10^{22}

16. A sample originally contained 10^{20} radioactive atoms, which emit α-particles. The ratio of α-particles emitted in the third year to that emitted during the second year is 0.3. How many α-particles were emitted in the first year?

(a) 3×10^{18} (b) 3×10^{19}

(c) 5×10^{18} (d) 7×10^{19}

17. A radioactive nuclei with decay constant 0.5/s is being produced at a constant rate of 100 nuclei/s. If at t = 0 there were no nuclei, the time when there are 50 nuclei is:

(a) 1s   (b) $2ln\left(\dfrac{4}{3}\right)$ s

(c) $ln\,2$ s   (d) $ln\left(\dfrac{4}{3}\right)$ s

18. The binding energy per nucleon for $^{2}_{1}H$ and $^{4}_{2}He$ respectively are 1.1 MeV and 7.1 MeV. The energy released in MeV when two $^{2}_{1}H$ nuclei fuse to form $^{4}_{2}He$ is

(a) 4.4   (b) 8.2   (c) 24   (d) 28.4

19. A gamma ray photon creates an electron-positron pair. If the rest mass energy of an electron is 0.5 MeV and the total kinetic energy of the electron-positron pair is 0.78 MeV, then the energy of the gamma ray photon must be

(a) 0.78 MeV   (b) 1.78 MeV

(c) 1.28 MeV   (d) 0.28 MeV

20. In a fission reaction $^{236}_{92}U \rightarrow ^{117}X + ^{117}Y + n + n$ the binding energy per nucleon of X and Y is 8.5 MeV whereas of ^{236}U is 7.6 MeV. The total energy liberated will be about

(a) 2000 MeV (b) 200 MeV

(c) 2 MeV (d) 200 keV

21. A heavy nucleus having mass number 200 gets disintegrated into two small fragments of mass number 80 and 120. If binding energy per nucleon for parent atom is 6.5 MeV and for daughter nuclei is 7 MeV and 8 MeV respectively, then the energy released in the decay is X × 110 MeV. Find the value of X.

(a) 3 (b) 4 (c) 2 (d) 1

22. A radioactive source of half-life 2 hours emits radiation of intensity which is 64 times the permissible safe level. The minimum time in hours after which it would be possible to work safely with the source is

(a) 12 (b) 8 (c) 6 (d) 24

23. The activity of a freshly prepared radioactive sample is 10^{10} disintegrations per second, whose mean life is 10^9 s. The mass of an atom of this radioisotope is 10^{-25} kg. The mass (in mg) of the radioactive sample is

(a) 1 (b) 3 (c) 5 (d) 6

24. Using a nuclear counter the count rate of emitted particles from a radioactive source is measured. At t = 0 it was 1600 counts per second and t = 8 seconds it was 100 counts per second. The count rate observed, as counts per second, at t = 6 seconds is close to:

(a) 200 (b) 150 (c) 400 (d) 360

25. The half life of a radioactive substance is 20 minutes. The approximate time interval $(t_2 - t_1)$ between the time t_2 when $\frac{2}{3}$ of it had decayed and time t_1 when $\frac{1}{3}$ of it had decayed is :

(a) 14 min (b) 20 min (c) 28 min (d) 7 min

ANSWER KEY																	
1	(b)	4	(c)	7	(d)	10	(c)	13	(a)	16	(b)	19	(b)	22	(a)	25	(b)
2	(c)	5	(d)	8	(c)	11	(a)	14	(a)	17	(b)	20	(b)	23	(a)		
3	(a)	6	(a)	9	(c)	12	(c)	15	(b)	18	(c)	21	(c)	24	(a)		

SEMICONDUCTOR ELECTRONICS: MATERIALS, DEVICES AND SIMPLE CIRCUITS

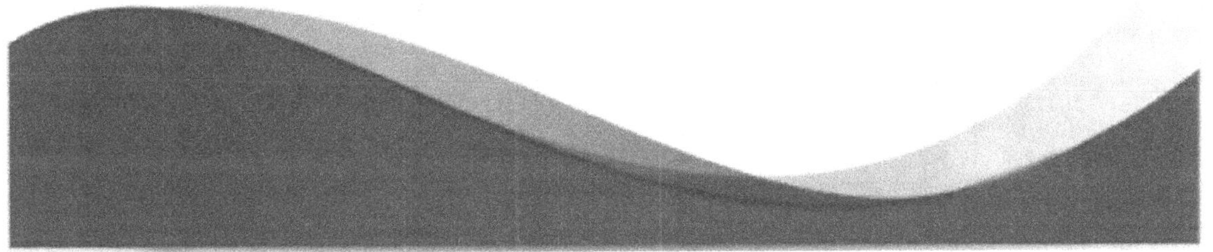

1. The conductivity of intrinsic semiconductor germanium at $27°$ is $2.13\ \text{mho m}^{-1}$ and mobilities of electrons and holes are 0.38 and $0.18\ \text{m}^2\text{V}^{-1}\text{s}^{-1}$ respectively. The density of charge carriers is

   (a) $2.37 \times 10^{19}\ \text{m}^{-3}$
   (b) $3.28 \times 10^{19}\ \text{m}^{-3}$
   (c) $7.83 \times 10^{19}\ \text{m}^{-3}$
   (d) $8.47 \times 10^{19}\ \text{m}^{-3}$

2. Pure Silicon at 500 K has equal electron (n_e) and hole (n_h) concentration of $1.5 \times 10^{16}\ \text{m}^{-3}$. Doping by indium increases n_h to $4.5 \times 10^{22}\ \text{m}^{-3}$. The n_e in the doped silicon is

   (a) 9×10^5
   (b) 5×10^9
   (c) 2.25×10^{11}
   (d) 3×10^{19}

3. The I-V characteristic of a P-N junction diode is shown below. The approximate dynamic resistance of the p-n junction when a forward bias of 2 volt is applied is

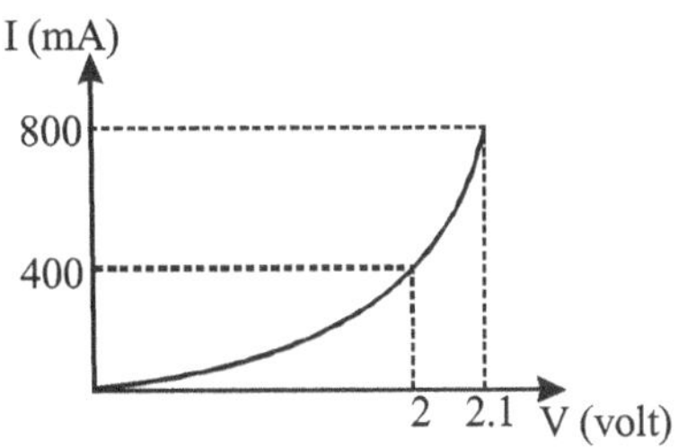

4. A zener diode of voltage V_Z (= 6V) is used to maintain a constant voltage across a load resistance R_L (= 1000 Ω) by using a series resistance R_s (= 100Ω). If the e.m.f. of source is E (= 9 V), what is the power being dissipated in Zener diode ?

   (a) 0.144 watt
   (b) 0.324 watt
   (c) 0.244 watt
   (d) 0.544 watt

   (a) $1\,\Omega$
   (b) $0.25\,\Omega$
   (c) $0.5\,\Omega$
   (d) $5\,\Omega$

5. The electric conductivity of an intrinsic semiconductor increases when the electromagnetic waves of wavelength equal or shorter than 3895 nm is incident on it. The band gap of the semiconductor is

   (a) 1.2 eV
   (b) 0.3 eV
   (c) 1.0 eV
   (d) 1.5 eV

6. What is the conductivity of a semiconductor sample having electron concentration of $5 \times 10^{18}\ \text{m}^{-3}$, hole concentration of $5 \times 10^{19}\ \text{m}^{-3}$, electron mobility of $2.0\ \text{m}^2\ \text{V}^{-1}\ \text{s}^{-1}$ and hole mobility of $0.01\ \text{m}^2\ \text{V}^{-1}\ \text{s}^{-1}$?

   (Take charge of electron as $1.6 \times 10^{-19}\ \text{C}$)

   (a) $1.68\ (\Omega - m)^{-1}$
   (b) $1.83\ (\Omega - m)^{-1}$
   (c) $0.59\ (\Omega - m)^{-1}$
   (d) $1.20\ (\Omega - m)^{-1}$

7. A p-n photodiode is made of a material with a band gap of 2.0eV. The minimum frequency of the radiation that can be absorbed by the material is nearly

(a) $1 \times 10^{14} \, Hz$ (b) $20 \times 10^{14} \, Hz$

(c) $10 \times 10^{14} \, Hz$ (d) $5 \times 10^{14} \, Hz$

8. Figure shows a circuit in which three identical diodes are used. Each diode has forward resistance of 20 Ω and infinite backward resistance. Resistors $R_1 = R_2 = R_3 = 50 \, \Omega$. Battery voltage is 6 V. The current through R_3 is :

(a) 50 mA

(b) 100 mA

(c) 60 mA

(d) 25 mA

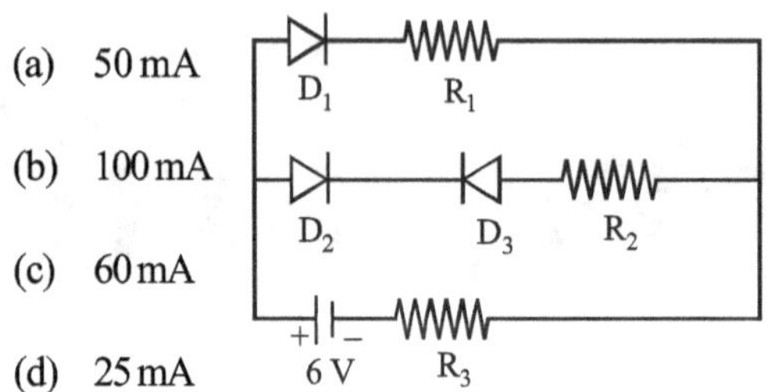

9. In a transistor, a change of 8.0 mA in the emitter current produces a change of 7.8 mA in the collector current. What change in the base current is necessary to produce the same change in the collector current?

(a) 50 μA   (b) 100 μA

(c) 150 μA   (d) 200 μA

10. In a *CE* transistor amplifier, the audio signal voltage across the collector resistance of 2 kΩ is 2 V. If the base resistance is 1 kΩ and the current amplification of the transistor is 100, the input signal voltage is :

(a) 0.1 V   (b) 1.0 V

(c) 1mV   (d) 10 mV

11. A Zener diode is connected to a battery and a load as shown below:

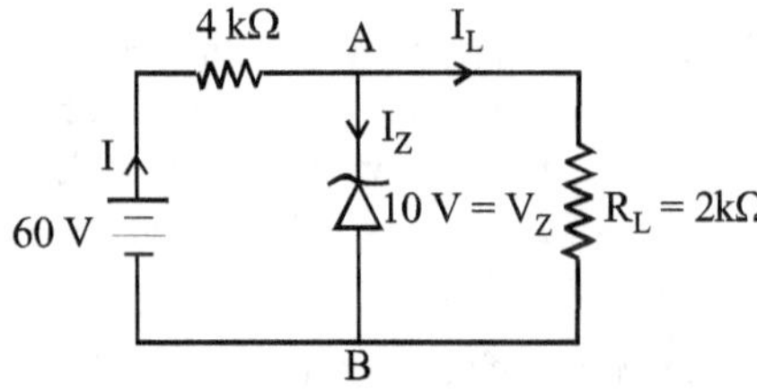

The currents, I, I_Z and I_L are respectively.

(a) 15 mA, 5 mA, 10 mA

(b) 15 mA, 7.5 mA, 7.5 mA

(c) 12.5 mA, 5 mA, 7.5 mA

(d) 12.5 mA, 7.5 mA, 5 mA

12. In a common emitter configuration with suitable bias, it is given than R_L is the load resistance and R_{BE} is small signal dynamic resistance (input side). Then, voltage gain, current gain and power gain are given, respectively, by:

(β is current gain, I_B, I_C, I_E are respectively base, collector and emitter currents)

(a) $\beta \dfrac{R_L}{R_{BE}}, \dfrac{\Delta I_E}{\Delta I_B}, \beta^2 \dfrac{R_L}{R_{BE}}$

(b) $\beta^2 \dfrac{R_L}{R_{BE}}, \dfrac{\Delta I_C}{\Delta I_B}, \beta \dfrac{R_L}{R_{BE}}$

(c) $\beta^2 \dfrac{R_L}{R_{BE}}, \dfrac{\Delta I_C}{\Delta I_E}, \beta^2 \dfrac{R_L}{R_{BE}}$

(d) $\beta \dfrac{R_L}{R_{BE}}, \dfrac{\Delta I_C}{\Delta I_B}, \beta^2 \dfrac{R_L}{R_{BE}}$

13. The input resistance of a silicon transistor is 100 Ω. Base current is changed by 40 μA which results in a change in collector current by 2 mA. This transistor is used as a common emitter amplifier with a load resistance of 4 kΩ. The power gain of the amplifier is :

(a) 10^5 (b) 10^3

(c) 10^6 (d) 10^2

14. With increasing biasing voltage of a photodiode, the photocurrent magnitude :

(a) remains constant

(b) increases initially and after attaining certain value, it decreases

(c) Increases linearly

(d) increases initially and saturates finally

15. In the given circuit, the current through zener diode is:

(a) 2.5mA

(b) 3.3mA

(c) 5.5mA

(d) 6.7mA

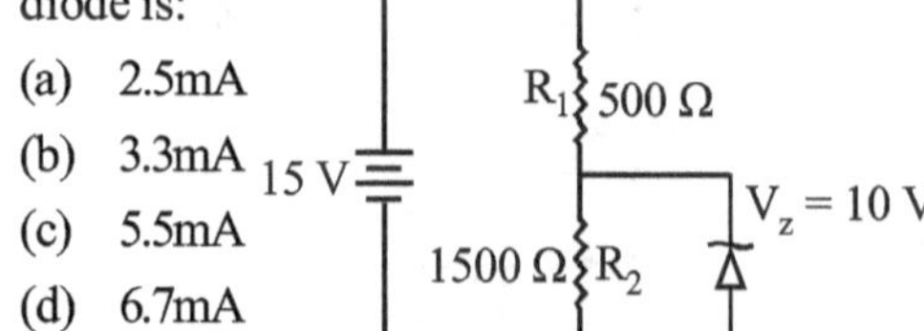

16. The I-V characteristic of an LED is

(a)
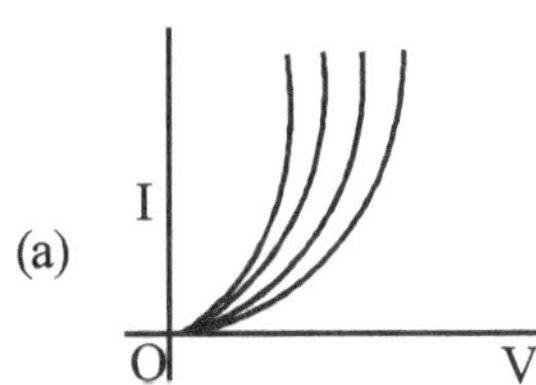

(b)
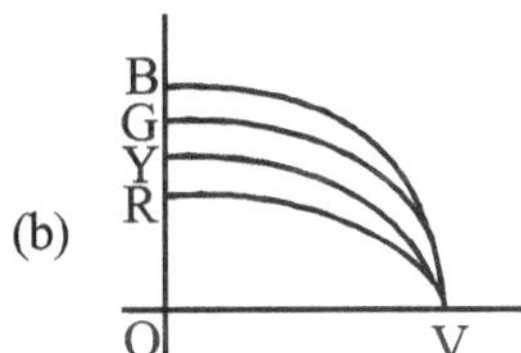

(c)
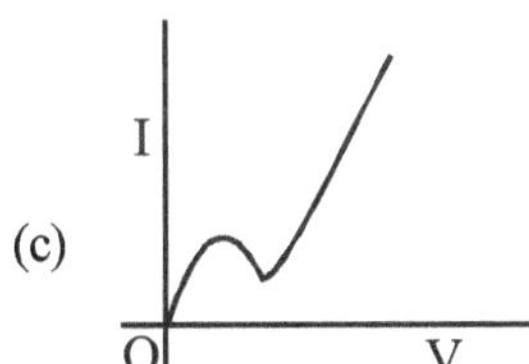

(d)
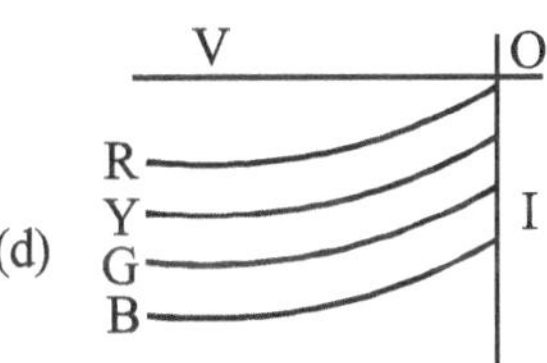

17. A pure semiconductor has equal electron and hole concentration of 10^{16} m^{-3}. Doping by gallium increases n_h to 5×10^{22} m^{-3}. Then, the value of n_e in the doped semiconductor is

(a) 10^6/m^3

(b) 10^{22}/m^3

(c) 2×10^6/m^3

(d) 2×10^9/m^3

18. A diode having potential difference 0.5 V across its junction which does not depend on current, is connected in series with resistance of 20Ω across source. If 0.1 A current passes through resistance then what is the voltage of the source?

(a) 1.5 V

(b) 2.0 V

(c) 2.5 V

(d) 5 V

19. A common emitter amplifier has a voltage gain of 49, an input impedance of 100Ω and an output impedance of 490Ω. The power gain of the amplifier is

(a) 500

(b) 499

(c) 490

(d) 501

20. If the given transistor is used as an amplifier then for input resistance of 80Ω and load resistance of 16kΩ, the output voltage corresponding to the input voltage of 12mV will be

(a) 37.5 mV

(b) 37500 V

(c) 300 V

(d) 300mV

21. Figure consists of two NOT gates followed by a NOR gate. This combination is equivalent to a single

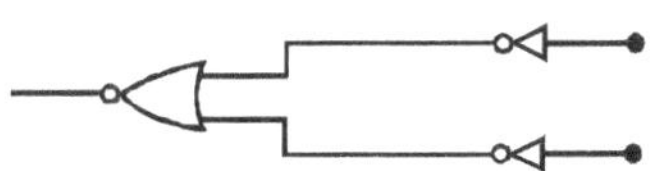

(a) NAND gate

(b) AND gate

(c) OR gate

(d) XOR gate

22. The load resistance and the input resistance of a CE amplifier are respectively 10 kΩ and 2 kΩ. If β of the transistor is 49, the voltage gain of the amplifier is

(a) 125

(b) 150

(c) 175

(d) 245

23. A logic gate and its truth table are shown below:

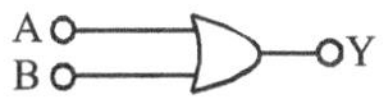

A	B	Y
0	0	0
0	1	1
1	0	1
1	1	1

The gate is :

(a) NOR

(b) AND

(c) OR

(d) NOT

24. The given figure shows the wave forms for two inputs A and B and that for the output Y of a logic circuit. The logic circuit is a/an.

(a) AND gate

(b) OR gate

(c) NAND

(d) NOT gate

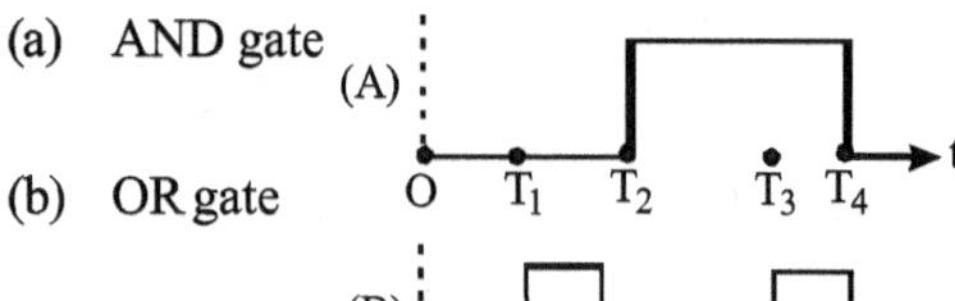

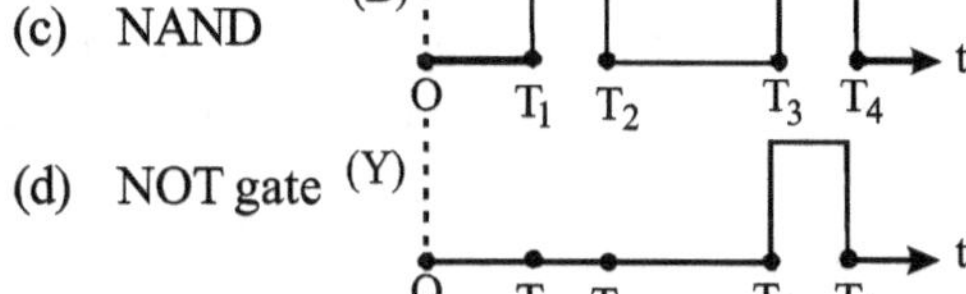

25. To get an output 1 from the circuit shown in the figure, the input must be

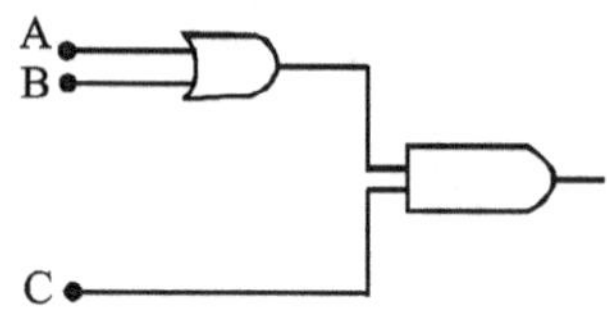

(a) $A = 0, B = 1, C = 0$ (b) $A = 1, B = 0, C = 0$

(c) $A = 1, B = 0, C = 1$ (d) $A = 1, B = 1, C = 0$

								ANSWER KEY									
1	(a)	**4**	(a)	**7**	(d)	**10**	(d)	**13**	(a)	**16**	(a)	**19**	(c)	**22**	(d)	**25**	(c)
2	(b)	**5**	(b)	**8**	(a)	**11**	(d)	**14**	(d)	**17**	(d)	**20**	(c)	**23**	(c)		
3	(b)	**6**	(a)	**9**	(d)	**12**	(d)	**15**	(b)	**18**	(c)	**21**	(b)	**24**	(a)		

1 Physical World, Units and Measurements

1. **(b)** The work done = force × displacement

$\therefore$ unit, $u_1 = Fs$

and $u_2 = 4F \times 4s = 16u$.

2. **(b)** $\vec{E} \times \vec{B} \rightarrow (MLT^{-3}A^{-1}) \times (MT^{-2}A^{-1})$

$= M^2LT^{-5}A^{-2}$.

3. **(c)**

4. **(b)** Maximum number of significant figures should be only 3 digits.

5. **(d)** For angular momentum, the dimensional formula is $[ML^2T^{-1}]$. For other three, it is $[ML^{-1}T^{-2}]$.

6. **(b)**

7. **(b)** $\dfrac{\text{Planck's constant}}{\text{Moment of inertia}} = \dfrac{\dfrac{2\pi I\omega}{n}}{I} \left[\text{As } \dfrac{nh}{2\pi} = I\omega \right]$

$= \dfrac{2\pi I(2\pi f)}{nI} = \left(\dfrac{4\pi^2}{n}.f \right) = [T^{-1}]$

8. **(c)**

9. **(d)** $\dfrac{\Delta Q}{Q} \times 100$

$= \dfrac{2\Delta I}{I} \times 100 + \dfrac{\Delta R}{R} \times 100 + \dfrac{\Delta t}{t} \times 100$

$= 2 \times 2\% + 1\% + 1\% = 6\%$.

10. **(a)** Let $m = KF^a L^b T^c$

Substituting the dimensions of

$[F] = [MLT^{-2}]$, $[L] = [L]$ and $[T] = [T]$ and comparing both side, we get $m = FL^{-1}T^2$

11. **(d)**

12. **(b)** In $p = p_0 \exp(-\alpha t^2)$, αt^2 dimensionless

$\therefore \alpha = \dfrac{1}{t^2} = \dfrac{1}{T^2} = [T^{-2}]$

13. **(a)** Here, at is dimensionless

$\Rightarrow a = \dfrac{1}{t} = \left[\dfrac{1}{T} \right] = [T^{-1}]$, $\quad x = \dfrac{V_0}{a}$

and $V_0 = xa = [LT^{-1}] = [M^0 LT^{-1}]$

14. **(a)** $\tau = F \times r \times \sin\theta$; $W = F \times d \times \cos\theta$

Dimensionally, light year = wavelength = $[L]$

15. **(a)** $\dfrac{[ML^2T^{-2}][ML^2T^{-1}]^2}{[M^5][M^{-1}L^3T^{-2}]^2} = [M^0L^0T^0]$

$= $ angle.

16. **(b)**

17. **(a)** $\sqrt{\dfrac{\mu_0}{\varepsilon_0}} = \sqrt{\dfrac{\mu_0^2}{\varepsilon_0\mu_0}} = \mu_0 c$ $\quad \left(\dfrac{1}{\sqrt{\mu_0\varepsilon_0}} = c \right)$

$\mu_0 c \rightarrow MLT^{-2}A^{-2} \times LT^{-1}$

$ML^2T^{-3}A^{-2}$

Dimensions of resistance

18. **(c)** Given, Length of simple pendulum,

$l = 25.0$ cm

Time of 40 oscillation, $T = 50s$

Time period of pendulum

$T = 2\pi\sqrt{\dfrac{\ell}{g}}$

$$\Rightarrow T^2 = \frac{4\pi^2 \ell}{g} \Rightarrow g = \frac{4\pi^2 \ell}{T^2}$$

$\Rightarrow$ Fractional error in $g = \dfrac{\Delta g}{g} = \dfrac{\Delta l}{l} + \dfrac{2\Delta T}{T}$

$$\Rightarrow \frac{\Delta g}{g} = \left(\frac{0.1}{25.0}\right) + 2\left(\frac{1}{50}\right) = 0.044$$

$\therefore$ Percentage error in $g = \dfrac{\Delta g}{g} \times 100 = 4.4\%$

19. **(d)** $A = 7 \times 5.29 = 37.03 \text{ cm}^2$

The result should have three significant figures, so $A = 37.0 \text{ cm}^2$

20. **(a)** Thickness = M.S. Reading + Circular Scale Reading (L.C.)

Here $LC = \dfrac{\text{Pitch}}{\text{Circular scale division}}$

$$= \frac{0.1}{50} = 0.002 \text{ cm per division}$$

So, correct measurement is measurement of integral multiple of L.C.

21. **(b)** According to question

$$E_y \propto J_x B_z$$

$\therefore$ Constant of proportionality

$$K = \frac{E_y}{B_z J_x} = \frac{C}{J_x} = \frac{m^3}{As}$$

$$\left[\text{As } \frac{E}{B} = C \text{ (speed of light) and } J = \frac{I}{\text{Area}}\right]$$

22. **(a)** Momentum, $p = m \times v$

Given, mass of a body = 3.513 kg speed of body

$= (3.513) \times (5.00) = 17.565 \text{ kg m/s}$

= 17.6 (Rounding off to get three significant figures)

23. **(d)** Given : $Z = \dfrac{a^2 b^{2/3}}{\sqrt{c}\, d^3}$

Percentage error in Z,

$$= \frac{\Delta Z}{Z} = \frac{2\Delta a}{a} + \frac{2}{3}\frac{\Delta b}{b} + \frac{1}{2}\frac{\Delta c}{c} + \frac{3\Delta d}{d}$$

$$= 2 \times 2 + \frac{2}{3} \times 1.5 + \frac{1}{2} \times 4 + 3 \times 2.5 = 14.5\%.$$

24. **(c)** $x = at + bt^2 - ct^3$

$$\therefore \quad ct^3 = x \Rightarrow c = \frac{x}{t^3} = \frac{[L]}{[T^3]} = \left[LT^{-3}\right]$$

25. **(c)** Given, $y = \cos(\omega t + kx)$

$(\omega t + kx)$ is an angle and hence it is a dimension less quantity.

$$[(\omega t + kx)] = [M^0 L^0 T^0]$$

or $[\omega t] = [M^0 L^0 T^0]$

$$[\omega] = \frac{[M^0 L^0 T^0]}{[T]} = [M^0 L^0 T^{-1}]$$

2   Motion in a Straight Line

1.   **(c)** $\bar{v} = \dfrac{(8 \times 1 - 3 \times 1 \times 1) - 0}{1} = 5\,\text{ms}^{-1}$

2.   **(b)** $|\text{Average velocity}| = \dfrac{|\text{displacement}|}{\text{time}}$

$$= \dfrac{2r}{t} = 2 \times \dfrac{1}{1} = 2\,\text{m/s}.$$

3.   **(b)**

4.   **(b)** $\sqrt{x} = (t+7)$ or $x = (t+7)^2$

$\dfrac{dx}{dt} = 2(t+7)$, $\therefore$ velocity $\propto$ time

5.   **(d)**   At E, the slope of the curve is negative as

$$v = \dfrac{ds}{dt}.$$

6.   **(a)** $v = \alpha\sqrt{x} \Rightarrow \dfrac{dx}{dt} = \alpha\sqrt{x}$

$$\dfrac{dx}{\sqrt{x}} = \alpha\,dt \Rightarrow \int_0^x \dfrac{dx}{\sqrt{x}} = \alpha\int_0^t dt$$

$$\Rightarrow \left[\dfrac{2\sqrt{x}}{1}\right]_0^x = \alpha[t]_0^t$$

$$\Rightarrow 2\sqrt{x} = \alpha t \Rightarrow x = \dfrac{\alpha^2}{4}t^2$$

7.   **(b)**   From $v^2 = u^2 + 2as \Rightarrow 0 = u^2 + 2as$

$$\Rightarrow a = \dfrac{-u^2}{2s} = \dfrac{-(20)^2}{2 \times 10} = -20\,\text{m/sec}^2$$

8.   **(c)** $s_x = u_x t + \dfrac{1}{2}a_x t^2 \Rightarrow s_x = \dfrac{1}{2} \times 6 \times 16 = 48\,\text{m}$

$$s_y = u_y t + \dfrac{1}{2}a_y t^2 \Rightarrow s_y = \dfrac{1}{2} \times 8 \times 16 = 64\,\text{m}$$

$$s = \sqrt{s_x^2 + s_y^2} = 80\,\text{m}$$

9.   **(b)** $8 = a\,t_1$ and $0 = 8 - a\,(4 - t_1)$

or $t_1 = \dfrac{8}{a}$ $\therefore$ $8 = a\left(4 - \dfrac{8}{a}\right)$

$8 = 4\,a - 8$ or $a = 4$ and $t_1 = 8/4 = 2$ sec

Now, $s_1 = 0 \times 2 + \dfrac{1}{2} \times 4\,(2)^2$ or $s_1 = 8\,\text{m}$

$$s_2 = 8 \times 2 - \dfrac{1}{2} \times 4 \times (2)^2 \quad \text{or} \quad s_2 = 8\,\text{m}$$

$\therefore$ $s_1 + s_2 = 16\,\text{m}$

10.   **(b)**   In one dimensional motion, the body can have at a time one velocity but not two values of velocities.

11.   **(a)** $v = \sqrt{3x + 16} \Rightarrow v^2 = 3x + 16$

$$\Rightarrow v^2 - 16 = 3x$$

Comparing with $v^2 - u^2 = 2ax$, we get, u = 4 units, 2a = 3 or a = 1.5 units

12.   **(c)**   The speed of an object, falling freely due to gravity, depends only on its height and not on its mass. Since the paths are frictionless and all the objects fall through the same height, therefore, their speeds on reaching the ground will be in the ratio of $1 : 1 : 1$.

13.   **(a)**   Since total displacement is zero, hence average velocity is also zero.

14.   **(d)** $V_m = L\,\dfrac{(t_1 + t_2)}{t_1\,t_2}$

$$t = \dfrac{L}{V_m} = \left[\dfrac{t_1\,t_2}{t_1 + t_2}\right]$$

15. **(c)** Initial relative velocity $v_A - v_B$, is reduced to 0 in distance d' ($<d$) with retardation a.

$$\therefore \quad 0^2 - (v_A - v_B)^2 = -2\,ad'$$

$$d' = \frac{(v_A - v_B)^2}{2a} \quad \therefore \quad d > \frac{(v_A - v_B)^2}{2a}$$

16. **(c)**

17. **(c)** **Fir first case :** Initial velocity,

$$u = 50 \times \frac{5}{18}\,m/s,$$

$$v = 0, s = 6m, a = a$$

Using, $v^2 - u^2 = 2as$

$$\Rightarrow 0^2 - \left(50 \times \frac{5}{18}\right)^2 = 2 \times a \times 6$$

$$\Rightarrow -\left(50 \times \frac{5}{18}\right)^2 = 2 \times a \times 6$$

$$a = -\frac{250 \times 250}{324 \times 2 \times 6} \approx -16\,ms^{-2}.$$

Case-2 : Initial velocity, $u = 100\,km/hr$

$$= 100 \times \frac{5}{18}\ m/sec$$

$$v = 0, s = s, a = a$$

As $v^2 - u^2 = 2as$

$$\Rightarrow 0^2 - \left(100 \times \frac{5}{18}\right)^2 = 2as$$

$$\Rightarrow -\left(100 \times \frac{5}{18}\right)^2 = 2 \times (-16) \times 5$$

$$s = \frac{500 \times 500}{324 \times 32} = 24m$$

18. **(b)**

19. **(c)** According to question, object is moving with constant negative acceleration i.e., a = – constant (C)

$$\frac{v\,dv}{dx} = -C$$

$$v\,dv = -C\,dx$$

$$\frac{v^2}{2} = -Cx + k \qquad x = -\frac{v^2}{2C} + \frac{k}{C}$$

Hence, graph (c) represents correctly.

20. **(c)** Average speed

$$= \frac{\text{Total distance travelled}}{\text{Total time taken}} = \frac{x}{T}$$

$$= \frac{x}{\dfrac{x}{2 \times 40} + \dfrac{x}{2 \times 60}} = 48\ km/h$$

21. **(c)** Let time taken by A to reach finishing point is t_0

$\therefore$ Time taken by B to reach finishing point

$$= t_0 + t$$

$$v_A - v_B = v$$

$$\Rightarrow v = a_1 t_0 - a_2 (t_0 + t) = (a_1 - a_2)t_0 - a_2 t \ ...(i)$$

$$x_B = x_A = \frac{1}{2} a_1 t_0^2 = \frac{1}{2} a_2 (t_0 + t)^2$$

$$\Rightarrow \sqrt{a_1} t_0 = \sqrt{a_2} (t_0 + t)$$

$$\Rightarrow \left(\sqrt{a_1} - \sqrt{a_2}\right) t_0 = \sqrt{a_2} t$$

$$\Rightarrow t_0 = \frac{\sqrt{a_2} t}{\sqrt{a_1} - \sqrt{a_2}}$$

Putting this value of t_0 in equation (i)

$$v = (a_1 - a_2)\frac{\sqrt{a_2} t}{\sqrt{a_1} - \sqrt{a_2}} - a_2 t$$

$$= \left(\sqrt{a_1} + \sqrt{a_2}\right)\sqrt{a_2} t - a_2 t = \sqrt{a_1 a_2} t + a_2 t - a_2 t$$

or, $v = \sqrt{a_1 a_2}\, t$

22. **(c)** Acceleration $a = \tan\theta$, where θ is the angle of tangent drawn on the velocity-time graph.

23. **(a)**

24. **(c)** We have, $S_n = u + \dfrac{a}{2}(2n-1)$

or $\quad 65 = u + \dfrac{a}{2}(2\times5-1)$

or $\quad 65 = u + \dfrac{9}{2}a \qquad\qquad .....\text{(i)}$

Also, $105 = u + \dfrac{a}{2}(2\times9-1)$

or $\quad 105 = u + \dfrac{17}{2}a \qquad\qquad .....\text{(ii)}$

Equation (ii) – (i) gives,

$40 = \dfrac{17}{2}a - \dfrac{9}{2}a = 4a$ or $a = 10\ \text{m/s}^2$.

Substitute this value in (i) we get,

$u = 65 - \dfrac{9}{2}\times10 = 65 - 45 = 20\ \text{m/s}$

$\therefore$ The distance travelled by the body in 20 s is,

$s = ut + \dfrac{1}{2}at^2 = 20\times20 + \dfrac{1}{2}\times10\times(20)^2$

$\quad = 400 + 2000 = 2400\ \text{m}.$

25. **(b)** $x = 40 + 12\,t - t^3, \quad V = \dfrac{dx}{dt} = 12 - 3t^2$

For $V = 0; \quad t = \sqrt{\dfrac{12}{3}} = 2\ \text{sec}$

So, after 2 seconds velocity becomes zero.

Value of x in 2 secs $= 40 + 12.2 - 2^3 = 40 + 24 - 8$

$= 56\ \text{m}$

26. **(d)**

27. **(b)** For stone to be dropped from rising balloon of velocity 29 m/s, $u = -29$ m/s, $t = 10$ sec.

$\therefore\ h = -29\times10 + \dfrac{1}{2}\times9.8\times100$

$\qquad = -290 + 490 = 200\ \text{m}.$

28. **(c)** For first body, $16 = \dfrac{1}{2}gt_1^{\,2}$; second body,

$25 = \dfrac{1}{2}gt_2^2$

$\therefore\ \dfrac{16}{25} = \dfrac{t_1^{\,2}}{t_2^{\,2}} \Rightarrow \dfrac{t_1}{t_2} = \dfrac{4}{5}.$

29. **(a)** Instantaneous velocity $v = \dfrac{\Delta x}{\Delta t}$

From graph, $v_A = \dfrac{\Delta x_A}{\Delta t_A} = \dfrac{4m}{8s} = 0.5\ \text{m/s}$

and $v_B = \dfrac{\Delta x_B}{\Delta t_B} = \dfrac{8m}{16s} = 0.5\ \text{m/s}$

30. **(c)** Distance travelled in fifth second for first body = distance travelled in 3rd second for second body, $S_5 = S_3$

$S_t = u + \dfrac{(2t-1)a}{2}; \quad S_5 = 0 + \dfrac{9}{2}a_1;$

$S_3 = 0 + \dfrac{5}{2}a_2$

$\dfrac{9}{2}a_1 = \dfrac{5}{2}a_2 \Rightarrow \dfrac{a_1}{a_2} = \dfrac{5}{9}$

3   Motion in a Plane

1. (b) Unit vector along y axis $= \hat{j}$, so the required vector

$$= \hat{j} - [(\hat{i} - 3\hat{j} + 2\hat{k}) + (3\hat{i} + 6\hat{j} + 7\hat{k})]$$

$$= -4\hat{i} - 2\hat{j} - 9\hat{k}$$

2. (a) Note that the given angles of projection add upto $90°$. So, the ratio of horizontal ranges is $1:1$.

3. (c) $\vec{A} = 3\hat{i} + 4\hat{j} + 5\hat{k}$, $\vec{B} = 3\hat{i} + 4\hat{j} - 5\hat{k}$

$$\vec{A}.\vec{B} = (3\hat{i} + 4\hat{j} + 5\hat{k}).(3\hat{i} + 4\hat{j} - 5\hat{k})$$

$$|\vec{A}|\,|\vec{B}|\cos\theta = 9 + 16 - 25 = 0$$

$|\vec{A}| \neq 0$, $|\vec{B}| \neq 0$, hence, $\cos\theta = 0 \Rightarrow \theta = 90°$

4. (c) $500\cos\theta = 250 \Rightarrow \cos\theta = \dfrac{1}{2}$

or $\theta = 60°$.

5. (a) The horizontal distance covered by bomb,

$$BC = u_H \times \sqrt{\frac{2h}{g}}$$

$$= 150\sqrt{\frac{2 \times 80}{10}} = 600\,\text{m}$$

∴ The distance of target from dropping point of bomb.

$$AC = \sqrt{AB^2 + BC^2} = \sqrt{(80)^2 + (600)^2}$$

$$= 605.3\,\text{m}$$

6. (d) Standard equation of projectile motion

$$y = x\tan\theta - \frac{gx^2}{2u^2\cos^2\theta}$$

Comparing with given equation

$$A = \tan\theta \quad \text{and} \quad B = \frac{g}{2u^2\cos^2\theta}$$

So $\dfrac{A}{B} = \dfrac{\tan\theta \times 2u^2\cos^2\theta}{g} = 40$

(As $\theta = 45°$, $u = 20$ m/s, $g = 10$ m/s^2)

7. (b) Maximum possible horizontal range $= v^2/g$

Maximum possible area of the circle

$$= \pi\left(\frac{v^2}{g}\right)^2 = \frac{\pi\,v^4}{g^2}$$

8. (b)

9. (d) $t = \dfrac{2u\sin 30°}{g\cos 30°} = \dfrac{2(10)\,(1/2)}{10\,(\sqrt{3}/2)} = \dfrac{2}{\sqrt{3}}$ sec

$$R = 10\cos 30°\,t - \frac{1}{2}\,g\sin 30°\,t^2$$

$$= \frac{10\sqrt{3}}{2}\left(\frac{2}{\sqrt{3}}\right) - \frac{1}{2}(10)\left(\frac{1}{2}\right)\frac{4}{3}$$

$$= 10 - \frac{10}{3} = \frac{20}{3}\,\text{m}$$

10. (c) When a particle moves on a circular path with a constant speed, then its motion is said to be a uniform circular motion in a plane. This motion has radial acceleration whose magnitude remains constant but whose direction changes continuously, So $a_r \neq 0$ and $a_t = 0$.

11. (c) Speed, $v = $ constant (from question)

Centripetal acceleration, $a = \dfrac{V^2}{r}$

$$ra = \text{constant}$$

Hence graph (c) correctly describes relation between acceleration and radius.

12. **(d)**

13. **(c)** If t is the time of flight, then

$$0 = v t - \frac{1}{2}(g \cos \theta)t^2.$$

$$\therefore \quad t = \frac{2v}{g \cos \theta}$$

Range , $R = 0 + \frac{1}{2}(g \sin \theta)t^2 = \frac{1}{2}g \sin \theta \left(\frac{2v}{g \cos \theta}\right)^2$

$$= \frac{2v^2 \tan \theta \sec \theta}{g}$$

14. **(d)** Centripetal acc,

$$a_c = \frac{v^2}{r} = \frac{(30)^2}{500} = 1.8 \, m/s^2$$

Tangentical acc, $a_t = 2 \, m/s^2$

$\therefore$ Resultant acc, $a = \sqrt{a_t^2 + a_c^2} = 2.7 \, m/s^2$

15. **(c)**

16. **(c)** $H_{max} = \frac{u^2 \sin^2 q}{2g}$

According to question,

$$\frac{u_1^2 \sin^2 45°}{2g} = \frac{u_2^2 \sin^2 60°}{2g}$$

$$\Rightarrow \frac{u_1^2}{u_2^2} = \frac{\sin^2 60°}{\sin^2 45°} \Rightarrow \frac{u_1}{u_2} = \frac{\sqrt{3}/2}{1/\sqrt{2}} = \sqrt{\frac{3}{2}}.$$

17. **(d)** As maximum height attained by each one is same, so u_y is also same. As

$$T = \frac{2u_y}{g},$$

So $T_1 = T_2 = T_3$.

18. **(b)** From equation, $\vec{v} = \hat{i} + 2\hat{j}$

$$\Rightarrow x = t \qquad \qquad \ldots(i)$$

$$y = 2t - \frac{1}{2}(10t^2) \qquad \qquad \ldots(ii)$$

From (i) and (ii), $y = 2x - 5x^2$

19. **(a)** Here, $R = 0.1 \, m$

$$\omega = \frac{2\pi}{T} = \frac{2\pi}{60} = 0.105 \, rad/s$$

Acceleration of the tip of the clock second's hand,

$$a = \omega^2 R = (0.105)^2 (0.1) = 0.0011$$

$$= 1.1 \times 10^{-3} \, m/s^2$$

Hence, average acceleration is of the order of 10^{-3}.

20. **(a)** Given $\vec{u} = 3\hat{i} + 4\hat{j}, \vec{a} = 0.4\hat{i} + 0.3\hat{j}, t = 10 \, s$

From 1st equatoin of motion.

$$a = \frac{v - u}{t}$$

$$\therefore v = at \, tu$$

$$\Rightarrow v = \left(0.4\hat{i} + 0.3\hat{j}\right) \times 10 + \left(3\hat{i} + 4\hat{j}\right)$$

$$\Rightarrow \quad 4\hat{i} + 3\hat{j} + 3\hat{j} + 4\hat{j}$$

$$\Rightarrow \quad v = 7\hat{i} + 7\hat{j}$$

$$\Rightarrow \quad |\vec{v}| = \sqrt{7^2 + 7^2} = 7\sqrt{2} \, \text{unit.}$$

21. **(d)**

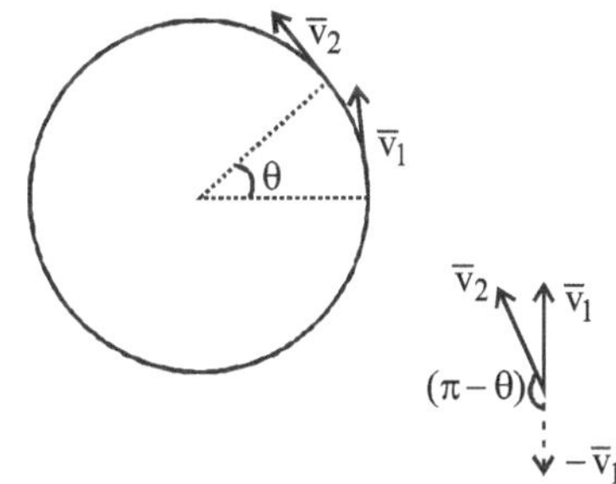

Change in velocity,

$$|\Delta \vec{v}| = \sqrt{v_1^2 + v_2^2 + 2v_1 v_2 \cos(\pi - \theta)}$$

$$= 2v \sin \frac{\theta}{2} \qquad \left(\because |\vec{v}_1| = |\vec{v}_2|\right) = v$$

$$= (2 \times 10) \times \sin(30°) = 2 \times 10 \times \frac{1}{2}$$

$$= 10 \, m/s$$

22. **(c)**

23. **(d)** Tower height and final height is same so, required range is:

$$R = \frac{u^2 \sin 2\theta}{g} = \frac{(20)^2 \sin(2 \times 45°)}{10} = 40 \text{ m}$$

24. **(a)**

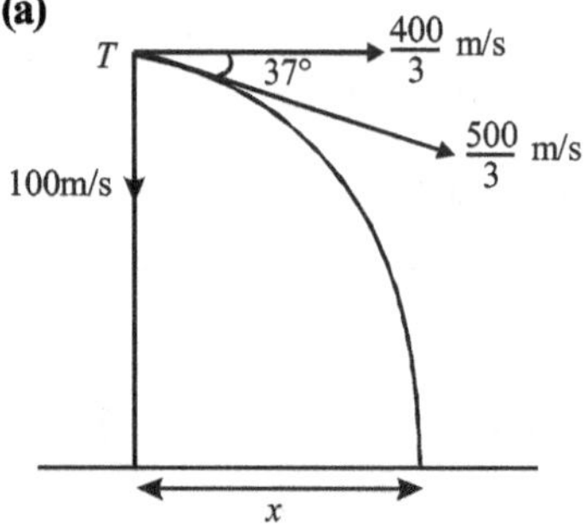

$$1500 = 100t + \frac{1}{2}10t^2 \; ; t = 10 \text{ sec.}$$

$$x = \frac{400}{3}t = \frac{4000}{3} \text{ m}$$

25. **(b)**

26. **(b)**

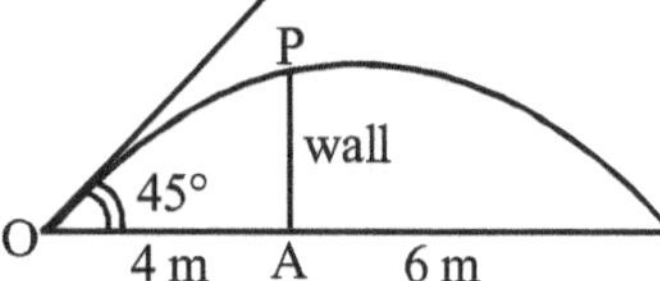

As ball is projected at an angle 45° to the horizontal therefore Range = 4H

or $\quad 10 = 4H \Rightarrow H = \dfrac{10}{4} = 2.5 \text{ m}$

$\quad(\because \text{Range} = 4\text{ m} + 6\text{ m} = 10\text{m})$

Maximum height, $H = \dfrac{u^2 \sin^2 \theta}{2g}$

$$\therefore \; u^2 = \frac{H \times 2g}{\sin^2 \theta} = \frac{2.5 \times 2 \times 10}{\left(\dfrac{1}{\sqrt{2}}\right)^2} = 100$$

or, $\quad u = \sqrt{100} = 10 \text{ ms}^{-1}$

Height of wall PA

$$= OA \tan \theta - \frac{1}{2}\frac{g(OA)^2}{u^2 \cos^2 \theta}$$

$$= 4 - \frac{1}{2} \times \frac{10 \times 16}{10 \times 10 \times \dfrac{1}{\sqrt{2}} \times \dfrac{1}{\sqrt{2}}} = 2.4 \text{ m}$$

27. **(a)**

28. **(c)** Yes, Man will catch the ball, if the horizontal component of velocity becomes equal to the constant speed of man.

$$\frac{v_o}{2} = v_o \cos\theta$$

or $\quad \theta = 60°$

29. **(d)** R will be same for θ and $90° - \theta$.

Time of flights:

$$t_1 = \frac{2u \sin \theta}{g} \text{ and}$$

$$t_2 = \frac{2u \sin(90° - \theta)}{g} = \frac{2u \cos \theta}{g}$$

Now, $t_1 t_2 = \left(\dfrac{2u \sin \theta}{g}\right)\left(\dfrac{2u \cos \theta}{g}\right)$

$$= \frac{2}{g}\left(\frac{u^2 \sin 2\theta}{g}\right) = \frac{2R}{g}$$

30. **(b)** For same range, the angle of projections are :

θ and $90° - \theta$. So,

$$h_1 = \frac{u^2 \sin^2 \theta}{2g} \text{ and}$$

$$h_2 = \frac{u^2 \sin^2(90° - \theta)}{2g} = \frac{u^2 \cos^2 \theta}{2g}$$

Also, $R = \dfrac{u^2 \sin 2\theta}{g}$

$$h_1 h_2 = \frac{u^2 \sin^2 \theta}{2g} \times \frac{u^2 \cos^2 \theta}{2g}$$

$$= \frac{u^2}{16} \frac{u^2 (2\sin \theta \cos \theta)^2}{g^2}$$

$$= \frac{R^2}{16}$$

or $R^2 = 16\, h_1 h_2$

4 — Laws of Motion

1. **(c)** $F = \dfrac{m(v-u)}{t} = \dfrac{0.15(0-20)}{0.1} = 30\,N$

2. **(d)** $v^2 = u^2 - 2gh$

   or $v = \sqrt{u^2 - 2gh}$

   Momentum, $P = mv$

   $= m\sqrt{u^2 - 2gh}$

   At $h = 0$, $P = mu$ and at $h = \dfrac{u^2}{f}, P = 0$

   upward direction is positive and downward direction is negative.

3. **(b)** As in fig. the mass of the rope : $m = 4 \times 1.5$ $= 6\,kg$

   Acceleration : $a = 12/6 = 2\,m/s^2$

   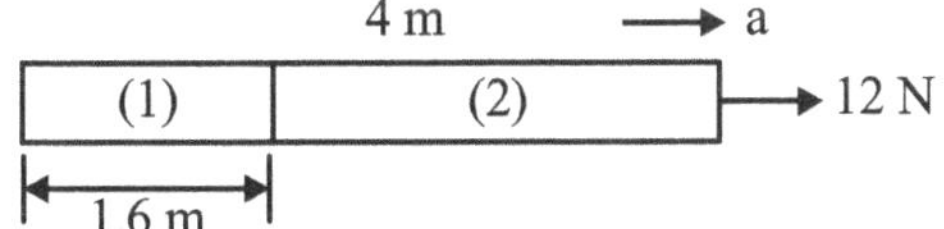

   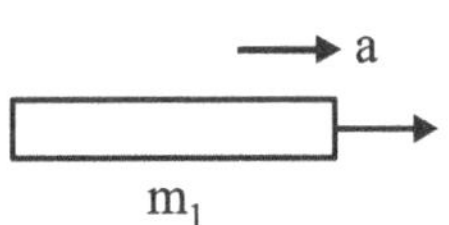

   Mass of part 1 as in fig. : $m_1 = 1.6 \times 1.5 = 2.4\,kg$ $T = m_1 a = 2.4 \times 2 = 4.8\,N$

4. **(d)** For 0.5 kg block, $6 = 0.5\,a$

5. **(d)** $T = m(g+a) = 6000(10+5) = 90000\,N$

6. **(b)** $a = \dfrac{m_2}{m_1 + m_2}\,g = \dfrac{3}{7+3} \times 10 = 3\,m/s^2$

7. **(d)** Taking the rope and the block as a system we get $P = (m + M)\,a$

   $\therefore a = \dfrac{P}{m+M}$

   Taking the block as a system,

   we get $T = Ma$ $\therefore T = \dfrac{MP}{m+M}$

8. **(c)** In series each spring will have same force. Here it is 4 kg-wt.

9. **(a)** $a = g(\sin\theta - \mu\cos\theta)$

   $= 9.8(\sin 45° - 0.5\cos 45°)$

   $= \dfrac{4.9}{\sqrt{2}}\,m/sec^2$

10. **(c)**

11. **(a)** Tension in the string when the body is at the top of the circle (T)

    $= \dfrac{mv^2}{r} - mg = 71.8\,N$

12. **(c)** $\dfrac{dM}{dt} = 0.1\,kg/s$, $v_{gas} = 50\,m/s$,

    Mass of the rocket = 2 kg. $Mv = $ constant

    $-v\dfrac{dM}{dt} + M\dfrac{dv}{dt} = 0$. $\therefore \dfrac{dv}{dt} = \dfrac{1}{M}v\dfrac{dM}{dt}$

    $\Rightarrow$ Acceleration $= \dfrac{1}{2} \times 50 \times 0.1 = 2.5\,m/s^2$

13. **(c)** Acceleration $a = \left(\dfrac{m_1 - m_2}{m_1 + m_2}\right)g$

    $= \dfrac{(5-4.8) \times 9.8}{(5+4.8)}\,m/s^2 = 0.2\,m/s^2$

14. **(b)** Here $u = 72\,km/h = 20\,m/s$; $v = 0$;

    $a = -\mu g = -0.5 \times 10 = -5\,m/s^2$

As $v^2 = u^2 + 2as$,

$$\therefore \quad s = \frac{\left(v^2 - u^2\right)}{2a} = \frac{(0 - (20)^2)}{2 \times (-5)} = 40\text{m}$$

15. **(c)**

16. **(c)** $\vec{F} = 6\,\hat{i} - 8\,\hat{j} + 10\,\hat{k}$,

$$|F| = \sqrt{36 + 64 + 100} = 10\sqrt{2} \ \text{N}$$

$$\left(\because F = \sqrt{F_x^2 + F_y^2 + F_z^2}\right)$$

$$\therefore \quad m = \frac{10\sqrt{2}}{1} = 10\sqrt{2} \ \text{kg}$$

17. **(a)** From $F = \dfrac{R}{t^2}\,v(t) \Rightarrow m\dfrac{dv}{dt} = \dfrac{R}{t^2}\,v(t)$

Integrating both sides $\displaystyle\int \frac{dv}{v} = \int \frac{Rdt}{mt^2}$

In $v = -\dfrac{R}{mt} \qquad \therefore \ln v \propto \dfrac{1}{t}$

18. **(d)** As shown in the figure, the three forces are represented by the sides of a triangle taken in the same order. Therefore the resultant force is zero. $\vec{F}_{net} = m\vec{a}$.

Therefore, acceleration is also zero i.e., velocity remains unchanged.

19. **(d)** During downward motion :

$$F = mg \sin\theta - \mu\, mg \cos\theta$$

During upward motion :

$$2F = mg \sin\theta + \mu\, mg \cos\theta$$

Solving above two equations, we get

$$\mu = \frac{1}{3}\tan\theta = \frac{1}{3}$$

20. **(c)** The tension in both strings will be same due to symmetry.

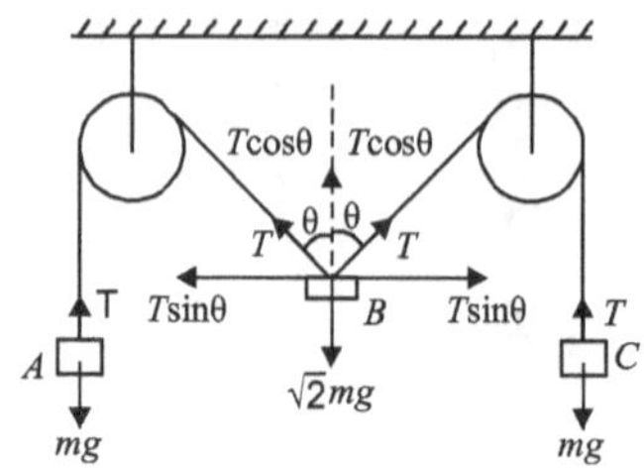

For equilibrium in vertical direction for body B we have

$$\sqrt{2}\, mg = 2T \cos\theta$$

$$\therefore \quad \sqrt{2}\, mg = 2(mg)\cos\theta$$

$$[\because T = mg, \text{ (at equilibrium)}]$$

$$\therefore \quad \cos\theta = \frac{1}{\sqrt{2}} \Rightarrow \theta = 45°$$

21. **(b)**

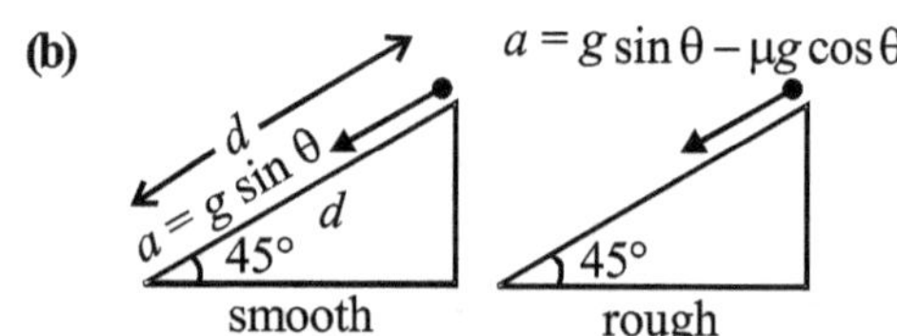

On smooth inclined plane, acceleration of the body $= g \sin\theta$. Let d be the distance travelled

$$\therefore \quad d = \frac{1}{2}(g\sin\theta)t_1^2,$$

$$t_1 = \sqrt{\frac{2d}{g\sin\theta}},$$

On rough inclined plane,

$$a = \frac{mg\sin\theta - \mu R}{m}$$

$$\Rightarrow \quad a = \frac{mg\sin\theta - \mu mg\cos\theta}{m}$$

$$\Rightarrow \quad a = g\sin\theta - \mu_k g\cos\theta$$

$$\therefore \quad d = \frac{1}{2}(g\sin\theta - \mu_k g\cos\theta)t_2^2$$

$$t_2 = \sqrt{\frac{2d}{g\sin\theta - \mu\hat{k}g\cos\theta}}$$

According to question, $t_2 = nt_1$

$$n\sqrt{\frac{2d}{g\sin\theta}} = \sqrt{\frac{2d}{g\sin\theta - \mu\hat{k}g\cos\theta}}$$

Here, μ is coefficient of kinetic friction as the block moves over the inclined plane.

$\therefore \quad \sin\theta = (\sin\theta - \mu\hat{k}\cos\theta)n^2$

$\Rightarrow \quad n = \dfrac{1}{\sqrt{1-\mu_k}} \Rightarrow n^2 = \dfrac{1}{1-\mu_k}$

$\Rightarrow \quad \mu_k = 1 - \dfrac{1}{n^2}$

22. (a) Given, initial velocity, $u = 100$m/s.

Final velocity, $v = 0$.

Acceleration, $a = \mu_k g = 0.5 \times 10$

$v^2 - u^2 = 2as$ or

$\Rightarrow 0^2 - u^2 = 2(-\mu_k g)s$

$\Rightarrow -100^2 = 2 \times -\dfrac{1}{2} \times 10 \times s$

$\Rightarrow s = 1000$ m

23. (c) When the incline is given an acceleration a towards the right, the block receives a reaction ma towards left.

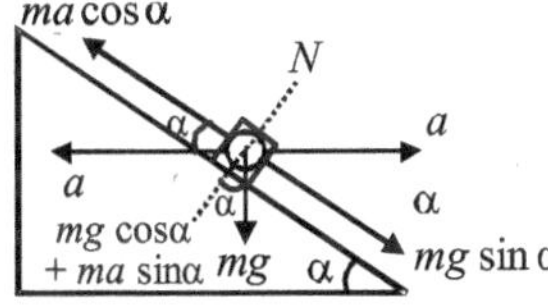

For block to remain stationary, Net force along the incline should be zero.

$mg\sin\alpha = ma\cos\alpha \Rightarrow a = g\tan\alpha$

24. (d) Using, $\mu mg = \dfrac{mv^2}{r} = mr\omega^2$

$\omega = 2\pi n = 2\pi \times 3.5 = 7\pi$ rad/sec

Radius, $r = 1.25$ cm

$\qquad = 1.25 \times 10^{-2}$ m

Coefficient of friction, $\mu = ?$

$$\mu mg = \frac{m(r\omega)^2}{r} \quad (\because \ v = r\omega)$$

$\mu mg = mr\omega^2$

$$\Rightarrow \quad \mu = \frac{r\omega^2}{g} = \frac{1.25 \times 10^{-2} \times \left(7 \times \dfrac{22}{7}\right)^2}{10}$$

$$= \frac{1.25 \times 10^{-2} \times 22^2}{10} = 0.6$$

25. (c) Tension, $T = 360$ N

Mass of a man m = 60 kg

$mg - T = ma$

$$\therefore \ a = g - \frac{T}{m}$$

$$= 10 - \frac{360}{60} = 4m/s^2$$

26. (d) For first half

acceleration $= g\sin\phi$;

For second half

acceleration $= -(g\sin\phi - \mu g\cos\phi)$

For the block to come to rest at the bottom, acceleration in I half = retardation in II half.

$g\sin\phi = -(g\sin\phi - \mu g\cos\phi)$

$\Rightarrow \mu = 2\tan\phi$

NOTE

According to work-energy theorem, $W = \Delta K = 0$

(Since initial and final speeds are zero)

$\therefore$ Workdone by friction + Work done by gravity = 0

$$i.e., \quad -(\mu\, mg \cos\phi)\frac{\ell}{2} + mg\ell \sin\phi = 0$$

or $\quad \dfrac{\mu}{2}\cos\phi = \sin\phi \quad$ or $\quad \mu = 2\tan\phi$

27.   **(d)**   The reading of the spring scale is the normal reaction between the man and the spring scale.

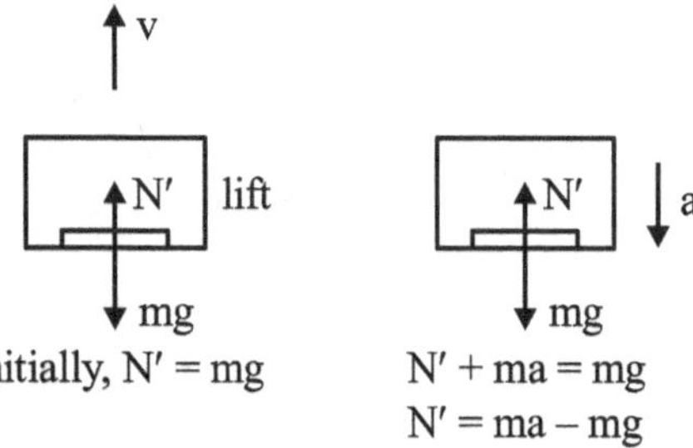

Initially, $N' = mg$

$N' + ma = mg$

$N' = ma - mg$

As the reading decreases, it means that the normal reaction is also decreasing. Firstly, the lift must be moving upwards with a constant velocity and then decelerated to rest.

28.   **(c)**   Thrust

$$F = u\left(\frac{dm}{dt}\right) = 5\times 10^4 \times 40 = 2\times 10^6\,N$$

29.   **(d)**   The particle is moving in circular path

From the figure,

$mg = R\sin\theta \quad \ldots (i)$

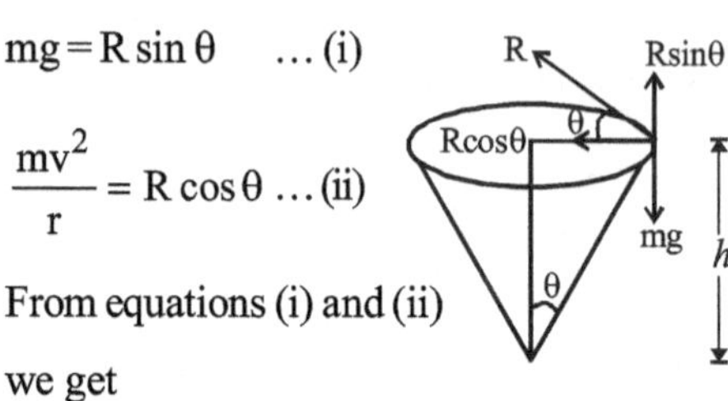

$\dfrac{mv^2}{r} = R\cos\theta \ldots (ii)$

From equations (i) and (ii) we get

$$\tan\theta = \frac{rg}{v^2} \text{ but } \tan\theta = \frac{r}{h}$$

$$\therefore h = \frac{v^2}{g} = \frac{(0.5)^2}{10} = 0.025\text{m} = 2.5\text{cm}$$

30.   **(d)**   Angle of banking is $\tan\theta$

$$= \frac{v^2}{rg} = \frac{20^2}{40\sqrt{3}\times 10}$$

$$\tan\theta = \frac{1}{\sqrt{3}}$$

$$\therefore \quad \theta = 30°$$

5 — Work, Energy and Power

1. **(d)** As the body moves in the direction of force therefore work done by gravitational force will be positive.
$$W = Fs = mgh = 10 \times 9.8 \times 10 = 980\,J$$

2. **(d)** Since height is same for both balls, their velocities on reaching the ground will be same
$$\therefore \frac{K.E_1}{K.E_2} = \frac{m_1 v_0^2}{m_2 v_0^2} = \frac{m_1}{m_2} = \frac{2}{4} = \frac{1}{2}$$

3. **(b)** $k = 5 \times 10^3\,N/m$
$$W = \frac{1}{2}k\left(x_2^2 - x_1^2\right)$$
$$= \frac{1}{2} \times 5 \times 10^3 \left[(0.1)^2 - (0.05)^2\right]$$
$$= \frac{5000}{2} \times 0.15 \times 0.05 = 18.75\,Nm$$

4. **(b)**

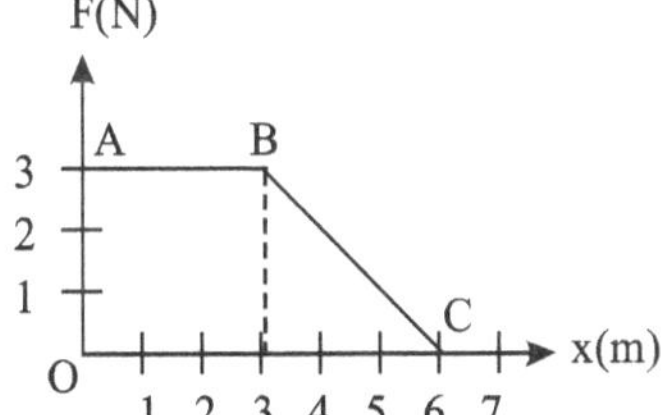

Work done = area under F-x graph
$$= \text{area of trapezium OABC}$$
$$= \frac{1}{2}(3+6)(3) = 13.5\,J$$

5. **(b)** Work done on the body = K. E. gained by the body
$$Fs\cos\theta = 1 \Rightarrow F\cos\theta = \frac{1}{s} = \frac{1}{0.4} = 2.5\,N$$

6. **(d)** In case of uniform circular motion, work done and power produced by a body is zero

7. **(d)** $P = F \times v \Rightarrow P = F\,at \quad \therefore\ P \propto t$
$$[\text{as } v = u + at = 0 + at = at]$$

8. **(b)** When the identical balls collide head-on, their velocities get interchanged.

9. **(b)**

10. **(d)** $\dfrac{e_1}{e_2} = \dfrac{3}{1}$ But, $e_1 = \dfrac{v}{2v} = \dfrac{1}{2}$
$$\therefore\ 3e_2 = \frac{1}{2} \text{ or } e_2 = \frac{1}{6}$$

Ratio between relative velocity of approach and relative velocity of separation = 6 : 1

11. **(b)** $h_n = e^{2n}h_0 \Rightarrow \dfrac{h}{2} = e^4 h \Rightarrow e = \left(\dfrac{1}{2}\right)^{1/4}$

12. **(d)** Due to the same mass of A and B as well as due to elastic collision, velocities of spheres get interchanged after the collision.

13. **(c)** If a is the retardation due to frictional force f, then $2ax = v^2$
$$\text{or } \frac{1}{2}mv^2 = \frac{1}{2}m(2ax) = max \qquad \text{..........(1)}$$
or kinetic energy = fx $(\because f = ma)$
Thus if kinetic energy is doubled, x is also doubled.

14. **(b)** From the Principle of energy conservation
$$\frac{1}{2}mv^2 = \frac{1}{2}kx^2$$
$$\text{or, } 2 \times (3)^2 = 144 \times x^2$$
$$\text{or, } x = \sqrt{\frac{2 \times 3 \times 3}{144}} = \frac{3\sqrt{2}}{12} = \frac{\sqrt{2}}{4} = \frac{1}{2\sqrt{2}}$$

So the length of compressed spring
$$= 2 - \frac{1}{2\sqrt{2}} = \frac{4\sqrt{2}-1}{2\sqrt{2}} \approx 1.5\,m$$

15. **(b)** From figure,

$h = OB \sin 30°$

$= \dfrac{l}{2} \times \dfrac{1}{2} = \dfrac{l}{4}$

$\therefore$ $P.E. = mgh = \dfrac{mgl}{4}$

16. **(b)** We know that $\Delta U = -W$ for conservative forces

$\therefore \Delta U = -\int_0^x F\,dx$ or $\Delta U = -\int_0^x k\,x\,dx$

$\Rightarrow U_{(x)} - U_{(0)} = -\dfrac{kx^2}{2} \Rightarrow U_{(x)} = -\dfrac{kx^2}{2}$

$$[\text{as } U_{(0)} = 0]$$

This is the equation of a parabola, which is symmetric to U-axis in negative direction.

17. **(c)** Apply conservation of Momentum

$m_1 v_1 = (m_1 + m_2)v$ or $v = \dfrac{m_1 v_1}{(m_1 + m_2)}$

Here $v_1 = 36$ km/hr $= 10$ m/s

$m_1 = 2\,Kg$, $m_2 = 3\,Kg$; $v = \dfrac{10 \times 2}{5} = 4\,m/s$

$K.E. \text{ (initial)} = \dfrac{1}{2} \times 2 \times (10)^2 = 100\,J$

$K.E. \text{ (Final)} = \dfrac{1}{2} \times (3+2) \times (4)^2 = 40\,J$

Loss in K.E. $= 100 - 40 = 60\,J$

18. **(c)** Mass, $m_1 = 2.0$ kg.

$V_1 = \dfrac{m_1 - m_2}{m_1 + m_2} u_1 = \dfrac{u_1}{4}$

Solving we get, $m_2 = M = 1.2$ kg

19. **(a)** Initial, $K.E. = \dfrac{1}{2} mv^2$

$= \dfrac{1}{2} \times \dfrac{20}{1000} \times 600 \times 600 = 3600\,J$

Change in K.E. $=$ P.E. $\Rightarrow \dfrac{1}{2} m(v^2 - v_1^2) = mgh$

$\Rightarrow 3600 - \dfrac{1}{2} \times \dfrac{20}{1000} \times v_1^2 = 4 \times 10 \times 80$

$\Rightarrow v_1 = 200\,m/s$

20. **(a)** For particle C,

According to law of conservation of linear momentum, Verticle component,

$2\,mv' \sin\theta = mv \sin 60° + mv \sin 45°$

$2mv'\sin\theta = \dfrac{mv}{\sqrt{2}} + \dfrac{mv\sqrt{3}}{2}$ ......(i)

Horizontal component,

$2\,mv' \cos\theta = mv \sin 60° - mv \cos 45°$

$2mv'\cos\theta = \dfrac{mv}{2} - \dfrac{mv}{\sqrt{2}}$ ......(ii)

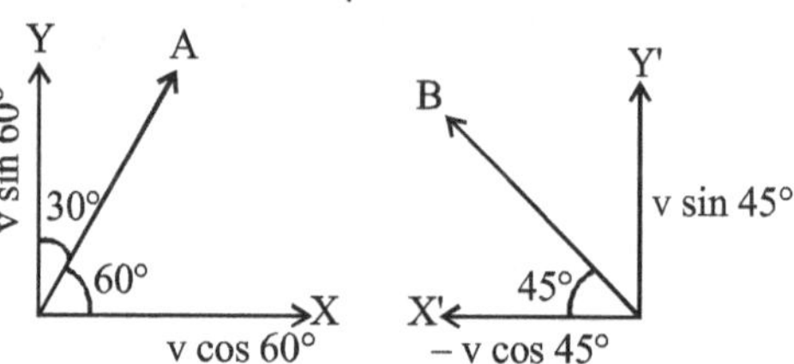

Dividing eq^n (i) by eq^n (ii),

$$\tan\theta = \dfrac{\dfrac{1}{\sqrt{2}} + \dfrac{\sqrt{3}}{2}}{\dfrac{1}{2} - \dfrac{1}{\sqrt{2}}} = \dfrac{\sqrt{2} + \sqrt{3}}{1 - \sqrt{2}}$$

21. **(a)** Potential energy

$V(x) = \dfrac{x^4}{4} \dfrac{-x^2}{2}$ joule

For maxima of minima

$\dfrac{dV}{dx} = 0 \Rightarrow x^3 - x = 0 \Rightarrow x = \pm 1$

$\Rightarrow$ Min. P.E. $= \dfrac{1}{4} - \dfrac{1}{2} = -\dfrac{1}{4}\,J$

$K.E._{(max.)} + P.E._{(min.)} = 2$ (Given)

$\therefore K.E._{(max.)} = 2 + \dfrac{1}{4} = \dfrac{9}{4}$

$K.E._{max.} = \dfrac{1}{2} mv_{max}^2$

$\Rightarrow \dfrac{1}{2} \times 1 \times v_{max}^2 = \dfrac{9}{4} \Rightarrow v_{max.} = \dfrac{3}{\sqrt{2}}$

22. **(d)** Work done by tension + Work done by force (applied) + Work done by gravitational force = change in kinetic energy
Work done by tension is zero

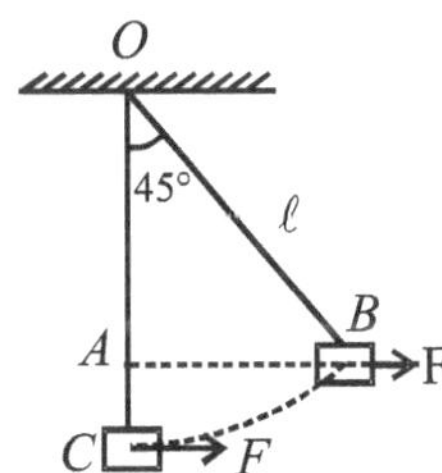

$$\Rightarrow 0 + F \times AB - Mg \times AC = 0$$

$$\Rightarrow F = Mg\left(\frac{AC}{AB}\right) = Mg\left[\frac{1 - \dfrac{1}{\sqrt{2}}}{\dfrac{1}{\sqrt{2}}}\right]$$

$$\left[\because AB = \ell \sin 45° = \frac{\ell}{\sqrt{2}} \text{ and}\right.$$

$$AC = OC - OA = \ell - \ell \cos 45° = \ell\left(1 - \frac{1}{\sqrt{2}}\right)$$

where ℓ = length of the string.]

$$\Rightarrow F = Mg(\sqrt{2} - 1)$$

23. **(d)** Let u be the velocity with which the particle is thrown and m be the mass of the particle. Then

$$K = \frac{1}{2}mu^2. \qquad \ldots (1)$$

At the highest point the velocity is u cos 60° (only the horizontal component remains, the vertical component being zero at the top-most point). Therefore kinetic energy at the highest point.

$$K' = \frac{1}{2}m(u\cos 60°)^2 = \frac{1}{2}mu^2 \cos^2 60° = \frac{K}{4}$$

[From 1]

24. **(b)** We know that Power, $P = Fv$

But $F = mav = m\dfrac{dv}{dt}v$

$$\therefore P = mv\frac{dv}{dt} \Rightarrow P\,dt = mv\,dv$$

Integrating both sides $\displaystyle\int_0^t P\,dt = m\int_0^v v\,dv$

$$P.\,t = \frac{1}{2}mv^2 \Rightarrow v = \left(\sqrt{\frac{2P}{m}}\right)t^{1/2}$$

Distance,

$$s = \int_0^t v\,dt = \sqrt{\frac{2P}{m}}\int_0^t t^{1/2}\,dt = \sqrt{\frac{2P}{m}}\cdot\frac{t^{3/2}}{3/2}$$

$$\Rightarrow s = \sqrt{\frac{8P}{9m}}\cdot t^{3/2} \Rightarrow s \propto t^{3/2}$$

So, graph (b) is correct.

25. **(b)** Let the velocity and mass of 4 kg piece be v_1 and m_1 and that of 12 kg piece be v_2 and m_2.

Applying conservation of linear momentum

$$16 \times 0 = 4 \times v_1 + 12 \times 4$$

$$\Rightarrow v_1 = -\frac{12 \times 4}{4} = -12 \; ms^{-1}$$

Kinetic energy of 4 kg mass

$$\therefore K.E. = \frac{1}{2}m_1 v_1^2 = \frac{1}{2} \times 4 \times 144 = 288 \; J$$

26. **(b)** Centripetal acceleration $a_c = n^2 R t^2$

$$a_c = \frac{v^2}{R} = n^2 R t^2$$

$$v^2 = n^2 R^2 t^2$$

$$v = nRt$$

$$a_c = \frac{dv}{dt} = nR$$

Power $= ma_t v = m\,nR\,nRt = Mn^2 R^2 t.$

27. **(b)** From principle of conservation of energy

[u = initial velocity, v = velocity after penetrating 1 cm

$$\frac{1}{2}mv^2 = (100\% - 20\%)\frac{1}{2}mu^2$$

$$v^2 = \frac{4}{5}u^2 \qquad \qquad ....(1)$$

From $v^2 = u^2 + 2as$

$$\frac{4}{5}u^2 = u^2 + 2as \Rightarrow a = -\frac{u^2}{10} \qquad ....(2)$$

Let it will penetrate total t distance before coming to rest then

$$v^2 = u^2 + 2as$$

$$0 = u^2 - 2\left(\frac{u^2}{10}\right)s \qquad \therefore s = 5\,cm$$

28. **(d)** If l is length of pendulum and θ be angular amplitude then from principle of conservation of energy

(Initial total energy) $0 + mgh = \frac{1}{2}mv^2 + 0$

(Final total energy)

$$\Rightarrow v = \sqrt{2gh} = \sqrt{2g\ell(1 - \cos\theta)}$$

29. **(a)** Given : $m = 2kg$, $u = 0$, $F = 7N$, $\mu_k = 0.1$, $t = 10s$,

$W = ?$

Acceleration produced by applied force

$$\Rightarrow a_1 = \frac{F}{m} = \frac{7}{2} = 3.5\ m/s^2.$$

Force of friction, $f = \mu_k R = \mu_k mg$

$$= 0.1 \times 2 \times 9.8 = 1.96\ N$$

Retardation produced by friction

$$= a_2 = \frac{-f}{m} = \frac{-1.96}{2} = -0.98\ m/s^2$$

Net acceleration $= a = a_1 + a_2 = 3.50 - 0.98$

$$= 2.52\ m/s^2$$

Distance moved by the body in 10 seconds

$$S = ut + \frac{1}{2}at^2 = 0 + \frac{1}{2} \times 2.52 \times (10)^2 = 126\ m.$$

Work done by the frictional force $= -f \times s$

$$= -1.96 \times 126 = -246.9\ J$$

Velocity at the end of 10 s is

$$v = u + at = 0 + 2.52 \times 10 = 25.2\ m/s$$

Final K.E. $= \frac{1}{2}mv^2 = \frac{1}{2} \times 2 \times (25.2)^2 = 635\ J$

Initial K.E. $= 0$

$\therefore$ Change in KE $= 635 - 0 = 635\ J$

30. **(b)** Power $= \dfrac{\text{Work done}}{\text{Time}} = \dfrac{\frac{1}{2}m\left(v^2 - u^2\right)}{t}$

$$P = \frac{1}{2} \times \frac{2.05 \times 10^6 \times \left[(25)^2 - (5^2)\right]}{5 \times 60}$$

$P = 2.05 \times 10^6\ W = 2.05\ MW$

System of Particles and Rotational Motion

1. **(b)** $\vec{v}_{cm} = \dfrac{m_1\vec{v}_1 + m_2\vec{v}_2}{m_1 + m_2}$

$= \dfrac{2\times 2 + 4\times 10}{2+4} = 7.3\,m/s$

2. **(a)** Angular momentum of system remains constant

$I \propto \dfrac{1}{\omega} \Rightarrow \dfrac{I_2}{I_1} = \dfrac{\omega_1}{\omega_2} = \dfrac{20}{10} \Rightarrow I_2 = 2I_1 = 2I$

3. **(c)** According to problem disc is melted and recasted into a solid sphere so their volume will be same.

$V_{Disc} = V_{Sphere} \Rightarrow \pi R_{Disc}^2 t = \dfrac{4}{3}\pi R_{Sphere}^3$

$\Rightarrow \pi R_{Disc}^2 \left(\dfrac{R_{Disc}}{6}\right) = \dfrac{4}{3}\pi R_{Sphere}^3$

$$\left[t = \dfrac{R_{Disc}}{6},\ \text{given} \right]$$

$\Rightarrow R_{Disc}^3 = 8R_{Sphere}^3 \Rightarrow R_{Sphere} = \dfrac{R_{Disc}}{2}$

Moment of inertia of disc

$I_{Disc} = \dfrac{1}{2}MR_{Disc}^2 = I$ (given)

$\therefore M(R_{Disc})^2 = 2I$

Moment of inertia of sphere $I_{Sphere} = \dfrac{2}{5}MR_{Sphere}^2$

$= \dfrac{2}{5}M\left(\dfrac{R_{Disc}}{2}\right)^2 = \dfrac{M}{10}(R_{Disc})^2 = \dfrac{2I}{10} = \dfrac{I}{5}$

4. **(c)** $JL = (I\omega - 0) \Rightarrow \omega = \dfrac{JL}{I}$

Also $J = m(v - 0) \Rightarrow v = \dfrac{J}{m}$

$\therefore K = \dfrac{1}{2}mv^2 + \dfrac{1}{2}I\omega^2$

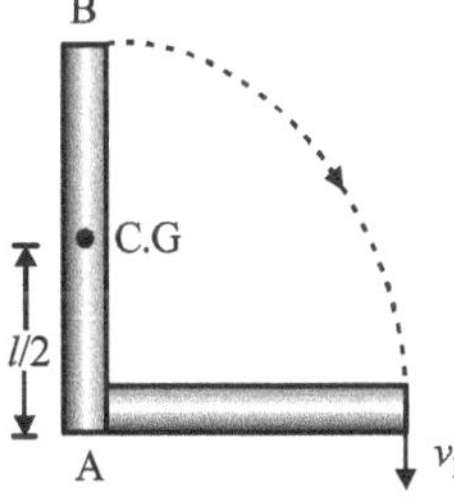

$= \dfrac{1}{2}m\left(\dfrac{J}{m}\right)^2 + \dfrac{1}{2}\left[\dfrac{m(2L)^2}{12}\right]\left[\dfrac{JL}{\dfrac{m(2L)^2}{12}}\right]^2$

$= 2\dfrac{J^2}{m}$

5. **(c)** From law of conservation of angular momentum

$I_1\omega_1 + I_2\omega_2 = (I_1 + I_2)\omega$

Angular velocity of system $\omega = \dfrac{I_1\omega_1 + I_2\omega_2}{I_1 + I_2}$

$\therefore$ Rotaional kinetic energy $= \dfrac{1}{2}(I_1 + I_2)\omega^2$

$\dfrac{1}{2}(I_1 + I_2)\left(\dfrac{I_1\omega_1 + I_2\omega_2}{I_1 + I_2}\right)^2 = \dfrac{(I_1\omega_1 + I_2\omega_2)^2}{2(I_1 + I_2)}$

6. **(b)** In this process potential energy of the metre stick will be converted into rotational kinetic energy.

P.E. of meter stick $= mg\left(\dfrac{l}{2}\right)$

Because its centre of gravity lies at the middle point of the rod.
Rotational kinetic energy

$E = \dfrac{1}{2}I\omega^2$

I = M.I. of metre stick about point $A = \dfrac{ml^2}{3}$

ω = Angular speed of the rod while striking the ground

v_B = Velocity of end B of metre stick while striking the ground

By the law of conservation of energy,

$$mg\left(\dfrac{l}{2}\right) = \dfrac{1}{2}I\omega^2 = \dfrac{1}{2}\dfrac{ml^2}{3}\left(\dfrac{v_B}{l}\right)^2$$

By solving we get,

$$v_B = \sqrt{3gl} = \sqrt{3 \times 10 \times 1} = 5.4\, m/s$$

7. **(a)** $\quad x_{CM} = \dfrac{m_1x_1 + m_2x_2 + \ldots \text{ to n terms}}{m_1 + m_2 + \ldots \text{ to n terms}}$

$$= \dfrac{m\ell + 2m.2\ell + 3m.3\ell + \ldots \text{ to n terms}}{m + 2m + 3m + \ldots \text{ to n terms}}$$

$$= \dfrac{m\ell\,(1 + 4 + 9 + \ldots \text{to n terms})}{m\,(1 + 2 + 3 + \ldots \text{to n terms})}$$

$$= \dfrac{\ell\,\dfrac{n\,(n+1)\,(2n+1)}{6}}{\dfrac{n\,(n+1)}{2}} = \dfrac{\ell\,(2n+1)}{3}$$

8. **(b)**

9. **(a)** $\quad$ (a =) OA = 6 cm , (c =) OO′ = 3.2 cm, (b =) O′B = 2 cm

Let m is mass/area

∴ Mass of the original disc

$$= \pi \times 6^2 \times m = 36\pi m$$

mass of the cut-out portion

$$= M' = \pi \times 2^2 \times m = 4\pi m$$

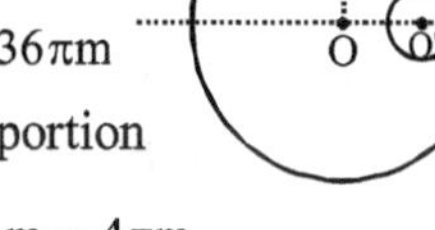

Centre of mass of the original disc is at O (0, 0)

If the C.M. of the cut-out portion is to the left of the disc at a distance x from O

$$\therefore\; x = \dfrac{M \times 0 - M' \times 3.2}{M - M'} = \dfrac{-4\pi m \times 3.2}{36\pi m - 4\pi m}$$

$$= \dfrac{-4 \times 3.2 \times \pi m}{32\pi m} = -0.4\,\text{cm}$$

−ve sign indicates it is left at a distance 0.4 cm from O. (Also, centre of mass after removal

$$= -\,cb^2/(a^2 - b^2))$$

10. **(d)** We know that both the cars take the same time to complete the circle, therefore ratio of angular speeds of the cars will be 1 : 1.

11. **(b)** By applying conservation of angular momentum about point O

$$MV\dfrac{a}{2} = \left[\dfrac{ma^2}{6} + \dfrac{ma^2}{2}\right]\omega$$

$$\Rightarrow \text{Angular velocity,}\,\omega = \dfrac{3V}{4a} = \dfrac{3 \times 2}{4 \times 0.3} = 5\,\text{rad/s}$$

12. **(b)** Given : m = 0.160 kg

$\theta = 60°$

v = 10 m/s

Angular momentum $\vec{L} = \vec{r} \times m\,\vec{v}$

$= H\,mv\cos\theta$

$$= mv\dfrac{v^2\sin^2\theta}{2g}\cos\theta \qquad \left[H = \dfrac{v^2\sin^2\theta}{2g}\right]$$

$$= \dfrac{10^2 \times \sin^2 60° \times \cos 60°}{2 \times 10} \times (0.16 \times 10)$$

$$= 3\ \text{kg m}^2/\text{s}$$

13. **(d)** We have, $\omega_2^2 = \omega_1^2 - 2\alpha\theta$ $\quad$ .....(1)

Here, $\omega_1 = \omega_0$, $\omega_2 = \dfrac{\omega_0}{2}$,

$\theta = 2\pi n = 36 \times 2\pi$ radian.

By substituting these values in eqn. (1) we get,

$$\left(\dfrac{\omega_0}{2}\right)^2 = \omega_0^2 - 2\alpha \times 36 \times 2\pi$$

$$4\pi\alpha \times 36 = \omega_0^2 - \dfrac{\omega_0^2}{4}$$

$$144\pi\alpha = \dfrac{3\omega_0^2}{4} \quad \text{or} \quad \alpha = \dfrac{\omega_0^2}{192\pi}$$

Again, applying third equation of angular momentum, $\omega_2^2 = \omega_1^2 - 2\alpha\theta$

Here, $\omega_2 = 0$, $\omega_1 = \dfrac{\omega_0}{2}$, $\theta = ?$

$$\Rightarrow \left(\dfrac{\omega_0}{2}\right)^2 = 2\left(\dfrac{\omega_0^2}{192\pi}\right)\theta$$

or $\theta = \dfrac{192\pi}{8} = 24\pi$ radian $= 12$ rotations

14. (c) Area of rectangular plate $A_2 = b\ell$

Area of triangular plate

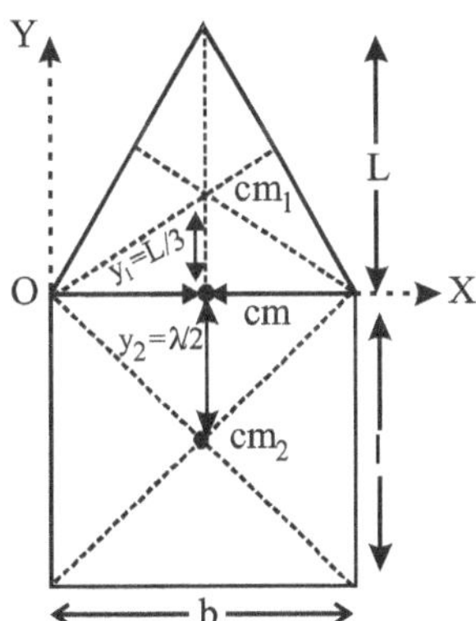

$A_1 = \dfrac{1}{2}bL$

For COM to be at common interface,
y-co-ordinate of COM $= 0$

$$\Rightarrow \dfrac{m_1 y_1 - m_2 y_2}{m_1 + m_2} = 0$$

$$\Rightarrow \dfrac{\rho A_1 y_1 - \rho A_2 y_2}{\rho A_1 + \rho A_2} = 0$$

(where $\rho = \dfrac{m}{A}$ = density of objects)

$$\Rightarrow A_1 y_1 = A_2 y_2 \quad \Rightarrow \ell = \dfrac{L}{\sqrt{3}}$$

$$[y_1 = L/3,\ y_2 = \ell/2]$$

15. (d) $I_1\omega_1 = I_2\omega_2$

or, $mk_1^2\omega_1 = mk_2^2\omega_2$ $\quad \therefore \dfrac{k_1}{k_2} = \sqrt{\dfrac{\omega_2}{\omega_1}}$

16. (b) According to theorem of perpendicular axes, moment of inertia of triangle (ABC)

$I_0 = km l^2$ ..... (i)

$BC = l$

Moment of inertia of a cavity DEF

$$I_{DEF} = K\dfrac{m}{4}\left(\dfrac{l}{2}\right)^2 = \dfrac{k}{16}ml^2$$

From equation (i),

$$I_{DEF} = \dfrac{I_0}{16}$$

Moment of inertia of remaining part

$$I_{remain} = I_0 - \dfrac{I_0}{16} = \dfrac{15 I_0}{16}$$

17. (b) M.I. of a thin rod about its mid-point, $\perp$ to its length (i.e., say inside the paper) is

given by $\dfrac{ml^2}{12}$.

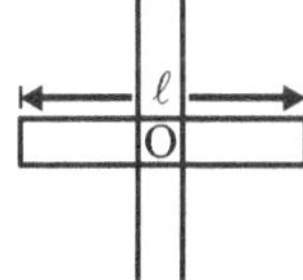

As the other rod $\perp$ to the first in the same plane has its axis of rotation common with the first, the M.I. of the two rods will add up

$$= \dfrac{ml^2}{12} + \dfrac{ml^2}{12} = \dfrac{ml^2}{6}$$

18. (d) M.I. of complete disc about its centre.

$$I_{Total} = \dfrac{1}{2}MR^2 \qquad ...(i)$$

M.I. of complete disc can also be written as

$I_{Total} = I_{removed\ hole} + I_{remaining\ disc}$

M.I. of removed hole about its own

$$axis = \dfrac{1}{2}\left(\dfrac{M}{4}\right)\left(\dfrac{R}{2}\right)^2 = \dfrac{1}{32}MR^2$$

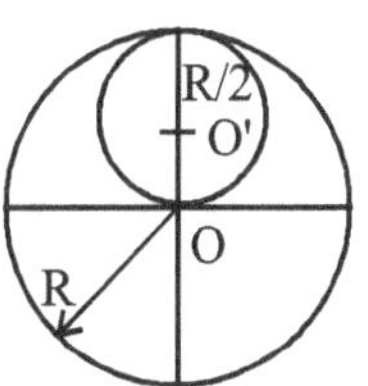

M.I. of removed hole about its own centre I

$$\text{removed hole} = I_{cm} + mx^2 = \frac{MR^2}{32} + \frac{M}{4}\left(\frac{R}{2}\right)^2$$

$$I_{Total} = \frac{3MR^2}{32} + I_{remaining\ disc} \qquad ...(ii)$$

From eq. (i) and (ii),

$$\frac{1}{2}MR^2 = \frac{3MR^2}{32} + I_{remaining\ disc}$$

$$\Rightarrow \quad I_{remaining\ disc}$$

$$= \frac{MR^2}{2} - \frac{3MR^2}{32} = \left(\frac{13}{32}\right)MR^2$$

19. (b) $\quad V = \sqrt{\dfrac{2gh}{1 + \dfrac{K^2}{R^2}}}$

20. (d) Minimum velocity for a body rolling without slipping

$$v = \sqrt{\frac{2gh}{1 + \dfrac{K^2}{R^2}}} = \sqrt{\frac{10}{7}gh}$$

For solid sphere, $\dfrac{K^2}{R^2} = \dfrac{2}{5}$

21. (c) Initially,

$$0 = \frac{m_1(-x_1) + m_2 x_2}{m_1 + m_2} \Rightarrow m_1 x_1 = m_2 x_2 \ ...(1)$$

Let the particles is displaced through distanced away from centre of mass

$$\therefore 0 = \frac{m_1(d - x_1) + m_2(x_2 - d')}{m_1 + m_2}$$

$$\Rightarrow 0 = m_1 d - m_1 x_1 + m_2 x_2 - m_2 d'$$

$$\Rightarrow d' = \frac{m_1}{m_2}d \qquad\qquad \text{[From (1).]}$$

22. (d) With respect to point θ, the CM of the cut-off portion $\left(\dfrac{a}{4}, \dfrac{b}{4}\right)$.

Using, $x_{CM} = \dfrac{MX - mx}{M - m}$

$$= \frac{M \times 0 - \dfrac{M}{4} \times \dfrac{a}{4}}{M - \dfrac{M}{4}} = -\frac{a}{12}$$

and $y_{CM} = -\dfrac{b}{12}$

So CM coordinates one

$$x_0 = \frac{a}{2} - \frac{a}{12} = \frac{5a}{12}$$

and $y_0 = \dfrac{b}{2} - \dfrac{b}{12} = \dfrac{5b}{12}$

23. (a) Torque about the origin $= \vec{\tau} = \vec{r} \times \vec{F}$

$= r\ F \sin\theta \Rightarrow 2.5 = 1 \times 5 \sin\theta$

$$\sin\theta = 0.5 = \frac{1}{2}$$

$$\Rightarrow \theta = \frac{\pi}{6}$$

24. (c) From figure,

$$ma = F - f \qquad\qquad ....(i)$$

And, torque $\tau = I\alpha$

$$\frac{mR^2}{2}\alpha = fR$$

$$\frac{mR^2}{2}\frac{a}{R} = fR \qquad\qquad \left[\because \alpha = \frac{a}{R}\right]$$

$$\frac{ma}{2} = f \qquad\qquad\qquad ...(ii)$$

Put this value in equation (i),

$$ma = F - \frac{ma}{2} \text{ or } F = \frac{3ma}{2}$$

25. **(b)** Acceleration of the body rolling down an inclined plane is given by.

$$a = \frac{g\sin\theta}{1 + \dfrac{I}{MR^2}}$$

26. **(a)**

27. **(a)** $M = 20$ kg., $R = 0.25$ m, $\omega = 100$ rad/s

M.I of the solid cylinder

$$= \frac{1}{2}MR^2 = \frac{1}{2}\times 20 \times (0.25)^2 = 0.625\ \text{kgm}^2$$

$$\text{K.E. of rotation} = \frac{1}{2}I\omega^2 = \frac{1}{2}\times 0.625 \times (100)^2$$

$$= 3125\ \text{J}.$$

28. **(d)** $\alpha = \dfrac{2\pi(n_2 - n_1)}{t}$

$$= \frac{2\pi\left(\dfrac{4500 - 1200}{60}\right)}{10}\,\text{rad}/\text{s}^2$$

$$= \frac{2\pi\dfrac{3300}{60}}{10} \times \frac{360}{2\pi}\frac{\text{degree}}{\text{s}^2} = 1980\ \text{degree/s}^2$$

29. **(d)** For a thin uniform square lamina

$$I_1 = I_2 = I_3 = \frac{ma^2}{12}$$

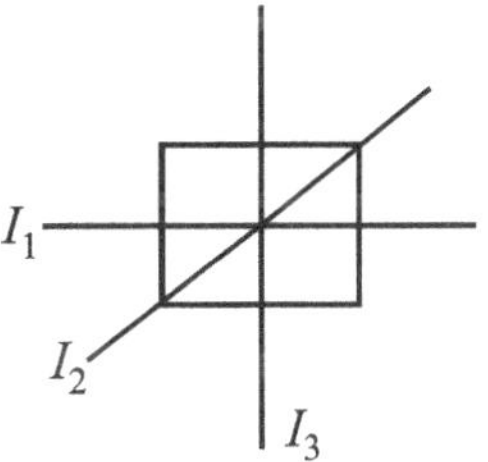

30. **(d)** $I_{AX} = m(AB)^2 + m(OC)^2$

$$= m\ell^2 + m\,(\ell\cos 60°)^2$$

$$= m\ell^2 + m\ell^2/4 = 5/4\ m\ell^2$$

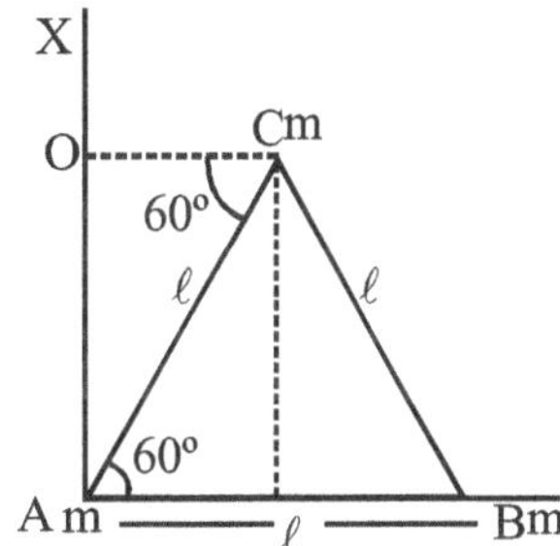

7   Gravitation

1.   **(c)** Centripetal force is provided by the gravitational force of attraction between two particles

i.e. $\dfrac{mv^2}{R} = \dfrac{Gm \times m}{(2R)^2}$

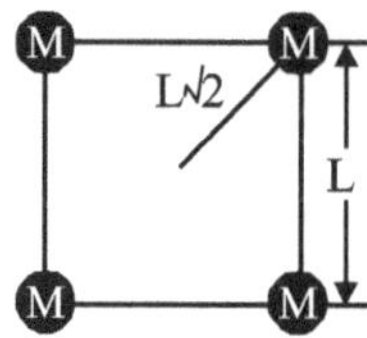

$\Rightarrow v = \dfrac{1}{2}\sqrt{\dfrac{Gm}{R}}$

2.   **(a)** $F = \dfrac{G m_1 m_2}{r^2} = \dfrac{G m_1 m_2}{(r_1 + r_2)^2}$.

3.   **(d)**

4.   **(a)** $g = g_p - R\omega^2 \cos^2 \lambda$

$= g_p - \omega^2 R \cos^2 60° = g_p - \dfrac{1}{4}R\omega^2$

5.   **(c)**

6.   **(b)** $g' = g - \omega^2 R \cos^2 \lambda$

To make effective acceleration due to gravity zero at equator $\lambda = 0$ and $g' = 0$

$\therefore 0 = g - \omega^2 R \Rightarrow \omega = \sqrt{\dfrac{g}{R}} = \dfrac{1}{800}\dfrac{rad}{s}$

7.   **(a)**

8.   **(d)** Let mass per unit light of wire, $\lambda = \dfrac{m}{\ell}$

and $\pi r = \ell$, $r = \dfrac{\ell}{\pi}$.

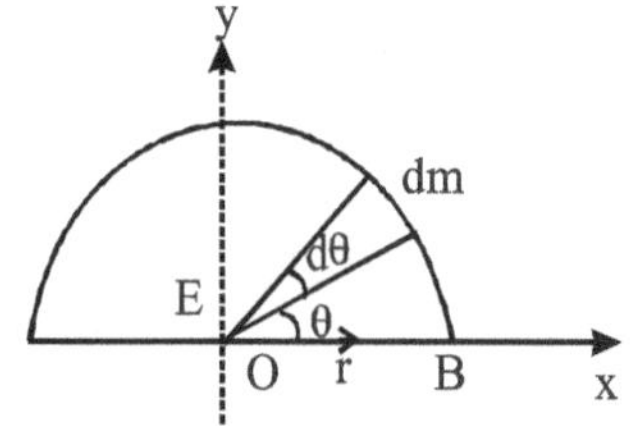

mass of element, $dm = \lambda r d\theta$ then $dE = \dfrac{Gdm}{r^2}$

$\displaystyle \int_0^\pi dE = \int_0^\pi \dfrac{G\lambda r d\theta}{r^2}(\hat{i}\cos\theta + \hat{j}\sin\theta)$

$E = \dfrac{G\lambda}{r}\left[\int_0^\pi \hat{i}\cos\theta + \int_0^\pi \hat{j}\sin\theta\right]$

$= \dfrac{2G\lambda}{r}\hat{j} = \dfrac{2GM}{\ell r}\hat{j} = \dfrac{2Gm\pi}{\ell^2}\hat{j}$ (along y-axis)

9.   **(a)** Potential at the centre due to single mass $=$

$\dfrac{-GM}{L/\sqrt{2}}$

Potential at the centre due to all four masses.

$= -4\dfrac{GM}{L/\sqrt{2}} = -4\sqrt{2}\dfrac{GM}{L} = -\sqrt{32}\times\dfrac{GM}{L}$

10.   **(d)**

11.   **(d)** Acceleration due to gravity on earth's surface

$g = G\dfrac{M}{R^2}$

This implies that as radius decreases, the acceleration due to gravity increases.

$\dfrac{\Delta g}{g} = -2\dfrac{\Delta R}{R}$ But $\dfrac{\Delta R}{R} = -1\%$

('−' sign is due to shrinking of earth)

$\therefore \quad \dfrac{\Delta g}{g} = -2 \times (-1\%) = 2\%$

12. **(c)**

13. **(c)** $v_e = \sqrt{2gR}$

Clearly escape velocity does not depend on the angle at which the body is projected.

14. **(b)** Gravitational potential energy (GPE) on the surface of earth, $E_1 = -\dfrac{GMm}{R}$

GPE at 3R, $E_2 = -\dfrac{GMm}{(R+3R)} = -\dfrac{GMm}{4R}$

$\therefore$ Change in GPE

$$= E_2 - E_1 = -\dfrac{GMm}{4R} + \dfrac{GMm}{R} = \dfrac{3GMm}{4R}$$

$$= \dfrac{3g\,R^2 m}{4R} \qquad \left(\because g = \dfrac{GM}{R^2} \right)$$

$$= \dfrac{3}{4} mg\,R$$

15. **(a)** For calculation of gravitational field intensity inside the cavity.

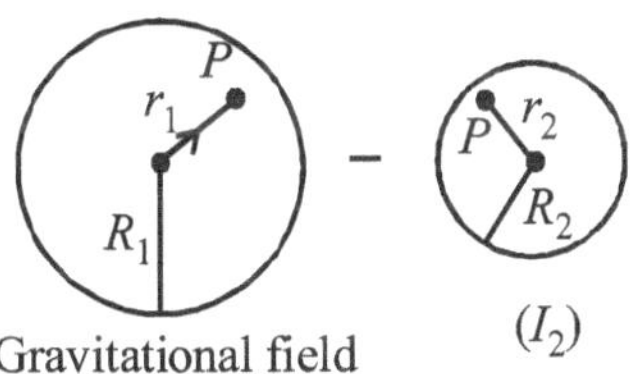

Gravitational field intensity without cavity (I_1)

(I_2)

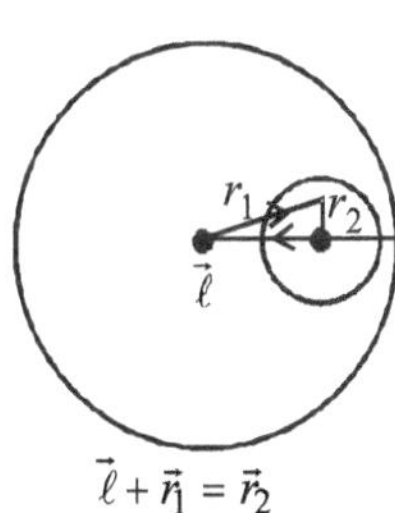

$\vec{\ell} + \vec{r_1} = \vec{r_2}$

$$\vec{I_1} = \dfrac{G\left(\dfrac{4}{3}\pi R_1^3\right)\rho\,(-\vec{r_1})}{R_1^3}$$

,

$$\vec{I_2} = \dfrac{G\left(\dfrac{4}{3}\pi R_2^3\right)\rho\,(-\vec{r_2})}{R_2^3}$$

$\vec{I} = \vec{I_1} - \vec{I_2}$ ($\vec{I}$ – intensity inside the cavity)

$$= \dfrac{4}{3} G\pi\rho\,[-\vec{r_1} + \vec{r_2}] = \dfrac{4}{3} G\pi\rho\,\vec{\ell}$$

16. **(a)**

17. **(d)** The energy required to remove the satellite from its orbit to infinity is called binding energy of the system.

Binding energy of satellite

$$= -E = \dfrac{GMm}{2r} = \dfrac{GMm}{2(R+h)}$$

18. **(d)**

19. **(c)** Areal velocity; $\dfrac{dA}{dt}$

$$dA = \dfrac{1}{2} r^2 d\theta$$

$$\Rightarrow \dfrac{dA}{dt} = \dfrac{1}{2} r^2 \dfrac{d\theta}{dt} = \dfrac{1}{2} r^2 \omega$$

Also, $L = mvr = mr^2\omega$

$$\therefore \dfrac{dA}{dt} = \dfrac{1}{2} \dfrac{L}{m}$$

20. **(a)**

21. **(b)** Variation of acceleration due to gravity, g with distance 'd' from centre of the earth

If $d < R, g = \dfrac{Gm}{R^2}.d$ $i.e., g \propto d$ (straight line)

If $d = R, g_s = \dfrac{Gm}{R^2}$

If $d > R, g = \dfrac{Gm}{d^2}$ $i.e., g \propto \dfrac{1}{d^2}$

22. **(a)**

23. **(d)**

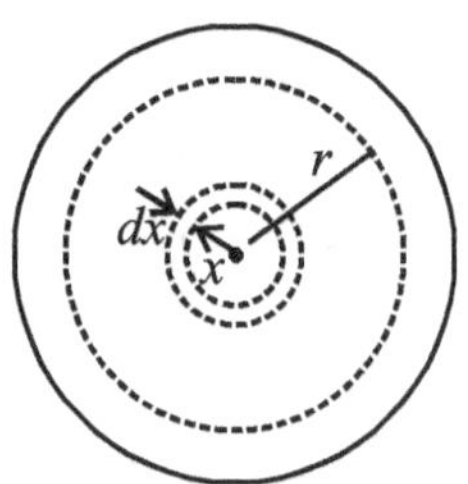

Mass of small element of planet of radius x and thickness dx.

$$dm = \rho \times 4\pi x^2 dx = \rho_0 \left(1 - \frac{x^2}{R^2}\right) \times 4\pi x^2 dx$$

Mass of the planet

$$M = 4\pi\rho_0 \int_0^r \left(x^2 - \frac{x^4}{R^2}\right) dx$$

$$\Rightarrow M = 4\pi\rho_0 \left|\frac{r^3}{3} - \frac{r^5}{5R^2}\right|$$

Gravitational field,

$$E = \frac{GM}{r^2} = \frac{G}{r^2} \times 4\pi\rho_0 \left(\frac{r^3}{3} - \frac{r^5}{5R^2}\right)$$

$$\Rightarrow E = 4\pi G\rho_0 \left(\frac{r}{3} - \frac{r^3}{5R^2}\right)$$

E is maximum when $\dfrac{dE}{dr} = 0$

$$\Rightarrow \frac{dE}{dr} = 4\pi G\rho_0 \left(\frac{1}{3} - \frac{3r^2}{5R^2}\right) = 0$$

$$\Rightarrow r = \frac{\sqrt{5}}{3} R$$

24. **(a)** Orbital speed of the body when it revolves very close to the surface of planet

$$V_0 = \sqrt{\frac{GM}{R}} \qquad \text{...(i)}$$

Here, G = gravitational constant
Escape speed from the surface of planet

$$V_e = \sqrt{\frac{2GM}{R}} \qquad \text{...(ii)}$$

Dividing (i) by (ii), we have

$$\frac{V_0}{V_e} = \frac{\sqrt{\dfrac{GM}{R}}}{\sqrt{\dfrac{2GM}{R}}} = \frac{1}{\sqrt{2}}$$

25. **(b)** Orbital, velocity, $v = \sqrt{\dfrac{GM}{r}}$

Kinetic energy of satellite A,

$$T_A = \frac{1}{2} m_A V_A^2$$

Kinetic energy of satellite B,

$$T_B = \frac{1}{2} m_B V_B^2$$

$$\Rightarrow \frac{T_A}{T_B} = \frac{m \times \dfrac{GM}{R}}{2m \times \dfrac{GM}{2R}} = 1$$

26. **(c)** $E_g = \dfrac{GM}{(3a)^2} + \dfrac{G(2M)}{(3a)^2} = \dfrac{GM}{3a^2}$

27. **(b)** $\dfrac{T_1^2}{T_2^2} = \dfrac{r_1^3}{r_2^3} = (4)^3 \qquad \therefore \quad T_2 = T_1/8.$

28. **(a)**

29. **(b)** $h = 32\,\text{km}, R = 6400\,\text{km}$, so $h \ll R$

$$g' = g\left(1 - \frac{2h}{R}\right) = g\left(1 - \frac{2 \times 32}{6400}\right)$$

$$\Rightarrow g' = \frac{99}{100} g = 0.99g$$

30. **(c)** According to Kepler's law of periods $T^2 \propto R^3$

$$\therefore \quad \left(\frac{T_2}{T_1}\right)^2 = \left(\frac{R_2}{R_1}\right)^3$$

$$\Rightarrow T_2 = T_1 \left(\frac{R_2}{R_1}\right)^{3/2} = 5 \times \left[\frac{4R}{R}\right]^{3/2}$$

$$= 5 \times 2^3 = 40\,\text{hours}$$

8

Mechanical Properties of Solids

1. **(c)** We know that Young's modulus

$$Y = \frac{F}{\pi r^2} \times \frac{L}{\ell}$$

Since Y, F are same for both the wires, we have,

$$\frac{1}{r_1^2} \frac{L_1}{\ell_1} = \frac{1}{r_2^2} \frac{L_2}{\ell_2}$$

or, $\quad \dfrac{\ell_1}{\ell_2} = \dfrac{r_2^2 \times L_1}{r_1^2 \times L_2} = \dfrac{(D_2/2)^2 \times L_1}{(D_1/2)^2 \times L_2}$

or, $\quad \dfrac{\ell_1}{\ell_2} = \dfrac{D_2^2 \times L_1}{D_1^2 \times L_2} = \dfrac{D_2^2}{(2D_2)^2} \times \dfrac{L_2}{2L_2} = \dfrac{1}{8}$

So, $\quad \ell_1 : \ell_2 = 1:8$

2. **(d)** The stress due to this weight is $S = L\rho g$

$$\therefore \quad L = \frac{S}{\rho g}$$

3. **(b)** For steel wire, $A_1 = 3 \times 10^{-5}\, m^2, l_1 = 4.7m$;

For copper wire, $A_2 = 4 \times 10^{-5}\, m^2, l_2 = 3.5m$

As $D l_1 = D l_2 = D l$ and $F_1 = F_2 = F$

$$\therefore \quad Y_1 = \frac{F_1 l_1}{A_1 D l_1} = \frac{F}{3 \times 10^{-5}} \times \frac{4.7}{\Delta l} \, ;$$

$$Y_2 = \frac{F_2 l_2}{A_2 D l_2} = \frac{F \times 3.5}{4 \times 10^{-5}\, \Delta l}$$

$$\therefore \quad \frac{Y_1}{Y_2} = \frac{4.7 \times 4 \times 10^{-5}}{3.5 \times 3 \times 10^{-5}} = \frac{18.8}{10.5} \approx 1.8$$

$$\therefore \quad Y_1 : Y_2 = \frac{18}{10} = \frac{9}{5}$$

4. **(a)** Given:

$A = 15.2 \times 19.1\ mm^2 = 15.2 \times 19.1 \times 10^{-6}\ m^2;$

$F = 44{,}500\ N, \ Y = 120 \times 10^9\ N/m^2$

Shearing strain $= \dfrac{F}{AY}$

$$= \frac{44500}{15.2 \times 19.1 \times 10^{-6} \times 120 \times 10^9} = 0.127 \times 10^{-2}$$

5. **(b)** The rod is uniform, the mid-point will lie at half of its height.

Tension at the mid point of the rod = weight of the suspended mass + weight of the half of the rod

$$= Mg + \frac{Mg}{2} = \frac{3Mg}{2}$$

$\therefore$ Stress at the mid-point

$$= \frac{F}{A} = \frac{3Mg/2}{A} = \frac{3Mg}{2A}$$

6. **(d)**

7. **(a)** $\quad W = \dfrac{1}{2} \dfrac{(\text{Stress})^2}{Y} \times \text{Volume}$

As F, A and Y are same $\Rightarrow W \propto$ Volume (area is same)

$$W \propto l \qquad\qquad (V = Al)$$

$$\frac{W_1}{W_2} = \frac{l_1}{l_2} = \frac{l}{2l} = \frac{1}{2}$$

8. **(d)**

9. **(b)** $\quad B = \dfrac{p}{\Delta V / V} \Rightarrow \dfrac{1}{B} \propto \dfrac{\Delta V}{V} \quad [p = \text{constant}]$

10. **(a)** From the graph, it is clear that for the given value of load, elongation is maximum for wire OA. Hence OA is the thinnest wire among the four wires.

11. **(d)**

12. **(a)** Given:

$L = 10$ cm $= 0.1$ m; $P = 7 \times 10^6$ Pa;

$B = 140$ GPa $= 140 \times 10^9$ Pa

$$B = \frac{P}{DV/V} = \frac{PV}{DV} = \frac{PL^3}{DV}$$

$$\Rightarrow DV = \frac{PL^3}{B} = \frac{7 \times 10^6 \times (0.1)^3}{140 \times 10^9} = 5 \times 10^{-8}\, m^3$$

13. **(a)** From question, $V = 1$ litre $= 10^{-3}$ m³,

$$\frac{DV}{V} = \frac{0.1}{100} = 10^{-3};\ B = \frac{PV}{DV}$$

$$\Rightarrow P = B\frac{DV}{V}$$

$$= 2.2 \times 10^9 \times 10^{-3} = 2.2 \times 10^6\ \text{N/m}^2$$

14. **(c)**

$$\ell = \frac{FL}{AY} \Rightarrow \ell \propto \frac{1}{r^2}\quad \text{(F, L and Y are same)}$$

$$\frac{\ell_1}{\ell_2} = \left(\frac{r_2}{r_1}\right)^2 \Rightarrow \frac{\ell_1}{\ell_2} = \left(\frac{r_2}{2r_2}\right)^2 = \frac{1}{4}$$

$$\Rightarrow \ell_2 = 4\ell_1 = 4\ \text{cm}$$

15. **(c)** Given,

Radius of wire, $r = 2$ mm

Mass of the load m $= 4$ kg

$$\text{Stress} = \frac{F}{A} = \frac{mg}{\pi(r)^2}$$

$$= \frac{4 \times 3.1\pi}{\pi \times (2 \times 10^{-3})^2} = 3.1 \times 10^6\ \text{N/m}^2$$

16. **(a)** If force F acts along the length L of the wire of cross-section A, then energy stored in unit volume of wire is given by

$$\text{Energy density} = \frac{1}{2}\ \text{stress} \times \text{strain}$$

$$= \frac{1}{2} \times \frac{F}{A} \times \frac{F}{AY} \quad \left(\because \text{stress} = \frac{F}{A} \text{ and strain} = \frac{X}{AY}\right)$$

$$= \frac{1}{2}\frac{F^2}{A^2 Y} = \frac{1}{2}\frac{F^2 \times 16}{(\pi d^2)^2 Y} = \frac{1}{2}\frac{F^2 \times 16}{\pi d^4 Y}$$

If u_1 and u_2 are the densities of two wires, then

$$\frac{u_1}{u_2} = \left(\frac{d_2}{d_1}\right)^4 \Rightarrow \frac{d_1}{d_2} = (4)^{1/4} \Rightarrow \frac{d_1}{d_2} = \sqrt{2}:1$$

17. **(c)** Poisson's ratio,

$$\sigma = \frac{\text{lateral strain } (\beta)}{\text{longitudinal strain } (\alpha)}$$

For material like copper, $\sigma = 0.33$

And, $Y = 3k(1 - 2\sigma)$

Also, $\dfrac{9}{Y} = \dfrac{1}{k} + \dfrac{3}{\eta}$

$Y = 2\eta(1 + \sigma)$

Hence, $\eta < Y < k$

18. **(c)**

19. **(a)** Energy stored in the wire per unit volume,

$$E = \frac{1}{2} \times \text{stress} \times \text{strain} \qquad ...(i)$$

We know that, $Y = \dfrac{\text{stress}}{\text{strain}}$

$$\Rightarrow \text{strain} = \frac{\text{stress}}{Y}$$

On substituting the expression of strain in equation (i) we get

$$E = \frac{1}{2} \times \text{stress} \times \frac{\text{stress}}{Y} = \frac{1}{2}\cdot\frac{S^2}{Y}$$

20. (a) Given: $F = 100\,\text{kN} = 10^5\,\text{N}$

$Y = 2 \times 10^{11}\,\text{Nm}^{-2}$

$\ell_0 = 1.0\,\text{m}$

radius $r = 10\,\text{mm} = 10^{-2}\,\text{m}$

From formula, $Y = \dfrac{\text{Stress}}{\text{Strain}}$

$\Rightarrow \quad \text{Strain} = \dfrac{\text{Stress}}{Y} = \dfrac{F}{AY}$

$$= \dfrac{10^5}{\pi r^2 Y} = \dfrac{10^5}{3.14 \times 10^{-4} \times 2 \times 10^{11}} = \dfrac{1}{628}$$

Therefore % strain $= \dfrac{1}{628} \times 100 = 0.16\%$

21. (c)

22. (c) The given graph does not obey Hooke's law and there is no well defined plastic region. So the graph represents elastomers.

23. (b) Here pressure,

$P = 10\,\text{atm} = 10 \times 1.013 \times 10^5\,\text{Pa}$,

$B = 37 \times 10^9\,\text{N/m}^2$

$\text{Vol. strain} = \dfrac{\text{stress}}{\text{bulk modulus}} = \dfrac{P}{B}$

$$= \dfrac{10 \times 1.013 \times 10^5}{37 \times 10^9} = 2.74 \times 10^{-5}$$

$\therefore$ Fractional change in volume $= \dfrac{DV}{V} = 2.74 \times 10^{-5}$

24. (c)

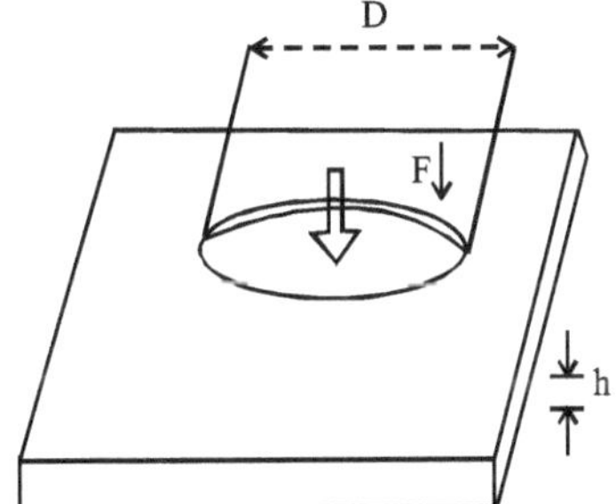

Shearing strain is created along the side surface of the punched disk. Note that the forces exerted on the disk are exerted along the circumference of the disk, and the total force exerted on its center only.

Let us assume that the shearing stress along the side surface of the disk is uniform, then

$$F = \int\limits_{\text{surface}} dF_{max} = \int\limits_{\text{surface}} \sigma_{max} dA = \sigma_{max} \int\limits_{\text{surface}} dA$$

$$= \int \sigma_{max}.A = \sigma_{max}.2\pi\left(\dfrac{D}{2}\right)h$$

$$= 3.5 \times 10^8 \times \left(\dfrac{1}{2} \times 10^{-2}\right) \times 0.3 \times 10^{-2} \times 2\pi$$

$$= 3.297 \times 10^4 \simeq 3.3 \times 10^4\,\text{N}$$

25. (d) $Y = 2\eta(1 + \sigma)$

$2.4\eta = 2\eta(1 + \sigma) \Rightarrow 1.2 = 1 + \sigma \Rightarrow \sigma = 0.2$

9   Mechanical Properties of Fluids

1. **(d)** Let, r = part or fraction of steel is inside the mercury. (Density of water = 1 gm/cc)

$$\therefore \quad V(7.8) = rV \times 13.6 + (1-r)V \times 1$$

or, $7.8 = 13.6\,r + 1 - r$

or, $12.6\,r = 6.8$

$$\therefore \quad r = \frac{6.8}{12.6} = 0.54$$

2. **(d)** According to principle of continuity, for a streamline flow of fluid through a tube of non-uniform cross-section the rate of flow of fluid (Q) is same at every point in the tube.

i.e., Av = constant $\Rightarrow A_1 v_1 = A_2 v_2$

Therefore, the rate of flow of fluid is same at M and N.

3. **(a)** Static potential energy = kinetic energy

$$mgh = \frac{1}{2}mv^2 \Rightarrow gh = \frac{1}{2}v^2$$

Pressure at bottom due to liquid column

$$= (3 \times 10^5 - 1 \times 10^5)\,\text{N m}^{-2} = 2 \times 10^5\,\text{N m}^{-2}$$

At bottom of tank,   Pressure P = ρgh

$$\therefore \quad v = \sqrt{\frac{2P}{\rho}} = \sqrt{\frac{2 \times 2 \times 10^5}{1 \times 10^3}} = \sqrt{400}\ \text{m/s}$$

Velocity of water v = 20 m/s

4. **(b)** When the temperature increases, the viscosity of gases increases and liquid decreases.

5. **(b)**

6. **(b)** $F_b + F_v = Mg$

Solving we get viscous force, $F_b = Mg\left(1 - \dfrac{d_2}{d_1}\right)$.

7. **(d)** Initially velocity increases with respect to time & becomes constant after some time, this constant velocity is called terminal velocity.

8. **(b)** When radius is doubled, increase in surface area

$$= 2 \times 4\pi\,(4R^2 - R^2) = 2 \times 4\pi \times 3R^2$$

$$= 24\pi R^2$$

Work done = Increase in area $\times$ T = $24\pi R^2$ T.

9. **(b)** Increment in area of soap film = $A_2 - A_1$

$$= 2 \times [(10 \times 0.6) - (10 \times 0.5)] \times 10^{-4}$$

$$= 2 \times 10^{-4}\,\text{m}^2$$

Work done = T $\times \Delta A$

$$= 7.2 \times 10^{-2} \times 2 \times 10^{-4} = 1.44 \times 10^{-5}\,\text{J}$$

10. **(c)**

11. **(a)** When two capillary tubes of same size are joined in parallel, then equivalent fluid resistance is

$$R_S = R_1 + R_2 = \frac{8\eta L}{\pi R^4} + \frac{8\eta \times 2L}{\pi(2R)^4} = \left(\frac{8\eta L}{\pi R^4}\right) \times \frac{9}{8}$$

Net rate of flow $= \dfrac{P}{R_S} = \dfrac{\pi P R^4}{8\eta L} \times \dfrac{8}{9}$

$$= \frac{8}{9}X \quad \left[\text{as } X = \frac{\pi P R^4}{8\eta L}\right]$$

12. **(d)** The volume of liquid flowing through both the tubes i.e., rate of flow of liquid is same.

Therefore, $V = V_1 = V_2$

i.e., $\dfrac{\pi P_1 r_1^4}{8\eta l_1} = \dfrac{\pi P_2 r_2^4}{8\eta l_2}$ or $\dfrac{P_1 r_1^4}{l_1} = \dfrac{P_2 r_2^4}{l_2}$

$\because$ $P_2 = 4P_1$ and $l_2 = l_1/4$

$$\frac{P_1 r_1^4}{l_1} = \frac{4P_1 r_2^4}{l_1/4} \Rightarrow r_2^4 = \frac{r_1^4}{16} \Rightarrow r_2 = r_1/2$$

13. **(b)**

14. **(b)** Time taken for the level to fall from H to H′,

$$t = \frac{A}{A_o}\sqrt{\frac{2}{g}}\left[\sqrt{H} - \sqrt{H'}\right]$$

15. **(a)** Suppose P_{gas} is the pressure of the gas on the oil. As the points A and B are at the same level in the mercury columns, so

$$P_A = P_B$$

or $\quad P_{gas} + \rho_{oil}\, gh_{oil} = P_a + \rho_{Hg}\, g\, h_{Hg}$

or $\quad P_{gas} + 820 \times 9.8 \times (1 + 1.50)$

$$= P_a + 13.6 \times 10^3 \times 9.8 \times (1.5 + 0.75)$$

or $\quad P_{gas} + 20.09 \times 10^3 = P_a + 299.88 \times 10^3$

$\therefore P_{gas} - Pa = 299.88 \times 10^3 - 20.09 \times 10^3$

or $[P_{gas}]_{gauge} = 279.8 \times 10^3\,\text{N/m}^2 = 2.8 \times 10^5\, P_a$

Absolute pressure of gas

$$[P_{gas}]_{absolute} = [P_{gas}]_{gauge} + P_a$$
$$= 2.8 \times 10^5 + 1.01 \times 10^5 = 3.81 \times 10^5\, P_a$$

16. **(a)** Acceleration due to gravity changes with the depth,

$$g' = g\left(1 - \frac{d}{R}\right)$$

And, $h = \dfrac{2T\cos\theta}{r\rho g}$

$\therefore$ Ratio, $\dfrac{x}{y}$ is $\left(1 - \dfrac{d}{R}\right)$

17. **(c)**

18. **(b)** Let the width of each plate is b and due to surface tension liquid will rise upto height h then upward force due to surface tension.

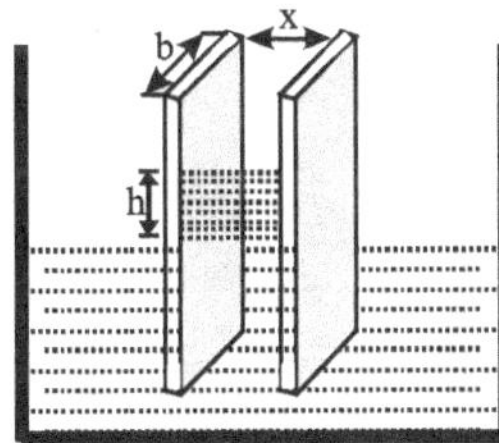

$$= 2Tb\cos\theta \qquad \ldots(i)$$

Weight of the liquid rises

in between the plates

$$= Vdg = (bxh)dg \qquad \ldots(ii)$$

Equating (i) and (ii) we get, $2T\cos\theta = xhdg$

$$\therefore \quad h = \frac{2T\cos\theta}{xdg}$$

19. **(c)** $\quad F = -\eta A\dfrac{dv}{dx}$ and $\dfrac{dv}{dx} = \dfrac{v_2 - v_1}{x_2 - x_1}$

$$= \frac{(0-3)\,\text{cm/s}}{(2-0)\,\text{mm}} = -\frac{3}{0.2}\,\text{s}^{-1} = -15\,\text{s}^{-1}$$

$$F = -15.5 \times 100 \times (-15) = 0.2325\,\text{N}$$

20. **(a)** $\quad V = \dfrac{KPr^4}{\eta\ell}$

21. **(a)**

22. **(c)** Angle of contact θ $\cos\theta = \dfrac{T_{SA} - T_{SL}}{T_{LA}}$

when water is on a waxy or oily surface

$T_{SA} < T_{SL}$ $\cos\theta$ is negative i.e., $90° < \theta < 180°$

i.e., angle of contact θ increases

And for $\theta > 90°$ liquid level in capillary tube fall. i.e., h decreases

23. **(c)**

24. **(b)** Here,

$$\left(\frac{3}{5}V_s\right)\rho_w g = \left(\frac{1}{4}V_s\right)\rho_\ell g \Rightarrow \frac{\rho_\ell}{\rho_w} = \frac{12}{5}$$

25. **(a)**

26. **(a)** Area of cross-section of tube, $a_1 = 8.0\,\text{cm}^2$

$$= 8 \times 10^{-4}\,\text{m}^2,$$

No. of holes = 40; Diameter of each hole,

$$D = 1\text{mm} = 10^{-3}\,\text{m}$$

$\therefore$ Radius of each hole, $r = \dfrac{D}{2} = \dfrac{1}{2} \times 10^{-3}\,\text{m}$

$$= 5 \times 10^{-4}\,\text{m}$$

Area of cross-section of each hole $= \pi r^2$
$= \pi(5 \times 10^{-4})^2\,\text{m}^2$

Total area of cross section of 40 holes,

$$a_2 = 40 \times \pi (5 \times 10^{-4})^2 \, m^2$$

Speed of liquid inside the tube, $v_1 = 1.5 \, m/min$

$$= \frac{1.5}{60} \, ms^{-1}$$

If v_2 is the velocity of the ejection of the liquid through the holes, then $a_1 \, v_1 = a_2 \, v_2$ 853

$$\text{or} \quad v_2 = \frac{(8 \times 10^{-4}) \times 1.5}{60 \times 40 \times \pi \times (5 \times 10^{-4})^2}$$

$$\Rightarrow v_2 = 0.637 \, ms^{-1}$$

27. **(b)** Given, $r = 3mm = 0.3 \, m$, $S = 4.65 \times 10^{-1} \, Nm^{-1}$,

$$P = 1.01 \times 10^5 \, Pa$$

Excess of pressure inside the drop of mercury is given by, $p = \dfrac{2S}{r} = \dfrac{2 \times 4.65 \times 10^{-1}}{3 \times 10^{-3}} = 310 \, Pa$

28. **(c)** Since pressure is transmitted undiminished throughout the fluid (Pascal's law)

$$F_1 = \frac{A_1}{A_2} F_2 = \frac{\pi (5 \times 5)}{\pi (15 \times 15)} (1350 \times 9.81)$$

$$\approx 1.5 \times 10^3 \, N$$

29. **(c)** According to equation of continuity

$$A_1 V_1 = A_2 V_2 + A_3 V_3$$

$$\Rightarrow 4 \times 0.2 = 2 \times 0.2 + 0.4 \times V_3 \Rightarrow V_3 = 1 \, m/s.$$

30. **(c)** For floating, we have

$$mg = \rho A v^2$$

$$\therefore \quad \rho = \frac{mg}{Av^2} = \frac{1.23 \times 10}{0.1 \times 10^2} = 1.23 \, kg/m^3$$

Thermal Properties of Matter

1. **(c)** $L = L_0 (1 + \alpha \Delta\theta) \Rightarrow \dfrac{L_1}{L_2} = \dfrac{1 + \alpha(\Delta\theta)_1}{1 + \alpha(\Delta\theta)_2}$

$\Rightarrow \dfrac{10}{L_2} = \dfrac{1 + 11 \times 10^{-6} \times 20}{1 + 11 \times 10^{-6} \times 19} \Rightarrow L_2 = 9.99989$

$\Rightarrow$ Length is shorten by

$10 - 9.99989 = 0.00011 = 11 \times 10^{-5}$ cm.

2. **(c)** $\dfrac{dQ}{dt} = \dfrac{kA\,(T_1 - T_2)}{L}$

$[(T_1 - T_2)$ is the temperature difference]

3. **(b)**

4. **(b)** $\dfrac{C}{5} = \dfrac{F - 32}{9}$; or $C = \dfrac{5}{9}F - \dfrac{160}{9}$. Equating

with $mx + c$

Thus the slope of line AB is 5/9.

5. **(c)** $\dfrac{\Delta Q_1}{\Delta t} = \dfrac{\Delta Q_2}{\Delta t}$

6. **(c)** Using Wein's law, $\lambda_m T = $ constant

$\lambda_1 T_1 = \lambda_2 T_2$

$\lambda_2 = \lambda_1 \dfrac{T_1}{T_2} \qquad \lambda_2 = \dfrac{\lambda_0 T}{2T} = \dfrac{\lambda_0}{2}$

7 **(b)**

8. **(c)** In parallel combination, the equivalent thermal conductivity is given by

$K = \dfrac{K_1 A_1 + K_2 A_2 + K_3 A_3 + \dots\dots + K_n A_n}{A_1 + A_2 + A_3 + \dots\dots + A_n}$

For two rods of equal area,

$K = \dfrac{(K_1 + K_2) A}{2A} = \dfrac{K_1 + K_2}{2}$ (if $A_1 = A_2 = A$)

9. **(c)**

10. **(d)** Mass of copper $= m_1 = 2.5$kg $= 2500$g,
Change in temperature $= \Delta t = 500 - 0 = 500°$C
Specific heat of copper $= c_1 = 0.39$ J/g/°C,
Latent heat of fusion of ice $= L = 335$ J/g

Let mass of ice melted $= m_2$

$\because$ Heat lost by copper = Heat gained by ice

$\Rightarrow m_1 c_1 \Delta t = m_2 L$

$m_2 = \dfrac{m_1 c_1 \Delta t}{L} = \dfrac{2500 \times 0.39 \times 500}{335} = 1455$g

11. **(c)** According to Newton's law of cooling, the temperature goes on decreasing with time non-linearly.

12. **(c)** From Newton's law of cooling

$\dfrac{dQ}{dt} = -KA \dfrac{dT}{dx}$

Area of cross-section A and thickness dx is the same.

Also $dQ = mCd\theta$

Thus in first case

$\dfrac{m \times C \times (61° - 59°)}{4} = \dfrac{-KA}{dx}\left[\left(\dfrac{61° + 51°}{2}\right) - 30°\right]$

(i) In second case,

$\dfrac{m \times C \times (51° - 49°)}{t} = \dfrac{-KA}{dx}\left[\left(\dfrac{51° + 49°}{2}\right) - 30°\right]$

(ii) Dividing equation (i) by equation (ii)

$\dfrac{t}{4} = \dfrac{30}{20}$ or $t = 6$ minutes.

13. **(a)**

14. **(a)** According to Newton's law of cooling,

$\dfrac{\theta_1 - \theta_2}{t} = K\left[\dfrac{\theta_1 + \theta_2}{2} - \theta_0\right]$

where θ_0 is the surrounding temperature.

$\therefore \dfrac{60 - 40}{7} = K\left(\dfrac{60 + 40}{2} - 10\right)$

$\Rightarrow \dfrac{20}{7} = 40K \Rightarrow K = \dfrac{1}{14}$

$$\therefore \ \frac{40-28}{t} = K\left[\frac{40+28}{2}-10\right] \Rightarrow \frac{12}{t} = 24K$$

or $\quad t = \dfrac{12}{24K} = \dfrac{12 \times 14}{24} = 7 \, \text{min}$

15. **(b)**

16. **(a)** Let the readings of two thermometers coincide at $C = F = x$

As $\dfrac{C}{5} = \dfrac{F-32}{9}$ $\qquad \therefore \dfrac{x}{5} = \dfrac{x-32}{9}$

or $9x = 5x - 160 \Rightarrow 4x = -160, \ \therefore x = -40°C$

17. **(c)**

18. **(b)** Area of the hole at 27°C

$$= \ S_1 = \frac{\pi D_1^2}{4} = \frac{\pi}{4} \times (4.24)^2 \, \text{cm}^2$$

Area of the hole at 227°C $= \ S_2 = \dfrac{\pi D_2^2}{4}$

$\beta = 2\alpha = 2 \times 1.70 \times 10^{-5} = 3.4 \times 10^{-5} \, / \, °C.$

Increase in area $= S_2 - S_1 = S_1 \beta \Delta T$

$\therefore \ \ S_2 = S_1 + S_1 \beta \Delta T = S_1 (1 + \beta \Delta T)$

$$\frac{\pi D_2^2}{4} = \frac{\pi}{4} \times (4.24)^2 \left[1 + 3.4 \times 10^{-5} \times (227 - 27)\right]$$

$\Rightarrow D_2^2 = (4.24)^2 \times 1.0068 \Rightarrow D_2 = 4.2544 \, \text{cm}$

$\therefore \quad$ Change in diameter

$\qquad = 4.2544 - 4.24 = 0.0144 \, \text{cm}$

19. **(a)** $\ F = Y \alpha t A$ or $F \propto \alpha$

$(\because \ Y t A$ is same for both copper and iron)

or $\ F_C \propto \alpha_C$ and $F_I \propto \alpha_I$

$\therefore \ \dfrac{F_C}{F_I} = \dfrac{3/2}{1} = \dfrac{3}{2}$

20. **(a)** $\ \dfrac{h_1}{h_2} = \dfrac{\rho_2}{\rho_1} = \dfrac{(1+\gamma\,\theta_1)}{(1+\gamma\,\theta_2)} \left[\because \rho = \dfrac{\rho_0}{(1+\gamma\,\theta)}\right]$

$\Rightarrow \dfrac{50}{60} = \dfrac{1+\gamma \times 50}{1+\gamma \times 100} \Rightarrow \gamma = 0.005/°C$

21. **(b)** According to Wien's law $\lambda_m \propto \dfrac{1}{T}$ and from the graph $(\lambda_m)_1 < (\lambda_m)_3 < (\lambda_m)_2$ therefore $T_1 > T_3 > T_2$.

22. **(a)** Heat given by water $= m_w C_w (T_{\text{mix}} - T_w)$

$$= 200 \times 1 \times (31 - 25)$$

Heat taken by steam $= m\,L_{\text{stem}} + m\,C_w (T_s - T_{\text{mix}})$

$= m \times 540 + m\,(1) \times (100 - 31)$

$= m \times 540 + m\,(1) \times (69)$

From the principal of calorimeter,

Heat lost = Heat gained

$\therefore (200)(31 - 25) = m \times 540 + m(1)(69)$

$\Rightarrow 1200 = m(609) \Rightarrow m \approx 2.$

23. **(c)** Heat loss = Heat gain = $mS\Delta\theta$

So, $m_A S_A \Delta\theta_A = m_B S_B \Delta\theta_B$

$\Rightarrow 100 \times S_A \times (100 - 90) = 50 \times S_B \times (90 - 75)$

$2S_A = 1.5S_B \Rightarrow S_A = \dfrac{3}{4} S_B$

Now, $100 \times S_A \times (100 - \theta) = 50 \times S_B \times (\theta - 50)$

$2 \times \left(\dfrac{3}{4}\right) \times (100 - \theta) = (\theta - 50)$

$300 - 3\theta = 2\theta - 100$

$400 = 5\theta \Rightarrow \theta = 80°C$

24. **(a)** $\ \Delta U = \Delta Q = mc\Delta T$

$$= \frac{100}{1000} \times 4184\,(50 - 30) \approx 8.4 \, \text{kJ}$$

25. **(d)** Let T be the temperature of the interface. In the steady state, $Q_1 = Q_2$

$$\begin{array}{cccc} T_1 & \ell_1 & \ell_2 & T_2 \\ \hline K_1 & & K_2 & \end{array}$$

$\therefore \ \dfrac{K_1 A(T_1 - T)}{\ell_1} = \dfrac{K_2 A(T - T_2)}{\ell_2},$

where A is the area of cross-section.

$\Rightarrow \quad K_1 A(T_1 - T)\ell_2 = K_2 A(T - T_2)\ell_1$

$\Rightarrow \quad K_1 T_1 \ell_2 - K_1 T \ell_2 = K_2 T \ell_1 - K_2 T_2 \ell_1$

$\Rightarrow \quad (K_2 \ell_1 + K_1 \ell_2)T = K_1 T_1 \ell_2 + K_2 T_2 \ell_1$

$$\Rightarrow \quad T = \frac{K_1 T_1 \ell_2 + K_2 T_2 \ell_1}{K_2 \ell_1 + K_1 \ell_2}$$

$$= \frac{K_1 \ell_2 T_1 + K_2 \ell_1 T_2}{K_1 \ell_2 + K_2 \ell_1}.$$

26. **(b)**

27. **(a)** Change in length of the metal wire (Δl) when its temperature is changed by ΔT is given by

$$\Delta l = l \alpha \Delta T$$

Here, α = Coefficient of linear expansion

Here, $\Delta l = 0.02\%$, $\Delta T = 10°C$

$$\therefore \alpha = \frac{\Delta l}{l \Delta T} = \frac{0.02}{100 \times 10}$$

$$\Rightarrow \alpha = 2 \times 10^{-5}$$

Volume coefficient of expansion,

$$\gamma = 3\alpha = 6 \times 10^{-5}$$

$$\because \rho = \frac{M}{V}$$

$$\frac{\Delta V}{V} \times 100 = \gamma \Delta T$$

$$= (6 \times 10^{-5} \times 10 \times 100) = 6 \times 10^{-2}$$

Volume increase by 0.06% therefore density decrease by 0.06%.

28. **(c)** The three curves AB, CD and EF meet at point P which is called the triple point of water. It is the point where all three states solid, liquid and gas of water co-exists.

29. **(a)** Let the piece of ice be fall from a height h.

Then $\quad mL = \dfrac{1}{4} mgh \Rightarrow h = \dfrac{4L}{g}$

$$= \frac{4 \times 3.4 \times 10^5}{10} = 136 \, \text{km}.$$

30. **(d)** $\ell = 10 \, \text{cm} = 0.1 \, \text{m}$, $d = 0.2 \, \text{mm}$,

$r = 0.1 \, \text{mm} = 1 \times 10^{-4} \, \text{m}$,

$e = 0.2$, $T = 2000 \, \text{K}$, $\sigma = 5.67 \times 10^{-8} \, \text{W/m}^2 \, \text{K}^4$

According to stefan's law of radiation, rate of emission of heat for an ordinary body,

$$E = \sigma A e T^4 = \sigma (2 \pi r \ell) e T^4 \quad [A = 2\pi r \ell]$$

$$= 5.67 \times 10^{-8} \times 2 \times 3.14 \times 1 \times 10^{-4} \times 0.1 \times 0.2 \times (2000)^4$$

$$= 11.4 \, \text{W}$$

$\therefore$ Power radiated by the filament = 11.4 W

11   Thermodynamics

1.   **(b)** $W = P(\Delta V) = m(C_p - C_v)\Delta T$

$$= 4(0.219 - 0.157) \times 4200 \times (120 - 20)$$

$$\simeq 104 \times 10^3 \text{J}$$

2.   **(a)**   From the first law of thermodynamics

$$dQ = dU + dW$$

Here $dW = 0$ (given)

$\therefore dQ = dU$

Now since $dQ < 0$ (given)

$\Rightarrow dU = -$ve $\Rightarrow dU$ decreases.

$\Rightarrow$ Temperature decreases.

3.   **(c)**

4.   **(d)**   Change in internal energy (ΔU) depends upon initial and final state of the function while ΔQ and ΔW are path dependent.

5.   **(a)**   PV = constant represents isothermal process.

6.   **(c)**

7.   **(c)**   For an adiabatic process of an ideal gas.

$$PV^{\gamma} = \text{const where} \quad \gamma = \frac{C_P}{C_V}$$

8.   **(c)**   For isothermal process

$$P_A V = P_B \frac{V}{2} \implies P_B = 2P_A \qquad ...(i)$$

For adiabatic process

$$P_A V^{\gamma} = P_B \left(\frac{V}{2}\right)^{\gamma} \implies P_B = 2^{\gamma} P_A \qquad ...(ii)$$

Since $\gamma > 1$, $P_B > P_A$

9.   **(b)**

10.   **(a)**   As we know,

$$\Delta Q = \Delta u + \Delta w \quad \text{(Ist law of thermodynamics)}$$

$$\implies \Delta Q = \Delta u + P\Delta v \quad \text{or}$$

$$150 = \Delta u + 100(1 - 2) = \Delta u - 100$$

$$\implies \Delta u = 150 + 100 = 250 \text{J}$$

Thus the internal energy of the gas increases by 250 J

11.   **(d)** $dU = dQ - dW = (8 \times 10^5 - 6.5 \times 10^5)$

$$= 1.5 \times 10^5 \text{ J}$$

$$dW = dQ - dU = 10^5 - 1.5 \times 10^5$$

$$= -0.5 \times 10^5 \text{ J}$$

$-$ ve sign indicates that work done on the gas is 0.5×10^5 J .

12.   **(b)**   For an adiabatic process, the temperature-volume relationship is

$$T_1 V_1^{\gamma-1} = T_2 V_2^{\gamma-1} \implies T_1 = T_2 \left(\frac{V_2}{V_1}\right)^{\gamma-1}$$

Here $\gamma = 1.4$ (for diatomic gas).

$$V_2 = \frac{V_1}{32}, T_1 = T_i, T_2 = aT_i$$

$$\therefore T_i = aT_i \left[\frac{1}{32}\right]^{1.4-1} \qquad \therefore T_i = aT_i \left[\frac{1}{2^5}\right]^{0.4} = \frac{aT_i}{4}$$

$$\therefore a = 4$$

13.   **(b)**   Volume $v = \dfrac{m}{d}$ and using $PV^{\gamma} = $ constant

$$\frac{P'}{P} = \frac{V}{V'} = \left(\frac{d'}{d}\right)^{\gamma}$$

or $128 = (32)^{\gamma}$ $\therefore \gamma = \dfrac{7}{5} = 1.4$

14. **(d)** Isochoric proceess $dV = 0$

$W = 0$ proceess 1

Isobaric : $W = P\,\Delta V = nR\Delta T$

Adiabatic $|W| = \dfrac{nR\Delta T}{\gamma - 1}$ $\quad 0 < \gamma - 1 < 1$

As workdone in case of adiabatic process is more so process 3 is adiabatic and process 2 is isobaric.

15. **(a)** From first law of thermodynamics

$Q_{adc} = \Delta U_{adc} + W_{adc}$

$50\,J = \Delta U_{adc} + 20\,J \quad \Rightarrow \Delta U_{adc} = 30\,J$

Again, $Q_{abc} = \Delta U_{abc} + W_{abc}$

$W_{abc} = Q_{abc} - \Delta U_{abc} = Q_{abc} - \Delta U_{adc}$

$\qquad = 36\,J - 30\,J = 6\,J$

16. **(a)** Given: Temperature of cold body, $T_2 = 250$ K temperature of hot body; $T_1 = 300$ K

Heat received, $Q_2 = 500$ cal work done, $W = ?$

Efficiency $= 1 - \dfrac{T_2}{T_1} = \dfrac{W}{Q_2 + W}$

$\Rightarrow 1 - \dfrac{250}{300} = \dfrac{W}{Q_2 + W}$

$W = \dfrac{Q_2}{5} = \dfrac{500 \times 4.2}{5} J = 420\,J$

17. **(b)**

18. **(a)** As we know $\eta = \dfrac{W}{Q_1} = 1 - \dfrac{T_2}{T_1}$

$\Rightarrow \eta = 1 - \dfrac{300\,K}{1200\,K} = \dfrac{3}{4}$

$\dfrac{3}{4} = \dfrac{W}{Q_1} \Rightarrow Q_1 = W \times \dfrac{4}{3} \Rightarrow Q_1 = 12.6 \times 10^6 \times \dfrac{4}{3}$

$Q_1 = 16.8 \times 10^6 J.$

19. **(a)**

20. **(b)** $\because \ \eta = 1 - \dfrac{T_2}{T_1} = \dfrac{W}{Q_1} = \dfrac{Q_1 - Q_2}{Q_1}$

where Q_1 = heat absorbed, Q_2 = heat rejected

$\Rightarrow 1 - \dfrac{T/3}{T} = \dfrac{W}{Q_1} \Rightarrow \dfrac{2}{3} = \dfrac{W}{Q_1} = \dfrac{Q_1 - Q_2}{Q_1}$

$\Rightarrow \dfrac{2}{3} = 1 - \dfrac{Q_2}{Q_1} \Rightarrow \dfrac{Q_2}{Q_1} = \dfrac{1}{3} \Rightarrow Q_2 = \dfrac{Q_1}{3} = \dfrac{Q}{3}$

21. **(c)**

22. **(b)** $\eta = 1 - \dfrac{T_2}{T_1} = 1 - \dfrac{(273 + 27)}{(273 + 627)}$

$= 1 - \dfrac{300}{900} = 1 - \dfrac{1}{3} = \dfrac{2}{3}$

But $\eta = \dfrac{W}{Q} = \dfrac{2}{3} \Rightarrow W = \dfrac{2}{3} \times Q = \dfrac{2}{3} \times 3 \times 10^6$

$= 2 \times 10^6 \, cal = 2 \times 10^6 \times 4.2\,J = 8.4 \times 10^6 J$

23. **(b)** Total work done by the gas during the cycle is equal to area of triangle ABC.

$\therefore \ \Delta W = \dfrac{1}{2} \times 4 \times 5 = 10\,J$

24. **(b)** Given, $V_1 = 1$ litre, $P_1 = 1$ atm

$V_2 = 3$ litre, $\gamma = 1.40,$

Using, $PV^\gamma = \text{constant} \Rightarrow P_1 V_1^\gamma = P_2 V_2^\gamma$

$\Rightarrow P_2 = P_1 \times \left(\dfrac{1}{3}\right)^{1.4} = \dfrac{1}{4.6555}\,atm$

$\therefore$ Work done, $W = \dfrac{P_1 V_1 - P_2 V_2}{\gamma - 1}$

$= \dfrac{\left(1 \times 1 - \dfrac{1}{4.6555} \times 3\right) 1.01325 \times 10^5 \times 10^{-3}}{0.4}$

$= 90.1\,J$

Closest value of $W = 90.5\,J$

25. **(a)**

26. **(d)** Volume of water does not change, no work is done on or by the system ($W = 0$)

According to first law of thermodynamics

$$Q = \Delta U + W$$

For Isochoric process $Q = \Delta U$

$$\Delta U = \mu c d T = 2 \times 4184 \times 20 = 16.7 \, kJ.$$

27. **(b)** Work done during the process $A \to B$

= Area of trapezium (= area bounded by indicator diagram with V-axis)

$$= \frac{1}{2}\left(2P_0 + P_0\right)\left(2V_0 - V_0\right) = \frac{3}{2}P_0V_0$$

Ideal gas eqn : $PV = nRT$

$$\Rightarrow \quad T = \frac{PV}{nR} = \frac{3P_0V_0}{2nR}$$

28. **(b)** $\Delta U_{ac} = -(\Delta U_{ca}) = -(-180) = 180 \, J$

$$Q = 250 + 60 = 310 \, J$$

Now $Q = \Delta U + W$

or $310 = 180 + W$

or $W = 130 \, J$

29. **(d)** The process is equivalent to $TV^{1/2} = C$

Compare with $TV^{\gamma-1} = C \Rightarrow x = 3/2$

$$\Rightarrow C = \frac{R}{\gamma - 1} + \frac{R}{1 - X} = \frac{R}{2/3} + \frac{R}{1 - (3/2)}$$

$$= \frac{3}{2}R - 2R = -\frac{1}{2}R$$

30. **(a)** $\Delta Q = \Delta U + \Delta W$

$$\Rightarrow \frac{\Delta W}{\Delta Q} = 1 - \frac{\Delta U}{\Delta Q} = 1 - \frac{nC_V dT}{nC_P dT}$$

$$\Rightarrow \frac{\Delta W}{\Delta Q} = 1 - \frac{C_V}{C_P} = 1 - \frac{3}{5} = \frac{2}{5} = 0.4$$

12   Kinetic Theory

1.   **(c)**   At constant pressure

$$V \propto T \;\Rightarrow\; \frac{\Delta V}{V} = \frac{\Delta T}{T}$$

Hence ratio of increase in volume per degree rise in kelvin temperature to it's origianl volume

$$= \frac{(\Delta V / \Delta T)}{V} = \frac{1}{T}$$

2.   **(c)** $\dfrac{PV}{T} = nR = \left(\dfrac{m}{M}\right)R$ or $\dfrac{PV}{T} = \left(\dfrac{R}{M}\right)m$

i.e. $\dfrac{PV}{T}$ versus m graph is straight line passing through origin with slope R/M, i.e. the slope depends on molecular mass of the gas M and is different for different gases.

3.   **(b)**

4.   **(a)** $P^2 V = $ constant   .... (1)

For an ideal gas, $PV = nRT$ .... (2)

Squaring equ. (2) and then divide equ. (1) by equ. (2), we get

$(T^2/V) = $ constant $\Rightarrow T \propto \sqrt{V}$

So, $T_2 = \sqrt{\dfrac{V_2}{V_1}}\, T_1 = \sqrt{2}\,T_0$ [as $v_2 = 2v_1$]

5.   **(b)**

6.   **(c)**   According to Dalton's law of partial pressures, we have $P = P_1 + P_2 + P_3$

7.   **(b)** $v_{rms} > v_{av} > v_{mp}$,

as $v_{mp} = 0.816\, v_{rms}$ and $v_{av} = 0.92\, v_{rms}$

8.   **(c)** $v \propto \sqrt{T}$ $\therefore \dfrac{v'}{v} = \sqrt{\dfrac{T'}{T}}$

Given $v' = 2v$ or, $\dfrac{2}{1} = \sqrt{\dfrac{T'}{T}}$

$\therefore \; T' = 4\,T = 4 \times 120\,K = 480\,K$

9.   **(a)** $P = \dfrac{1}{3}\rho \bar{v}^2 = \dfrac{1}{3} \times (6 \times 10^{-2}) \times (500)^2$

$\qquad\qquad = 5 \times 10^3 \, N/m^2$

10.   **(a)**

11.   **(c)**   From P-V graph,

$P \propto \dfrac{1}{V}$,   T = constant and Pressure is increasing from 2 to 1 so option (c) represents correct T-P graph.

12.   **(d)**   Using, $\gamma_{\text{mixture}} = \dfrac{n_1 C_{p_1} + n_2 C_{p_2}}{n_1 C_{v_1} + n_2 C_{v_2}}$

$\Rightarrow \dfrac{n_1}{\gamma_1 - 1} + \dfrac{n_2}{\gamma_2 - 1} = \dfrac{n_1 + n_2}{\gamma_m - 1}$

$\Rightarrow \dfrac{3}{\frac{4}{3} - 1} + \dfrac{2}{\frac{5}{3} - 1} = \dfrac{5}{\gamma_m - 1}$

$\Rightarrow \dfrac{9}{1} + \dfrac{2 \times 3}{2} = \dfrac{5}{\gamma_m - 1} \Rightarrow \gamma_m - 1 = \dfrac{5}{12}$

$\Rightarrow \gamma_m = \dfrac{17}{12} = 1.42$

13.   **(c)** $V = 25 \times 10^{-3}\, m^3$, $N = 1$ mole of O_2

$T = 300\,K$

$V_{rms} = 200\, m/s$

$\therefore \; \lambda = \dfrac{1}{\sqrt{2}\,N\pi r^2}$

Average time $\dfrac{1}{\tau} = \dfrac{<V>}{\lambda} = 200.N\pi r^2.\sqrt{2}$

$= \dfrac{\sqrt{2} \times 200 \times 6.023 \times 10^{23}}{25 \times 10^{-3}}.\pi \times 10^{-18} \times 0.09$

The closest value in the given option is $= 10^{10}$

14.   **(c)**   Relaxation time $(\tau) \propto \dfrac{\text{mean free path}}{\text{speed}}$

$\Rightarrow \tau \propto \dfrac{1}{v}$ and, $v \propto \sqrt{T}$

$\therefore \tau \propto \dfrac{1}{\sqrt{T}}$

Hence graph between τ v/s $\dfrac{1}{\sqrt{T}}$ is a straight line which is correctly depicted by graph shown in option (c).

15. **(b)** Let C_p and C_v be the specific heat capacity of the gas at constant pressure and volume.

At constant pressure, heat required

$$\Delta Q_1 = nC_p\Delta T$$

$$\Rightarrow 160 = nC_p \cdot 50 \qquad \text{...(i)}$$

At constant volume, heat required

$$\Delta Q_2 = nC_v\Delta T$$

$$\Rightarrow 240 = nC_v \cdot 100 \qquad \text{...(ii)}$$

Dividing (i) by (ii), we get

$$\frac{160}{240} = \frac{C_p}{C_v} \cdot \frac{50}{100} \Rightarrow \frac{C_p}{C_v} = \frac{4}{3}$$

$$\gamma = \frac{C_p}{C_v} = \frac{4}{3} = 1 + \frac{2}{f}$$

(Here, f = degree of freedom)

$$\Rightarrow f = 6.$$

16. **(c)** Total degree of freedom $f = 3 + 2 = 5$

Total energy, $U = \dfrac{nfRT}{2} = \dfrac{5RT}{2}$

And $\gamma = \dfrac{C_p}{C_v} = 1 + \dfrac{2}{f} = 1 + \dfrac{2}{5} = \dfrac{7}{5}$

17. **(d)** Here degree of freedom, $f = 3 + 3 = 6$ for triatomic non-linear molecule.

Internal energy of a mole of the gas at temperature T,

$$U = \frac{f}{2}nRT = \frac{6}{2}RT = 3RT$$

18. **(d)** The ratio of specific heats at constant pressure (C_p) and constant volume (C_v)

$$\frac{C_p}{C_v} = \gamma = \left(1 + \frac{2}{f}\right)$$

where f is degree of freedom

$$\frac{C_p}{C_v} = \left(1 + \frac{2}{5}\right) = \frac{7}{5}$$

19. **(b)** Using, $\tau = \dfrac{1}{2n\pi d^2 V_{avg}}$

$$\therefore t \propto \frac{\sqrt{T}}{P} \left[\therefore n = \frac{\text{no. of molecules}}{\text{Volume}}\right]$$

or, $\dfrac{t_1}{6\times10^{-8}} = \dfrac{\sqrt{500}}{2P} \times \dfrac{P}{\sqrt{300}} \approx 4\times10^{-8}$

20. **(c)** Heat transferred,

$$Q = nC_v\Delta T \text{ as gas in closed vessel}$$

To double the rms speed, temperature should be 4 times i.e., $T' = 4T$ as $v_{rms} = \sqrt{3RT/M}$

$$\therefore Q = \frac{15}{28} \times \frac{5\times R}{2} \times (4T - T)$$

$$\left[\therefore \frac{C_P}{C_V} = \gamma_{diatomic} = \frac{7}{5} \& C_p - C_v = R\right]$$

or, $Q = 10000\,J = 10\,kJ$

21. **(a)** $\because C = \sqrt{\dfrac{3RT}{M}}$

$$\Rightarrow (1930)^2 = \frac{3\times8.314\times300}{M}$$

$$M = \frac{3\times8.314\times300}{1930\times1930} \approx 2\times10^{-3}\,kg$$

The gas is H_2.

22. **(a)**

23. **(b)** Let n_1 and n_2 be the number of moles of each gas. Then

$$n_1 = \frac{PV}{RT} \text{ and } n_2 = \frac{PV}{RT}$$

When the two gases are mixed, total number of moles,

$$n = n_1 + n_2$$

$$\Rightarrow \frac{P'V}{RT} = \frac{PV}{RT} + \frac{PV}{RT} \qquad \Rightarrow P' = 2P$$

(where P' is the pressure of the mixture.)

24. **(c)** Given

$$C_P - C_V = 5000 \text{ J/mole}°C \quad \text{.....(i)}$$

$$\frac{C_P}{C_V} = 1.6 \qquad \text{.....(ii)}$$

From equations (i) & (ii),

$$\Rightarrow \frac{C_P}{C_V} - \frac{C_V}{C_V} = \frac{5000}{C_V} \quad \Rightarrow 1.6 - 1 = \frac{5000}{C_V}$$

$$\Rightarrow C_V = \frac{5000}{0.6} = 8.33 \times 10^3$$

Hence $C_p = 1.6\,C_V = 1.6 \times 8.33 \times 10^3$;

$C_p = 1.33 \times 10^4$

25. (c) $\quad C_{V\,mix} = \dfrac{n_1 C_{v_1} + n_2 C_{v_2}}{n_1 + n_2}$

$$\Rightarrow \frac{13R}{6} = \frac{n_1 C_{v_1} + 2n_1 C_{v_2}}{n_1 + 2n_1} \qquad \left[\because \frac{n_1}{n_2} = \frac{1}{2}\right]$$

$$\Rightarrow \frac{13R}{2} = C_{v_1} + 2C_{v_2}$$

Possible values are, $\quad C_{v_1} = \dfrac{3R}{2}, \; C_{v_2} = \dfrac{5R}{2}$

$\therefore$ Gases are monatomic (like He) and diatomic (like N_2)

26. (a) From $PV = nRT$

$$PV = \frac{m}{M}RT \Rightarrow P = \left(\frac{m}{V}\right) \times \frac{1}{M}RT \Rightarrow P = \rho \frac{RT}{m}$$

$$\Rightarrow \frac{P_A}{P_B} = \frac{\rho_A}{\rho_B} \frac{M_B}{M_A} \Rightarrow 2 = \frac{3}{2} \frac{M_B}{M_A}$$

So, $\dfrac{M_A}{M_B} = \dfrac{3}{4}$

27. (a) The speed of sound in a gas is given by

$$v = \sqrt{\frac{\gamma RT}{M}}$$

$$\therefore \; \frac{v_{O_2}}{v_{He}} = \sqrt{\frac{\gamma_{O_2}}{M_{O_2}} \times \frac{M_{He}}{\gamma_{He}}}$$

$$= \sqrt{\frac{1.4}{32} \times \frac{4}{1.67}} = 0.3237$$

$$\therefore \; v_{He} = \frac{v_{O_2}}{0.3237} = \frac{460}{0.3237} = 1421 \; m/s$$

28. (d) Since v_{rms} is doubled by increasing the temp. so by $v_{rms} = \sqrt{\dfrac{3KT}{m}}$, the temp. increase by four times.

Now for constant pressure $\dfrac{V_1}{T_1} = \dfrac{V_2}{T_2}$

$V_1 = V,\, T_1 = T^\circ K,\, T_2 = 4T^\circ K,\, V_2 = ?$

$V_2 = 4V$

29. (a) Mean KE of a diatomic gas $= \dfrac{5}{2}kT$

Therefore at constant temperature, ratio $\dfrac{E_1}{E_2} = 1$

30. (b) $\quad C_{rms} \propto \sqrt{\dfrac{1}{M}}; \; \therefore \dfrac{C_{rms_1}}{C_{rms_2}} = \sqrt{\left(\dfrac{m_2}{m_1}\right)}$

13 Oscillations

1. **(c)** $x = A \sin \omega t \cos \omega t = \dfrac{A}{2}\sin 2\omega t$, which is S.H.M.

2. **(a)** Equation of two simple harmonic motion

$$y = A\sin(\omega t + \phi) \qquad ....(1)$$

$$x = A\sin\left(\omega t + \phi + \frac{\pi}{2}\right) \Rightarrow x = A\cos(\omega t + \phi) \ ....(2)$$

On squaring and adding equations (1) and (2),

$$x^2 + y^2 = A^2$$

This is an equation of a circle. Hence, resulting motion will be a circular motion.

3. **(d)** $y = 5\sin(\pi t + 4\pi)$, comparing it with standard equation

$$y = a\sin(\omega t + \phi) = a\sin\left(\frac{2\pi t}{T} + \phi\right)$$

$$a = 5m \text{ and } \frac{2\pi t}{T} = \pi t \Rightarrow T = 2\sec .$$

4. **(d)** At mean position velocity is maximum

i.e., $v_{max} = \omega a \Rightarrow \omega = \dfrac{v_{max}}{a} = \dfrac{16}{4} = 4$

$\therefore v = \omega\sqrt{a^2 - y^2} \Rightarrow 8\sqrt{3} = 4\sqrt{4^2 - y^2}$

$\Rightarrow 192 = 16(16 - y^2) \Rightarrow 12 = 16 - y^2 \Rightarrow y = 2$ cm.

5. **(b)** $K = \dfrac{1}{2}m\omega^2(A^2 - x^2) = \dfrac{1}{2}m\omega^2 x^2$, at $x = \pm \dfrac{A}{\sqrt{2}}$.

6. **(d)** $\dfrac{U}{E} = \dfrac{\frac{1}{2}m\omega^2 y^2}{\frac{1}{2}m\omega^2 a^2} = \dfrac{y^2}{a^2}$

$$\Rightarrow \frac{U}{80} = \frac{\left(\frac{3}{4}a\right)^2}{a^2} = \frac{9}{16} \Rightarrow U = 45J$$

7. **(d)** $v^2 = \omega^2(A^2 - x^2) \qquad ...(i)$

and $a^2 = (\omega^2 x)^2 = \omega^4 x^2 \qquad ...(ii)$

From above equations, we have

$$v^2 = -\frac{a^2}{\omega^2} + \omega^2 A^2 \Rightarrow Y = mX + c$$

It represents straight line with negative slope.

8. **(c)** $T = 2\pi\sqrt{\dfrac{M}{k}}$; $T' = 2\pi\sqrt{\dfrac{M+m}{k}} = \dfrac{5T}{3}$

$\therefore 2\pi\sqrt{\dfrac{M+m}{k}} = \dfrac{5}{3} \times 2\pi\sqrt{\dfrac{M}{k}}$

$\Rightarrow M + m = \dfrac{25}{9} \times M$

$1 + \dfrac{m}{M} = \dfrac{25}{9} \Rightarrow \dfrac{m}{M} = \dfrac{25}{9} - 1 = \dfrac{16}{9}$

9. **(a)** Speed $= v = \omega\sqrt{a^2 - x^2}$

$$= \frac{2\pi}{T}\sqrt{a^2 - a^2/4} = \frac{\sqrt{3}a\pi}{T}$$

10. **(a)** In $x = A\cos\omega t$, the particle starts oscillating from extreme position. So at $t = 0$, its potential energy is maximum.

11. **(a)** Here, maximum mass that scale can read $= 50$ kg, max. extension $= y = 20 - 0$

$= 20$ cm $= 0.2$ m, $T = 0.6$ s

maximum force exerted an spring $= F = mg$

$$= 50 \times 9.8\,N$$

$$\therefore \quad k = \frac{F}{y} = \frac{50 \times 9.8}{0.2} = 2450 \ \text{N/m}$$

$$T = 2\pi\sqrt{\frac{m}{k}} \Rightarrow m = \frac{T^2 k}{4\pi^2} = \frac{(0.6)^2 \times 2450}{4 \times (3.14)^2}$$

$$= 22.36 \ \text{kg}$$

Weight of the body = mg = 22.36 × 9.8 = 219.1 N

12. (a) Here $T = 2\pi\sqrt{\dfrac{M+m}{k}}$

Where $k = \dfrac{mg}{x} \Rightarrow T = 2\pi\sqrt{\dfrac{(M+m)x}{mg}}$

13. (a) T = 0.04 sec

$$\text{Frequency} = \frac{1}{T} = \frac{1}{0.04} = 25\,\text{Hz} \qquad \Rightarrow f = 25 \ \text{Hz}$$

14. (a) Let initially in equilibrium y height of cylinder is inside the liquid. Then, weight of the cylinder = upthrust due to liquid displaced

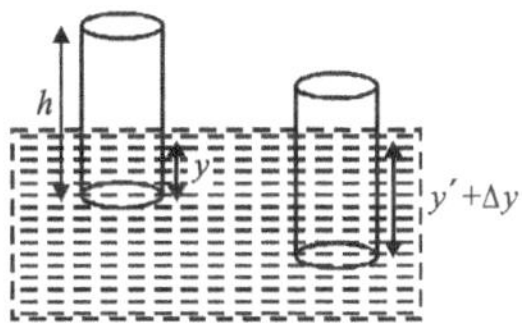

$$\therefore \quad Ah\rho g = Ay\rho_l\, g$$

When the cork cylinder is depressed slightly by Δy and released, a restoring force, equal to additional upthrust, acts on it. The restoring force

$$F = A(y + \Delta y)\,\rho_l\, g - Ay\rho_l g = A\, g\Delta y$$

$\therefore$ Acceleration,

$$a = \frac{F}{m} = \frac{A\rho_l g \Delta y}{Ah\rho} = \frac{\rho_l g}{h\rho}.\Delta y \qquad \text{and} \qquad \text{the}$$

acceleration is directed in a direction opposite to Δy. Obviously, as $a \propto -\Delta y$, the motion of cork cylinder is SHM, whose time period is given by

$$T = 2\pi\sqrt{\frac{\text{displacement}}{\text{acceleration}}} = 2\pi\sqrt{\frac{\Delta y}{a}} = 2\pi\sqrt{\frac{h\rho}{\rho_l g}}$$

15. (a) Let T_1 and T_2 be the time period of the two pendulums $T_1 = 2\pi\sqrt{\dfrac{1}{g}}$ and $T_2 = 2\pi\sqrt{\dfrac{4}{g}}$

As $\ell_1 < \ell_2$ therefore $T_1 < T_2$

Let at t = 0 they start swinging together. Since their time periods are different, the swinging will not be in unison always. Only when number of completed oscillations differ by an integer, the two pendulums will again begin to swing together.

Let longer length pendulum complete n oscillation and shorter length pendulum complete (n + 1) oscillation. For unison swinging

$$(n+1)T_1 = nT_2$$

$$\Rightarrow (n+1) \times 2\pi\sqrt{\frac{l}{g}} = (n) \times 2\pi\sqrt{\frac{4}{g}}$$

$$\Rightarrow n = 1 \quad \therefore \quad n + 1 = 1 + 1 = 2$$

16. (d)

17. (a) Let us consider the figure in which the block is displaced from equilibrium position by a distance (x) towards right.

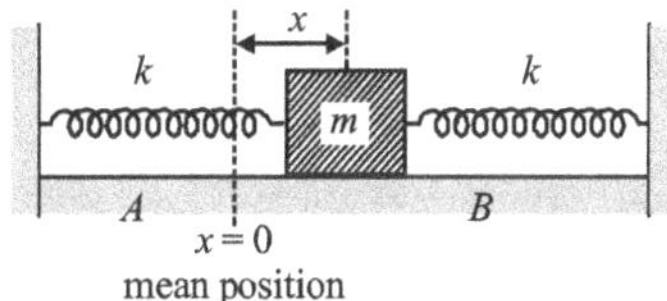

Then the right spring (B) gets compressed by x developing a restoring force (kx) towards left on the block. The left spring (A) is stretched by an amount x developing a restoring force kx towards left on the block as shown in the free body diagram of the block.

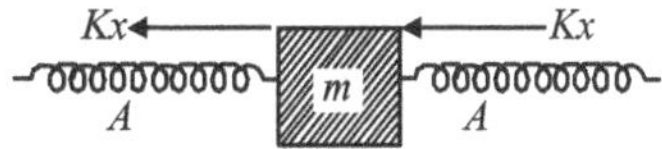

So net restoring force acting on block towards left side = $(kx + kx)$ [$\because$ Both forces are in same direction]

= $2\,kx$ towards left.

Hence restoring force towards left = $2kx$.

18. **(c)** As we know,

$$F = ma \Rightarrow a \propto F$$

or, $a \propto \sin t$

$$\Rightarrow \frac{dv}{dt} \propto \sin t$$

$$\Rightarrow \int_0^0 dV \propto \int_0^t \sin t \, dt$$

$$V \propto -\cos t + 1$$

$$\int_0^x dx = \int_0^t (-\cos t + 1) \, dt$$

$$x = \sin t - \frac{1}{2}\sin 2t$$

19. **(c)**

20. **(a)** Clearly $\sin 2\omega t$ is a periodic function with period $\dfrac{\pi}{\omega}$

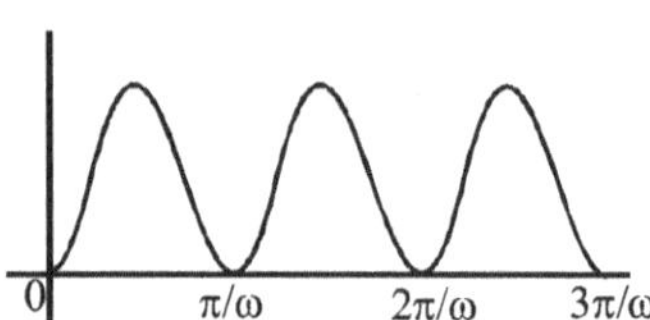

For SHM $\dfrac{d^2 y}{dt^2} \propto -y$

$$y = \sin^2 \omega t = \frac{1 - \cos 2\omega t}{2}$$

$$= \frac{1}{2} - \frac{1}{2}\cos 2\omega t$$

$$v = \frac{dy}{dt} = \frac{1}{2} \times 2\omega \sin 2\omega t = 2\omega \sin \omega t \cos \omega t$$

$$= \omega \sin 2\omega t$$

Acceleration, $a = \dfrac{d^2 y}{dt^2} = 2\omega^2 \cos 2\omega t$ which is not proportional to $-y$. Hence, it is not in SHM.

21. **(a)** $K = \dfrac{1}{2}m\omega^2 x^2$

$$\Rightarrow K_{max} = \frac{1}{2}m\omega^2 A^2$$

$$A = L\theta \qquad \omega = \sqrt{\frac{g}{L}}$$

$$\Rightarrow K = \frac{1}{2}m.\frac{g}{L}.L^2\theta^2$$

$$= \frac{1}{2}mgL\theta^2$$

$$\therefore \frac{K_1}{K_2} = \frac{L}{2L} = \frac{1}{2} \Rightarrow K_2 = 2K_1$$

22. **(c)** Potential energy $(U) = \dfrac{1}{2}kx^2$

Kinetic energy $(K) = \dfrac{1}{2}kA^2 - \dfrac{1}{2}kx^2$

According to the question, $U = k$

$$\therefore \frac{1}{2}kx^2 = \frac{1}{2}kA^2 - \frac{1}{2}kx^2$$

$$\Rightarrow x^2 = A^2 \text{ or, } x = \pm\frac{A}{\sqrt{2}}$$

23. **(d)** As we know, $E = E_0 e^{-\frac{bt}{m}}$

$$15 = 45e^{-\frac{b15}{m}}$$

[As no. of oscillations = 15 so t = 15sec]

$$\frac{1}{3} = e^{-\frac{b15}{m}}$$

Taking log on both sides

$$\frac{b}{m} = \frac{1}{15}\ell n\,3$$

24. (b) The kinetic energy of a particle executing S.H.M. at any instant t is given by

$$K = \frac{1}{2} ma^2 \omega^2 \sin^2 \omega t$$

where, m = mass of particle

a = amplitude

ω = angular frequency

t = time

The average value of $\sin^2 \omega t$ over a cycle is $\frac{1}{2}$.

$$\therefore KE = \frac{1}{2} m\omega^2 a^2 \left(\frac{1}{2}\right) \quad \left(\because <\sin^2\theta> = \frac{1}{2}\right)$$

$$= \frac{1}{4} m\omega^2 a^2 = \frac{1}{4} ma^2 (2\pi\nu)^2 \quad (\because \omega = 2\pi\nu)$$

or, $<K> = \pi^2 ma^2 \nu^2$

25. (a) K.E. of a body undergoing SHM is given by,

$$K.E. = \frac{1}{2} ma^2 \omega^2 \cos^2 \omega t$$

Here, a = amplitude of SHM

ω = angular velocity of SHM

Total energy in S.H.M $= \frac{1}{2} ma^2 \omega^2$

Given K.E. = 75% T.E.

$$\frac{1}{2} ma^2 \omega^2 \cos^2 \omega t = \frac{75}{100} \times \frac{1}{2} ma^2 \omega^2$$

$$\Rightarrow 0.75 = \cos^2 \omega t \Rightarrow \omega t = \frac{\pi}{6}$$

$$\Rightarrow t = \frac{\pi}{6 \times \omega} \Rightarrow t = \frac{\pi \times 2}{6 \times 2\pi} \Rightarrow t = \frac{1}{6} s$$

26. (a) Given : $y = 5\left[\sin(3\pi t) + \sqrt{3}\cos(3\pi t)\right]$

$$\Rightarrow y = 10\sin\left(3\pi t + \frac{\pi}{3}\right)$$

$\therefore$ Amplitude = 10 cm

Time period, $T = \dfrac{2\pi}{\omega} = \dfrac{2\pi}{3\pi} = \dfrac{2}{3} s$

27. (d) Acceleration due to gravity $g = \dfrac{GM}{R^2}$

$$\frac{g_p}{g_e} = \frac{M_p}{M_e}\left(\frac{R_e}{R_p}\right)^2 = 3\left(\frac{1}{3}\right)^2 = \frac{1}{3}$$

Also $T \propto \dfrac{1}{\sqrt{g}} \Rightarrow \dfrac{T_p}{T_e} = \sqrt{\dfrac{g_e}{g_p}} = \sqrt{3}$

$$\Rightarrow T_p = 2\sqrt{3}\ s$$

28. (c) Time of half the amplitude is = 2s

Using, $A = A_0 e^{-kt}$

$$\frac{A_0}{2} = A_e\, e^{-k \times 2} \qquad \text{...(i)}$$

and $\dfrac{A_0}{1000} = A_e\, e^{-kt}$ ...(ii)

Dividing (i) by (ii) and solving, we get

$t = 20$ s

29. (c) As energy $\propto$ (Amplitude)^2, the maximum for both of them occurs at the same frequency and this is only possible in case of resonance.

In resonance state $\omega_1 = \omega_2$

30. (a) Potential energy of spring $= \dfrac{1}{2} kx^2$

Here, x = distance of block from mean position,

k = spring constant

At mean position, potential energy $= \dfrac{1}{2} kA^2$

At equilibrium position, half of the mass of block breaks off, so its potential energy becomes half.

Remaining energy $= \dfrac{1}{2}\left(\dfrac{1}{2} kA^2\right) = \dfrac{1}{2} kA'^2$

Here, A' = New distance of block from mean position

$$\Rightarrow A' = \frac{A}{\sqrt{2}}$$

14   Waves

1.   **(b)** $y = 60 \cos(180t - 6x)$ ....(1)

$\omega = 180,\ k = 6 \Rightarrow \dfrac{2\pi}{\lambda} = 6$

$v = \dfrac{\omega}{k} = \dfrac{2\pi}{T} \times \dfrac{\lambda}{2\pi} = \dfrac{180}{6} = 30 \text{ m/s}$

$v_{max} = a\omega = 60 \times 180 \ \mu\text{m/s}$

$\qquad\qquad = 10800 \ \mu\text{m/s} = 0.0108 \text{ m/s}$

$\dfrac{v_{max}}{v} = \dfrac{0.0108}{30} = 3.6 \times 10^{-4}$

2.   **(b)** $v = \sqrt{\dfrac{\gamma P}{\rho}} = \sqrt{\dfrac{E}{\rho}}$ As per newton's formula,

$V = \sqrt{\dfrac{E'}{\rho}}$

Later, after
Laplace correction

$v = \sqrt{\dfrac{E}{\rho}}$

3.   **(a)** $L_0 = 60 \text{ cm}$ $v_0 = 256 \text{ Hz.}$

$v = \dfrac{1}{2L}\sqrt{\dfrac{T}{m}}$ $\therefore$ $v \propto \dfrac{1}{L}$

$\dfrac{v_1}{v_0} = \dfrac{L_0}{L_1}$

$v_1 = v_0 \dfrac{L_0}{L_1} = 256 \times \dfrac{60}{15} = 1024 \text{ Hz.}$

4.   **(c)** $\dfrac{I_{max}}{I_{min}} = \left(\dfrac{\sqrt{I_1} + \sqrt{I_2}}{\sqrt{I_1} - \sqrt{I_2}}\right)^2$

Given, $\dfrac{I_{max}}{I_{min}} = 25$

$\therefore \quad \dfrac{\sqrt{I_1} + \sqrt{I_2}}{\sqrt{I_1} - \sqrt{I_2}} = 5 \ \Rightarrow \ \dfrac{\sqrt{I_1}}{\sqrt{I_2}} = \dfrac{3}{2}$

$\Rightarrow \dfrac{I_1}{I_2} = \dfrac{9}{4}$

5.   **(a)** $n_{Last} = n_{First} + (N-1)x$

$2n = n + (41-1) \times 5$

$\Rightarrow n_{First} = 200 \text{ Hz and } n_{Last} = 400 \text{ Hz}$

6.   **(c)**   Using $n_{Last} = n_{First} + (N-1)x$

$\Rightarrow 3n = n + (26-1) \times 4$

$\Rightarrow n = 50 \text{ Hz}$

7.   **(a)** $v_{long.} = 100\,v_{trans.} \ \Rightarrow \ \sqrt{\dfrac{Y}{\rho}} = 100\sqrt{\dfrac{T}{m}}$

$\sqrt{\dfrac{Y}{\rho}} = 100\sqrt{\dfrac{\text{stress}}{\rho}} \quad \left[\because \dfrac{F}{A} = \text{stress}\right]$

$\sqrt{1 \times 10^{11}} = 100\sqrt{\text{stress}}$

$\Rightarrow \text{Stress} = \dfrac{10^{11}}{10^4} = 10^7 \text{ N/m}^2$

8.   **(b)**   Let the string vibrates in p loops, wavelength of the vibration is given by $\lambda_p = \dfrac{2l}{p}$

Given, $y = 2\sin\left(\dfrac{4\pi x}{15}\right)\cos(96\pi t)$

Comparing it with standard equation

$y = a\sin\left(\dfrac{2\pi x}{\lambda}\right)\cos\omega t$ we get

$\lambda = 7.5\,cm$

$$\lambda = \frac{2l}{p} \Rightarrow \lambda = \frac{2 \times 60}{7.5} \Rightarrow p = 16.$$

9. **(b)** Given : Frequency of tuning fork,

$n = 264$ Hz

Length of column $L = ?$

For closed organ pipe, $n = \dfrac{v}{4l}$

$$\Rightarrow l = \frac{v}{4n} = \frac{330}{4 \times 264} = 0.3125$$

or, $l = 0.3125 \times 100 = 31.25$ cm

In case of closed organ pipe only odd harmonics are possible.

Therefore value of l will be $(2n - 1)\,l$

Hence option (b) i.e. $3 \times 31.25 = 93.75$ cm is correct.

10. **(c)** $\omega_1 = 600\pi,\ \omega_2 = 604\pi,\ f_1 = 300\,Hz,$

$f_2 = 302\,Hz$

Beat frequency, $f_2 - f_1 = 2\,Hz$

$\Rightarrow$ number of beats in three seconds $= 6$

11. **(d)** Let the frequencies of tuning forks A, B and C be $\upsilon_A,\ \upsilon_B$ and υ_C respectively.

As, $\upsilon_A = \upsilon_C + \dfrac{1.5}{100}\upsilon_C$ and $\upsilon_B = \upsilon_C - \dfrac{2.5}{100}\upsilon_C$

Also, $\upsilon_A - \upsilon_B = 12\,Hz$

$$\left(\upsilon_C \times \frac{1.5}{100}\upsilon_C\right) - \left(\upsilon_C - \frac{2.5}{100}\upsilon_C\right) = 12$$

$$\frac{4\upsilon_C}{100} = 12 \text{ or } \upsilon_C = \frac{12 \times 100}{4} = 300\,Hz$$

12. **(a)**

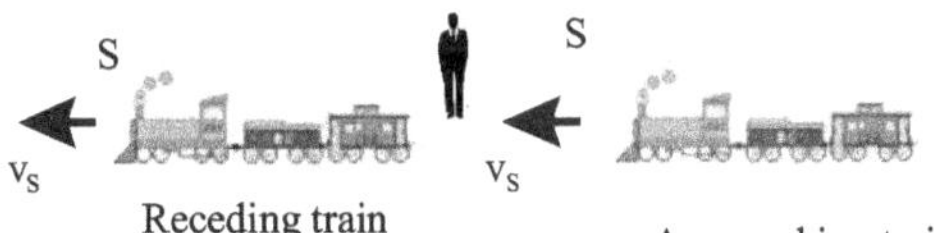

Frequency of sound heard by the man from approaching train.

$$n_a = n\left(\frac{v}{v - v_s}\right) = 240\left(\frac{320}{320 - 4}\right) = 243\,Hz$$

Frequency of sound heard by the man from receding train

$$n_r = n\left(\frac{v}{v + v_s}\right) = 240\left(\frac{320}{320 + 4}\right) = 237\,Hz$$

Hence, number of beats heard by man per sec
$= n_a - n_r = 243 - 237 = 6$

13. **(b)** Frequency heard by the observer

$$v_{observed} = \left(\frac{v_{sound}}{v_{sound} - v\cos\theta}\right)v_0$$

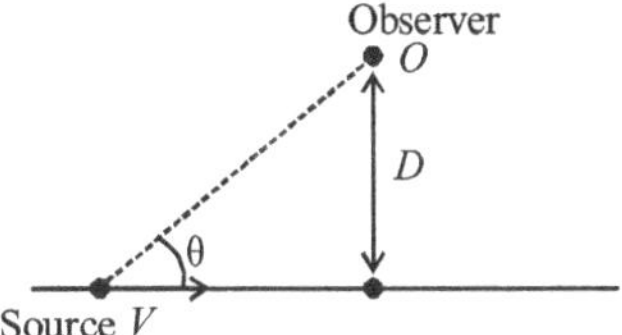

Initially θ will be less so $\cos\theta$ more.

$\therefore\ v_{observed}$ more, then it will decrease.

14. **(b)** Here $v_A = 72\,km/hr = 20\,m/sec$

$v_B = 36\,km/hr = 10\,m/sec$

$$n' = n\left(\frac{v + v_B\cos 45°}{v - v_A\cos 45°}\right)$$

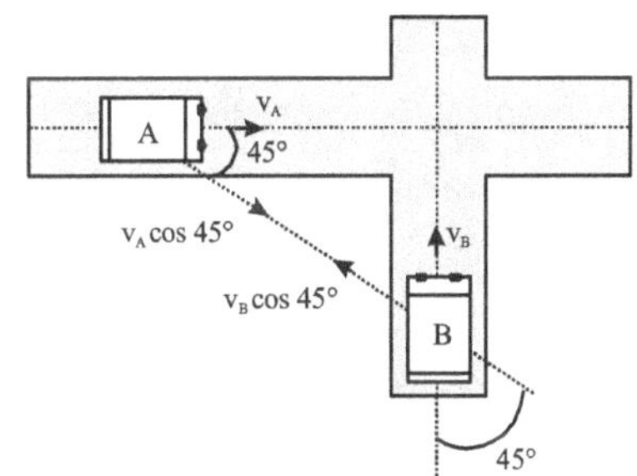

$$\Rightarrow n' = 280\left(\frac{340 + 10/\sqrt{2}}{340 - 20/\sqrt{2}}\right) = 298\,Hz$$

15. **(d)** $T = \dfrac{1}{f} = \dfrac{1}{500}\,s;$

Since compression alternates with rarefaction so again compression appears after

$$t = \frac{T}{2} = \frac{1}{1000}\,s$$

16. **(b)** Here, $T = 0.05$ sec, $v = 300$ ms^{-1}.

Now $1 = \dfrac{v}{\nu} = vT = (300 \times 0.05)$m   or, $\lambda = 15$ m

Phase of the point at 10 m from the source

$= \dfrac{2\pi}{\lambda} \times x = \dfrac{2\pi}{15} \times 10 = \dfrac{4\pi}{3}$ rad

Phase of the point at 15 m from the source

$\dfrac{2\pi}{\lambda} \times x = \dfrac{2\pi}{15} \times 15 = 2\pi$ rad

$\therefore$ The phase difference between the points

$= 2\pi - \dfrac{4\pi}{3} = \dfrac{2\pi}{3}$ rad

17. **(b)** Total length of sonometer wire, $l = 110$ cm $= 1.1$ m

Length of wire is in ratio, $6 : 3 : 2$ i.e. 60 cm, 30 cm, 20 cm.

Tension in the wire, $T = 400$ N

Mass per unit length, $m = 0.01$ kg

Minimum common frequency $= ?$

As we know,

Frequency, $v = \dfrac{1}{21}\sqrt{\dfrac{T}{m}} = \dfrac{1000}{11}$ Hz

$v_1 = \dfrac{1000}{6}$ Hz ; $v_2 = \dfrac{1000}{3}$ Hz ; $v_3 = \dfrac{1000}{2}$ Hz

Hence common frequency $= 1000$ Hz

18. **(b)** Let $n - 1 (= 400), n (= 401)$ and $n + 1 (= 402)$ be the frequencies of the three waves. If a be the amplitude of each then $y_1 = a \sin 2\pi(n-1)t$, $y_2 = a \sin 2\pi nt$ and $y_3 = a \sin 2\pi(n+1)t$

Resultant displacement due to all three waves is

$y = y_1 + y_2 + y_3$

$= a \sin 2\pi nt + a[\sin 2\pi(n-1)t + \sin 2\pi(n+t)t]$

$\Rightarrow y = a(1 + \cos 2\pi t)\sin 2\pi nt$

This is the resultant wave having amplitude $=$

$a(1 + \cos 2\pi t)$

For maximum amplitude,

$\cos 2\pi t = 1 \Rightarrow 2\pi t = 2m\pi$

where $m = 0, 1, 2, 3, \ldots\ldots$ $\Rightarrow t = 0, 1, 2, 3\ldots\ldots$

Hence, time interval between two successive maximum is $1\sec$. So, beat frequency $= 1$

Also for minimum amplitude $(2\cos 2\pi t) = 0$

$\Rightarrow \cos 2\pi t = -\dfrac{1}{2}$

$\Rightarrow 2\pi t = 2m\pi + \dfrac{2\pi}{3} \Rightarrow t = +\dfrac{1}{3}$

$\Rightarrow t = \dfrac{1}{3}, \dfrac{4}{3}, \dfrac{7}{3}, \dfrac{10}{3}\ldots\ldots$ (for $m = 0, 1, 2, \ldots$)

Hence time interval between two successive minima is 1 sec, so, number of beats per second $= 1$.

19. **(d)** Velocity of sound $\propto \dfrac{1}{\sqrt{\text{Density of gas}}}$

$\therefore \dfrac{v_0}{v_H} = \sqrt{\dfrac{\rho_H}{\rho_0}} = \sqrt{\dfrac{1}{16}} = \dfrac{1}{4} \Rightarrow \dfrac{v_H}{v_0} = \dfrac{4}{1}$

20. **(d)** With the propagation of a longitudinal wave, energy and linear momentum are propagated.

21. **(c)** Beat frequency

$=$ difference in frequencies of two waves

$= 11 - 9 = 2$ Hz

22. **(a)** Loudness of sound. $L_1 = 10\log\left(\dfrac{I_1}{I_0}\right)$;

$L_2 = 10\log\left(\dfrac{I_2}{I_0}\right)$

$\therefore L_1 - L_2 = 10\log\left(\dfrac{I_1}{I_0}\right) - 10\log\left(\dfrac{I_2}{I_0}\right)$

or, $\Delta L = 10\log\left(\dfrac{I_1}{I_0} \times \dfrac{I_0}{I_2}\right)$

or, $\Delta L = 10\log\left(\dfrac{I_1}{I_2}\right)$

The sound level attenuated by 20 dB ie

$L_1 - L_2 = 20 \, dB$

or, $20 = 10 \log\left(\dfrac{I_1}{I_2}\right)$ or, $2 = \log\left(\dfrac{I_1}{I_2}\right)$

or, $\dfrac{I_1}{I_2} = 10^2$ or, $I_2 = \dfrac{I_1}{100}$.

$\Rightarrow$ Intensity decreases by a factor 100.

23. (a) In solids, Velocity of wave

$$V = \sqrt{\dfrac{Y}{\rho}} = \sqrt{\dfrac{9.27 \times 10^{10}}{2.7 \times 10^3}}$$

$v = 5.85 \times 10^3 \, m/sec$

Since rod is clamped at middle fundamental wave shape is as follow

$\dfrac{\lambda}{2} = L \Rightarrow \lambda = 2L$ 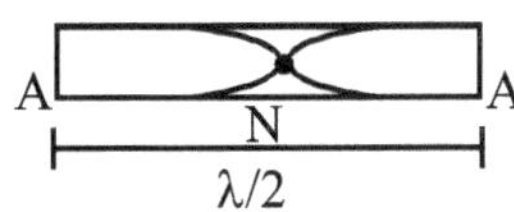

$\lambda = 1.2\,m \,(\because \, L = 60\,cm = 0.6m \, (given)$

Using $v = f\lambda$

$\Rightarrow \quad f = \dfrac{v}{\lambda} = \dfrac{5.85 \times 10^3}{1.2}$

$= 4.88 \times 10^3 \, Hz \simeq 5 \, KHz$

24. (a) For first resonance, $\dfrac{\lambda}{4} = \ell_1 + e = 11\,cm$

$(\because \, end \, correction \, e = 1 \, cm \, given)$

For second resonance, $\dfrac{3\lambda}{4} = \ell_2 + e$

$\Rightarrow \ell_2 = 3 \times 11 - 1 = 32 \, cm$

25. (a) We know that velocity in string is given by

$$v = \sqrt{\dfrac{T}{\mu}} \qquad ...(i)$$

where $\mu = \dfrac{m}{1} = \dfrac{mass \, of \, string}{length \, of \, string}$

The tension $T = \dfrac{m}{\ell} \times x \times g \qquad ..(ii)$

From (1) and (2)

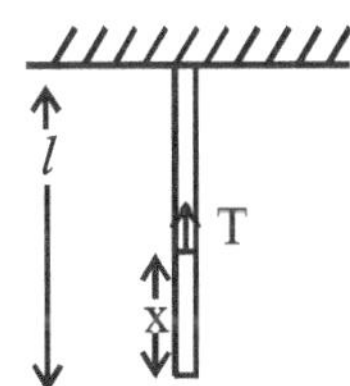

$\dfrac{dx}{dt} = \sqrt{gx}$

$x^{-1/2} dx = \sqrt{g} \, dt$

$\therefore \displaystyle\int_0^\ell x^{-1/2} dx - \sqrt{g} \int_0^\ell dt$

$\Rightarrow 2\sqrt{1}$

$= \sqrt{g} \times t \quad \therefore \, t = 2\sqrt{\dfrac{\ell}{g}} = 2\sqrt{\dfrac{20}{10}} = 2\sqrt{2}$

26. (b)

The fundamental frequency in case (a) is

$f = \dfrac{v}{2\ell}$

The fundamental frequency in case (b) is

$f' = \dfrac{v}{4(\ell/2)} = \dfrac{v}{2\ell} = f$

27. (c) Length of pipe $= 85 \, cm = 0.85m$

Frequency of oscillations of air column in closed organ pipe is given by,

$f = \dfrac{(2n-1)\upsilon}{4L}$

$$f = \frac{(2n-1)\upsilon}{4L} \le 1250$$

$$\Rightarrow \quad \frac{(2n-1)\times 340}{0.85\times 4} \le 1250$$

$$\Rightarrow \quad 2n-1 \le 12.5 \approx 6$$

28. **(b)** Maximum number of beats

= Maximum frequency – Minimum frequency

$= (v+1)-(v-1) = 2$ Beats per second

29. **(c)** It is given that tuning fork of frequency 256 Hz makes 5 beats/second with the vibrating string of a piano. Therefore, possible frequency of the piano are (256 ± 5) Hz. i.e., either 261 Hz or 251 Hz. When the tension in the piano string increases, its frequency will increases. As the original frequency was 261 Hz, the beat frequency should decreases, we can conclude that the frequency of piano string is 251 Hz

30. **(a)** Reflected frequency of sound reaching bat

$$= \left[\frac{V-(-V_0)}{V-V_s}\right]f = \left[\frac{V+V_0}{V-V_s}\right]f = \frac{V+10}{V-10}f$$

$$= \left(\frac{320+10}{320-10}\right)\times 8000 = 8516 \text{ Hz}$$

15   Electric Charges and Fields

1. **(a)** $F = \dfrac{1}{4\pi\varepsilon_0} \dfrac{(+7\times10^{-6})(-5\times10^{-6})}{r^2}$

$= -\dfrac{1}{4\pi\varepsilon_0}\dfrac{35\times10^{12}}{r^2} N$

$F' = \dfrac{1}{4\pi\varepsilon_0}\dfrac{(+5\times10^{-6})(-7\times10^{-6})}{r^2}$

$= -\dfrac{1}{4\pi\varepsilon_0}\dfrac{35\times10^{12}}{r^2} N$

2. **(b)** We have $E_a = \dfrac{2kp}{r^3}$ and $E_e = \dfrac{kp}{r^3}$;

$\therefore E_a = 2E_e$

3. **(d)** Charge $(q) = 0.2$ C; Distance $(d) = 2$ m; Angle $\theta = 60°$ and Work done $(W) = 4J$

Work done in moving the charge (W)

$= F.d \cos\theta = qEd \cos\theta$

or, $E = \dfrac{W}{qd\cos\theta} = \dfrac{4}{0.2\times2\times\cos60°} = \dfrac{4}{0.4\times0.5}$

$= 20$ N/C

4. **(d)** Net flux through the surface $= \phi_2 - \phi_1$

By Gauss's law, $\phi_2 - \phi_1 = \dfrac{q_{enc}}{\varepsilon_0}$

$q_{enc} = (\phi_2 - \phi_1)\varepsilon_0$

5. **(b)**

For equilibrium, charge should be placed on the left side of $-Q$ charge.

6. **(b)** $\dfrac{-K2q}{(x-L)^2} + \dfrac{K8q}{x^2} = 0 \Rightarrow \dfrac{1}{(x-L)^2} = \dfrac{4}{x^2}$

or, $\dfrac{1}{x-L} = \dfrac{2}{x} \Rightarrow x = 2x - 2L$ or $x = 2L$

7. **(c)** The total charge on the outer surface will be $Q + q$. So charge density will be

$\left[\dfrac{Q+q}{4\pi b^2}\right]$

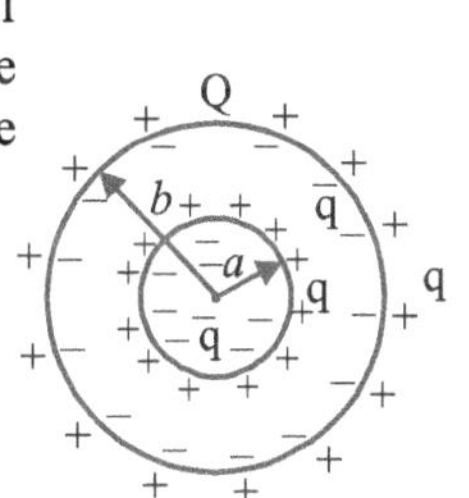

8. **(c)** Maximum torque on dipole is given by $\tau = p \times E$

Here $p = q.2\ell = (1.0\times10^{-6}\,C)(0.02m)$

$= 2\times10^{-8}\,Cm$

$\therefore \tau = (2\times10^{-8})(1.0\times10^5\,N/C)$

$= 2.0\times10^{-3}\,N-m$

9. **(b)** a = distance between centre of both spheres

By principle of superposition the net electric field at point P

$\vec{E} = \dfrac{\rho\vec{r}}{3\,\epsilon_0} - \dfrac{\rho\vec{r}\,'}{3\,\epsilon_0}$

$\therefore \vec{r} - \vec{r}\,' = \vec{a}$

$\therefore \vec{E} = \dfrac{\rho\vec{a}}{3\,\epsilon_0} = $ uniform

10. **(d)** For the drop to be stationary, $qE = mg$

$\therefore q = \dfrac{1.6\times10^{-6}\times10}{100} = 1.6\times10^{-7}C$

Number of electrons in drop

$$= \frac{q}{e} = \frac{1.6 \times 10^{-7}\,C}{1.6 \times 10^{-19}\,C} = 10^{12}\ \text{electrons}$$

11. **(d)** From figure

$$T \cos \theta = mg \qquad\qquad ....(i)$$

$$T \sin \theta = F_e \qquad\qquad ....(ii)$$

Dividing equation (ii) by (i), we get

$$\Rightarrow \frac{\sin\theta}{\cos\theta} = \frac{F_e}{mg} \qquad\qquad \Rightarrow F_e = mg \tan\theta$$

$$\Rightarrow \frac{kq^2}{x^2} = mg \tan\theta \qquad \Rightarrow q^2 = \frac{x^2 mg \tan\theta}{k}$$

Since θ is small

$$\therefore \tan\theta \approx \sin\theta = \frac{x}{2l}$$

$$\therefore q^2 = \frac{x^3 mg}{2kl} \qquad \Rightarrow \qquad q^2 \propto x^{3/2}$$

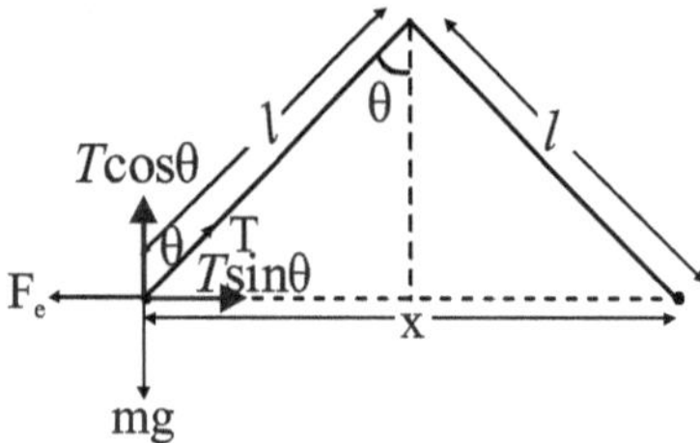

$$\Rightarrow \frac{dq}{dt} \alpha \frac{3}{2}\sqrt{x}\frac{dx}{dt} = \frac{3}{2}\sqrt{x}V$$

Since $\dfrac{dq}{dt} = \text{const.}$

$$\Rightarrow v \propto x^{-1/2} \qquad\qquad [\because q^2 \propto x^3]$$

12. **(d)** At equilibrium net force is zero,

$$\therefore\ k\frac{Q \times Q}{(2x)^2} + k\frac{Qq}{x^2} = 0$$

$$\Rightarrow\ q = -\frac{Q}{4}$$

13. **(b)** When cube is of side a and point charge Q is at the center of the cube then the total electric flux due to this charge will pass evenly through the six faces of the cube. So, the electric flux through one face will be equal to 1/6 of the total electric flux due to this charge.

Flux through 6 faces $= \dfrac{Q}{\epsilon_0}$

$\therefore$ Flux through 1 face, $= \dfrac{Q}{6\,\epsilon_0}$

14. **(b)** Potential energy of a dipole is given by

$$U = -\vec{P}.\vec{E}$$

$$= -PE \cos\theta$$

[Where θ = angle between dipole and perpendicular to the field]

$$= -(10^{-29})\,(10^3) \cos 45°$$

$$= -0.707 \times 10^{-26}\,J = -7 \times 10^{-27}\,J$$

15. **(a)** Let us consider a spherical shell of radius x and thickness dx.

Charge on this shell

$$dq = \rho.4\pi x^2 dx = \rho_0\left(\frac{5}{4} - \frac{x}{R}\right).4\pi x^2 dx$$

$\therefore$ Total charge in the spherical region from centre to $r\,(r<R)$ is

$$q = \int dq = 4\pi\rho_0 \int_0^r \left(\frac{5}{4} - \frac{x}{R}\right)x^2 dx$$

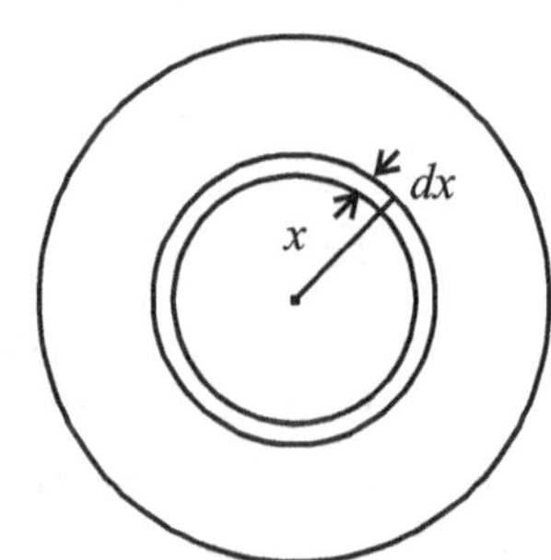

$$= 4\pi\rho_0\left[\frac{5}{4}.\frac{r^3}{3} - \frac{1}{R}.\frac{r^4}{4}\right] = \pi\rho_0 r^3\left(\frac{5}{3} - \frac{r}{R}\right)$$

$\therefore$ Electric field at r,

$$E = \frac{1}{4\pi \in_0} \cdot \frac{q}{r^2}$$

$$= \frac{1}{4\pi \in_0} \cdot \frac{\pi\rho_0 r^3}{r^2}\left(\frac{5}{3} - \frac{r}{R}\right) = \frac{\rho_0 r}{4 \in_0}\left(\frac{5}{3} - \frac{r}{R}\right)$$

16. (b) $\tau = -PE \sin\theta$

or $\quad I\alpha = -PE\,(\theta)$

$$\alpha = \frac{PE}{I}(-\theta)$$

On comparing with

$$\alpha = -\omega^2\theta$$

$$\omega = \sqrt{\frac{PE}{I}} = \sqrt{\frac{qdE}{2m\left(\frac{d}{2}\right)^2}} = \sqrt{\frac{2qE}{md}}$$

17. (b)

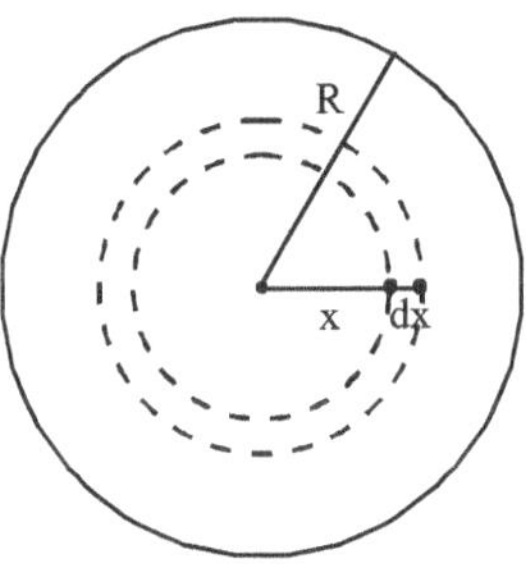

Let us consider a spherical shell of thickness dx and radius x. The area of this spherical shell $= 4\pi x^2$.

The volume of this spherical shell $= 4\pi x^2 dx$. The charge enclosed within shell

$$dq = \left[\frac{Qx}{\pi R^4}\right][4\pi x^2 dx] = \frac{4Q}{R^4} x^3 dx$$

The charge enclosed in a sphere of radius r_1 can be calculated by

$$Q = \int dq = \frac{4Q}{R^4}\int_0^{r_1} x^3 dx = \frac{4Q}{R^4}\left[\frac{x^4}{4}\right]_0^{r_1} = \frac{Q}{R^4} r_1^4$$

$\therefore$ The electric field at point P inside the sphere at a distance r_1 from the centre of the sphere is

$$E = \frac{1}{4\pi E} \frac{Q}{r_1^2}$$

$$\Rightarrow E = \frac{1}{4\pi \in_0} \frac{\left[\frac{Q}{R^4} r_1^4\right]}{r_1^2} = \frac{1}{4\pi \in_0} \frac{Q}{R^4} r_1^2$$

18. (a)

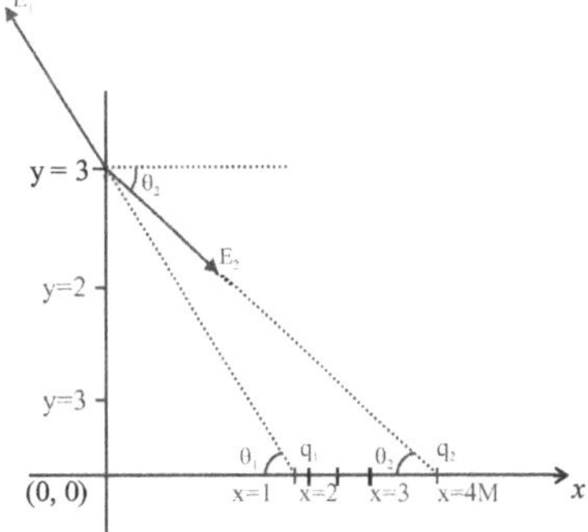

Let $\vec{E}_1$ and $\vec{E}_2$ are the vaues of electric field due to charge, q_1 and q_2 respectively

magnitude of $E_1 = \dfrac{1}{4\pi \in_0} \dfrac{q_1}{r_1^2}$

$$= \frac{1}{4\pi \in_0} \frac{\sqrt{10} \times 10^{-6}}{\left(1^2 + 3^2\right)}$$

$$= \left(9 \times 10^9\right) \times \sqrt{10} \times 10^{-7}$$

$$= 9\sqrt{10} \times 10^2$$

$$\therefore \vec{E}_1 = 9\sqrt{10} \times 10^2 \left[\cos\theta_1\left(-\vec{i}\right) + \sin\theta_1 \vec{j}\right]$$

$$\Rightarrow E_1 = 9 \times \sqrt{10} \times 10^2 \left[\frac{1}{\sqrt{10}}(-\hat{i}) + \frac{3}{\sqrt{10}}\hat{j}\right]$$

$$\Rightarrow E_1 = 9 \times 10^2\left[-\hat{i} + 3\hat{j}\right] = \left[-9\hat{i} + 27\hat{j}\right]10^2$$

Similarly, $E_2 = \dfrac{1}{4\pi \in_0}\dfrac{q_2}{r^2}$

$$E_2 = \frac{9 \times 10^9 \times (25) \times 10^{-6}}{\left(4^2 + 3^2\right)} \qquad E_2 = 9 \times 10^3 \text{ V/m}$$

$$\therefore \vec{E}_2 = 9 \times 10^3 \left(\cos\theta_2 \hat{i} - \sin\theta_2 \hat{j}\right) \quad \because \tan\theta_2 = \frac{3}{4}$$

$$\therefore \vec{E}_2 = 9 \times 10^3 \left(\frac{4}{5}\hat{i} - \frac{3}{5}\hat{j}\right) = \left(72\hat{i} - 54\hat{j}\right) \times 10^2$$

$$\therefore \vec{E} = \vec{E}_1 + \vec{E}_2 = \left(63\hat{i} - 27\hat{j}\right) \times 10^2 \, V/m$$

19. **(b)** According to Gauss's theorem electric flux through a closed surface $S = q/\varepsilon_0$

Where q = total charge enclosed by S

Electric flux pass through the spherical of Gaussian surface is independent on the radius of a Gaussian surface but depends on the charge enclosed by a Gaussian surface. On increasing the radius of Gaussian surface three times, but the charge enclosed by a Gaussian surface remain the same. Therefore, the electric flux pass through the Gaussian surface remains the same.

20. **(d)** By Gauss's law $\phi = \dfrac{1}{\varepsilon_0}(Q_{enclosed})$

$$\Rightarrow Q_{enclosed} = \phi\varepsilon_0 = (-8\times10^3 + 4\times10^3)\varepsilon_0$$

$$= -4\times10^3\,\varepsilon_0 \text{ coulomb.}$$

21. **(c)** Electric field between the sheets

$$= \frac{(\sigma_1 - \sigma_2)}{2\,\epsilon_0} \quad \text{(from Gauss's theorem)}$$

Here, $\sigma_1 = \sigma_2$ $E = 0$

22. **(c)**

23. **(d)** Total charge $Q = 80 + 40 = 120 \, \mu C$.

By using the formula $Q_1' = Q\left[\dfrac{r_1}{r_1 + r_2}\right]$.

New charge on sphere A is,

$$Q_A' = Q\left[\frac{r_A}{r_A + r_B}\right] = 120\left[\frac{4}{4+6}\right] = 48\,\mu C$$

Initially it was 80 μC i.e., 32 μC charge flows from A to B.

24. **(a)**

25. **(a)** $-eE = mg$

$$\overline{E} = -\frac{9.1\times10^{-31}\times10}{1.6\times10^{-19}} = -5.6\times10^{-11}\,N/C$$

26. **(c)**

27. **(d)** They will not experience any force if $|\vec{F}_G| = |\vec{F}_e|$

$$\Rightarrow G\frac{m^2}{(16\times10^{-2})^2} = \frac{1}{4\pi\varepsilon_0}\cdot\frac{q^2}{(16\times10^{-2})^2}$$

$$\Rightarrow \frac{q}{m} = \sqrt{4\pi\varepsilon_0 G}$$

28. **(d)**

29. **(c)** Work done in rotating a dipole $= PE\,(\cos\theta_1 - \cos\theta_2)$

If $\theta_1 = 0$ and $\theta_2 = 90°$, work done $= pE\,(1-0) = pE$

30. **(c)** With the increase in the spacing between the field lines, intensity of electric field decreases. So

$$F_A > (F_B = F_C)$$

16 Electrostatic Potential and Capacitance

1. **(c)** Let q_1 and q_2 be charge on two spheres of radius $'r'$ and $'R'$ respectively

As, $q_1 + q_2 = Q$

and $\sigma_1 = \sigma_2$ [Surface charge density are equal]

$$\therefore \frac{q_1}{r\pi r^2} = \frac{q_2}{4\pi R^2}$$

So, $q_1 = \dfrac{Qr^2}{R^2 + r^2}$ and $q_2 = \dfrac{QR^2}{R^2 + r^2}$

Now, potential, $V = \dfrac{1}{4\pi\varepsilon_0}\left[\dfrac{q_1}{r} + \dfrac{q_2}{R}\right]$

$$= \frac{1}{4\pi\varepsilon_0}\left[\frac{Qr}{R^2 + r^2} + \frac{QR}{R^2 + r^2}\right]$$

$$= \frac{Q(R+r)}{R^2 + r^2}\frac{1}{4\pi\varepsilon_0}$$

2. **(a)**

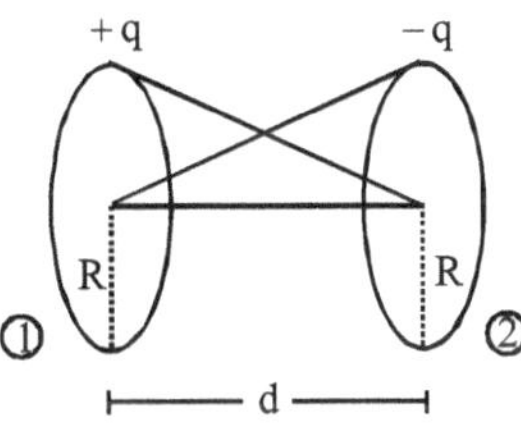

At (1) using, potential $(V_1) = V_{\text{self}} + V_{\text{due to (2)}}$

$$\Rightarrow V_1 = \frac{1}{4\pi\varepsilon_0}\left[\frac{q}{R} - \frac{q}{\sqrt{R^2 + d^2}}\right]$$

At (2) using potential $(V_2) = V_{\text{self}} + V_{\text{due to (1)}}$

$$\Rightarrow V_2 = \frac{1}{4\pi\varepsilon_0}\left[\frac{-q}{R} + \frac{q}{\sqrt{R^2 + d^2}}\right]$$

$$\Delta V = V_1 - V_2$$

$$= \frac{1}{4\pi\varepsilon_0}\left[\frac{q}{R} + \frac{q}{R} - \frac{q}{\sqrt{R^2 + d^2}} - \frac{q}{\sqrt{R^2 + d^2}}\right]$$

$$= \frac{1}{2\pi\varepsilon_0}\left[\frac{q}{R} - \frac{q}{\sqrt{R^2 + d^2}}\right]$$

3. **(a)**

4. **(a)** $\phi_1 = \dfrac{kq_1}{a_1} + \dfrac{kq_2}{a_2}$

or $\phi_2 = \dfrac{kq_1}{a_2} + \dfrac{kq_2}{a_2}$

Solve to get

$$q_1 = 4\pi\varepsilon_0\left(\frac{\phi_1 - \phi_2}{a_2 - a_1}\right)a_1 a_2$$

5. **(a)**

6. **(b)** $U_i = k\left[\dfrac{(-3q)\,q}{L}\times 3 + \dfrac{(q)\times(q)}{L}\times 3\right]$

$$= \frac{-6kq^2}{L}$$

$U_f = 0$

Work done by electric field $= -$ Change in potential energy

$$= U_i - U_f = \frac{-6kq^2}{L}$$

7. **(d)** $U = \dfrac{1}{4\pi\varepsilon_0}\left(\dfrac{2q^2}{a} - \dfrac{8q^2}{a} - \dfrac{4q^2}{a}\right)$

$$U = -\frac{9\times10^9 \times 10\times(0.1\times10^{-6})^2}{\left(\dfrac{10}{100}\right)} = -9\times10^{-3}\text{J}$$

8. **(c)** We know that potential energy of discrete system of charges is given by

$$U = \frac{1}{4\pi \in_0}\left(\frac{q_1q_2}{r_{12}} + \frac{q_2q_3}{r_{23}} + \frac{q_3q_1}{r_{31}}\right)$$

According to question,

$$U_{initial} = \frac{1}{4\pi \in_0}\left(\frac{q_1q_2}{0.3} + \frac{q_2q_3}{0.5} + \frac{q_3q_1}{0.4}\right)$$

$$U_{final} = \frac{1}{4\pi \in_0}\left(\frac{q_1q_2}{0.3} + \frac{q_2q_3}{0.1} + \frac{q_3q_1}{0.4}\right)$$

$$U_f - U_i = \frac{1}{4\pi \in_0}\left(\frac{q_1q_2}{0.1} - \frac{q_2q_3}{0.5}\right)$$

$$= \frac{q_3}{4\pi \in_0}(8q_2)$$

9. **(c)** Length of body diagnonal $= \sqrt{3}\,b$

Distance of centre of cube from each corner,

$$r = \frac{\sqrt{3}}{2}b$$

Total P.E. of charge $+ q$ at the centre

$$= \frac{8q(-q)}{4\pi\varepsilon_0 r} = \frac{-8q^2}{4\pi\varepsilon_0(\sqrt{3}\,b/2)} = \frac{-4q^2}{\pi\varepsilon_0\sqrt{3}\,b}$$

10. **(b)** Capacitors are parallel

so $C = \dfrac{\varepsilon_0 A}{t \times 2}(k_1 + k_2)$

11. **(a)** Charge $Q = C_1V$
Total capacity of combination (parallel)

$$C = C_1 + C_2$$

$$\text{P.D.} = \frac{Q}{C} = \frac{C_1V}{C_1 + C_2}$$

12. **(a)** Equivalent capacitance in series combination (C') is given by

$$\frac{1}{C'} = \frac{1}{C_1} + \frac{1}{C_2} \Rightarrow C' = \frac{C_1C_2}{C_1 + C_2}$$

For parallel combination equivalent capacitance
$C'' = C_1 + C_2$
For parallel combination
$q = 10(C_1 + C_2)$
$q_1 = 500\ \mu C$

$500 = 10(C_1 + C_2)$
$C_1 + C_2 = 50\mu F$ ....(i)
For Series Combination–

$$q_2 = 10\frac{C_1C_2}{(C_1 + C_2)}$$

$$80 = 10\frac{C_1C_2}{50} \quad \text{From equation} \quad ....(ii)$$

$C_1C_2 = 400$ ....(iii)
From equation (i) and (ii)
$C_1 = 10\mu F \qquad C_2 = 40\mu F$

13. **(c)** In parallel combination, $C_{eq} = C_1 + C_2$
$\qquad = 10\ \mu F$

When connected across $1\ V$ battery, then

$$\frac{U_1}{U_2} = \frac{\left(\frac{1}{2}C_1V^2\right)}{\left(\frac{1}{2}C_2V^2\right)} = \frac{1}{4}$$

$$\Rightarrow \frac{C_1}{C_2} = \frac{1}{4}$$

$\therefore C_2 = 8\ \mu F$ and $C_1 = 2\ \mu F$
Now C_1 and C_2 are connected in series combination,

$$\therefore C_{equivalent} = \frac{C_1C_2}{C_1 + C_2} = \frac{2 \times 8}{2 + 8} = \frac{16}{10} = 1.6\mu F$$

14. **(b)** Energy stored in the system initially

$$U_i = \frac{1}{2}CE^2$$

$$U_f = \frac{1}{2}\frac{Q^2}{C_{eq}} = \frac{(CE)^2}{2 \times 4C} = \frac{1}{2}\frac{CE^2}{4}$$

[As $Q = CE$, and $C_{eq} = 4C$]

$$\Delta U = \frac{1}{2}CE^2 \times \frac{3}{4} = \frac{3}{8}CE^2 = \frac{3}{8}\frac{Q^2}{C}$$

15. **(c)** $E = \dfrac{\sigma}{\varepsilon_0} = \dfrac{Q}{A\varepsilon_0}$

$\therefore Q = \varepsilon_0 . E. A = 8.85 \times 10^{-12} \times 100 \times 1$
$\qquad = 8.85 \times 10^{-10}C$

16. (d) In equilibrium, $F = q\,E = (n\,e)\dfrac{V}{d} = mg$

$$n = \frac{mg\,d}{eV} = \frac{1.96 \times 10^{-15} \times 9.8 \times 0.02}{1.6 \times 10^{-19} \times 800} = 3$$

17. (a) As $x = t\left(1 - \dfrac{1}{K}\right)$, where x is the addition distance of plate, to restore the capacity of original value.

$\therefore \quad 3.5 \times 10^{-5} = 4 \times 10^{-5}\left(1 - \dfrac{1}{K}\right) \cdot \Rightarrow K = 8.$

18. (c) $\quad Q_1 = C_1 V_1 = 6 \times 10^{-3}\,C$
$\qquad\quad Q_2 = C_2 V_2 = 12 \times 10^{-3}\,C$

As the capators are now in series θ_1 should flow through the battery

so, $V = \dfrac{Q_1}{C_{eq}} = \dfrac{6 \times 10^{-3}}{\dfrac{1 \times 3}{1+3} \times 10^{-6}} = 8\,kV$

19. (c) Initial charge on C_1 is $Q_1 = C_1 V = 110\,\mu C$
Let x charge flow through wires.

$$\frac{Q_1 - x}{C_1} = \frac{x}{C_{eq}}$$

where $C_{eq} = \dfrac{C_2 \times C_3}{C_2 + C_3} = \dfrac{2 \times 3}{2+3} = \dfrac{6}{5}\mu F$

Solve to get $x = 60\,\mu C.$

20. (c) Initially potential difference across both the capacitor is same hence energy of the system is

$$U_1 = \frac{1}{2}CV^2 + \frac{1}{2}CV^2 = CV^2 \qquad ...(i)$$

In the second case when key K is opened and dielectric medium is filled between the plates, capacitance of both the capacitors becomes $3C$, while potential difference across A is V and potential difference across B is $\dfrac{V}{3}$ hence energy of the system now is

$$U_2 = \frac{1}{2}(3C)V^2 + \frac{1}{2}(3C)\left(\frac{V}{3}\right)^2 = \frac{10}{6}CV^2 \ ... (ii)$$

So, $\dfrac{U_1}{U_2} = \dfrac{3}{5}$

21. (a) Capacitors $2\mu F$ and $2\mu F$ are parallel, their equivalent $= 4\ \mu F$
$6\mu F$ and $12\ \mu F$ are in series, their equivalent $= 4\ \mu F$

Now $4\mu F$ (2 and 2 μF) and $8\mu F$ in series $= \dfrac{8}{3}$

And $4\mu F$ (12 & 6 μF) and $4\mu F$ in parallel $= 4 + 4 = 8\mu F$

$8\mu F$ in series with $1\mu F = \dfrac{8}{9}\mu F$

Now $C_{eq} = \dfrac{8}{9} + \dfrac{8}{3} = \dfrac{32}{9}\mu F$

$\dfrac{1}{C_{eq}} = \dfrac{1}{C} + \dfrac{9}{32} = 1 \Rightarrow C = \dfrac{32}{23}\ \mu F$

22. (d) Given, $C_1 = 5\ \mu F$ and $V_1 = 220$ Volt
When capacitor C_1 fully charged it is disconnected from the supply and connected to uncharged capacitor C_2.
$C_2 = 2.5\ \mu F,\ V_2 = 0$
Energy change during the charge redistribution,

$$\Delta U = U_i - U_f = \frac{1}{2}\frac{C_1 C_2}{C_1 + C_2}(V_1 - V_2)^2$$

$$= \frac{1}{2} \times \frac{5 \times 2.5}{(5 + 2.5)}(220 - 0)^2\ \mu J$$

$$= \frac{5}{2 \times 3} \times 22 \times 22 \times 100 \times 10^{-6}\ J$$

$$= \frac{5 \times 11 \times 22}{3} \times 10^{-4}\ J = \frac{55 \times 22}{3} \times 10^{-4}\ J$$

$$= \frac{1210}{3} \times 10^{-4}\ J = \frac{1210}{3} \times 10^{-3}\ J \simeq 4 \times 10^{-2}\ J$$

23. (c) To get a capacitance of $2\mu F$ arrangement of capacitors of capacitance $1\mu F$ as shown in figure 8 capacitors of $1\mu F$ in parallel with four such branches in series i.e., 32 such capacitors are required.

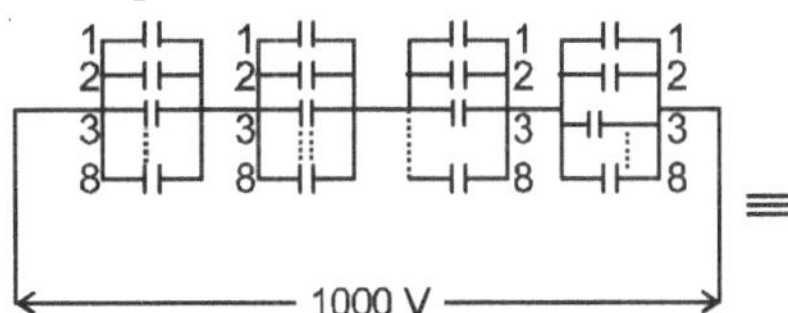

$$\frac{1}{C_{eq}} = \frac{1}{8} + \frac{1}{8} + \frac{1}{8} + \frac{1}{8} \qquad \therefore \ C_{eq} = 2\,\mu F$$

24. (c) Given area of Parallel plate capacitor,
$A = 200\,cm^2$

Separation between the plates, $d = 1.5\,cm$

Force of attraction between the plates,

$$F = 25 \times 10^{-6} N$$

$$F = QE$$

$$F = \frac{Q^2}{2A\,\epsilon_0}$$

(E due to parallel plate $= \dfrac{\sigma}{2\,\epsilon_0} = \dfrac{Q}{A2\,\epsilon_0}$)

But $Q = CV = \dfrac{\epsilon_0 A(V)}{d}$

$$\therefore \quad F = \frac{(\epsilon_0\,AV)^2}{d^2 \times 2A\,\epsilon_0}$$

$$= \frac{(\epsilon_0\,A)^2 \times V^2}{d^2 \times 2 \times (A\,\epsilon_0)} = \frac{(\epsilon_0\,A) \times V^2}{d^2 \times 2}$$

$$\text{or, } 25 \times 10^{-6} = \frac{(8.85 \times 10^{-12}) \times (200 \times 10^{-4}) \times V^2}{2.25 \times 10^{-4} \times 2}$$

$$\Rightarrow V = \sqrt{\frac{25 \times 10^{-6} \times 2.25 \times 10^{-4} \times 2}{8.85 \times 10^{-12} \times 200 \times 10^{-4}}} \approx 250\ V$$

25. (a) In the first condition, electrostatic energy is

$$U_i = \frac{1}{2} CV_0^2 = \frac{1}{2} \times 60 \times 10^{-12} \times 400$$

$$= 12 \times 10^{-9}\, J$$

In the second condition $U_F = \dfrac{1}{2} C'V'^2$

$$U_f = \frac{1}{2} 2C \cdot \left(\frac{V_0}{2}\right)^2 \qquad \left(\because\ C' = 2C,\, V' = \frac{V_0}{2}\right)$$

$$= \frac{1}{4} \times 60 \times 10^{-12} \times (20)^2 \qquad = 6 \times 10^{-9}\, J$$

Energy lost $= U_i - U_f = 12 \times 10^{-9} J - 6 \times 10^{-9} J = 6\,nJ$

17   # Current Electricity

1. **(b)** $R_t = R_0(1 + \alpha t)$

Initially, $R_0(1 + 30\alpha) = 10\,\Omega$

Finally, $R_0(1 + \alpha t) = 11\,\Omega$

$$\therefore \frac{11}{10} = \frac{1 + \alpha t}{1 + 30\alpha}$$

or, $10 + (10 \times 0.002 \times t) = 11 + 330 \times 0.002$

or, $0.02t = 1 + 0.66$ or $t = \dfrac{1.66}{0.02} \simeq 83°C$.

2. **(c)** Charge = area under the current – time graph

$q_1 = 2 \times 1 = 2,\ q_2 = 1 \times 2 = 2,$

and $q_3 = \dfrac{1}{2} \times 2 \times 2 = 2$

$q_1 : q_2 : q_3 = 2 : 2 : 2 = 1 : 1 : 1$

3. **(b)** Let the internal resistance of the battery be r. Then the current flowing through the circuit is given by

$$i = \frac{E}{R + r}$$

In first case, $2 = \dfrac{E}{2 + r}$ ...(1)

In second case, $0.5 = \dfrac{E}{9 + r}$ ...(2)

From (1) & (2),

$4 + 2r = 4.5 + 0.5\,r \Rightarrow 1.5\,r = 0.5 \Rightarrow r = \dfrac{1}{3}\,\Omega.$

4. **(c)**

5. **(d)** Given : Number of cells, $n = 5$, emf of each cell $= E$

Internal resistance of each cell $= r$

In series, current through resistance R

$$I = \frac{nE}{nr + R} = \frac{5E}{5r + R}$$

In parallel, current through resistance R

$$I' = \frac{E}{\dfrac{r}{n} + R} = \frac{nE}{r + nR} = \frac{5E}{r + 5R}$$

According to question, $I = I'$

$$\therefore \frac{5E}{5r + R} = \frac{5E}{r + 5R} \Rightarrow 5r + R = r + 5R$$

or $R = r$ $\therefore \dfrac{R}{r} = 1$

6. **(b)** Case 1 $P_1 = \dfrac{V^2}{R}$

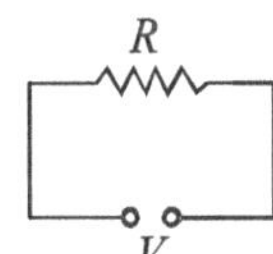

Case 2

The wire is cut into two equal pieces. Therefore, the resistance of the individual wire is $\dfrac{R}{2}$. These are connected in parallel

$$\therefore R_{eq} = \frac{R/2}{2} = \frac{R}{4}$$

$$\therefore P_2 = \frac{V^2}{R/4} = 4\left(\frac{V^2}{R}\right) = 4P_1$$

7. **(c)**

8. **(c)** $\dfrac{R_1}{R_2} = \dfrac{\ell_1}{\ell_2}$ where $\ell_2 = 100 - \ell_1$

In the first case $\dfrac{X}{Y} = \dfrac{20}{80}$

In the second case $\dfrac{4X}{Y} = \dfrac{\ell}{100 - \ell} \Rightarrow \ell = 50$ cm

9. **(b)** If ℓ_1 = length from one end then

$$\frac{\ell_1}{1 - \ell_1} = \frac{X}{R} = \frac{12}{18}$$

$$\ell_1 = \frac{12}{30}\,m = 40cm.$$

and ℓ'_1 = length from one end in second case

$$\frac{\ell'_1}{1 - \ell'_1} = \frac{X}{R'} = \frac{12}{8} = 60\,cm.;\ shift = 20\,cm$$

10. **(a)** $R_{eq} = \dfrac{R_1 R_2}{R_1 + R_2} = \dfrac{\left(\dfrac{R}{2} \cdot \dfrac{R}{2}\right)}{\dfrac{R}{2} + \dfrac{R}{2}} = \dfrac{R}{4}$

11. **(a)** The terminal potential difference of a cell is given by $V + Ir = E$

$V = V_A - V_B$ or $V = E - Ir \Rightarrow \dfrac{dV}{dI} = -r$,

Also for, $i = 0$ then $V = E$ slope $= -r$,

intercept $= E$

12. **(c)** If a heater boils m kg water in time t_1 and another heater boils the same water in t_2, then both connected in series will boil the same water

in time $t_s = t_1 + t_2$ and if in parallel $t_p = \dfrac{t_1 t_2}{t_1 + t_2}$

[Use time taken $\propto$ Resistance]

13. **(d)**

14. **(c)** $i = neAV_d$ and $V_d \propto \sqrt{E}$ (Given)

or, $i \propto \sqrt{E}$

$i^2 \propto E$

$i^2 \propto V$

Hence graph (c) correctly dipicts the *V-I* graph for a wire made of such type of material.

15. **(c)**

16. **(c)** Total power consumed by electrical appliances in the building, $P_{total} = 2500W$

Watt $=$ Volt $\times$ ampere

$\Rightarrow 2500 = V \times I \Rightarrow 2500 = 220\,I$

$\Rightarrow I = \dfrac{2500}{220} = 11.36 \approx 12A$

(Minimum capacity of main fuse)

17. **(a)**

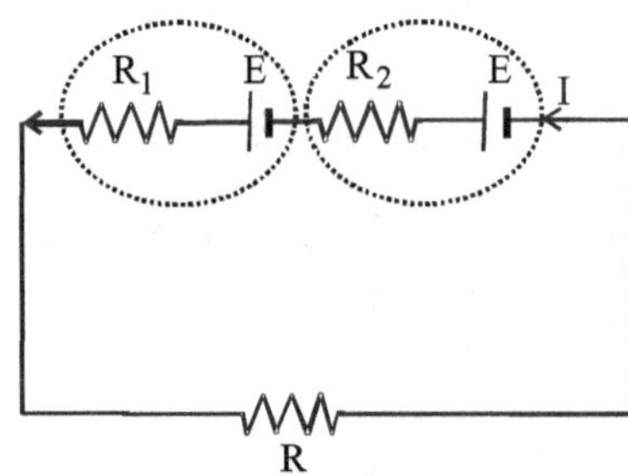

Let *E* be the emf of each source of current

Current in the circuit $I = \dfrac{2E}{R + R_1 + R_2}$

Potential difference across cell having internal resistance R_2

$V = E - iR_2 = 0$

$E - \dfrac{2E}{R + R_1 + R_2} \cdot R_2 = 0$

$\Rightarrow R + R_1 + R_2 - 2R_2 = 0$

$\Rightarrow R + R_1 - R_2 = 0$

$\Rightarrow R = R_2 - R_1$

18. **(d)** Charge mobility

$(\mu) = \dfrac{V_d}{E}$ [Where $V_d =$ drift velocity]

and resistivity $(\rho) = \dfrac{E}{j} = \dfrac{EA}{I} \Rightarrow E = \dfrac{I(\rho)}{A}$

$\Rightarrow \mu = \dfrac{V_d}{E} = \dfrac{V_d A}{I\rho}$

$= \dfrac{1.1 \times 10^{-3} \times \pi \times \left(5 \times 10^{-3}\right)^2}{5 \times 1.7 \times 10^{-8}}$

$\mu = 1.0 \dfrac{m^2}{V_s}$

19. **(b)** Given: $\dfrac{\ell_1}{\ell_2} = \dfrac{4}{3}$ $\qquad \dfrac{r_1}{r_2} = \dfrac{2}{3}$

Since the two wires are connected in parallel, potential remains same. i.e.,

$V =$ constant.

$IR =$ Constant

i.e., $I_1 R_1 = I_2 R_2 \Rightarrow \dfrac{I_1}{I_2} = \dfrac{R_2}{R_1}$ ..... (a)

But we know that, $R = \dfrac{\rho\ell}{A}$

$\therefore \dfrac{R_1}{R_2} = \left(\dfrac{\ell_1}{A_1}\right)\left(\dfrac{A_2}{\ell_2}\right)$ (since area, $A = \pi r^2$) $= 3$

Substitute this value in equation (a) we get,

$\dfrac{I_1}{I_2} = \dfrac{1}{3}$.

20. **(d)** Case (I) : $E + E = (r + r + 5)\,1$

or $2E = 2r + 5$ ...(i)

Case (II) : $E = \left(\dfrac{r \times r}{r + r} + 5\right) \times 0.8$

or $E = \left(\dfrac{r}{2} + 5\right)0.8$

or $E = 0.4r + 4.0$ ...(ii)

Multiplying (ii) by 2 and equating with (i), we get

$$2r + 5 = 0.8\,r + 8 \text{ or } 1.2\,r = 3 \text{ or } r = \frac{3}{1.2} = 2.5$$

21. (a) $\eta = \dfrac{5 \times 15 \times 14}{10 \times 8 \times 15} = 0.875$ or $87.5\,\%$

22. (b) In case of internal resistance measurement by potentiometer,

$$\frac{V_1}{V_2} = \frac{\ell_1}{\ell_2} = \frac{\left[ER_1/(R_1+r)\right]}{\left[ER_2/(R_2+r)\right]} = \frac{R_1(R_2+r)}{R_2(R_1+r)}$$

$$\Rightarrow \quad \frac{2}{3} = \frac{5}{10}\left[\frac{10+r}{5+r}\right] \Rightarrow r = 10\,\Omega$$

23. (b) $V = IR = (neAv_d)\rho\dfrac{\ell}{A}$

$$\therefore \quad \rho = \frac{V}{V_d\,lne}$$

Here V = potential difference
l = length of wire
n = no. of electrons per unit volume of conductor.
e = no. of electrons
Placing the value of above parameters we get resistivity

$$r = \frac{5}{8 \prime 10^{28} \prime 1.6 \prime 10^{-19} \prime 2.5 \prime 10^{-4} \prime 0.1}$$
$$= 1.6 \times 10^{-5}\,\Omega m$$

24. (a)

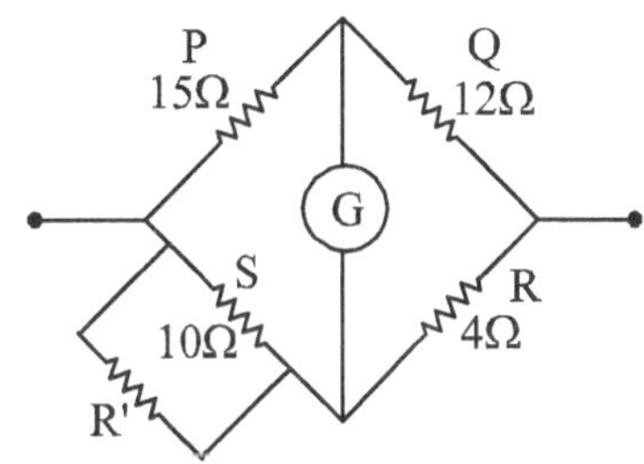

As per Wheatstone bridge balance condition

$$\frac{P}{Q} = \frac{S}{R}$$

Let resistance R' is connected in parallel with resistance S of 10Ω

$$\therefore \quad \frac{15}{12} = \frac{\dfrac{10R'}{10+R'}}{4} \Rightarrow 5 = \frac{10R'}{10+R'}$$

$$\Rightarrow 50 + 5R' = 10R'$$

$$\therefore \quad R' = \frac{50}{5} = 10\,\Omega$$

25. (a) Potential gradient, $x = \dfrac{\text{Potential drop}}{\text{length}}$

Here, Potential drop = 1.02
Balancing length from P = 100 − 49

$$\therefore x = \frac{1.02}{100-49} = 0.02 \text{ volt/cm}$$

18 Moving Charges and Magnetism

1. **(a)** $F = ma = qvB$ ⮕ $a = \dfrac{qvB}{m}$

$$= \dfrac{1.6 \times 10^{-19} \times 2 \times 3.4 \times 10^{7}}{1.67 \times 10^{-27}} = 6.5 \times 10^{15} \text{ m/sec}^2$$

2. **(c)** $r = \dfrac{mv}{qB}$ or $r \propto v$

As v is doubled, the radius also becomes double. Hence radius $= 2 \times 2 = 4$ cm

3. **(c)** Equating magnetic force to centripetal force,

$$\dfrac{mv^2}{r} = qvB \sin 90°$$

Time to complete one revolution,

$$T = \dfrac{2\pi r}{v} = \dfrac{2\pi m}{qB}$$

4. **(a)** $B \propto \dfrac{1}{r}$

$$\therefore B' = \dfrac{1}{3} B = \dfrac{1}{3} \times 10^{-3} = 3.33 \times 10^{-4} \text{T}$$

5. **(d)**

6. **(d)** Magnetic field at a point on the axis of a current carrying wire is always zero.

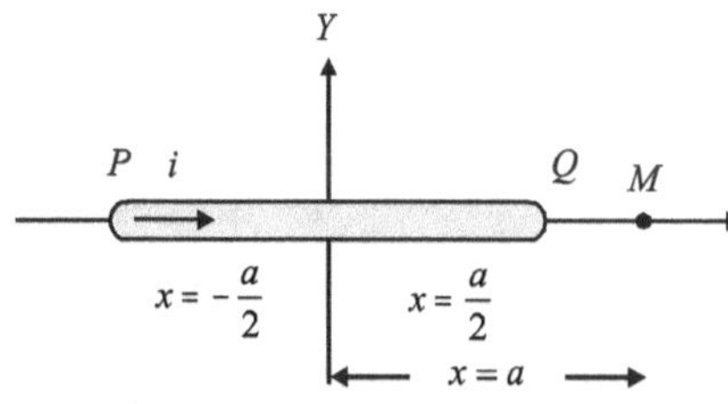

7. **(c)** $B = \mu_0 ni$

$$B_1 = (\mu_0)\left(\dfrac{n}{2}\right)(2\,i) = \mu_0 ni = B$$

$$\Rightarrow B_1 = B$$

8. **(b)** $F = Bi\ell = 2 \times 1.2 \times 0.5 = 1.2$ N

9. **(a)** $F = \dfrac{\mu_0}{4\pi} \times \dfrac{2i_1 i_2}{r}$

$= 50 \times 10^{-7}$ N/m. Here F is force per unit length.

10. **(c)** $R = \dfrac{V}{I_g} - G = \dfrac{10}{0.01} - 10 = 990 \ \Omega$ in series.

11. **(a)** $\dfrac{F}{\ell} = \dfrac{\mu_0 i^2}{2\pi d} = 9.8 \times 4 \times 10^{-6}$

$$\Rightarrow i = \sqrt{\dfrac{4 \times 10^{-6} \times 9.8 \times 0.12}{2 \times 10^{-7}}} = 4.85 \,\text{A}$$

12. **(d)** $Bqv = mv^2/r$ or $q/m = v/rB$.

13. **(a)**

14. **(d)** For a charged particle orbiting in a circular path in a magnetic field

$$\dfrac{mv^2}{r} = Bqv \Rightarrow v = \dfrac{Bqr}{m}$$

or $mv^2 = Bqvr$

Also,

$$E_K = \dfrac{1}{2}mv^2 = \dfrac{1}{2}Bqvr = Bq\dfrac{r}{2}\cdot\dfrac{Bqr}{m} = \dfrac{B^2q^2r^2}{2m}$$

For deuteron, $E_1 = \dfrac{B^2q^2r^2}{2 \times 2m}$, For proton,

$$E_2 = \dfrac{B^2q^2r^2}{2m}$$

$$\dfrac{E_1}{E_2} = \dfrac{1}{2} \Rightarrow \dfrac{50\,\text{keV}}{E_2} = \dfrac{1}{2} \Rightarrow E_2 = 100\,\text{keV}$$

15. **(c)** Since particle is moving undeflected

So, $q_E = qvB \Rightarrow B = \dfrac{E}{V} = \dfrac{10^4}{10} = 10^3 \text{ wb}/\text{m}^2$

16. **(d)** $m = 1.67 \times 10^{-27}$ kg; $e = 1.60 \times 10^{-19}$ C; $v = 10\,\text{MHz} = 10^7$ Hz; R = 60 cm = 0.6 m

$$B = \frac{2\pi\, mv}{e} = \frac{2\pi \times 1.67 \times 10^{-27} \times 10^7}{1.60 \times 10^{-19}}$$

$$= 0.656 \text{ Tesla}$$

$$E_{max} = \frac{B^2 e^2 R^2}{2\,m}$$

$$= \frac{(0.656)^2 \times (1.60 \times 10^{-19})^2 (0.6)^2}{2 \times 1.67 \times 10^{-27}}$$

$$= 11.874 \times 10^{-13}\,J = \frac{11.874 \times 10^{-13}}{1.6 \times 10^{-13}} = 7.421\,MeV$$

17. (a) According to Ampere's circuit law

$$\oint \vec{B}.d\vec{I} = \mu_0 I_{enclosed} = \mu_0(2A - 1A) = \mu_0$$

18. (c) The magnetic field at a point on the axis of a circular loop at a distance x from centre is,

$$B = \frac{\mu_0 i\, a^2}{2(x^2 + a^2)^{3/2}}$$

$$B' = \frac{\mu_0 i}{2a} = \frac{B.(x^2 + a^2)^{3/2}}{a^3}$$

Put $x = 4$ & $a = 3 \Rightarrow B' = \frac{54(5^3)}{3 \times 3 \times 3} = 250\,\mu T$

19. (d) Current in a small element, $dI = \frac{d\theta}{\pi} I$

Magnetic field due to the element

$$dB = \frac{\mu_0}{4\pi} \frac{2dI}{R}$$

The component $dB \cos\theta$, of the field is cancelled by another opposite component.
Therefore,

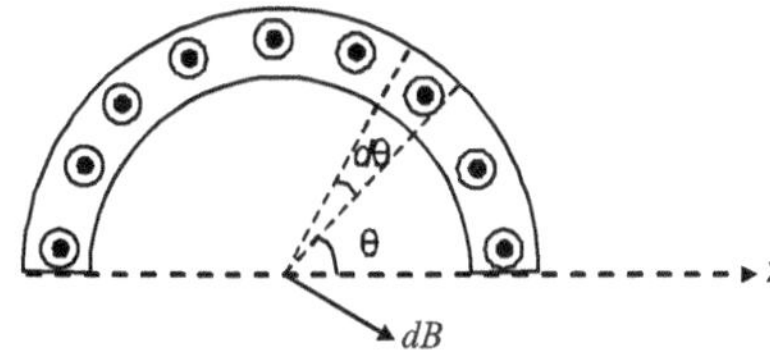

$$B_{net} = \int dB \sin\theta = \frac{\mu_0 I}{2\pi^2 R} \int_0^\pi \sin\theta d\theta = \frac{\mu_0 I}{\pi^2 R}$$

20. (c)

21. (c) $I_g G = (I - I_g)s$

$\therefore 10^{-3} \times 100 = (10 - 10^{-3}) \times S$

$\therefore S \approx 0.01\,\Omega$

22. (c)

23. (b) The centripetal force is provided by the magnetic force

$$\therefore \frac{mv^2}{R} = qvB \Rightarrow r = \frac{mv}{Bq} \qquad \therefore r \propto \frac{\sqrt{m}}{q}$$

$$\therefore r_p : r_d : r_\alpha = \frac{\sqrt{m_p}}{q_p} : \frac{\sqrt{m_d}}{q_d} : \frac{\sqrt{m_\alpha}}{q_\alpha} = 1 : \sqrt{2} : 1$$

Thus we have, $r_\alpha = r_p < r_d$

24. (a) When a moving charged particle is subjected to a perpendicular magnetic field, then it describes a circular path of radius.

$$r = \frac{p}{qB}$$

where q = Charge of the particle
$\qquad p$ = Momentum of the particle
$\qquad B$ = Magnetic field
Here p, q and B are constant for electron and proton, therefore the radius will be same.

25. (d) The magnetic field due to circular coil (1) is

$$B_1 = \frac{\mu_0 i_1}{2r} = \frac{\mu_0 i_1}{2(2\pi \times 10^{-2})}$$

$$= \frac{\mu_0 \times 3 \times 10^2}{4\pi}$$

Magnetic field due to coil (2)
Total magnetic field

$$B_2 = \frac{\mu_0 i_2}{2(2\pi \times 10^{-2})} = \frac{\mu_0 \times 4 \times 10^2}{4\pi}$$

Total magnetic field, $B = \sqrt{B_1^2 + B_2^2}$

$$= \frac{\mu_0}{4\pi} \cdot 5 \times 10^2$$

$$\Rightarrow B = 10^{-7} \times 5 \times 10^2 \Rightarrow B = 5 \times 10^{-5}\,Wb/m^2$$

26. (c) $F = \frac{\mu_0}{2\pi} \left(\frac{i_1 i_2}{a} - \frac{i_1 i_2}{2a} \right) \times a = \frac{\mu_0 i_1 i_2}{4\pi}$

27. (a) Force acting between two long conductor carrying current,

$$F = \frac{\mu_0}{4\pi} \frac{2I_1 I_2}{d} \times \ell \qquad \qquad ...(i)$$

Where d = distance between the conductors
ℓ = length of conductor

In second case, $F' = -\frac{\mu_0}{4\pi} \frac{2(2I_1)I_2}{3d} \ell \qquad ..(ii)$

From equation (i) and (ii), we have

$$\therefore \quad \frac{F'}{F} = \frac{-2}{3}$$

28. **(a)** Here, side of the triangle, $l = 4.5 \times 10^{-2}$ m, current, $I = 1$ A
magnetic field at the centre of the triangle 'O' B = ?

From figure, $\tan 60° = \sqrt{3} = \dfrac{1}{2d}$

$$\Rightarrow \quad d = \frac{l}{2\sqrt{3}}$$

$$= \left(\frac{4.5 \times 10^{-2}}{2\sqrt{3}} \right) \text{m}$$

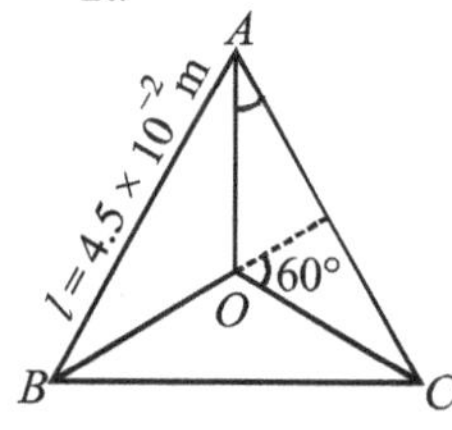

Magnetic field, $B = \dfrac{\mu_0 i}{4\pi d}(\cos\theta_1 + \cos\theta_2)$

Putting value of $\mu = 4\pi \times 10^{-7}$ and θ_1 and θ_2 we will get $B = 4 \times 10^{-5}$ Wb/m²

29. **(a)** Magnetic field induction at the centre of current carrying circular coil of radius r is

$$B = \frac{\mu_0}{4\pi} \frac{I}{R} \times 2\pi$$

Here $B_A = \dfrac{\mu_0}{4\pi} \dfrac{I}{R} \times 2\pi$ and $B_B = \dfrac{\mu_0}{4\pi} \dfrac{2I}{2R} \times 2\pi$

$$\Rightarrow \quad \frac{B_A}{B_B} = \frac{I/R}{2I/2R} = 1$$

30. **(d)** $C\theta = NBiA \sin 90°$

or $10^{-6}\left(\dfrac{\pi}{180}\right) = 175 B(10^{-3}) \times 10^{-4}$

$$\therefore \quad B = 10^{-3}\,\text{T}$$

19

Magnetism and Matter

1. **(c)** Let the actual angle of dip (in the magnetic meridian) be θ. If B_H and B_v be the horizontal and vertical component of the earth's magnetic field respectively, then $\tan\theta = \left(\dfrac{B_v}{B_H}\right)$

In the plane situated at $30°$ with the magnetic meridian, the horizontal component of the earth's magnetic field will be $B_H\cos 30°$ while the vertical component will be Bv. The angle of dip in this plane is,

$$\tan 45° = \frac{B_v}{B_H\cos 30°}$$

$$\frac{\tan\theta}{\tan 45°} = \cos 30° \Rightarrow \theta = \tan^{-1}\left(\frac{\sqrt{3}}{2}\right)$$

2. **(c)** $M_{net} = \sqrt{M_0^2 + M_0^2 + 2M_0^2\cos 60°}$

$$= \sqrt{3M_0^2} = \sqrt{3}M_0$$

3. **(a)** The torque acting on the magnet of magnetic moment M, when held at angle θ to magnetic field B,

$\tau = MB\sin\theta$

$\tau_1 = MB\sin 90° = MB = 10^{-5}$ Nm.

$\tau_2 = MB\sin 30° = 0.5 \times 10^{-5}$ Nm $= 5 \times 10^{-6}$ Nm

4. **(d)** For a temporary magnet the hysteresis loop should be long and narrow.

5. **(a)** Magnetic moment, M $= 8.7 \times 10^{-2}$ Am^2 moment of inertia, I $= 11.5 \times 10^{-6}$ kg m^2 Time period of oscillation is

$$T = \frac{6.70}{10} = 0.6755$$

As, $T = 2\pi\sqrt{\dfrac{I}{MB}}$; $B = \dfrac{4\pi^2 I}{MT^2}$

$$\therefore \quad B = \frac{4 \times (3.14)^2 \times 11.5 \times 10^{-6}}{8.7 \times 10^{-2} \times (0.67)^2} = 0.012\,\text{T}$$

6. **(d)** As $F \propto \dfrac{1}{r^4}$ and r becomes twice, therefore,

F becomes $\dfrac{1}{2^4} = \dfrac{1}{16}$ times $\Rightarrow$

$$\therefore \quad \frac{1}{16} \times 8 = 0.5 \text{ N}.$$

7. **(b)** $\tau = MB\sin\theta = 0.1 \times 3 \times 10^{-4}\sin 30°$

or $\tau = 1.5 \times 10^{-5}$ N–m.

8. **(a)** Torque $\tau = MB_H\sin\theta$

$= 0.1 \times 10^{-3} \times 4\pi \times 10^{-3} \times \sin 30°$

$= 10^{-7} \times 4\pi \times \dfrac{1}{2}$

$= 2\pi \times 10^{-7}$ N $\times$ m

9. **(a)** Given that : $B_1 = 1.2 \times 10^{-2}$ T, orientation of dipole with the field B_1, $\theta_1 = 15°$
Hence, orientation of dipole with B_2,
$\theta_2 = 60° - 15° = 45°$ (figure)
As the dipole is in equilibrium, therefore, the torque on the dipole due to the two fields must be equal and opposite.

If M be the magnetic dipole moment of the dipole, then

$\tau_1 = \tau_2$

or $MB_1\sin\theta_1 = MB_2\sin\theta_2$

or, $B_2 = \dfrac{B_1\sin\theta_1}{\sin\theta_2} = \dfrac{1.2 \times 10^{-2}\sin 15°}{\sin 45°}$

$= \dfrac{1.2 \times 10^{-2} \times 0.2588}{0.7071} = 4.4 \times 10^{-3}$ Tesla

10. **(a)**

11. **(b)** $\tau = MB\sin\theta$

$\tau = iAB\sin 90°$

$\therefore \quad A = \dfrac{\tau}{iB}$

Also, $A = 1/2\,(BC)\,(AD)$

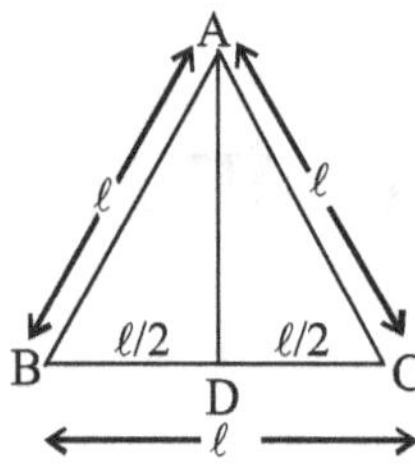

But $\dfrac{1}{2}(BC)(AD) = \dfrac{1}{2}(l)\sqrt{l^2 - \left(\dfrac{l}{2}\right)^2} = \dfrac{\sqrt{3}}{4}l^2$

$\Rightarrow \quad \dfrac{\sqrt{3}}{4}(l)^2 = \dfrac{\tau}{Bi} \quad \therefore \quad l = 2\left(\dfrac{\tau}{\sqrt{3}\,B.i}\right)^{\frac{1}{2}}$

12. **(d)**

From figure $B_{net} = \sqrt{B_a^2 + B_e^2}$

$= \sqrt{\left(\dfrac{\mu_0}{4\pi}\cdot\dfrac{2M}{d^3}\right)^2 + \left(\dfrac{\mu_0}{4\pi}\cdot\dfrac{M}{d^3}\right)^2}$

$= \sqrt{5}\cdot\dfrac{\mu_0}{4\pi}\cdot\dfrac{M}{d^3} = \sqrt{5}\times 10^{-7}\times\dfrac{10}{(0.1)^3}$

$= \sqrt{5}\times 10^{-3}$ tesla

13. **(a)** $\tan\theta = \dfrac{V}{H}, \tan\theta' = \dfrac{V}{H\cos x}$;

$\dfrac{\tan\theta'}{\tan\theta} = \dfrac{1}{\cos x}$

14. **(b)** Ferromagnetic substance has magnetic domains whereas paramagnetic substances have magnetic dipoles which get attracted to a magnetic field.

Diamagnetic substances do not have magnetic dipole but in the presence of external magnetic field due to their orbital motion of electrons these substances are repelled.

15. **(a)** The volume of the cube is
$V = (10^{-6}\,m)^3 = 10^{-18}\,m^3$

Net dipole moment m_{net}
$= 8 \times 10^{10} \times 9 \times 10^{-24}\,A\,m^2$
$= 72 \times 10^{-14}\,A\,m^2$

Intensity of magnetization is magnetic moment developed per unit volume.

$\therefore \quad$ magnetization, $M = \dfrac{m_{net}}{volume}$

$= \dfrac{72\times 10^{-14}\,A\,m^2}{10^{-18}\,m^3} = 72\times 10^4\;A\;m^{-1}$

$= 7.2 \times 10^5\,A\,m^{-1}$

16. **(b)** Diamagnetic materials are repelled in an external magnetic field.

Bar B represents diamagnetic materials.

17. **(d)** The magnetic permeability of the material

$\mu = \dfrac{B}{H} = \dfrac{4H}{H} = 4$

18. **(d)** Time period of a vibration magnetometer,

$T \propto \dfrac{1}{\sqrt{B}} \quad \Rightarrow \quad \dfrac{T_1}{T_2} = \sqrt{\dfrac{B_2}{B_1}}$

$\Rightarrow \quad T_2 = T_1\sqrt{\dfrac{B_1}{B_2}} = 2\sqrt{\dfrac{24\times 10^{-6}}{6\times 10^{-6}}} = 4s$

19. **(d)** In magnetic dipole

Force $\propto \dfrac{1}{r^4}$

In the given question,

Force $\propto x^{-n}$

Hence, $n = 4$

20. **(a)** Given, $B = 4 \times 10^{-5}$ T

$R_E = 6.4 \times 10^6\,m$

Dipole moment of the earth $M = ?$

$B = \dfrac{\mu_0}{4\pi}\dfrac{M}{d^3}$

$4\times 10^{-5} = \dfrac{4\pi\times 10^{-7}\times M}{4\pi\times\left(6.4\times 10^6\right)^3}$

$\therefore \quad M \cong 10^{23}\,Am^2$

21. **(a)** Given $M = 8 \times 10^{22}\,Am^2$

$d = R_e = 6.4 \times 10^6\,m$

Earth's magnetic field, $B = \dfrac{\mu_0}{4\pi} \cdot \dfrac{2M}{d^3}$

$= \dfrac{4\pi \times 10^{-7}}{4\pi} \times \dfrac{2 \times 8 \times 10^{22}}{(6.4 \times 10^6)^3} \cong 0.6\,Gauss$

22. **(a)** $M = 60\,Am^2$

$\tau = 1.2 \times 10^{-3}\,Nm,\ B_H = 40 \times 10^{-6}\,Wb/m^2$

$\vec{\tau} = \vec{M} \times \vec{B}_H \implies \tau = MB_H \sin\theta$

$\implies 1.2 \times 10^{-3} = 60 \times 40 \times 10^{-6}\sin\theta$

$\implies \sin\theta = \dfrac{1.2 \times 10^{-3}}{60 \times 40 \times 10^{-6}} = \dfrac{1}{2} = \sin 30°$

$\implies \theta = 30°$

23. **(c)** As the magnet is placed with its south pole pointing south, hence the neutral point lies on the equatorial line. At the neutral point, the magnetic field B due to the magnet becomes equal and opposite to horizontal component of earth's magnetic field i.e., B_H.

Hence, if M be magnetic dipole moment of the magnet of length 2ℓ and r the distance of the neutral point from its centre, then

$B = \dfrac{\mu_0}{4\pi} \dfrac{M}{(r^2 + \ell^2)^{3/2}} = B_H$

Given that $\mu_0 = 4\pi \times 10^{-7}\,T\,mA^{-1}, M = 1.34\,Am^2,$

$r = 15\,cm = 0.15\,m$ and $\ell = 5.0\,cm = 0.05\,m$

$\therefore\quad B_H = 10^{-7} \times \dfrac{1.34}{[(0.15)^2 + (0.5)^2]^{3/2}}$

$= 10^{-7} \times \dfrac{1.34}{0.025\sqrt{0.025}} = 0.34 \times 10^{-4}\,T$

24. **(c)** Here, $r = 30\,cm = 0.3\,m$

we know $\dfrac{\mu_0 M}{4\pi r^3} = B_H = 3.6 \times 10^{-5}$

$\implies M = \dfrac{3.6 \times 10^{-5}}{10^{-7}}(0.3)^3 = 9.7\,Am^2$

25. **(b)** For a tangent galvanometer, $i = \dfrac{2rH}{\mu_0 N}\tan\theta$

Now $8\,\Omega$ and $8\,\Omega$ in parallel $= 4\,\Omega$.

$i = \dfrac{emf}{resistance} = \dfrac{4}{4} = 1\,ampere$

$\therefore$ For T.G. $\dfrac{r\tan\theta}{N} = \dfrac{\mu_0 i}{2H},$

$r = radius$

$\therefore\quad \dfrac{r_A \tan\theta_A}{N_A} = \dfrac{r_B \tan\theta_B}{N_B}$

$\implies \dfrac{r_A \tan 30°}{N_A} = \dfrac{r_B \tan 60°}{N_B}$

$N = $ number of turns $\implies \dfrac{8 \times 1}{\sqrt{3}N_A} = \dfrac{16 \times \sqrt{3}}{N_B}$

$\implies \dfrac{8}{\sqrt{3} \times 2} = \dfrac{16\sqrt{3}}{N_B} \implies N_B = 12\,turns$

20 Electromagnetic Induction

1. **(d)** Induced emf $e = \dfrac{\mu_0 N_1 N_2 A}{\ell}\dfrac{di}{dt}$

$$= \dfrac{4 \times 3.14 \times 10^{-7} \times 2000 \times 300 \times 1.2 \times 10^{-3} \times [2-(-2)]}{0.30}$$

$$= 48.2 \times 10^{-3}\,\text{V} \approx 48\,\text{mV}$$

2. **(c)** Induced emf $= vB_H l = 1.5 \times 5 \times 10^{-5} \times 2$
$$= 15 \times 10^{-5} = 0.15\,\text{mV}$$

3. **(b)** $\dfrac{d\phi}{dt} = \dfrac{(W_2 - W_1)}{t}$,

$R_{tot} = (R + 4R)\Omega = 5R\ \Omega$

$i = \dfrac{nd\varphi}{R_{tot}dt} = \dfrac{-n(W_2 - W_1)}{5Rt}$. $(\because W_2\ \&\ W_1$ are

magnetic flux)

4. **(a)** According to right hand palm rule, the Lorentz force on free electrons in the conductor will be directed towards end B. Hence, the end A gets positively charged.

5. **(c)** Relative velocity $= v + v = 2v$

$\therefore$ emf. $= B.l\,(2v)$

6. **(a)** Given : $n = 10$ turns, $R_{coil} = 20\Omega$,
$R_G = 30\Omega$, Total resistance in the circuit
$= 20 + 30 = 50\Omega$.
$A = 10^{-2}\,\text{m}^2,\quad B = 10^{-2}\,\text{T},\ \phi_1 = 0°,\ \phi_2 = 60°$

$q = \dfrac{\phi_1 - \phi_2}{R} = \dfrac{BnA\cos\theta_1 - BnA\cos\theta_2}{R}$

$= \dfrac{BnA(\cos 0 - \cos 60)}{R} = \dfrac{BnA\,(1 - 0.5))}{R}$

$= 1 \times 10^{-5}\,\text{C}$

7. **(d)**

8. **(d)** Given that $\phi = at\,(T - t)$

Induced emf, $E = \dfrac{d\phi}{dt} = \dfrac{d}{dt}\big[at\,(T - t)\big]$

$= at\,(0 - 1) + a\,(T - t)$

$= a\,(T - 2t)$

So, induced emf is also a function of time.

$\therefore$ Heat generated in time T is

$$H\int_0^T \dfrac{E^2}{R}\,dt = \dfrac{a^2}{R}\int_0^T (T - 2t)^2\,dt = \dfrac{a^2 T^3}{3R}$$

9. **(a)** Area of the loop $= 0.1 \times 0.1 = 0.01\,\text{m}^2$

$$\varepsilon = -\dfrac{d\phi}{dt} = \dfrac{-d}{dt}(BA)$$

Magnitude of emf

$$\varepsilon = A\dfrac{dB}{dt} = (0.01\text{m}^2)\,(0.02\ \text{T}/\text{s}) = 2 \times 10^{-4}\,\text{V}$$

Resistance of the loop is

$$R = \rho\dfrac{\ell}{A} = \dfrac{1.7 \times 10^{-8} \times 40 \times 10^{-2}}{3.14 \times 10^{-6}}$$

$$= 2.16 \times 10^{-3}\,\Omega$$

Current induced in the loop

$$I = \dfrac{\varepsilon}{R} = \dfrac{2 \times 10^{-4}\,\text{V}}{2.16 \times 10^{-3}\,\Omega} = 9.3 \times 10^{-2}\,\text{amp.}$$

10. **(d)** The magnetic field is increasing in the downward direction. Therefore, according to Lenz's law the current I_1 will flow in the direction ab and I_2 in the direction dc.

11. **(c)**

12. **(a)** In case of both the circular and the elliptical loops, the rate of change of area of the loops during their passage out of the field is not constant, hence induced emf will not remain constant for them.

13. **(c)** Induced emf in the coil, $e = -L\left(\dfrac{di}{dt}\right)$.

Initialy, $\dfrac{di}{dt} = 0$, then $\dfrac{di}{dt} = -ve$ and finally

$\dfrac{di}{dt} = +ve$

Accordingly $e = 0$, $e = +ve$, and finally $e = -ve$.

14. **(d)** Inductance $= \dfrac{\mu_0 N^2 A}{L}$

15. **(a)** $Q_{\text{coil}} = (NQ) \propto i$

So, $\dfrac{Q_1}{Q_2} = \dfrac{i_1}{i_2} = \dfrac{3}{2}$

or $Q_2 = \dfrac{2}{3} Q_1 = \dfrac{2}{3} \times 10^{-3} = 6.67 \times 10^{-4}$ Wb

16. **(b)** We have given, time period, $T = 10$s

$\therefore$ Angular velocity, $\omega = \dfrac{2\pi}{10} = \dfrac{\pi}{5}$

Magnetic flux, $\phi(t) = BA \cos \omega t$
Emf induced,

$E = \dfrac{-d\phi}{dt} = BA\omega \sin \omega t = BA\omega \sin(\omega t)$

Induced emf, $|\varepsilon|$ is maximum when $\omega t = \dfrac{\pi}{2}$

$\Rightarrow$ $t = \dfrac{\dfrac{\pi}{2}}{\dfrac{\pi}{5}} = 2.5$ s

For induced emf to be minimum i.e zero

$\omega t = \pi$ $\Rightarrow$ $t = \dfrac{\pi}{\dfrac{\pi}{5}} = 5\ s$

$\therefore$ Induced emf is zero at t = 5 s

17. **(c)** Power $= \dfrac{B^2 v^2 l^2}{R}$

$= \dfrac{0.5 \times 0.5 \times 12 \times 12 \times 15 \times 15 \times 10^{-8}}{9 \times 10^{-3}}$

$= 9 \times 10^{-3}$ watt

Current $= \dfrac{Bvl}{R}$

$= \dfrac{0.5 \times 12 \times 10^{-2} \times 15 \times 10^{-2}}{9 \times 10^{-3}} = 1A$

18. **(d)** $e_0 = \omega NBA = (2\pi v)NBA$
$-2 \times 3.14 \times 100 \times 5000 \times 0.2 \times 0.25 - 157$ kV

19. **(c)** $A = 200\ cm^2 = 200 \times 10^{-4}\ m^2; N = 100;$
$R = 2\Omega$
Initial magnetic flux linked with the coil is
$\phi_i = BA \cos \theta = 0.1 \times 200 \times 10^{-4} \times \cos 0°$
$= 2 \times 10^{-3}$ Wb
Final magnetic flux linked with the coil is $\phi_f = 0$

$\varepsilon = -\dfrac{N\Delta\phi}{\Delta t} = \dfrac{-N(\phi_f - \phi_i)}{\Delta t}$

$= \dfrac{-100(0 - 2 \times 10^{-3})}{1} = 0.2 V$

Induced current $I = \dfrac{\varepsilon}{R} = \dfrac{0.2V}{2\Omega} = 0.1A$

Induced charge q = It = 0.1 × 1 = 0.1 C

20. **(b)** $L = \mu_0 nI$

$\therefore$ $\dfrac{L_2}{L_1} = \dfrac{\mu}{\mu_0}$ ----($\because$ n and I are same)

$\therefore$ $L_2 = \mu_r L_1 = 900 \times 0.18 = 162$ mH

21. **(c)**

22. **(c)** As total length L of the wire will remain constant
L = (3a) N   (N = total turns)
and length of winding = (d) N
  (d = diameter of wire)
self inductance $= \mu_0 n^2 A\ell$

$= \mu_0 n^2 \left(\dfrac{\sqrt{3}a^2}{4}\right) dN$

$\propto a^2 N \propto a$ [as N = L/3a $\Rightarrow$ N$\propto \dfrac{1}{a}$]

Now 'a' increased to '3a'
So self inductance will become 3 times

23. **(d)** Given, Area of cross-section of pipe,
$A = 10\ cm^2$

Length of pipe, $\ell = 20$ cm

$$M = \frac{\mu_0 N_1 N_2 A}{\ell}$$

$$= \frac{4\pi \times 10^{-7} \times 300 \times 400 \times 100 \times 10^{-4}}{0.2}$$

$$M = \frac{\mu_0 N_1 N_2 A}{\ell}$$

$$= 2.4\pi \times 10^{-4} \text{H}$$

24. (d) Induced emf,

$$e = -\frac{\Delta\phi}{\Delta t} = \frac{-\Delta(LI)}{\Delta t} = -L\frac{\Delta I}{\Delta t}$$

$$\therefore \ |e| = L\frac{\Delta I}{\Delta t}$$

$$\Rightarrow 8 = L \times \frac{[2-(-2)]}{0.05} \Rightarrow L = \frac{8 \times 0.05}{4} = 0.1\text{H}$$

25. (a) Net charge

$$Q = \frac{\Delta\phi}{R} = \frac{1}{10}A(B_f - B_i) = \frac{1}{10} \times 3.5 \times 10^{-3}$$

$$\left(0.4\sin\frac{\pi}{2} - 0\right) = \frac{1}{10}(3.5 \times 10^{-3})(0.4 - 0)$$

$$= 1.4 \times 10^{-4} \text{mC}$$

21

Alternating Current

1. **(b)** $V = 50 \times 2 \sin 100\pi \cos 100\pi t = 50 \sin 200\pi t$

   $\Rightarrow V_0 = 50 \; Volts$ and $\nu = 100 \; Hz$

2. **(a)** Initially, when steady state is achieved,

   $$i = \frac{E}{R}$$

   Let E is short circuited at $t = 0$. Then

   At $t = 0$, $i_0 = \dfrac{E}{R}$

   Let during decay of current at any time the current flowing is $-L\dfrac{di}{dt} - iR = 0$

   $$\Rightarrow \frac{di}{i} = -\frac{R}{L}dt \Rightarrow \int_{i_0}^{i}\frac{di}{i} = \int_{0}^{t} -\frac{R}{L}dt$$

   $$\Rightarrow \log_e \frac{i}{i_0} = -\frac{R}{L}t \Rightarrow i = i_0 \, e^{-\frac{R}{L}t}$$

   $$\Rightarrow i = \frac{E}{R}e^{-\frac{R}{L}t} = \frac{100}{100}e^{\frac{-100\times10^{-3}}{100\times10^{-3}}} = \frac{1}{e}$$

3. **(d)**

4. **(d)** Current is maximum when $X_L = X_C$

   $$\Rightarrow \omega L = \frac{1}{\omega C}$$

   $$\Rightarrow \omega = \frac{1}{\sqrt{LC}} = \frac{1}{\sqrt{0.5\times8\times10^{-6}}}$$

   $$= \frac{1}{2\times10^{-3}} = 500 \text{ rad/s.}$$

5. **(d)** From figure,

   $$\tan 45° = \frac{\dfrac{1}{\omega C} - \omega L}{R}$$

   $$\Rightarrow \frac{1}{\omega C} - \omega L = R$$

   $$\Rightarrow \frac{1}{\omega C} = R + \omega L$$

   $$C = \frac{1}{\omega(R + \omega L)} = \frac{1}{2\pi f(R + 2\pi f L)}$$

6. **(b)**

7. **(b)** $i = i_0 (1 - e^{-Rt/L})$

   $$i_o = \frac{E}{R} \text{(Steady current)} \qquad \text{when } t = \infty$$

   $$i_\infty = \frac{E}{R}(1 - e^{-\infty}) = \frac{15}{10} = 1.5$$

   $$i_1 = 1.5(1 - e^{-R/L}) = 1.5(1 - e^{-2})$$

   $$\Rightarrow \frac{i_\infty}{i_1} = \frac{1}{1 - e^{-2}} = \frac{e^2}{e^2 - 1}$$

8. **(c)** $I_0 = \dfrac{E_0}{R} = \dfrac{nBA\omega}{R}$

   Given, $n = 1$, $B = 10^{-2}$ T,

   $A = \pi(0.3)^2 \text{m}^2$, $R = \pi^2$

   $f = (200/60)$ and $\omega = 2\pi(200/60)$

   Substituting these values and solving, we get

   $I_0 = 6 \times 10^{-3} \text{A} = 6\text{mA}$

9. **(b)** Here, $X_L = \omega_L = 2\pi f L = 2\pi \times 50 \times 1 = 100\pi\,\Omega$

   $$X_c = \frac{1}{\omega C} = \frac{1}{2\pi f C} = \frac{1}{2\pi\times50\times10\times10^{-6}}$$

   $$= \frac{10^3}{\pi}\,\Omega$$

So, $X = |X_L - X_C| = \left|100\pi - \dfrac{10^3}{\pi}\right|$

$$= \left|10^2\left[\dfrac{\pi^2 - 10}{\pi}\right]\right|\Omega$$

10. **(d)** From the rating of the bulb, the resistance of the bulb can be calculated.

$$R = \dfrac{V_{rms}^2}{P} = 100\Omega$$

For the bulb to be operated at its rated value the rms current through it should be 1A

Also, $I_{rms} = \dfrac{V_{rms}}{Z}$

$$\therefore \quad 1 = \dfrac{200}{\sqrt{100^2 + (2\pi 50.L)^2}}$$

$$L = \dfrac{\sqrt{3}}{\pi}H$$

11. **(c)** Av. electric field energy $= \left(\dfrac{1}{2}CV_{rms}^2\right)$

$$= 25 \times 10^{-3}\,J$$

$$\therefore \dfrac{1}{2}C \times (I_{rms}X_C)^2$$

$$\therefore \dfrac{1}{2} \times C.I_{rms}^2 \times \dfrac{1}{4\pi^2 v^2 C^2} = 25 \times 10^{-3}\,J$$

$$\therefore C = 20\mu F$$

12. **(d)** Power factor $_{(old)}$

$$= \dfrac{R}{\sqrt{R^2 + X_L^2}} = \dfrac{R}{\sqrt{R^2 + (2R)^2}} = \dfrac{R}{\sqrt{5}R}$$

Power factor$_{(new)} = \dfrac{R}{\sqrt{R^2 + (X_L - X_C)^2}}$

$$= \dfrac{R}{\sqrt{R^2 + (2R - R)^2}} = \dfrac{R}{\sqrt{2}R}$$

$$\therefore \dfrac{\text{New power factor}}{\text{Old power factor}} = \dfrac{\dfrac{R}{\sqrt{2}R}}{\dfrac{R}{\sqrt{5}R}} = \sqrt{\dfrac{5}{2}}$$

13. **(b)** Given,

$V_0 = 283$ volt, $\omega = 320, R = 5\,\Omega, L = 25$ mH, $C = 1000\,\mu F$

$x_L = \omega L = 320 \times 25 \times 10^{-3} = 8\,\Omega$

$x_C = \dfrac{1}{\omega C} = \dfrac{1}{320 \times 1000 \times 10^{-6}} = 3.1\,\Omega$

Total impedance of the circuit :

$$Z = \sqrt{R^2 + (X_L - X_C)^2} = \sqrt{25 + (4.9)^2} = 7\,\Omega$$

Phase difference between the voltage and current

$$\tan\phi = \dfrac{X_L - X_C}{R}$$

$$\tan\phi = \dfrac{4.9}{5} \approx 1 \Rightarrow \phi = 45°$$

14. **(a)** $i = \dfrac{V}{\sqrt{R^2 + \left(\dfrac{1}{\omega C}\right)^2}}$

or $\quad I = \dfrac{V}{\sqrt{R^2 + \dfrac{1}{\omega^2 C^2}}}$ ...(i)

and $\quad \dfrac{I}{2} = \dfrac{V}{\sqrt{R^2 + \dfrac{\omega^2 C^2}{9}}}$ ...(ii)

On simplifying above equations, we get

$$\dfrac{X_L}{R} = \dfrac{\omega L}{R} = \sqrt{\dfrac{3}{5}}.$$

15. **(c)** Across resistor, $I = \dfrac{V}{R} = \dfrac{100}{1000} = 0.1\,A$

At resonance,

$$X_L = X_C = \dfrac{1}{\omega C} = \dfrac{1}{200 \times 2 \times 10^{-6}} = 2500$$

Voltage across L is

$$I X_L = 0.1 \times 2500 = 250 \, V$$

16. **(d)** $V = \dfrac{V_0}{T/4} t \Rightarrow V = \dfrac{4V_0}{T} t$

$$\Rightarrow V_{rms} = \sqrt{<V^2>} = \frac{4V_0}{T}\sqrt{<t^2>} = \frac{4V_0}{T}\left\{ \frac{\int_0^{T/4} t^2 dt}{\int_0^{T/4} dt} \right\}^{1/2}$$

$$= \frac{V_0}{\sqrt{3}}$$

17. **(b)** We have, $V = V_0(1 - e^{-t/RC})$

$$\Rightarrow 120 = 200(1 - e^{-t/RC})$$

$$e^{-t/r} = \frac{200 - 120}{200} = \frac{80}{200}$$

$$t = \log_e(2.5)$$
$$\Rightarrow t = RC \, \text{in} \, (2.5) \qquad [\because r = RC]$$
$$\Rightarrow R = 2.71 \times 10^6 \, \Omega$$

18. **(b)** Given that $E_0 = 10 \, V, t = \dfrac{1}{600} s$

$$\therefore \quad E = E_0 \cos 2\pi ft$$

$$= 10 \cos\left[2\pi \times 50 \times \frac{1}{600} \right]$$

$$= 10 \cos(\pi/6) = 10(\sqrt{3}/2) = 5\sqrt{3} \, V$$

19. **(a)** From Kirchoff's current law,

$$i_3 = i_1 + i_2 = 3\sin \omega t + 4\sin(\omega t + 90°)$$
$$\Rightarrow \quad i_3 = i_0 \sin(\omega t + \phi)$$

where $i_0 = \sqrt{3^2 + 4^2 + 2(3)(4)\cos 90°}$

and $\tan \phi = \dfrac{4\sin 90°}{3 + 4\cos 90°} = \dfrac{4}{3}$

$$\therefore \quad i_3 = 5 \sin(\omega t + 53°)$$

20. **(c)** Time constant for parallel combination
$= 2RC$

Time constant for series combination $= \dfrac{RC}{2}$

In first case :

$$V = V_0\left(1 - e^{-\frac{t}{CR}} \right) \Rightarrow \frac{V_0}{2} = V_0 - V_0 e^{-\frac{t}{CR}}$$

$$V = V_0 e^{-\frac{t_1}{2RC}} = \frac{V_0}{2} \qquad \text{...(1)}$$

In second case :

In series grouping, equivalent capacitance $= \dfrac{C}{2}$

$$V = V_0 e^{-\frac{t_2}{(RC/2)}} = \frac{V_0}{2} \qquad \text{....(2)}$$

From (1) and (2)

$$\frac{t_1}{2RC} = \frac{t_2}{(RC/2)}$$

$$\Rightarrow \quad t_2 = \frac{t_1}{4} = \frac{10}{4} = 2.5 \, \text{sec.}$$

21. **(c)** 

when L is removed from the circuit

$$\frac{X_C}{R} = \tan\frac{p}{3}$$

$$X_C = R\tan\frac{\pi}{3} \qquad \text{....(1)}$$

when C is remove from the circuit

$$\frac{X_L}{R} = \tan\frac{p}{3}$$

$$X_C = R\tan\frac{\pi}{3} \qquad \text{...(2)}$$

net impedence $Z = \sqrt{R^2 + (X_L - X_C)^2} = R$

power factor $\cos \phi = \dfrac{R}{Z} = 1$

22. **(c)** Time constant for parallel combination = $2RC$

Time constant for series combination $= \dfrac{RC}{2}$

In first case :

$$V = V_0 e^{-\frac{t_1}{2RC}} = \frac{V_0}{2} \qquad ...(1)$$

In second case :

$$V = V_0 e^{-\frac{t_2}{(RC/2)}} = \frac{V_0}{2} \qquad ....(2)$$

From (1) and (2)

$$\frac{t_1}{2RC} = \frac{t_2}{(RC/2)} \Rightarrow t_2 = \frac{t_1}{4} = \frac{10}{4} = 2.5 \text{ sec.}$$

23. **(a)** Given,

Reactance of inductance coil, $Z = 100\Omega$

Frequency of AC signal, $v = 1000$ Hz

Phase angle, $\phi = 45°$

$$\tan\phi = \frac{X_L}{R} = \tan 45° = 1$$

$$\Rightarrow X_L = R$$

Reactance, $Z = 100 = \sqrt{X_L^2 + R^2}$

$$\Rightarrow 100 = \sqrt{R^2 + R^2}$$

$$\Rightarrow \sqrt{2}R = 100 \Rightarrow R = 50\sqrt{2}$$

$$\therefore X_L = 50\sqrt{2}$$

$$\Rightarrow L\omega = 50\sqrt{2} \qquad (\because X_L = \omega L)$$

$$\Rightarrow L = \frac{50\sqrt{2}}{2\pi \times 1000} \qquad (\because \omega = 2\pi v)$$

$$= \frac{25\sqrt{2}}{\pi} \text{ mH}$$

$$= 1.1 \times 10^{-2}\,\text{H}$$

24. **(c)** Given, $V_L : V_C : V_R = 1 : 2 : 3$

$V = 100\,\text{V}$

$V_R = ?$

As we know,

$$V = \sqrt{V_R^2 + (V_L - V_C)^2}$$

Solving we get, $V_R \approx 90\text{V}$

25. **(b)**

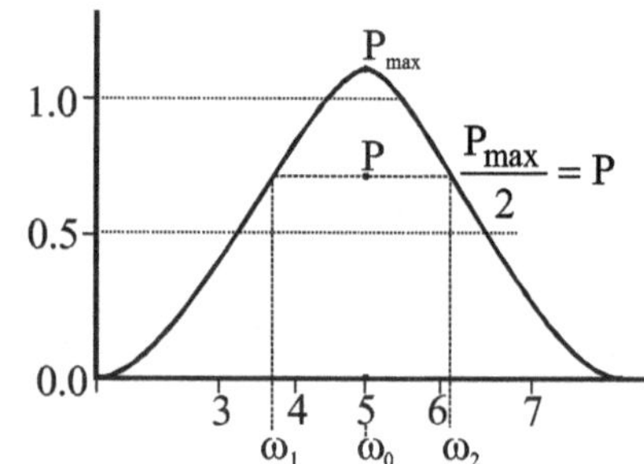

Quality factor of the circuit

$$= \frac{\omega_0}{\omega_2 - \omega_1} = \frac{5}{2.5} = 2.0$$

22   Electromagnetic Waves

1. **(a)** Electromagnetic waves carry momentum and hence can exert pressure (P) on surfaces, which is called **radiation pressure**. For an electromagnetic wave with poynting vector $\vec{S}$, incident on a perfectly absorbing surface then,

   $P = \dfrac{S}{c}$ and if incident on a perfectly reflecting surface then, $P = \dfrac{2S}{c}$

2. **(a)** Energy density (EM waves)

   $$= \varepsilon_0 E_{rms}^2 = \varepsilon_0 \left(\dfrac{E_0}{\sqrt{2}}\right)^2 = \dfrac{1}{2}\varepsilon_0 E_0^2$$

3. **(c)** Incident momentum, $p = \dfrac{E}{c}$

   For perfectly reflecting surface with normal incidence

   $$\Delta p = 2p = \dfrac{2E}{c} \; ; \quad F = \dfrac{\Delta p}{\Delta t} = \dfrac{2E}{ct}$$

4. **(b)** EM waves carry momentum and hence can exert pressure on surfaces. They also transfer energy to the surface so $p \neq 0$ and $E \neq 0$.

5. **(c)**

6. **(b)** Here, $k = \dfrac{2\pi}{\lambda}$, $\omega = 2\pi\upsilon$

   $$\therefore \quad \dfrac{k}{\omega} = \dfrac{2\pi/\lambda}{2\pi\upsilon} = \dfrac{1}{\lambda\upsilon} = \dfrac{1}{c} \qquad (\because c = \upsilon\lambda)$$

   where c is the speed of electromagnetic wave in vacuum. It is a constant whose value is 3×10^8 $m\ s^{-1}$

7. **(c)** $E_0 = B_0 C = 20 \times 10^{-9} \times 3 \times 10^8 = 6$ v/m

8. **(c)** Relation between E_0 and B_0

   $$\dfrac{B_0}{E_0} = \dfrac{1}{c} = \sqrt{\mu_0 \varepsilon_0} \ \text{ i.e. } B_0 = E_0 \sqrt{\varepsilon_0 \mu_0}$$

9. **(c)**

10. **(c)** Gamma rays < X-rays < Ultra violet < Visible rays < Infrared rays < Microwaves < Radio waves.

11. **(a)** $\dfrac{E_0}{B_0} = c$. also $k = \dfrac{2\pi}{\lambda}$ and $\omega = 2\pi v$

    These relation gives $E_0 k = B_0 \omega$

12. **(d)** Given : $\vec{B} = 1.2 \times 10^{-8}\hat{k}\,T$

    $\vec{E} = ?$

    From formula,

    $E = Bc = (1.2 \times 10^{-8}\,T)(3 \times 10^8\,ms^{-1}) = 3.6\,Vm^{-1}$

    $\vec{B}$ is along Z-direction and the wave propagates along X-direction. Therefore $\vec{E}$ should be along Y-direction.

    Thus, $\vec{E} = 3.6\hat{j}\,Vm^{-1}$

13. **(d)** $B_y = 2 \times 10^{-7}\sin(0.5 \times 10^3\,z + 1.5 \times 10^{11}\,t)\,T$

    The electric vector is perpendicular to B as well as direction of propagation of electromagnetic wave.

    Therefore E_x has to be taken.

    Further, $E_0 = B_0 \times c = 2 \times 10^{-7} \times 3 \times 10^8\,V/m$

    $\qquad E_0 = 2 \times 10^{-7} \times 3 \times 10^8 = 60\,V/m$

    $\therefore$ The corresponding value of the electric field is

    $E_x = 60\sin(0.5 \times 10^3\,z + 1.5 \times 10^{11}\,t)\,V/m$

14. **(b)** $\omega = 2\pi v = \dfrac{2\pi c}{\lambda} = \dfrac{2\pi \times 3 \times 10^8}{6 \times 10^{-3}} = \pi \times 10^{11}$ rad/sec

    The equation for the electric field, along y-axis in the electromagnetic wave is

$$E_y = E_0 \sin \omega\left(t - \frac{x}{c}\right)$$

$$= 33\sin\left[\pi \times 10^{11}\left(t - \frac{x}{c}\right)\right]$$

15. (b)

16. (b) Wavelength of monochromatic green light
$= 5.5 \times 10^{-5}$ cm

$$\text{Intensity } I = \frac{\text{Power}}{\text{Area}} = \frac{100 \times (3/100)}{4\pi(5)^2}$$

$$= \frac{3}{100\pi} \, \text{Wm}^{-2}$$

Now, half of this intensity (I) belongs to electric field and half of that to magnetic field, therefore,

$$\frac{I}{2} = \frac{1}{4}\varepsilon_0 E_0^2 C \quad \text{or} \quad E_0 = \sqrt{\frac{2I}{\varepsilon_0 C}}$$

$$= \sqrt{\frac{2 \times \left(\dfrac{3}{100\pi}\right)}{\left(\dfrac{1}{4\pi \times 9 \times 10^9}\right) \times (3 \times 10^8)}} = \sqrt{\frac{6}{25} \times 30}$$

$$= \sqrt{7.2}$$

$$\therefore \quad E_0 = 2.68 \, \text{V/m}$$

17. (c) Given: Amplitude of electric field,
$$E_0 = 4 \, \text{V/m}$$
Absolute permitivity,
$$\varepsilon_0 = 8.8 \times 10^{-12} \, c^2/\text{N-m}^2$$
Average energy density $u_E = ?$
Applying formula,

$$\text{Average energy density } u_E = \frac{1}{4}\varepsilon_0 E_0^2$$

$$\Rightarrow \quad u_E = \frac{1}{4} \times 8.8 \times 10^{-12} \times (4)^2$$

$$= 35.2 \times 10^{-12} \, \text{J/m}^3$$

18. (a) Velocity of light

$$c = \frac{E}{B} \Rightarrow B = \frac{E}{c} = \frac{9.3}{3 \times 10^8} = 3.1 \times 10^{-8}\,\text{T}$$

19. (a) On comparing the given equation to

$$\vec{E} = a_0 \hat{i}\,\cos(\omega t - kz), \ \omega = 6 \times 10^8, \ k = \frac{2p}{1} = \frac{w}{c}$$

$$k = \frac{\omega}{c} = \frac{6 \times 10^8}{3 \times 10^8} = 2\,\text{m}^{-1}$$

20. (d) EM wave intensity

$$\Rightarrow I = \frac{\text{Power}}{\text{Area}} = \frac{1}{2}\varepsilon_0 E_0^2 c$$

[where E_0 = maximum electric field]

$$\Rightarrow \frac{27 \times 10^{-3}}{10 \times 10^{-6}} = \frac{1}{2} \times 9 \times 10^{-12} \times E_0^2 \times 3 \times 10^8$$

$$\Rightarrow E_0 = \sqrt{2} \times 10^3 \, \text{kV/m} = 1.4\,\text{kV/m}$$

21. (b) Using, formula $E_0 = B_0 \times C$
$= 100 \times 10^{-6} \times 3 \times 10^8$
$= 3 \times 10^4 \text{N/C}$
Here we assumed that
$B_0 = 100 \times 10^{-6}$ is in tesla (T) units

22. (b) As we know,

$$|\vec{B}| = \frac{|\vec{E}|}{C} = \frac{6.3}{3 \times 10^8} = 2.1 \times 10^{-8}\,\text{T}$$

and $\hat{E} \times \hat{B} = \hat{C}$

$\hat{j} \times \hat{B} = \hat{i}$ [$\because$ EM wave travels along +(ve) x-direction.]

$$\therefore \quad \hat{B} = \hat{k} \quad \text{or} \quad \vec{B} = 2.1 \times 10^{-8}\hat{k}\,\text{T}$$

23. (d) $\quad I = \dfrac{B_0^2}{2\mu_0} \cdot C$

$$\Rightarrow \frac{B_0^2}{2} = \frac{I\mu_0}{C}$$

$$\Rightarrow \; B_{rms} = \sqrt{\frac{I\mu_0}{C}}$$

$$= \sqrt{\frac{10^8 \times 4\pi \times 10^{-7}}{3 \times 10^8}}$$

$$\simeq 6 \times 10^{-4}\,\text{T}$$

Which is closest to 10^{-4}.

24. (c) In electromagnetic wave, $\dfrac{E_0}{B_0} = C$

$\therefore$ Maximum value of magnetic field, $B_0 = \dfrac{E_0}{C}$

$$F_{max} = qVB_{max}\sin 90° = \frac{qV_0 E_0}{C}$$

(Given $V_0 = 0.1\,C$ and $E_0 = 30$)

$$= \frac{1.6 \times 10^{-19} \times 0.1 \times 3 \times 10^8 \times 30}{3 \times 10^8} = 4.8 \times 10^{-19}\,\text{N}$$

25. (b) Energy density $= \dfrac{1}{2}\dfrac{B^2}{\mu_0}$

$$\Rightarrow B = \sqrt{2 \times \mu_0 \times \text{Energy density}}$$

$$\mu_0 = \frac{1}{C^2 \varepsilon_0} = 4\pi \times 10^{-7}$$

$$\therefore B = \sqrt{2 \times 4\pi \times 10^{-7} \times 1.02 \times 10^{-8}} = 160 \times 10^{-9}$$

$$= 160\,\text{nT}$$

23 Ray Optics and Optical Instruments

1. (a) From mirror formula

$$\frac{1}{v}+\frac{1}{-280}=\frac{1}{20}$$

$$\frac{1}{v}=\frac{1}{20}+\frac{1}{280}$$

$$\frac{1}{v}=\frac{14+1}{280}$$

$$v=\frac{280}{15}$$

$$v_I=-\left(\frac{v}{u}\right)^2 v_0$$

$$\therefore\ v_I=-\left(\frac{280}{15\times280}\right)^2\times15$$

$$\therefore\ v_I=\frac{-15}{15\times15}$$

$$v_I=-\frac{1}{15}\ \text{m/sec}$$

2. (a) $\sin\theta_c=\dfrac{1}{\mu}=\dfrac{3}{4}$

or $\quad\tan\theta_c=\dfrac{3}{\sqrt{16-9}}=\dfrac{3}{\sqrt{7}}=\dfrac{R}{12}$

$$\Rightarrow R=\frac{36}{\sqrt{7}}\ \text{cm}$$

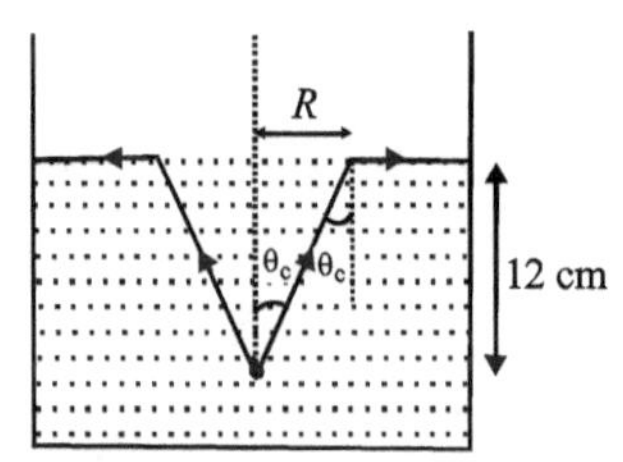

3. (a) Considering refraction at the curved surface,

$$u=-20,\ \mu_2=1;\ \mu_1=3/2,\ R=+20$$

$$\frac{\mu_2}{v}-\frac{\mu_1}{u}=\frac{\mu_2-\mu_1}{R}$$

$$\Rightarrow\quad\frac{1}{v}-\frac{3/2}{-20}=\frac{1-3/2}{20}\Rightarrow v=-10$$

i.e., 10 cm below the curved surface or 10 cm above the actual position of flower.

4. (b) The focal length (f_1) of the lens with $n=1.5$ is given by

$$\frac{1}{f_1}=(n_1-1)\left[\frac{1}{R_1}-\frac{1}{R_2}\right]=\frac{1}{28}$$

The focal length (f_2) of the lens with $n=1.2$ is given by

$$\frac{1}{f_2}=(n_2-1)\left[\frac{1}{R_1}-\frac{1}{R_2}\right]=\frac{1}{70}$$

The focal length f of the combination is

$$\frac{1}{f}=\frac{1}{f_1}+\frac{1}{f_2}=\frac{1}{20}$$

Applying lens formula for the combination of lens

$$\frac{1}{v}-\frac{1}{u}=\frac{1}{f}\quad\Rightarrow\quad\frac{1}{v}-\frac{1}{-40}=\frac{1}{20}$$

$$\Rightarrow\quad v=40\ \text{cm}$$

5. (d)

6. (c)

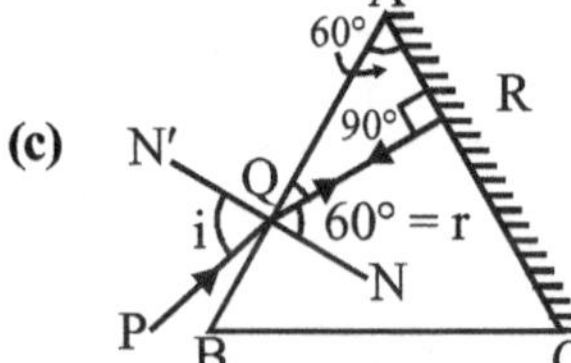

It is clear from the figure that the ray will retrace the path when the refracted ray QR is incident normally on the polished surface AC. Thus, angle of refraction $r=60°$

We know that $\mu = \dfrac{\sin i}{\sin r}$

$\therefore \sin i = \mu \times \sin r = \sqrt{2} \times \sin 60°$

$= \sqrt{2} \times \dfrac{\sqrt{3}}{2}$ or $i = \sin^{-1}\sqrt{\dfrac{3}{2}}$

7. (a) We have,

$$\mu = \dfrac{\sin\left(\dfrac{A+\delta_m}{2}\right)}{\sin\left(\dfrac{A}{2}\right)} \Rightarrow \cot\dfrac{A}{2} = \dfrac{\sin\left(\dfrac{A+\delta_m}{2}\right)}{\sin\left(\dfrac{A}{2}\right)}$$

or $\cos\dfrac{A}{2} = \cos\left[\dfrac{\pi}{2} - \left(\dfrac{A+\delta_m}{2}\right)\right]$

or $A = \pi - A - \delta_m \Rightarrow \delta_m = \pi - 2A$.

8. (c) For least distance of distinct vision, the magnifying power

$$M = -\dfrac{f_0}{f_e}\left(1+\dfrac{f_e}{D}\right) = -\dfrac{60}{5}\left(1+\dfrac{5}{25}\right) = -14.4$$

Now, $\dfrac{1}{f_e} = \dfrac{1}{v_e} - \dfrac{1}{u_e}$

v_e and u_e are negative

$\therefore \dfrac{1}{f_e} = -\dfrac{1}{25} - \left(-\dfrac{1}{u_e}\right) \Rightarrow \dfrac{1}{u_e} = \dfrac{1}{25} + \dfrac{1}{5}$ or, u_e

$= 4.17\,\text{cm}$

The length of telescope in this position

$L = f_0 + u_e = 60 + 4.17 = 64.17\,\text{cm}$

9. (d) $|M| = \dfrac{f_0}{f_e} = 5$, $L = f_0 + f_e = 36$

$\therefore f_e = 6\,\text{cm}, f_0 = 30\,\text{cm}$

10. (c)

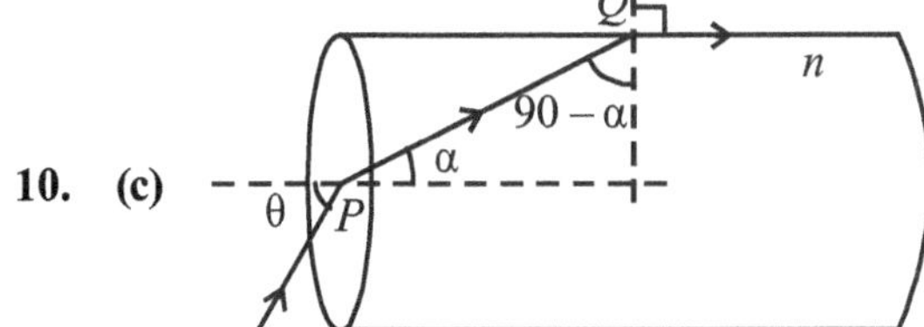

Applying Snell's law
for medium inside the cylinder and air at Q we get

$$n = \dfrac{\sin 90°}{\sin(90° - \alpha)} = \dfrac{1}{\cos\alpha}$$

$\therefore \cos\alpha = \dfrac{1}{n}$

$\therefore \sin\alpha = \sqrt{1-\cos^2\alpha} = \sqrt{1-\dfrac{1}{n^2}} = \dfrac{\sqrt{n^2-1}}{n}$ ...(i)

Applying Snell's Law for air and medium inside the cylinder at P we get

$$n = \dfrac{\sin\theta}{\sin\alpha}$$

$\Rightarrow \sin\theta = n \times \sin\alpha = \sqrt{n^2 - 1}$; [from (i)]

$\therefore \sin\theta = \sqrt{\left(\dfrac{2}{\sqrt{3}}\right)^2 - 1} = \sqrt{\dfrac{4}{3} - 1} = \dfrac{1}{\sqrt{3}}$

or $\theta = \sin^{-1}\left(\dfrac{1}{\sqrt{3}}\right)$

11. (b) According to lens maker's formula in air

$$\dfrac{1}{f_a} = \left(_a\mu_g - 1\right)\left(\dfrac{1}{R_1} - \dfrac{1}{R_2}\right)$$

$\Rightarrow \dfrac{1}{f_a} = \left(\dfrac{1.5}{1} - 1\right)\left(\dfrac{1}{R_1} - \dfrac{1}{R_2}\right)$ .... (i)

Using lens maker's formula in liquid medium,

$$\dfrac{1}{f_m} = \left(\dfrac{\mu_g}{\mu_m} - 1\right)\left(\dfrac{1}{R_1} - \dfrac{1}{R_2}\right)$$

$\Rightarrow \dfrac{1}{f_m} = \left(\dfrac{1.5}{1.6} - 1\right)\left(\dfrac{1}{R_1} - \dfrac{1}{R_2}\right)$ .... (ii)

Dividing (i) by (ii),

$$\dfrac{f_m}{f_a} = \left(\dfrac{\dfrac{1.5-1}{1.5}}{\dfrac{1.5}{1.6} - 1}\right) = -8$$

$$P_a = -5 = \frac{1}{f_a}$$

$$\Rightarrow f_a = -\frac{1}{5}$$

$$\Rightarrow f_m = -8 \times f_a = -8 \times -\frac{1}{5} = \frac{8}{5}$$

$$P_m = \frac{\mu}{f_m} = \frac{1.6}{8} \times 5 = 1D$$

12. **(d)** From the equation of line

$$m = k_1 v + k_2 \qquad (\because y = mx + c)$$

$$\Rightarrow \frac{v}{u} = k_1 v + k_2 \qquad \left(\because m = \frac{v}{u}\right)$$

$$\Rightarrow \frac{1}{u} = k_1 + \frac{k_2}{v} \text{ (Dividing both sides by v)}$$

$$\Rightarrow \frac{k_2}{v} - \frac{1}{u} - k_1$$

Comparing with lens formula $\dfrac{1}{v} - \dfrac{1}{u} = \dfrac{1}{f}$, we get

$$k_1 = \frac{1}{-f} \text{ and } k_2 = 1$$

$$\therefore f = \frac{1}{\text{slope of } m - v \text{ graph}} = -\frac{b}{c}$$

13. **(b)**

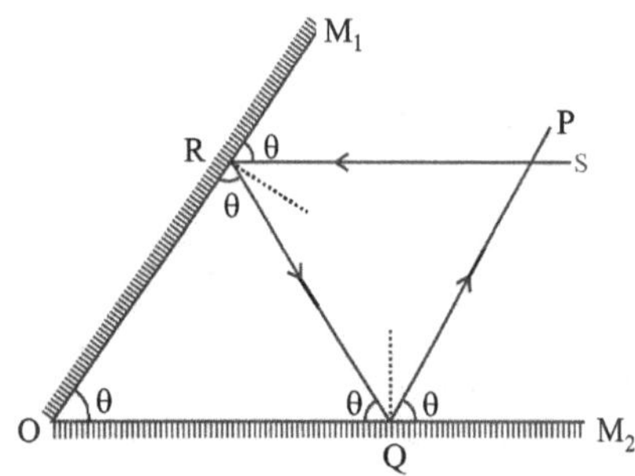

Let angle between the two mirrors be θ.

Ray PQ ∥ mirror M_1 and Rs ∥ mirror M_2

$$\therefore \quad M_1 Rs = \angle ORQ = \angle M_1 OM_2 = \theta$$

Similarly, $\angle M_2 QP = \angle OQR = \angle M_2 OM_1 = \theta$

$$\therefore \quad \text{In } \Delta ORQ, 3\theta = 180° \Rightarrow \theta = \frac{180°}{3} = 60°$$

14. **(c)** Real depth $= 5\,cm + 1cm = 6\,cm$

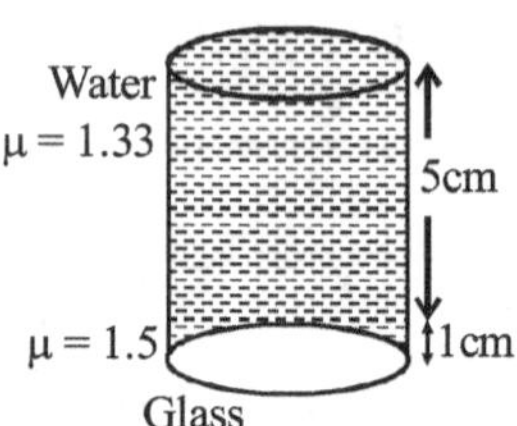

Apparent depth $= \dfrac{d_1}{\mu_1} + \dfrac{d_2}{\mu_2} + ...$

$$= \frac{5}{1.33} + \frac{1}{1.5}$$

$$\simeq 3.8 + 0.7 \simeq 4.5\,cm$$

$$\therefore \text{ Shift} = 6\,cm - 4.5\,cm \cong 1.5\,cm$$

15. **(d)** For light to come out through face 'AC', total internal reflection must not take place.

i.e., $\theta < c \Rightarrow \sin\theta < \sin c$

$$\Rightarrow \sin\theta < \frac{1}{\mu}$$

$$\text{or} \quad \mu < \frac{1}{\sin\theta} \Rightarrow \mu < \frac{1}{\sin 45°}$$

$$\Rightarrow \quad \mu < \sqrt{2} \quad \Rightarrow \quad \mu < 1.414$$

16. **(b)** For the convex spherical refracting surface of oil we apply

$$\frac{-\mu_1}{u} + \frac{\mu_2}{v} = \frac{\mu_2 - \mu_1}{R}$$

$$\therefore \quad \frac{-1}{(-24)} + \frac{7/4}{v} = \frac{\frac{7}{4} - 1}{6}$$

$$\therefore \quad v = 21\,cm$$

For water-oil interface

$$\frac{\frac{-7}{4}}{+21} + \frac{\frac{4}{3}}{V'} = 0$$

$$\therefore \quad V' = 16\,cm.$$

This is the image distance from water-oil interface. Therefore the distance of the image from the bottom of the tank is $18 - 16 = 2$ cm.

17. **(a)** Given $AQ = AR$ and $\angle A = 60°$

$\therefore \quad \angle AQR = \angle ARQ = 60°$

$\therefore \quad r_1 = r_2 = 30°$

Applying Snell's law on face AB.

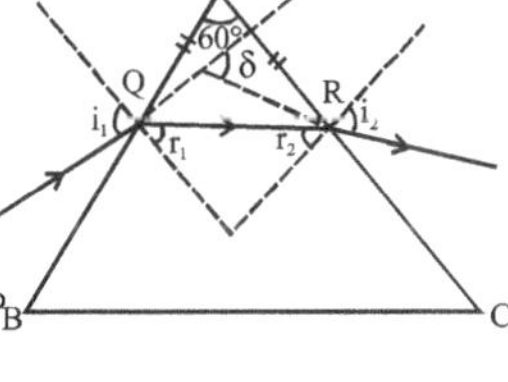

1. $\sin i_1 = \mu \sin r_1$

$\Rightarrow \quad \sin i_1 = \sqrt{3} \sin 30°$

$$= \sqrt{3} \times \frac{1}{2} = \frac{\sqrt{3}}{2}$$

$\therefore \quad i_1 = 60°$

Similarly, $i_2 = 60°$

In a prism, deviation

$\delta = i_1 + i_2 - A = 60° + 60° - 60° = 60°$

18. **(d)** $f_1 = \dfrac{R}{2(\mu - 1)} = 30 \text{cm.} \; ; \; f_2 = \dfrac{R}{2\mu} = 10 \text{cm.}$

Solving we get, $\mu = 1.5 \quad \left[\because \; \dfrac{1}{f_{eq}} = \dfrac{1}{f_1} + \dfrac{1}{f_2} \right]$

19. **(a)** Given $i = 60°$

$\qquad A = \delta = e$

$\delta = i + e - A \Rightarrow \delta = i \quad (\because e = A)$

$$\mu = \frac{\sin\left(\dfrac{A + \delta_m}{2}\right)}{\sin \dfrac{A}{2}}$$

Here angle of deviation is min.$(\because i = e)$

$$\therefore \quad \mu = \frac{\sin\left(\dfrac{60° + 60°}{2}\right)}{\sin \dfrac{60°}{2}} = 1.73$$

20. **(a)** Given,

Distance between an object and screen,

$D = 100$ cm

Distance between the two position of lens,

$d = 40$ cm

Focal length of lens,

$$f = \frac{D^2 - d^2}{4D} = \frac{100^2 - 40^2}{4(100)}$$

$$= \frac{(100 + 40)(100 - 40)}{4(100)} = 21 \text{ cm}$$

Power, $P = \dfrac{1}{f} = \dfrac{100}{21} = \dfrac{N}{100}$

$\therefore N = 476.19 \approx 476$

21. **(c)** Given : $\mu = 1.5$; $R_{curved} = 30$ cm

Using, Lens-maker formula

$$\frac{1}{f} = (\mu - 1)\left(\frac{1}{R_1} - \frac{1}{R_2}\right)$$

For plano-convex lens

$R_1 \to \infty$ then $R_2 = -R$

$$\therefore f = \frac{R}{\mu - 1} = \frac{30}{1.5 - 1} = 60 \text{ cm}$$

22. **(b)** Using, $M = \dfrac{v}{u}$

or $\quad -2 = \dfrac{v_1}{x_1} \Rightarrow v_1 = -2x_1$

We have $\dfrac{1}{v} - \dfrac{1}{u} = \dfrac{1}{f}$ or $\dfrac{1}{-2x_1} - \dfrac{1}{x_1} = \dfrac{1}{20}$

$x_1 = 30$ cm

And $\dfrac{1}{2x_2} - \dfrac{1}{x_2} = \dfrac{1}{20}$ or $x_2 = -10$ cm

So, $\dfrac{x_1}{x_2} = \dfrac{30}{10} = 3$

23. **(a)** Given : Length of compound microscope,

$\qquad L = 10$ cm

Focal length of objective $f_0 = 1$ cm and of eye-piece, $f_e = 5$ cm

$u_0 = f_e = 5$ cm

Final image formed at infinity (∞), $v_e = \infty$

$v_0 = 10 - 5 = 5$

Using lens formula, $\dfrac{1}{v} - \dfrac{1}{u} = \dfrac{1}{f}$

$$\dfrac{1}{v_0} - \dfrac{1}{u_0} = \dfrac{1}{f_0} \Rightarrow \dfrac{1}{5} - \dfrac{1}{u_0} = \dfrac{1}{1} \Rightarrow u_0 = -\dfrac{5}{4}\ \text{cm}$$

24. **(a)** According to question, final image i.e.,

　　$v_2 = 25$ cm,

　　$f_0 = 1$ cm, magnification, $m = m_1 m_2 = 100$

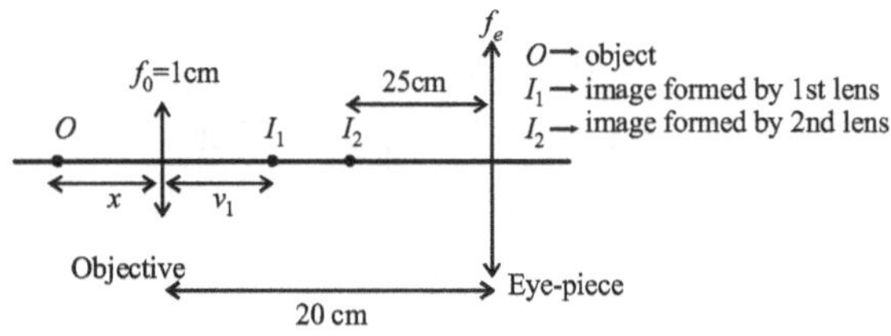

Using lens formula,

For first lens or objective

$$= \dfrac{1}{v_1} - \dfrac{1}{-x} = \dfrac{1}{1} \Rightarrow v_1 = \dfrac{x}{x-1}$$

Also magnification $|m_1| = \left|\dfrac{v_1}{u_1}\right| = \dfrac{1}{x-1}$

For 2nd lens or eye-piece, this is acting as object

$$\therefore u_2 = -(20 - v_1) = -\left(20 - \dfrac{x}{x-1}\right)$$

and $v_2 = -25$ cm

Angular magnification $|m_A| = \left|\dfrac{D}{u_2}\right| = \dfrac{25}{|u_2|}$

Total magnification $m = m_1 m_A = 100$

$$\left(\dfrac{1}{x-1}\right)\left(\dfrac{25}{20 - \dfrac{x}{x-1}}\right) = 100$$

$$\Rightarrow \dfrac{25}{20(x-1) - x} = 100 \Rightarrow 1 = 80(x-1) - 4x$$

$$\Rightarrow 76x = 81 \Rightarrow x = \dfrac{81}{76}$$

$$\Rightarrow u_2 = -\left(20 - \dfrac{\dfrac{81}{76}}{\dfrac{81}{76} - 1}\right) = \dfrac{-19}{5}$$

Again using lens formula for eye-piece

$$\dfrac{1}{-25} - \dfrac{1}{-\dfrac{19}{5}} = \dfrac{1}{f_e} \Rightarrow f_e = \dfrac{25 \times 19}{106} \approx 4.48\ \text{cm}$$

25. **(c)** Here $i = 60°$. As the angle between reflected and refracted ray is 90°, then $i + r = 90°$ or $r = 30°$
Now

$$\mu = \dfrac{\sin i}{\sin r} = \dfrac{\sin 60°}{\sin 30°} = \dfrac{\sqrt{3}/2}{1/2} = \sqrt{3} = 1.732$$

24

Wave Optics

1. **(b)** $I_A = I + 4I + 2\sqrt{I \times 4I}\cos\pi/2 = 5I$

and $I_B = I + 4I + 2\sqrt{I \times 4I}\cos\pi = I$

So $I_A - I_B = 5I - I = 4I$

2. **(b)** P to Q: convergence increasing; Q to R : direction changing.

3. **(c)** $I_{max} = \left(\sqrt{I_1} + \sqrt{I_2}\right)^2 = \left(\sqrt{nI} + \sqrt{I}\right)^2$

$$= \left(\sqrt{n} + 1\right)^2 I$$

$$I_{min} = \left(\sqrt{n} - 1\right)^2 I$$

$$\frac{I_{max} - I_{min}}{I_{max} + I_{min}} = \frac{2\sqrt{n}}{(n+1)}$$

4. **(b)** Effective path difference is $\mu_1 L_1 - \mu_2 L_2$.

5. **(a)**

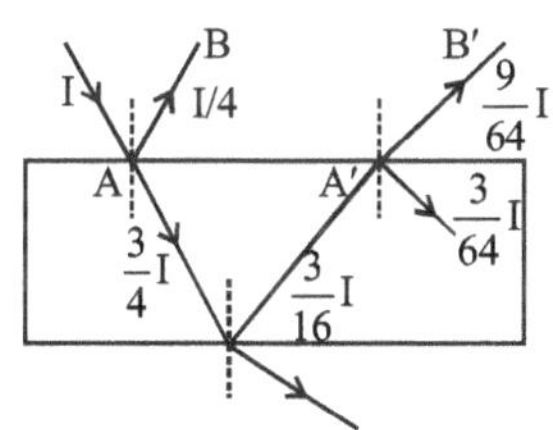

From figure $I_1 = \dfrac{I}{4}$ and $I_2 = \dfrac{9I}{64}$

$$\Rightarrow \frac{I_2}{I_1} = \frac{9}{16}$$

By using $\dfrac{I_{max}}{I_{min}} = \left(\dfrac{\sqrt{\dfrac{I_2}{I_1}} + 1}{\sqrt{\dfrac{I_2}{I_1}} - 1}\right)^2 = \left(\dfrac{\sqrt{\dfrac{9}{16}} + 1}{\sqrt{\dfrac{9}{16}} - 1}\right)^2$

$$= \frac{49}{1}$$

6. **(c)** $2I_0 = 4I_0 \cos^2\left(\dfrac{\Delta\phi}{2}\right)$ here, $\Delta\phi = \dfrac{\pi}{2}$

But, $\Delta\phi = \dfrac{2\pi}{\lambda}\Delta x$ so, $\Delta x = \dfrac{\lambda}{4}$

$$\frac{dy}{D} = \frac{\lambda}{4}$$

$$\frac{\lambda D}{d} = \beta$$

Multiplying equation (i) and (ii) we get, $y = \dfrac{\beta}{4}$

7. **(c)** For first minimum, $a\sin\theta = n\lambda = 1\lambda$

$$\sin\theta = \frac{\lambda}{a} = \frac{5000 \times 10^{-10}}{0.001 \times 10^{-3}} = 0.5$$

$$\theta = 30°$$

8. **(c)** Wavelength for which maximum obtained at the hole has the maximum intensity on passing. So,

$$x = \frac{n\lambda D}{d} = \lambda = \frac{xd}{nD}$$

$$= \frac{1 \times 10^{-3} \times 0.5 \times 10^{-3}}{n \times 50 \times 10^{-2}} = \frac{1 \times 10^{-6}}{n} = \frac{1000nm}{n}$$

$n = 1$, $\lambda = 1000$ nm $\rightarrow$ Not in the given range

$n = 2, \lambda = 500$nm

9. **(c)**

10. **(c)** Here Angle of incidence, $i = (90 - 33)° = 57°$

$$\tan 57° = 1.54$$

$$\mu_{glass} = \tan i$$

It means, here Breswster's law is followed and the reflected ray is completely polarised.

Now, when reflected ray is analysed through a polaroid then intensity of light is given by malus law.

i.e. $I = I_0 \cos^2\theta$

on rotating polaroid 'θ' changes. Due to which intensity first decreases and then increases.

11. (b) For minima,

$$b \sin \theta = n\lambda \Rightarrow \sin \theta = \frac{n\lambda}{b}$$

Distance of nth minima $x = D \sin \theta$

for second minima

or $\sin \theta_1 = \frac{x_1}{D}$

for $n = 2$

$$\sin \theta_1 = \frac{2\lambda}{b}$$

Also, for $n = 4$

$$\sin \theta_2 = \frac{4\lambda}{b} = \frac{x_2}{D}$$

$$x_2 - x_1 = \frac{4\lambda}{b} - \frac{2\lambda}{b} = \frac{2\lambda}{b}$$

$$3 = \frac{2\lambda}{b} \Rightarrow b = \frac{2\lambda}{3} \qquad \text{..... (i)}$$

Width of central maxima $= \frac{2\lambda}{b}$

$$= \frac{2\lambda}{\frac{2\lambda}{3}} = 3 \text{ cm}. \text{ ... from eq. (i)}$$

12. (a) $\Delta\theta = \frac{1.22\lambda}{a} = \frac{l}{R}$

The minimum distance between them

$$l = \frac{R \times 1.22 \times \lambda}{a}$$

$$= \frac{9.46 \times 10^{15} \times 10 \times 1.22 \times 600 \times 10^{-9}}{0.3}$$

$$l = 2.3 \times 10^{11} \text{ m}$$

$$\Rightarrow l = 2.3 \times 10^{8} \text{ km}$$

13. (b) Angle between polarizer P_1 and $P_2 = 30°$ (given)

Angle between polarizer P_2 and $P_3 = \theta = 90° - 30° = 60°$

The intensity of light transmitted by P_1 is

$$I_1 = \frac{I_0}{2} = \frac{32}{2} = 16 \frac{W}{m^2}$$

According to Malus law the intensity of light transmitted by P_2 is $I_2 = I_1 \cos^2 30°$

$$= 16\left(\frac{\sqrt{3}}{2}\right)^2 = 12 \frac{W}{m^2}$$

Similarly intensity of light transmitted by P_3 is

$$I_3 = I_2 \cos^2 \theta = 12 \cos^2 60° = 12\left(\frac{1}{2}\right)^2 = 3\frac{W}{m^2}$$

14. (a) $x = \frac{1.22\lambda}{2\mu \sin\theta}$

$$= \frac{1.22 \times 5000}{2 \times 1.25} = 0.24 \ \mu m$$

15. (a) Here, $x_1 = 2d$ and $x_2 = \sqrt{5}d$

For, first minima, $\Delta x = \frac{\lambda}{2}$

$$\therefore \Delta x = x_2 - x_1 = \sqrt{5}d - 2d = \frac{\lambda}{2}$$

$$\Rightarrow d = \frac{\lambda}{2\left(\sqrt{5} - 2\right)}$$

16. (a) If angular position of 2nd maxima from central maxima is θ then

$$\sin \theta = \frac{(2n-1)\lambda}{2a} = \frac{3\lambda}{20} = \frac{3 \times 550 \times 10^{-9}}{2 \times 22 \times 10^{-7}}$$

$$\therefore \quad \theta \simeq \frac{\pi}{8} \text{rad}$$

17. (a) Polariser A and B have same alignment of transmission axis.

Lets assume polariser c is introduced at θ angle

$$\frac{1}{2}\cos^2 \theta \times \cos^2 \theta = \frac{1}{3}$$

or, $\cos^4 \theta = \frac{2}{3} \Rightarrow \cos\theta = \left(\frac{2}{3}\right)^{1/4}$

18. **(a)** $\theta = \dfrac{1.22\lambda}{d} = \dfrac{1.22 \times 500 \times 10^{-9}}{2}$

$= 305 \times 10^{-9}$ rad.

19. **(c)** Change in path difference for any point on screen is $|\mu - 1.8|\, t$.

For central maxima, phase difference $= 0$.

Hence,

$d \sin\theta - |\mu - 1.8|\, t.$

$\Rightarrow\quad d\theta = |\mu - 1.8|\, t$

$\qquad\qquad$ [θ is very small and is in radian]

$\Rightarrow\quad |\mu - 1.8| = \dfrac{10^{-3} \times 0.1}{0.5 \times 10^{-3}} = 0.2$

$\Rightarrow\quad \mu = 2\ $ or 1.6

20. **(c)**

21. **(b)** $w_a = \lambda/d \Rightarrow w_a\, \alpha\, \lambda$

$\dfrac{(w_a)_{\text{water}}}{w_a} = \dfrac{\lambda_{\text{water}}}{\lambda} = \dfrac{\lambda}{\mu_{\text{water}}\lambda}$

$(w_a)_{\text{water}} = \dfrac{2 \times 3}{4} = 0.15^\circ.$

22. **(a)** $n_1\,\lambda_1 = n_2\,\lambda_2$ for bright fringe

$n\,(7.5 \times 10^{-5}) = (n+1)(5 \times 10^{-5})$

$\Rightarrow\quad 1.5\,n = n + 1$

$\Rightarrow\quad 3\,n = 2\,n + 2$

$\Rightarrow\quad n = 2$

23. **(a)** In young's double slit experiment, intensity at a point is given by

$I = I_0 \cos^2 \dfrac{\phi}{2} \qquad\qquad \text{...(i)}$

where, $\phi =$ phase difference,

Using phase difference, $\phi = \dfrac{2\pi}{\lambda} \times$ path difference

For path difference λ, phase difference $\phi_1 = 2\pi$

For path difference, $\dfrac{\lambda}{6}$, phase difference

$\phi_2 = \dfrac{\pi}{3}$

Using equation (i),

$\dfrac{I_1}{I_2} = \dfrac{\cos^2\left(\dfrac{\phi_1}{2}\right)}{\cos^2\left(\dfrac{\phi_2}{2}\right)} = \dfrac{\cos^2\left(\dfrac{2\pi}{2}\right)}{\cos^2\left(\dfrac{\pi}{3}\right)}$

$\Rightarrow \dfrac{K}{I_2} = \dfrac{1}{\dfrac{3}{4}} = \dfrac{4}{3} \Rightarrow I_2 = \dfrac{3K}{4} = \dfrac{9K}{12}$

$\therefore\quad n = 9.$

24. **(b)**

25. **(c)** Here, $\sin\theta_{ic}/\sin\theta_{iB} = 1.28$

As we know,

$\mu = \dfrac{\sin\theta_{iB}}{\sin\left(\dfrac{\pi}{2} - \theta_{iB}\right)}$

where, θ_{iB} is Brewster's angle of incidence,

And, $\mu = \dfrac{1}{\sin\theta_{ic}}$

On solving we get, relative refractive index of the two media.

25 Dual Nature of Radiation and Matter

1. **(a)** From the de-Broglie relation,

$$p_1 = \frac{h}{\lambda_1}$$

$$p_2 = \frac{h}{\lambda_2}$$

Momentum of the final particle (p_f) is given by

$$\therefore \ p_f = \sqrt{p_1^2 + p_2^2}$$

$$\Rightarrow \frac{h}{\lambda} = \sqrt{\frac{h^2}{\lambda_1^2} + \frac{h^2}{\lambda_2^2}}$$

$$\Rightarrow \frac{1}{\lambda^2} = \frac{1}{\lambda_1^2} + \frac{1}{\lambda_2^2}$$

2. **(a)** Here, $u = 0$; $a = \dfrac{eE}{m}$; $v = ?$; $t = t$

$$\therefore \ v = u + at = 0 + \frac{eE}{m}t$$

de-Broglie wavelength,

$$\lambda = \frac{h}{mv} = \frac{h}{m(eEt/m)} = \frac{h}{eEt}$$

Rate of change of de-Broglie wavelength

$$\frac{d\lambda}{dt} = \frac{h}{eE}\left(-\frac{1}{t^2}\right) = \frac{-h}{eEt^2}$$

3. **(c)** $K_A = \dfrac{hc}{\lambda_A} - \phi_0$; $K_B = \dfrac{hc}{\lambda_B} - \phi_0$

But $\lambda_A = 2\lambda_B$, therefore

$$\therefore \ K_A < \frac{K_B}{2}$$

4. **(a)** $\lambda = 667 \times 10^{-9}\,\text{m}, P = 9 \times 10^{-3}\,\text{W}$

$$P = \frac{Nhc}{\lambda}, N = \text{No. of photons emitted/sec.}$$

$$N = \frac{9 \times 10^{-3} \times 667 \times 10^{-9}}{6.6 \times 10^{-34} \times 3 \times 10^8} = 3 \times 10^{16}\,/\,\text{sec}$$

5. **(c)**

6. **(d)** Energy $= $ charge $\times$ potential diff.
$E_{\text{electron}} = q_e V$ and $E_{\text{proton}} = q_p\,4V$

de-Broglie wavelength $\lambda = \dfrac{h}{P} = \dfrac{h}{\sqrt{2mE}}$

$$\lambda_e = \frac{h}{\sqrt{2m_e eV}} \ \text{and} \ \lambda_P = \frac{h}{\sqrt{2m_P e4V}}$$

$$(\because q_e = q_P)$$

$$\therefore \ \frac{\lambda_e}{\lambda_P} = \frac{\dfrac{h}{\sqrt{2m_e eV}}}{\dfrac{h}{\sqrt{2m_P e4V}}} = 2\sqrt{\frac{m_P}{m_e}}$$

7. **(d)** $W_0 = h\nu_1 - eV_1 = h\,\nu_2 - eV_2$
$eV_2 = h(\nu_2 - \nu_1) + eV_1$

$$\Rightarrow V_2 = \frac{h(n_2 - n_1)}{e} + V_1$$

8. **(d)** $eV_0 = \dfrac{hc}{\lambda_0} - W_0$ and $eV' = \dfrac{hc}{2\lambda_0} - W_0$

Subtracting them we have

$$e(V_0 - V') = \frac{hc}{\lambda_0}\left[1 - \frac{1}{2}\right] = \frac{hc}{2\lambda_0}$$

or $\quad V' = V_0 - \dfrac{hc}{2e\lambda_0}$

9. **(d)** From question, $m_A = m$; $m_B = \dfrac{m}{2}$

$u_A = V \quad u_B = 0$
Let after collision velocity of $A = V_1$ and velocity of $B = V_2$
Applying law of conservation of momentum,

$$mu = mv_1 + \left(\frac{m}{2}\right)v_2$$

or, $2u = 2v_1 + v_2 \qquad \qquad ....(i)$

By law of collision

$$e = \frac{v_2 - v_1}{u - 0}$$

or, $u = v_2 - v_1$ ....(ii)

$[\because$ collision is elastic, $e = 1]$

using eqns (i) and (ii)

$$v_1 = \frac{u}{3} \text{ and } v_2 = \frac{4}{3}u$$

de-Broglie wavelength $\lambda = \dfrac{h}{p}$

$$\therefore \quad \frac{\lambda_A}{\lambda_B} = \frac{P_B}{P_A} = \frac{\dfrac{m}{2} \times \dfrac{4}{3}u}{m \times \dfrac{u}{3}} = 2$$

10. (a) Retarding potential depends on the frequency of incident radiation but is independent of intensity.

11. (a) For one photo cathode

$$hf_1 - W = \frac{1}{2}mv_1^2 \qquad \text{....(i)}$$

For another photo cathode

$$hf_2 - W = \frac{1}{2}mv_2^2 \qquad \text{....(ii)}$$

Subtracting (ii) from (i) we get

$$(hf_1 - W) - (hf_2 - W) = \frac{1}{2}mv_1^2 - \frac{1}{2}mv_2^2$$

$$h(f_1 - f_2) = \frac{m}{2}(v_1^2 - v_2^2)$$

$$\Rightarrow \ v_1^2 - v_2^2 = \frac{2h}{m}(f_1 - f_2)$$

12. (a) Number of photons emitted is $\dfrac{Pt}{\left(\dfrac{hc}{\lambda}\right)} = n_0$

$$= \frac{P\lambda t}{hc}$$

Since the radiation is spherical symmetric, so total number of photons entring the sensor is n_0 times the ratio of aperture area to the area of a sphere of radius ℓ.

$$N = n_0 \frac{\pi(2d)^2}{4\pi\ell^2} = \frac{P\lambda t}{hc} \frac{d^2}{\ell^2}$$

13. (d) $h\upsilon - h\upsilon_0 = E_K$, according to photoelectric equation, when $\upsilon = \upsilon_0$, $E_K = 0$.

Graph (d) represents $E_K - \upsilon$ relationship.

14. (c) As the metal surface is same, work function (ϕ) is same for both the case.

Initially $KE_{max} = nh - \phi$ ..... (i)

After increase

$KE'_{max} = 3\,nh - \phi$ .... (ii)

For work function ϕ – not to be –ve or zero, v' > $\sqrt{3}v$

15. (a) Energy of photon (E) is given by

$$E = \frac{hc}{\lambda}$$

Number of photons of wavelength λ emitted in t second from laser of power P is given by

$$n = \frac{Pt\lambda}{hc}$$

$$\Rightarrow n = \frac{2 \times \lambda}{hc} = \frac{2 \times 10^{-3} \times 5 \times 10^{-7}}{2 \times 10^{-25}} \ (\because t = 1S)$$

$$\Rightarrow n = 5 \times 10^{15}$$

16. (a) Given, $\lambda = 660\,nm$, Power $= 0.5\,kW$, $t = 60\,ms$

Power $P = \dfrac{nhc}{\lambda t} \Rightarrow n = \dfrac{p\lambda t}{hc}$

$$= 0.5 \times 10^3 \times \frac{660 \times 10^{-9} \times 60 \times 10^{-3}}{6.6 \times 10^{-34} \times 3 \times 10^8}$$

$$= 100 \times 10^{18} = 10^{20}$$

17. (d) From Einstein's photoelectric equation, we have

$$\frac{hc}{\lambda_1} = \frac{hc}{\lambda_0} + eV \qquad ...(1)$$

$$\frac{hc}{\lambda_2} = \frac{hc}{\lambda_0} + eV \qquad ...(2)$$

$$\frac{hc}{\lambda_3} = \frac{hc}{\lambda_0} + 3eV' \qquad ...(3)$$

From equation (1) & (2)

$$\frac{3}{2\lambda_1} - \frac{2}{2\lambda_2} = \frac{1}{\lambda_0}$$

$$\frac{hc}{\lambda_1} - hc\left[\frac{3}{2\lambda_1} - \frac{1}{2\lambda_2}\right] = eV'$$

$$\frac{hc}{e}\left[\frac{1}{\lambda_3} - \frac{3}{2\lambda_1} + \frac{1}{2\lambda_2}\right] = V'$$

18. **(c)** $h\nu - \phi = K_{max} = \dfrac{1}{2}mv_{max}^2$

According to question $\dfrac{5h\nu_0 - h\nu_0}{2h\nu_0 - h\nu_0} = \dfrac{v_2^2}{v_1^2}$

$v_2 = 2v_1 = 2 \times 4 \times 10^6 = 8 \times 10^6$ m/s.

19. **(b)** $E - W_0 = \dfrac{1}{2}mv^2 = eV_s$

or $\dfrac{hc}{\lambda} - W_0 = eV_s$

Hence, $\dfrac{hc}{0.6 \times 10^{-6}} - W_0 = e(0.5)$ ....(i)

and $\dfrac{hc}{0.4 \times 10^{-6}} - W_0 = e(1.5)$ ....(ii)

Solving, we get $W_0 = 1.5$ eV

20. **(b)** $E = W_0 + eV_0$

For hydrogen atom, $E = +13.6$ eV $= 4.2 + eV_0$

$\Rightarrow V_0 = \dfrac{(13.6 - 4.2)eV}{e} = 9.4$V

Potential at anode $= -9.4$ V

21. **(d)** The electron ejected with maximum speed v_{max} are stopped by electric field E $=4$N/C after travelling a distance d $=1$m

$$\dfrac{1}{2}mv_{max}^2 = eEd = 4eV$$

The energy of incident photon $= \dfrac{1240}{200} = 6.2$ eV

From equation of photo electric effect

$$\phi = h\upsilon - \dfrac{1}{2}mv^2 = 6.2 - 4 = 2.2 \text{ eV}$$

22. **(a)** From the Einstein's photoelectric equation

Energy of photon

= Kinetic energy of photoelectrons + Work function

$\Rightarrow$ Kinetic energy = Energy of Photon – Work Function

Let ϕ_0 be the work function of metal and v_1 and v_2 be the velocity of photoelectrons. Using Einstein's photoelectric equation we have

$$\dfrac{1}{2}mv_1^2 = 4 - \phi_0 \qquad ...(i)$$

$$\dfrac{1}{2}mv_2^2 = 2.5 - \phi_0 \qquad ...(ii)$$

$$\Rightarrow \dfrac{\frac{1}{2}mv_1^2}{\frac{1}{2}mv_2^2} = \dfrac{4 - \phi_0}{2.5 - \phi_0}$$

$$\Rightarrow (2)^2 = \dfrac{4 - \phi_0}{2.5 - \phi_0} \Rightarrow 10 - 4\phi_0 = 4 - \phi_0$$

$$\phi_0 = 2eV$$

23. **(a)** de-Broglie wavelength (λ),

Momentum, $mv = \dfrac{h}{\lambda} = p = \sqrt{2m(KE)}$

$\therefore \lambda = \dfrac{h}{\sqrt{2mKE}} \Rightarrow \lambda \propto \dfrac{1}{\sqrt{KE}}$

$\therefore \dfrac{\lambda_A}{\lambda_B} = \sqrt{\dfrac{K_B}{K_A}} = \sqrt{\dfrac{T_A - 1.5}{T_A}}$ (as given)

Also, $\dfrac{\lambda_A}{\lambda_B} = \dfrac{1}{2}$

On solving we get, $T_A = 2\ eV$

$\therefore KE_B = T_A - 1.5 = 2 - 1.5 = 0.5\ eV$

$\therefore$ Work function of metal B is

$\phi_B = E_B - KE_B = 4.5 - 0.5 = 4\ eV$

24. **(c)** Here w $= 2\pi \times 6 \times 10^{14}$ or f$= 6 \times 10^{14}$ Hz

Wavelength $\lambda = \dfrac{C}{f} = \dfrac{3 \times 10^8}{6 \times 10^{14}} = 0.5 \times 10^{-6}\,m$

$= 5000 A^0$

Now $E = \dfrac{12374}{5000} = 2.48\,eV$

Using $E = w + eV_s$

$2.48 = 2 + eV_s$ or $V_s = 0.48$ V

25. **(a)** From Einstein's photoelectric equation,

$$\dfrac{hc}{l_1} = f + \dfrac{1}{2}m(2v)^2 \qquad ....(i)$$

and $\dfrac{hc}{l_2} = f + \dfrac{1}{2}mv^2 \qquad ....(ii)$

As per question, maximum speed of photoelectrons in two cases differ by a factor 2

From eqn. (i) & (ii)

$$\Rightarrow \dfrac{\frac{hc}{\lambda_1} - \phi}{\frac{hc}{\lambda_2} - \phi} = 4 \Rightarrow \dfrac{hc}{\lambda_1} - \phi = \dfrac{4hc}{\lambda_2} - 4\phi$$

$$\Rightarrow \dfrac{4hc}{\lambda_2} - \dfrac{hc}{\lambda_1} = 3\phi \Rightarrow \phi = \dfrac{1}{3}hc\left(\dfrac{4}{\lambda_2} - \dfrac{1}{\lambda_1}\right)$$

$$= \dfrac{1}{3} \times 1240\left(\dfrac{4 \times 350 - 540}{350 \times 540}\right) = 1.8\,eV$$

26   Atoms

1. **(d)**

$$n = 3, (-1.51\,eV)$$
$$E_3$$
$$n = 2, (-3.4\ eV)$$
$$n = 1, (-13.6\ eV)$$

$E_{3\to2} = -1.51 - (-3.4) = 1.89\ eV$

$\Rightarrow |E_{3\to2}| \approx 1.9\ eV$

2. **(a)**

3. **(b)** The smallest frequency and largest wavelength in ultraviolet region will be for transition of electron from orbit 2 to orbit 1.

$$\therefore \quad \frac{1}{\lambda} = R\left(\frac{1}{n_1^2} - \frac{1}{n_2^2}\right)$$

$$\Rightarrow \quad \frac{1}{122\times10^{-9}} = R\left[\frac{1}{1^2} - \frac{1}{2^2}\right] = R\left[1 - \frac{1}{4}\right] = \frac{3R}{4}$$

$$\Rightarrow \quad R = \frac{4}{3\times122\times10^{-9}}$$

The highest frequency and smallest wavelength for infrared region will be for transition of electron from ∞ to 3rd orbit.

$$\therefore \quad \frac{1}{\lambda} = R\left(\frac{1}{n_1^2} - \frac{1}{n_2^2}\right)$$

$$\Rightarrow \quad \frac{1}{\lambda} = \frac{4}{3\times122\times10^{-9}}\left(\frac{1}{3^2} - \frac{1}{\infty}\right)$$

$$\therefore \quad \lambda = \frac{3\times122\times9\times10^{-9}}{4} = 823.5\ nm$$

4. **(b)**

5. **(b)** $\dfrac{1}{\lambda} = R\left(\dfrac{1}{n_1^2} - \dfrac{1}{n_2^2}\right)$

$$\frac{1}{\lambda_0} = R\left(\frac{1}{2^2} - \frac{1}{3^2}\right) = R\left(\frac{1}{4} - \frac{1}{9}\right) = \frac{5R}{36}$$

$$\frac{1}{\lambda} = R\left(\frac{1}{2^2} - \frac{1}{4^2}\right) = R\left(\frac{1}{4} - \frac{1}{16}\right) = \frac{3R}{16}$$

$$\frac{\lambda}{\lambda_0} = \frac{5}{36}\times\frac{16}{3} = \frac{20}{27}$$

6. **(a)**

7. **(a)** $\dfrac{1}{\lambda_{max}} = R\left[\dfrac{1}{(1)^2} - \dfrac{1}{(2)^2}\right]$

$$\Rightarrow \quad \lambda_{max} = \frac{4}{3R} \approx 1213\text{Å}$$

8. **(c)** $\dfrac{n(n-1)}{2} = 6$

$n^2 - n - 12 = 0$

$(n-4)(n+3) = 0$

or $\quad n = 4$

$$\begin{array}{l} \underline{\hspace{6cm}}\ 4 \\ \underline{\hspace{6cm}}\ 3 \\ \underline{\hspace{6cm}}\ 2 \\ \underline{\hspace{6cm}}\ 1 \end{array}$$

9. **(b)** $E = \dfrac{hc}{\lambda}$

10. **(b)**

11. **(b)** $E = Rhc\left[\dfrac{1}{n_1^2} - \dfrac{1}{n_2^2}\right]$

E will be maximum for the transition for which

$\left[\dfrac{1}{n_1^2} - \dfrac{1}{n_2^2}\right]$ is maximum. Here n_2 higher energy level.

Clearly, $\left[\dfrac{1}{n_1^2} - \dfrac{1}{n_2^2}\right]$ is maximum for the third transition, $1 \to 3$. I transition represents the absorption of energy.

12. **(a)** We know that $\dfrac{1}{\lambda} = RZ^2\left[\dfrac{1}{n_1^2} - \dfrac{1}{n_2^2}\right]$

The wave length of first spectral line in the Balmer series of hydrogen atom is 6561Å. Here $n_2 = 3$ and $n_1 = 2$

$$\therefore \ \frac{1}{6561} = R(1)^2\left(\frac{1}{4} - \frac{1}{9}\right) = \frac{5R}{36} \qquad ...(i)$$

For the second spectral line in the Balmer series of singly ionised helium ion $n_2 = 4$ and $n_1 = 2$; $Z = 2$

$$\therefore \ \frac{1}{\lambda} = R(2)^2\left[\frac{1}{4} - \frac{1}{16}\right] = \frac{3R}{4} \qquad ...(ii)$$

Dividing equations (i) and (ii), we get

$$\frac{\lambda}{6561} = \frac{5R}{36} \times \frac{4}{3R} = \frac{5}{27} \qquad \therefore \ \lambda = 1215\,\text{Å}$$

So, $n_2 = 4$

$n_1 = 2$ is verified.

13. (c) Centripetal force = Coulombian force

$$\frac{mv^2}{a_0} = \frac{1}{4\pi\varepsilon_0}\cdot\frac{e \times e}{a_0^2}$$

$$\Rightarrow v^2 = \frac{e^2}{4\pi\varepsilon_0.a_0.m} \Rightarrow v = \frac{e}{\sqrt{4\pi\varepsilon_0.a_0.m}}$$

14. (c) Energy of photon $= \dfrac{hc}{\lambda} = \dfrac{12500}{980} = 12.75\,\text{eV}$

Energy of electron in n^{th} orbit is given by

$$\text{En} = \frac{-13.6}{n^2} \Rightarrow E_n - E_1 = -13.6\left[\frac{1}{n^2} \frac{-1}{1^2}\right]$$

$$\Rightarrow 12.75 = 13.6\left[\frac{1}{1^2} \frac{-1}{n^2}\right] \Rightarrow n = 4$$

$\therefore$ Electron will excite to $n = 4$

We know that 'R' $\propto n^2$

$\therefore$ Radius of atom will be $16a_0$

15. (c) $E_n = -13.6\dfrac{Z^2}{n^2}$

For He^+, $E_2 = \dfrac{-13.6(2)^2}{2^2} = -13.60\,\text{eV}$

Ionization energy $= 0 - E2 = 13.60\,\text{eV}$

16. (d) Spectral lines obtained on account of transition from nth orbit to various lower orbits is $\dfrac{n(n-1)}{2}$

$$\Rightarrow 6 = \frac{n(n-1)}{2} \Rightarrow n = 4$$

$$\Delta E = \frac{hc}{\lambda} = \frac{-Z^2}{n^2}(13.6eV)$$

$$\Rightarrow \frac{1}{\lambda} = Z^2\left(\frac{13.6eV}{hc}\right)\left(\frac{1}{n_2^2} - \frac{1}{n_1^2}\right)$$

$$= (13.4)(3)^2\left[1 - \frac{1}{16}\right]eV$$

$$\Rightarrow \lambda = \frac{1242 \times 16}{(13.4) \times (9)(15)}\,\text{nm} \simeq 10.8\,\text{nm}$$

17. (a) $\dfrac{1}{\lambda_1} = R\left(\dfrac{1}{3^2} - \dfrac{1}{4^2}\right) = \dfrac{7R}{16 \times 9}$

And $\dfrac{1}{\lambda_2} = R\left(\dfrac{1}{2^2} - \dfrac{1}{3^2}\right) = \dfrac{5R}{36}$

Now $\dfrac{\lambda_1}{\lambda_2} = \dfrac{(5R/36)}{7R/(16 \times 9)} = \dfrac{20}{7}$

18. (b) For first excited state n' = 3

Time period $T \propto \dfrac{n^3}{z^2}$

$$\Rightarrow \frac{T_2}{T_1} = \frac{n'^3}{n^3}$$

$\therefore$ T2 $= 8$T1 $= 8 \times 1.6 \times 10{-16}$s

$\therefore$ Frequency, $v = \dfrac{1}{T_2} = \dfrac{1}{8 \times 1.6 \times 10^{-16}}$

$\approx 7.8 \times 10^{14}\,\text{Hz}$

19. (d) V $= (12.1 - 5.1)$ volt

$V_{stopping} = 7V$

20. (a) Velocity of electron in n^{th} orbit of hydrogen atom is given by :

$$v_n = \frac{2\pi KZe^2}{nh}$$

Substituting the values we get,

$$v_n = \frac{2.2 \times 10^6}{n}\,\text{m/s}$$

or $\quad v_n \propto \dfrac{1}{n}$ Hyperbolic relation.

21. (b) For 2nd line of Balmer series in hydrogen spectrum

$$\frac{1}{\lambda} = R\,(1)\left(\frac{1}{2^2} - \frac{1}{4^2}\right) = \frac{3}{16}R$$

For Li^{2+} $\left[\dfrac{1}{\lambda} = R \times 9\left(\dfrac{1}{x^2} - \dfrac{1}{12^2}\right) = \dfrac{3R}{16}\right]$

which is satisfied by $n = 12 \to n = 6$.

22. **(d)**

23. **(a)** $\dfrac{mv^2}{r} = \dfrac{3q^2}{4\pi\varepsilon_0 r^2} \Rightarrow mvr = \dfrac{3q^2}{4\pi\varepsilon_0 v}$ ...(i)

and $\dfrac{nh}{2\pi} = mvr$ ...(ii)

Using (i) and (ii) and putting n = 1

$\dfrac{h}{2\pi} = \dfrac{3q^2}{4\pi\varepsilon_0 v} \Rightarrow v = \dfrac{3q^2}{2\varepsilon_0 h}$

24. **(b)** A hydrogen atom makes a transition from n = 2 to n = 1

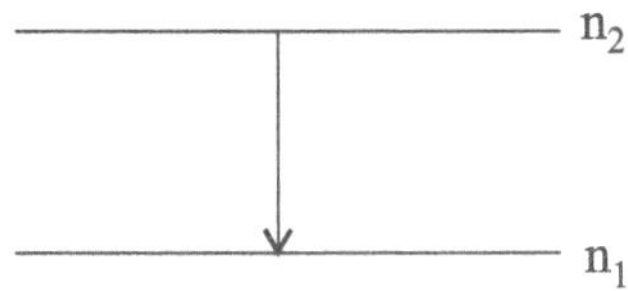

Then wavelength

$= Rcz^2\left[\dfrac{1}{n_1^2} - \dfrac{1}{n_2^2}\right] = Rc(1)^2\left[1 - \dfrac{1}{4}\right]$

$\lambda = Rc\left[\dfrac{3}{4}\right]$ ...(1)

For ionized lithium

$\lambda = Rc(3)^2\left[\dfrac{1}{n^2}\right] = Rc\,9\left[\dfrac{1}{n^2}\right]$ ...(2)

$Rc\left[\dfrac{3}{4}\right] = Rc\,9\left[\dfrac{1}{n^2}\right]$

$\Rightarrow \dfrac{3}{4} = \dfrac{9}{n^2} \Rightarrow n = \sqrt{12} = 2\sqrt{3}$

$\therefore$ The least quantum number must be 4.

25. **(c)** The energy required to remove the electron from the nth orbit of hydrogen is given by

$E_n = \dfrac{13.6}{n^2}$ eV /atom

For $n = 2$, $E_n = \dfrac{13.6}{4} = 3.4\,eV$

Therefore the energy required to remove electron from $n = 2$ is $+3.4$ eV.

1. **(b)** For nucleus of $_8O^{16}$
Mass $= (16)\,(1.67 \times 10^{-27})\,kg$

$$\text{Volume} = \frac{4}{3}\pi R^3$$

$$= \frac{4}{3}\pi(3\times10^{-15})^3\,m^3 = 36\pi \times 10^{-45}\,m^3$$

$$\text{Density} = \frac{\text{mass}}{\text{volume}} = \frac{16 \times 1.67 \times 10^{-27}\,kg}{36\pi \times 10^{-45}\,m^3}$$
$$= 2.35 \times 10^{17}\,kgm^{-3}$$

2. **(c)**

3. **(a)** Nuclear density is independent of atomic number.

4. **(c)** $_1^2H$ and $_1^3H$ requires a and b amount of energies for their nucleons to be separated.

$_2^4He$ releases c amount of energy in its formation i.e., in assembling the nucleons as nucleus.
Hence, Energy released $= c - (a+b) = c - a - b$

5. **(d)** $\lambda_A = 5\lambda$ and $\lambda_B = \lambda$
At $t = 0$, $(N_0)_A = (N_0)_B$

$$\text{Given,}\ \frac{N_A}{N_B} = \left(\frac{1}{e}\right)$$

According to radioactive decay, $\dfrac{N}{N_0} = e^{-\lambda t}$

$$\therefore\ \frac{N_A}{(N_0)_A} = e^{-\lambda_A t} \qquad \text{..... (1)}$$

$$\frac{N_B}{(N_0)_B} = e^{-\lambda_B t} \qquad \text{..... (2)}$$

From (1) and (2), $\dfrac{N_A}{N_B} = e^{-(5\lambda-\lambda)t}$

$$\Rightarrow \left(\frac{1}{e}\right) = e^{-4\lambda t} = \left(\frac{1}{e}\right)^{4\lambda t} \Rightarrow 4\lambda t = 1 \ \therefore t = \frac{1}{4\lambda}.$$

6. **(a)** Let no. of α-particles emitted be x and no. of β particles emitted be y.
Diff. in mass no. $4x = 238 - 206 = 32 \Rightarrow x = 8$
Diff. in atomic no. $2x - 1y = 92 - 82 = 10$
$16 - y = 10, y = 6$

7. **(d)** Let initially there are total N_0 number of nuclei

At time t $\dfrac{N_B}{N_A} = 0.3(\text{given})$

$$\Rightarrow\ N_B = 0.3N_A$$
$$N_0 = N_A + N_B = N_A + 0.3N_A$$

$$\therefore\ N_A = \frac{N_0}{1.3}$$

As we know $N_t = N_0\,e^{-\lambda t}$

$$\text{or,}\ \frac{N_0}{1.3} = N_0\,e^{-\lambda t}$$

$$\frac{1}{1.3} = e^{-\lambda t} \Rightarrow ln(1.3) = \lambda t$$

$$\text{or,}\ t = \frac{ln(1.3)}{\lambda} \Rightarrow t = \frac{ln(1.3)}{\dfrac{ln(2)}{T}} = \frac{ln(1.3)}{ln(2)}T$$

8. **(c)** **Given:** $\dfrac{dN_0}{dt} = 20\ \text{decays/min}$

$$\frac{dN}{dt} = 2\ \text{decays/min}$$
$$T_{1/2} = 5730\ \text{years}$$
As we know,

$$N = N_0 e^{-\lambda t} \Rightarrow \text{Log}\frac{N_0}{N} = \lambda t$$

$$\therefore\ t = \frac{1}{\lambda}\text{Log}\frac{N_0}{N}$$

$$= \frac{2.303 \times T_{1/2}}{0.693} \times \text{Log}_{10}\frac{N_0}{N}$$

$$\text{But}\ \frac{\dfrac{dN_0}{dt}}{\dfrac{dN}{dt}} = \frac{N_0}{N} = \frac{20}{2} = 10$$

$$\therefore\ t = \frac{2.303 \times 5730}{0.693} \times 1 = 19039\ \text{years}$$

9. **(c)** As we know, for first order decay,

$$N(t) = N_0 e^{-\lambda t}$$

According to question,

$$\frac{N(t)}{N_0} = \frac{9}{16} = e^{-\lambda t}$$

After time, $t/2$;

$$N(t/2) = N_0 e^{-\lambda(t/2)}$$

$$\frac{N(t/2)}{N_0} = \sqrt{e^{-\lambda t}} = \sqrt{\frac{9}{16}}$$

$$\therefore N(t/2) = \frac{3}{4} N_0$$

10. **(c)**

11. **(a)** $\text{B.E}_H = \dfrac{2.22}{2} = 1.11$

$\text{B.E}_{He} = \dfrac{28.3}{4} = 7.08$

$\text{B.E}_{Fe} = \dfrac{492}{56} = 8.78 = \text{maximum}$

$\text{B.E}_U = \dfrac{1786}{235} = 7.6$

$^{56}_{26}Fe$ is most stable as it has maximum binding energy per nucleon.

12. **(c)** We use the formula,

$$R = R_0 A^{1/3}$$

This represents relation between atomic mass and radius of the nucleus.

For berillium, $R_1 = R_0 (9)^{1/3}$

For germanium, $R_2 = R_0 A^{1/3}$

$$\frac{R_1}{R_2} = \frac{(9)^{1/3}}{(A)^{1/3}} \Rightarrow \frac{1}{2} = \frac{(9)^{1/3}}{(A)^{1/3}}$$

$$\Rightarrow \frac{1}{8} = \frac{9}{A} \Rightarrow A = 8 \times 9 = 72.$$

13. **(a)** $\text{B.E.} = \Delta mc^2 = \Delta m \times 931\,\text{MeV}$

$$= [2(1.0087 + 1.0073) - 4.0015] \times 931$$

$$= 28.4\,\text{MeV}$$

14. **(a)** Let λ_1 and λ_2 be the decay constants of two process. N be the number of nuclei left undecayed after two process. From the law of radioactive decay we have

$$-\frac{dN}{dt} = \lambda_1 N + \lambda_2 N \qquad \left[\because -\frac{dN}{dt} = \lambda N\right]$$

$$\Rightarrow -\frac{dN}{dt} = (\lambda_1 + \lambda_2) N$$

$$\Rightarrow \lambda_{eq.} = (\lambda_1 + \lambda_2)$$

$$\Rightarrow \frac{\ln 2}{T} = \frac{\ln 2}{T_1} + \frac{\ln 2}{T_2} \qquad \left(\because \lambda = \frac{\ln 2}{T}\right)$$

$$\Rightarrow \frac{1}{T} = \frac{1}{T_1} + \frac{1}{T_2}$$

$$\Rightarrow \frac{1}{T} = \frac{1}{10} + \frac{1}{100} = \frac{11}{100}$$

[Given: $T_1 = 10\,\text{s}$ & $T_2 = 100\,\text{s}$]

$$\Rightarrow T = \frac{100}{11} = 9\,\text{sec.}$$

15. **(b)** We know that $N_\beta = N_0 (1 - e^{-\lambda t})$

$$N_\beta = \frac{6.023 \times 10^{23}}{24}\left[1 - e^{\frac{\ell n\,2}{15} \times 7.5}\right]$$

on solving we get,

$N_\beta = 7.4 \times 10^{21}$

16. **(b)**

17. **(b)** Let N be the number of nuclei at any time t then,

$$\frac{dN}{dt} = 100 - \lambda N \quad \text{or} \quad \int_0^N \frac{dN}{(100 - \lambda N)} = \int_0^t dt$$

$$-\frac{1}{\lambda}\left[\log (100 - \lambda N)\right]_0^N = t$$

$$\log (100 - \lambda N) - \log 100 = -\lambda t$$

$$\log \frac{100 - \lambda N}{100} = -\lambda t$$

$$\frac{100 - \lambda N}{100} = e^{-\lambda t} \quad 1 - \frac{\lambda N}{100} = e^{-\lambda t}$$

$$N = \frac{100}{\lambda}(1 - e^{-\lambda t})$$

As, $N = 50$ and $\lambda = 0.5/\text{sec}$

$$\therefore \quad 50 = \frac{100}{0.5}(1 - e^{-0.5t})$$

Solving we get,

$$t = 2\ln\left(\frac{4}{3}\right)\,\text{sec}$$

18. **(c)** The chemical reaction of process is

$$2\,^2_1H \rightarrow\,^4_2He$$

Energy released $= 4 \times (7.1) - 4(1.1) = 24\,\text{eV}$

19. **(b)**

20. **(b)** Binding energy

$$= 117 \times 8.5 + 117 \times 8.5 - 236 \times 7.6$$

$$= 234 \times 8.5 - 236 \times 7.6$$

$$= 1989 - 1793.6 = 195.4\,\text{MeV}$$

Thus, in per fission of Uranium nearly 200 MeV energy is liberated

21. **(c)** Energy released

$$= (80 \times 7 + 120 \times 8 - 200 \times 6.5)$$

$$= 220 \text{ MeV}$$

22. **(a)** No. of half life required to reduce material to safe level.

$$2^n = 64 \Rightarrow n = 6$$

$\therefore$ Minimum time required to work safely

$$= 6\, T_{1/2}$$

$$= 6 \times 2 = 12 \text{ hours.}$$

23. **(a)** We know that, $\left|\dfrac{dN}{dt}\right| = \lambda N = \dfrac{1}{T_{mean}} N$

$$\therefore \quad 10^{10} = \dfrac{1}{10^9} \times N \qquad \therefore \quad N = 10^{19}$$

i.e. 10^{19} radioactive atoms are present in the freshly prepared sample.

The mass of the sample

$$= 10^{19} \times 10^{-25} \text{ kg} = 10^{-6} \text{kg} = 1 \text{ mg}$$

24. **(a)** According to question, at $t = 0$, $A0 = \dfrac{dN}{dt}$

$$= 1600 \text{ C/s}$$
and at $t = 8$s, $A = 100$ C/s

$$\therefore \quad \dfrac{A}{A_0} = \dfrac{1}{16} \text{ in 8s}$$

Therefore half life period, $t1/2 = 2$s

$$\therefore \text{ Activity at } t = 6s = 1600 \left(\dfrac{1}{2}\right)^3 = 200\text{C/s}$$

25. **(b)** Number of undecayed atom after time t_2 ;

$$\dfrac{N_0}{3} = N_0 e^{-\lambda t_2} \qquad \qquad \ldots\text{(i)}$$

Number of undecayed atom after time t_1 ;

$$\dfrac{2N_0}{3} = N_0 e^{-\lambda t_1} \qquad \qquad \ldots\text{(ii)}$$

Dividing (ii) by (i), we get

$$2 = e^{\lambda(t_2 - t_1)}$$
$$\Rightarrow \ln 2 = \lambda(t_2 - t_1)$$
$$\Rightarrow t_2 - t_1 = \ln 2/\lambda$$

28. Semiconductor Electronics: Materials, Devices and Simple Circuits

1. **(a)** Conductivity, $\sigma = \dfrac{1}{\rho} = e(n_e\mu_e + n_h\mu_h)$

ie, $2.13 = 1.6 \times 10^{-19}(0.38 + 0.18)\,n_i$

(Since in intrinsic semi-conductor, $n_e = n_h = n_i$)

$\therefore$ density of charge carriers,

$$n_i = \frac{2.13}{1.6 \times 10^{-19} \times 0.56} = 2.37 \times 10^{19}\,\text{m}^{-3}.$$

2. **(b)** $n_i^2 = n_e \cdot n_h$

3. **(b)** $R = \dfrac{\Delta V}{\Delta I} = \dfrac{2.1 - 2}{(800 - 400) \times 10^{-3}} = \dfrac{1}{4} = 0.25\,\Omega$

4. **(a)** Here, $E = 9V$; $V_z = 6$; $R_L = 1000\Omega$ and $R_s = 100\Omega$,

Potential drop across series resistor

$V = E - V_Z = 9 - 6 = 3V$

Current through series resistance R_S is

$$I = \frac{V}{R} = \frac{3}{100} = 0.03\,\text{A}$$

Current through load resistance R_L is

$$I_L = \frac{V_Z}{R_L} = \frac{6}{1000} = 0.006\,\text{A}$$

Current through Zener diode is

$I_z = I - I_L = 0.03 - 0.006 = 0.024$ amp.

Power dissipated in Zener diode is

$P_Z = V_Z I_Z = 6 \times 0.024 = 0.144$ Watt

5. **(b)** Forbidden energy gap

$$\Rightarrow \frac{hc}{\lambda} = \frac{6.6 \times 10^{-34} \times 3 \times 10^8}{3895 \times 10^{-9} \times 1.6 \times 10^{-19}}$$

$= 0.003 \times 10^2\,\text{eV} = 0.3\,\text{eV}$

6. **(a)** The conductivity of semiconductor

$\sigma = e\,(\eta_e\mu_e + \eta_h\mu_h)$

$= 1.6 \times 10^{-19}(5 \times 10^{18} \times 2 + 5 \times 10^{19} \times 0.01)$

$= 1.6 \times 1.05 = 1.68$

7. **(d)**

8. **(a)** Here, diodes D_1 and D_2 are forward biased and D_3 is reverse biased. Therefore current through R_3

$$i = \frac{V}{R'} = \frac{6}{120} = \frac{1}{20}\,\text{A} = 50\,\text{mA}$$

9. **(d)**

10. **(d)** Given, $R_C = 2\,\text{k}\Omega$

$V_C = 2\,\text{V}$

$R_B = 1\,\text{k}\Omega$

$\beta = 100$

$$\frac{V_C}{V_i} = \beta \cdot \frac{R_C}{R_B} \Rightarrow \frac{2}{V_i} = 100 \cdot \frac{2}{1}$$

$\Rightarrow V_i = 10\,\text{mV}$

11. **(d)** Here, $R = 4\,\text{k}\Omega = 4 \times 10^3\,\Omega$

$V_i = 60\,\text{V}$

Zener voltage $V_z = 10\,\text{V}$

$R_L = 2\,\text{k}\Omega = 2 \times 10^3\,\Omega$

Load current, $I_L = \dfrac{V_Z}{R_L} = \dfrac{10}{2 \times 10^3} = 5\,\text{mA}$

Current through R, $I = \dfrac{V_i - V_z}{R}$

$= \dfrac{60 - 10}{4 \times 10^3} = \dfrac{50}{4 \times 10^3} = 12.5\,\text{mA}$

Fom circuit diagram,

$I = I_Z + I_L \Rightarrow 12.5 = I_Z + 5 \Rightarrow I_z = 7.5\,\text{mA}$

12. **(d)** Curent gain $\beta = \dfrac{\Delta I_C}{I_B}$

Voltage gain A_v = Current gain × Resistance gain

$\Rightarrow \beta \dfrac{R_L}{R_{BE}}$

Power gain A_p = (Current gain)^2 × Resistance gain

$\Rightarrow \beta^2 \dfrac{R_L}{R_{BE}}$

13. **(a)**

14. **(d)** I-V characteristic of a photodiode is as follows :

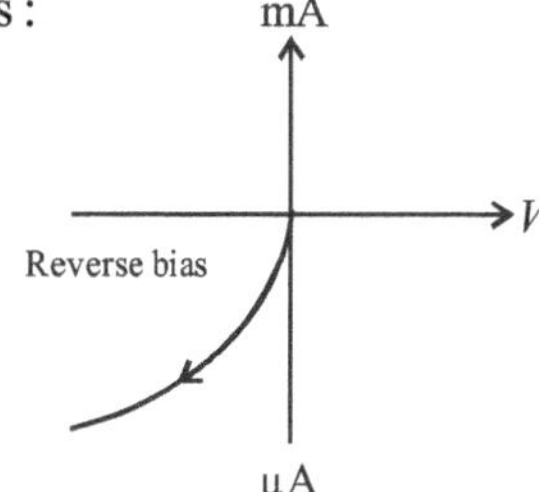

On increasing the biasing voltage of a photodiode, the magnitude of photocurrent first increases and then attains a saturation.

15. (b)

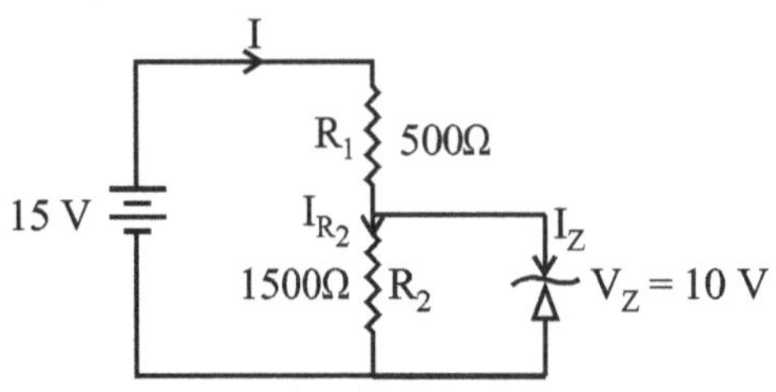

The voltage drop across R_2 is $V_{R_2} = V_Z = 10\,V$

The current through R_2 is

$$I_{R_2} = \frac{V_{R_2}}{R_2} = \frac{10\,V}{1500\Omega} = 0.667 \times 10^{-2}\,A$$
$$= 6.67 \times 10^{-3}\,A = 6.67\,mA$$

The voltage drop across R_1 is

$$V_{R_1} = 15V - V_{R_2} = 15V - 10V = 5V$$

The current through R_1 is

$$I_{R_1} = \frac{V_{R_1}}{R_1} = \frac{5\,V}{500\Omega} = 10^{-2}\,A$$

$$= 10 \times 10^{-3}\,A = 10\,mA$$

The current through the zener diode is

$$I_Z = I_{R_1} - I_{R_2} = (10 - 6.67)mA = 3.3\,mA$$

16. (a) For same value of current higher value of voltage is required for higher frequency hence (a) is correct answer.

17. (d) Here, $n_i = 10^{16}\,m^{-3}$, $n_h = 5 \times 10^{22}\,m^{-3}$
As $n_e n_h = n_i^2$

$$\therefore\ n_e = \frac{n_i^2}{n_h} = \frac{(10^{16}\,m^{-3})^2}{5 \times 10^{22}\,m^{-3}} = 2 \times 10^9\,m^{-3}$$

18. (c) $V' = V + IR = 0.5 + 0.1 \times 20 = 2.5\,V$

19. (c) Power gain = voltage gain × current gain

$$= V_G \cdot I_G = \frac{V_0}{V_i} \cdot \frac{I_0}{I_i}$$

$$= \frac{V_0^2}{V_i^2} \cdot \frac{R_i}{R_0} = 49 \times 49 \times \frac{100}{490} = 490$$

20. (c) Current gain, $\beta = \dfrac{\Delta I_C}{\Delta I_B} = \dfrac{(15-10)\,mA}{(80-40)\,\mu A}$

$$= \frac{5 \times 10^{-3}}{40 \times 10^{-6}} = \frac{5000}{40} = 125$$

Voltage gain, $A_v = \beta \dfrac{R_L}{R_{in}}$;

$$\frac{V_{out}}{V_{in}} = 125 \left(\frac{16 \times 10^3}{80} \right)$$

$$V_{out} = 125 \times \frac{16000}{80} \times 12 \times 10^{-3} = 300V$$

21. (b)

$$A \to \overline{A}, \quad B \to \overline{B}, \quad \overline{\overline{A} + \overline{B}} = C$$

A	B	$\overline{A}$	$\overline{B}$	$\overline{A} + \overline{B}$	C	
0	0	1	1	1	0	
0	1	1	0	1	0	≡ AND gate
1	0	0	1	1	0	
1	1	0	0	0	1	

22. (d) Output resistance, $R_0 = 10\,k\Omega$
Input resistance, $R_i = 2\,k\Omega$ and $\beta = 49$

Voltage gain, $A_V = \beta \times \dfrac{R_0}{R_i} = 49 \times \dfrac{10}{2} = 245$

23. (c) The truth table of OR gate is given as

A	B	Y
0	0	0
0	1	1
1	0	1
1	1	1

24. (a) When both A and B are high between time T_3 and T_4 the output Y is high, otherwise zero. Thus the logic gate is AND gate

25. (c) A and B are the inputs of an OR gate. If A = 1, and B = 0, the output of OR gate will be 1. Now the output of OR gate along with C make the inputs of an AND gate.
Thus output of OR gate = 1, and C = 1, give the final output of AND gate as 1.